.NET Standard 2.0 Cookbook

Develop high quality, fast and portable applications by leveraging the power of .NET Standard Library

Fiqri Ismail

BIRMINGHAM - MUMBAI

.NET Standard 2.0 Cookbook

Commissioning Editor: Richa Tripathi
Acquisition Editors: Denim Pinto/Nitin Dasan
Content Development Editor: Nikhil Borkar
Technical Editor: Jijo Maliyekal
Copy Editor: Safis Editing
Project Coordinator: Ulhas Kambali
Proofreader: Safis Editing
Indexer: Priyanka Dhadke
Graphics: Tania Dutta
Production Coordinator: Shraddha Falebhai

First published: May 2018

Production reference: 1090518

Published by Packt Publishing Ltd.
Livery Place
35 Livery Street
Birmingham
B3 2PB, UK.

ISBN 978-1-78883-466-7

www.packtpub.com

Mapt

Contributors

About the author

Fiqri Ismail is an experienced architect with a demonstrated history of working in the information technology and services industry. Skilled in ASP.NET, ASP.NET MVC, ASP.NET Core, Entity Framework, C#, Microsoft Azure, PHP, and Delphi, he is a Microsoft MVP in Visual Studio and Related Technologies for 11 concussive years to date. He is also a community leader and a speaker at Sri Lanka Developer Forum and in Global Events such as Microsoft Tech Summit and Global Azure Bootcamp.

I would love thank Mr. Arjuna Seneviratna, my first teacher on web-related technologies and Mr. Saman Chandana Silva, who helped me buy my first computer. Also, I would like to thank my wife and daughter for giving their time to complete this book.

About the reviewer

Hansamali Gamage is an experienced professional and Microsoft MVP in Visual Studio and technologies from Sri Lanka. She possesses over 5 years of experience in. NET stack and Azure-related services. She is a frequent speaker at local and global tech events, a tech enthusiast, and an award winning writer on the Microsoft Tech Net forum. She works at TIQRI, previously known as Exilesoft, a technology-focused software engineering company with offices in Scandinavia, Asia, and Australia.

I would like to thank my loving family for their continuous help and support.

Packt is searching for authors like you

If you're interested in becoming an author for Packt, please visit `authors.packtpub.com` and apply today. We have worked with thousands of developers and tech professionals, just like you, to help them share their insight with the global tech community. You can make a general application, apply for a specific hot topic that we are recruiting an author for, or submit your own idea.

Table of Contents

Preface

This book is a step-by-step guide to building .NET Standard 2.0 Library and its usage in various .NET platforms. Also, we will demonstrate the usage of the library using ASP.NET, ASP.NET Core, ASP.NET MVC, Xamarin iOS, and Xamarin Android. Finally, we will guide you through how to package and send your library using the NuGet package manager.

Who this book is for

This book is for developers who need to get in touch with the new .NET Standard 2.0 Library. If you have a basic knowledge of C# and what a library can do to your code, that's enough to understand this book. Also, if you are a developer who writes third-party libraries, this will give you a fair idea of what .NET Standard 2.0 Library is and how you can cater to various .NET based platforms in Windows, Linux, and macOS using it.

What this book covers

`Chapter 1`, *Back to Basics*, gives an overview of where it all began for the starters trying to build their first .NET based class library. It talks about the problems with this approach. Getting started with a simple project and using it with a console application and a classic Windows based application, the chapter talks about the issues with the current approach of libraries available. It introduces readers to .NET Standard 2.0 and its versions. How to create the first .NET Standard 2.0 library and use it with various .NET flavors such as .NET Framework and .NET Core applications is covered.

`Chapter 2`, *Primitives, Collections, LINQ, and More*, explores the Core of .NET Standard 2.0. It talks about Primitives, Collections, Reflection, and LINQ. The areas supported so far are covered. It makes use of features among different flavors of .NET Framework.

`Chapter 3`, *Working with Files*, provides an explanation of System.IO and System.Security within the .NET Standard 2.0 and the usage of read write operations using the filesystem. Also, it introduces usage in cross-platform versions of .NET Core in Ubuntu and macOS.

`Chapter 4`, *Functional Programming*, introduces functional programming capabilities in C# and how to use them in .NET Standard 2.0 Library.

`Chapter 5`, *XML and Data*, explains the usage of System.XML and System.Data within .NET Standard 2.0 for creating XML Documents and the usage of Data Tables.

`Chapter 6`, *Exploring Threading,* talks about Thread support for creating a multithreaded .NET Standard 2.0 library. This is in addition to the usage of Tasks as asynchronous capabilities of C# within the library.

`Chapter 7`, *Networking,* focuses on the usage of System.Net within .NET Standard 2.0. It dives into Sockets, Http, and Mail and how to use them in a .NET Standard Library 2.0.

`Chapter 8`, *To iOS with Xamarin,* outlines creating a simple mobile-based application using Visual Studio for Mac mobile iOS tools. The chapter guides through to create a .NET Standard 2.0 library and use it with the built iOS application.

`Chapter 9`, *To Android with Xamarin,* takes you through creating a simple mobile-based application using Visual Studio for Mac and Android tools. It showcases how to create a .NET Standard 2.0 library and use it with the built Android application.

`Chapter 10`, *Let's Fine-Tune Our Library,* demonstrates how to fine-tune .NET Standard 2.0 library using Debugging tools and Diagnostics tools. Also, it helps you capture exceptions and ensure that the end user has a solid experience using our .NET Standard Library 2.0.

`Chapter 11`, *Packaging and Delivery,* discusses how to deliver a completed .NET Standard 2.0 Library to the world. How to use NuGet package manager, creating a package, and delivering it is covered.

`Chapter 12`, *Deploying,* informs how to create a .NET Standard Library 2.0, use it with ASP.NET Core web applications, and deploy it to Azure Cloud.

To get the most out of this book

This book assumes that readers have basic knowledge of C#. Also, it assumes basic knowledge of using Visual Studio, installing packages using NuGet, and referencing libraries within projects from other projects.

Basic knowledge of using command-line tools such as bash on Ubuntu and terminal in macOS will be an added advantage but not a must.

Download the example code files

You can download the example code files for this book from your account at `www.packtpub.com`. If you purchased this book elsewhere, you can visit `www.packtpub.com/support` and register to have the files emailed directly to you.

You can download the code files by following these steps:

1. Log in or register at `www.packtpub.com`.
2. Select the **SUPPORT** tab.
3. Click on **Code Downloads & Errata**.
4. Enter the name of the book in the **Search** box and follow the onscreen instructions.

Once the file is downloaded, please make sure that you unzip or extract the folder using the latest version of:

- WinRAR/7-Zip for Windows
- Zipeg/iZip/UnRarX for Mac
- 7-Zip/PeaZip for Linux

The code bundle for the book is also hosted on GitHub at `https://github.com/PacktPublishing/DotNET-Standard-2-Cookbook`. We also have other code bundles from our rich catalog of books and videos available at `https://github.com/PacktPublishing/`. Check them out!

Code in Action

Visit the following link to check out videos of the code being run:
`https://goo.gl/GwN5Xq`

Conventions used

There are a number of text conventions used throughout this book.

`CodeInText`: Indicates code words in text, database table names, folder names, filenames, file extensions, pathnames, dummy URLs, user input, and Twitter handles. Here is an example: "Mount the downloaded `WebStorm-10*.dmg` disk image file as another disk in your system."

A block of code is set as follows:

```
public void WriteLog(string message)
{
logFile.WriteLine($"{DateTime.Now} Log Message: {message} ");
}
```

When we wish to draw your attention to a particular part of a code block, the relevant lines or items are set in bold:

```
if (!File.Exists(logFileName))
{
  logFile = File.CreateText(logFileName);
}
else
{
  logFile = File.AppendText(logFileName);
}
```

Any command-line input or output is written as follows:

```
$ dotnet build
```

Bold: Indicates a new term, an important word, or words that you see onscreen. For example, words in menus or dialog boxes appear in the text like this. Here is an example: "Select **System info** from the **Administration** panel."

Warnings or important notes appear like this.

Tips and tricks appear like this.

Sections

In this book, you will find several headings that appear frequently (*Getting ready*, *How to do it...*, *How it works...*, *There's more...*, and *See also*).

To give clear instructions on how to complete a recipe, use these sections as follows:

Getting ready

This section tells you what to expect in the recipe and describes how to set up any software or any preliminary settings required for the recipe.

How to do it...

This section contains the steps required to follow the recipe.

How it works...

This section usually consists of a detailed explanation of what happened in the previous section.

There's more...

This section consists of additional information about the recipe in order to make you more knowledgeable about the recipe.

See also

This section provides helpful links to other useful information for the recipe.

Get in touch

Feedback from our readers is always welcome.

General feedback: Email `feedback@packtpub.com` and mention the book title in the subject of your message. If you have questions about any aspect of this book, please email us at `questions@packtpub.com`.

Errata: Although we have taken every care to ensure the accuracy of our content, mistakes do happen. If you have found a mistake in this book, we would be grateful if you would report this to us. Please visit `www.packtpub.com/submit-errata`, selecting your book, clicking on the Errata Submission Form link, and entering the details.

Piracy: If you come across any illegal copies of our works in any form on the internet, we would be grateful if you would provide us with the location address or website name. Please contact us at `copyright@packtpub.com` with a link to the material.

If you are interested in becoming an author: If there is a topic that you have expertise in and you are interested in either writing or contributing to a book, please visit `authors.packtpub.com`.

Reviews

Please leave a review. Once you have read and used this book, why not leave a review on the site that you purchased it from? Potential readers can then see and use your unbiased opinion to make purchase decisions, we at Packt can understand what you think about our products, and our authors can see your feedback on their book. Thank you!

For more information about Packt, please visit `packtpub.com`.

1
Back to Basics

In this chapter, we will cover the following recipes:

- Creating a C#-based console application
- Creating a C# class library
- Creating a classic Windows application to use the library
- Creating a WPF-based application to use the library
- Hello Universe – My first .NET Standard class library
- Creating a Windows console-based application to use the library
- Creating a ASP.NET Core-based web application to use the library

Technical requirements

Readers should have a basic knowledge of C#. They should also have a basic knowledge of using Visual Studio, installing packages using NuGet, and referencing libraries within projects from other projects.

The code files for this chapter can be found on GitHub:
`https://github.com/PacktPublishing/DotNET-Standard-2-Cookbook/tree/master/Chapter01`

Check out the following video to see the code in action:
`https://goo.gl/PoR4HM`

Introduction

Microsoft .NET is a general-purpose development platform with support for multiple programming languages, which is a key feature. Other key features include asynchronous and concurrent programming models and native interoperability. The .NET Framework supports multiple programming languages, such as C#, VB.NET, and F#, which are actively developed and supported by Microsoft. In this book, we are going to look at C#.

C# is a modern, object-oriented, type-safe programming language that helps developers build robust, secure applications using the .NET Framework. C# was introduced with .NET Framework 1.0 in 2002. Since that time, C# has evolved and matured. At the time of writing, the current version of C# is 7.0 and .NET has various flavors to use with the following:

- **.NET Framework**: The full flavor of .NET that is distributed with Windows. Used by developers to build ASP.NET 4.5/4.6 under Windows or desktop Windows applications.
- **.NET Core**: Another flavor of .NET that runs under Windows, Mac, and Linux. Used by developers to build cross-platform .NET-based applications including cross-platform web applications, using ASP.NET Core.
- **Xamarin**: A mono-based framework used for mobile applications for iOS, Android, and Windows phone devices. macOS desktop applications are supported with this flavor.
- **.NET Standard**: A replacement for **Portable Class Libraries** (**PCL**) used by developers to share code among all platforms, but supported with APIs in the latest version, 2.0. Also, you should note that .NET Standard 2.0 is supported in .NET Core 2.0, .NET Framework 4.6.1, and later versions, as well as in Visual Studio 2017 (version 15.3).

Creating a C#-based console application

Let's get started with a simple C#-based console application. This console application will introduce some basic C# code and get things up and running for the library we are going to build in the next recipe. Our main focus is to get to the C# coding and prepare ourselves for all the excitement we are going to have later.

Getting ready

To step through this recipe, you will need a running copy of Visual Studio 2017 with the latest version of .NET Framework. If you don't have a copy of Visual Studio 2017, you can download it from `https://www.visualstudio.com/`.

This will take you to Microsoft's Visual Studio website. Follow the instructions on the site to get a copy of Visual Studio and get things started.

How to do it...

1. Open Visual Studio 2017.
2. Click **File** | **New** | **Project** and, in the **New Project** template dialog box, select **Visual C#** in the left-hand pane and **Console App (.NET Framework)** in the right-hand pane:

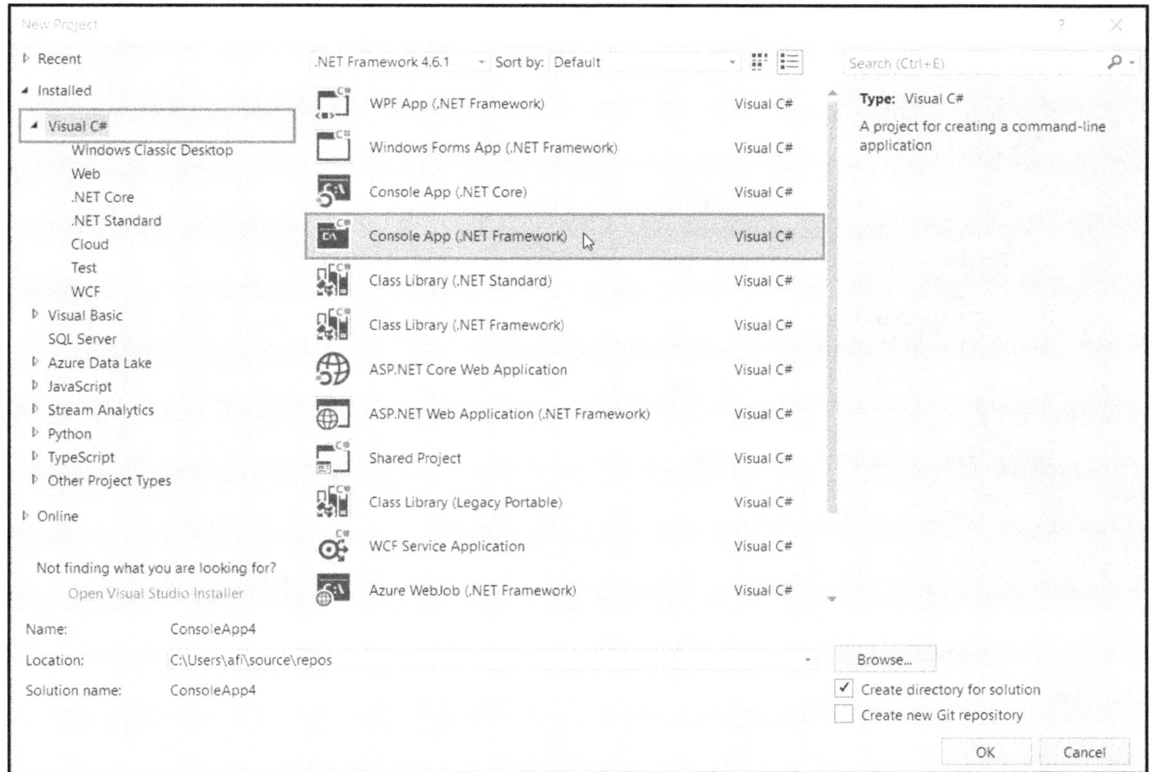

3. In the **Name:** text box, type a name for your application. In this case, type `HelloCSharp`. Select a preferred location in the **Location:** drop-down list or click the **Browse...** button and select a location. Leave the defaults as they are:

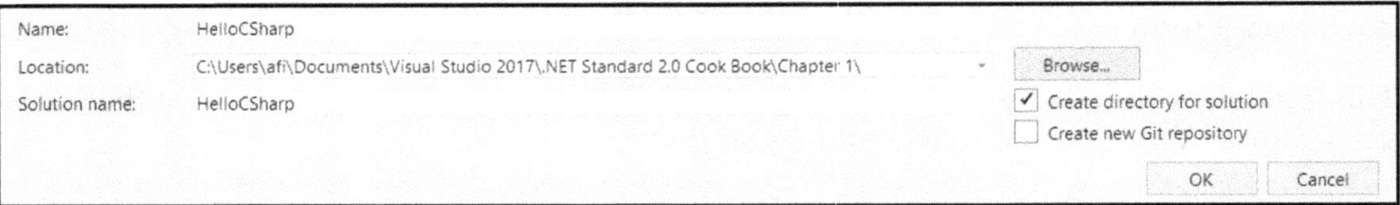

4. Now Click **OK**.
5. You will be presented with a default code template for a C# console application. Let's hit *F5* to give it a test run. If everything is fine, a console will pop up and close.
6. At the end of the `Main` method, type the following code snippet:

```
private static string SayHello(string yourName)
{
    return $"Hello, {yourName}";
}
```

7. Now, inside your `Main` method, type the code that calls the previous method we just created:

```
var message = SayHello("Fiqri Ismail");
Console.WriteLine(message);
Console.ReadLine();
```

8. Now we have written our first C# code. The code of the console app should look like the following after you are done coding:

```
static void Main(string[] args)
{
  var message = SayHello("Fiqri Ismail");
  Console.WriteLine(message);
  Console.ReadLine();
}

private static string SayHello(string yourName)
{
  return $"Hello, {yourName}";
}
```

9. Let's hit *F5* and test the application. If everything is OK, you should see the following screen. Press *Enter* to exit:

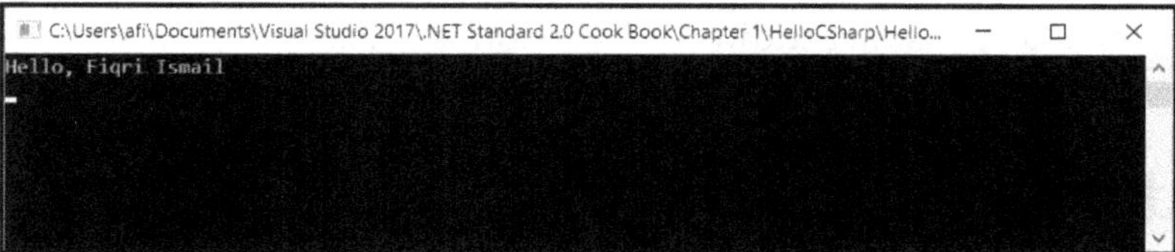

How it works...

Let us take a quick look at what we did in the previous recipe. In steps 1 to 4, we created a C#-based console application. The skeleton for a console application already comes with Visual Studio as a template. Giving a proper name to your project and a location is a good habit. These things will help you to track down your project easily for future use. In step 5, we just make sure the default console application template works fine and that there are no surprises waiting for us before doing any actual coding.

In step 6, we created a static method that takes a `string` parameter and returns a message with that parameter; this is called **String Interpolation**. It's a new feature introduced in C# 6.0 and can be used instead of the traditional `string.format()` method. Step 7 uses that method inside the main method. As in a normal console application, `Console.ReadLine()` will wait till any key is pressed before exiting. Finally, in step 9, we debug the code to check that everything works fine and as expected.

See also

- C# fundamentals (`Chapter 2`, *Primitives, Collections, LINQ, and More*)
- Creating Windows-based applications using C# (Creating a classic Windows-based application to use the Library—`Chapter 1`, *Back to Basics*)

Creating a C# class library

In this recipe, we are going to build a simple C# class library. This library will have a simple public method that takes a parameter and returns a string. Also, we will be creating a blank Visual Studio solution and adding the library project. This solution will be used in later recipes.

Getting ready

Make sure you have installed a flavor of Visual Studio 2017 and its latest updates. At the time of writing, the latest Visual Studio 2017 version is 15.3.5.

How to do it...

1. Open Visual Studio 2017.
2. Click **File** | **New** | **Project** and, in the **New Project** template dialog box, select **Visual Studio Solutions** under the **Other Project Types** node in the left-hand pane, and select **Blank Solution** in the right-hand pane:

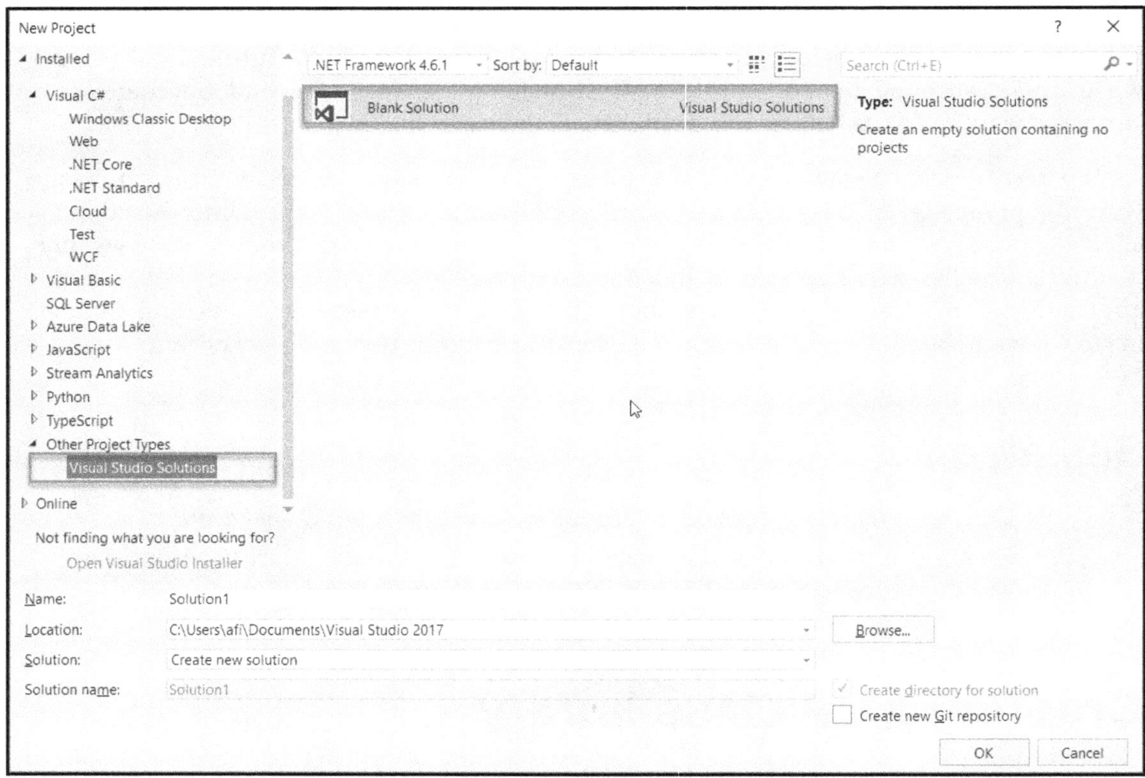

3. In the **Name:** textbox, type a name for your application. In this case, type `Chapter1.Library`. Select a preferred location under the **Location:** drop-down list or click the **Browse...** button and select a location. Leave the defaults as they are:

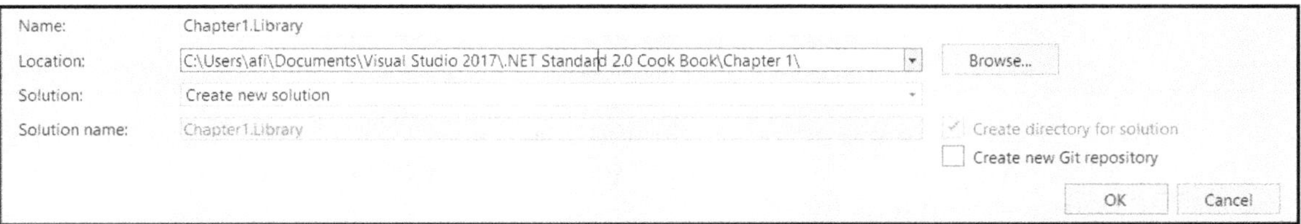

4. Now you have a blank solution. Let's add a C# class library project to the solution. Click **Project** | **Add New Item...** or you can right-click on the `Chapter1.Library` solution label in the **Solution Explorer**, and select **Add** | **New Project....**
5. In the **Add New Project** template dialog box, select **Visual C#** in the left side, pane and select **Class Library (.NET Framework)** in the right-hand pane:

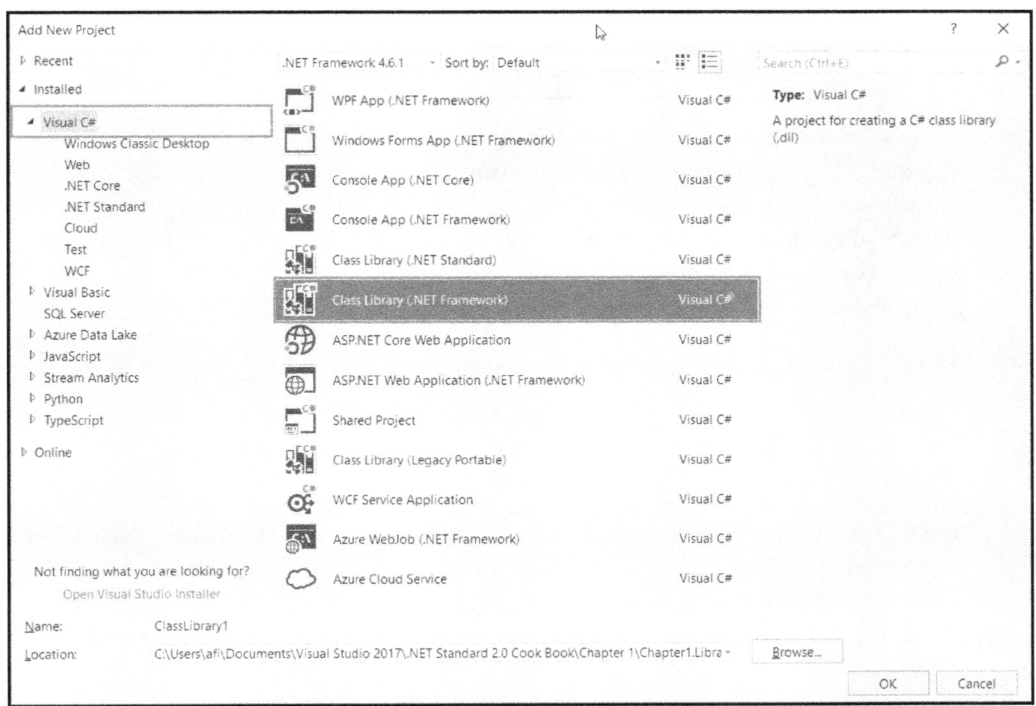

6. In the **Name:** textbox, type a name for your class library. In this case, type `Chapter1.Library.HelloLib` as the name of the project. Leave the current location under the **Location:** drop-down list and click **OK** to create the project:

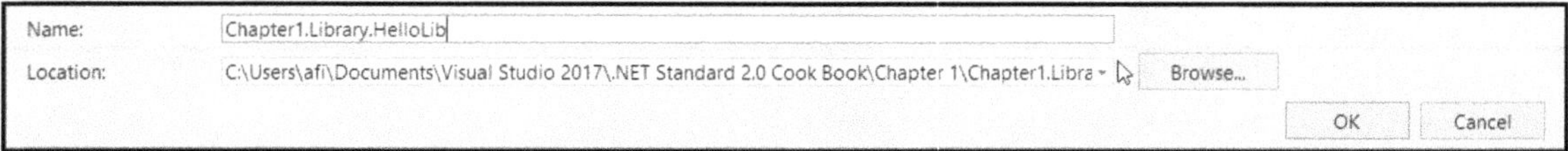

7. Now we have a brand new .NET Framework-based class library. In the **Solution Explorer** (press *Ctrl* + *Alt* + *L* if you don't see the **Solution Explorer**), the default structure should look like this:

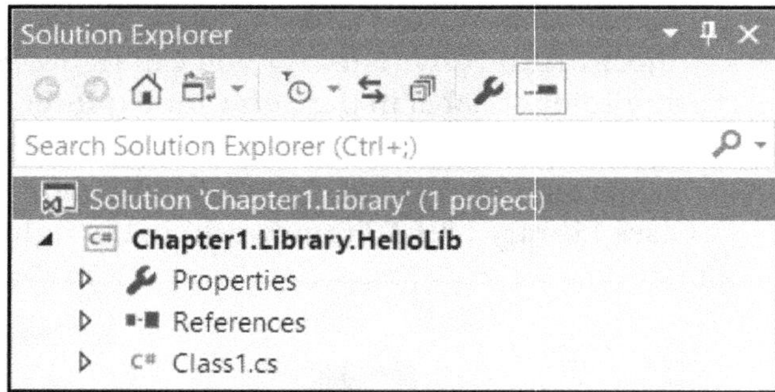

8. Now we have a default template for a class library project. Let's rename `Class1.cs` to something more meaningful. Rename it `HelloWorld.cs`. You can simply soft click on the label of the file in the **Solution Explorer** and type the new name (or click on the filename label and press *F2*). Click **Yes** in the confirmation box to confirm the renaming.
9. Type the following code snippet in the `HelloWorld` class body:

```
public string SayHello(string name)
{
    return $"Hello {name}, congratulations !!!,
    this message is from the class library you created.";
}
```

10. Let's build our code to check that everything is fine. Click **Build** | **Build Solution**, or press *Ctrl* + *Shift* + *B*, and the solution should build successfully. Let's test our class library in the next recipe.
11. Click **File** | **Save All**, or press *Ctrl* + *Shift* + *S*, to save the solution and the class library project.

How it works...

Let's see what we have done so far in this recipe and how it works. In steps 1 to 3, you have created a blank solution. Blank solutions are a very good starting point for any size of project. It gives you a whole new solution to start with. Later on, you can add more bits and pieces to your solution. Even though this is a simple introduction to class libraries, it is good practice to stick with proper naming conventions. It's not a must, but good practice. As you can see, we have given a name `Chapter1.Library`, so the name is meaningful and it says what our solution is about.

In the next steps, from 4 to 8, we have added a class library project to our blank solution. Now you have an idea how a solution will grow over time, from start to end. The template we have chosen is a full .NET Framework class library. We renamed the default `Class1.cs` template provided by Visual Studio. It's good practice to give a meaningful name to classes and the files we work with.

In steps 9 and 10, we added code to our class and checked all the syntax was correct by building the solution. It is also good practice to check for typos and other errors in syntax once in a while.

Creating a classic Windows-based application to use the library

So far, from the previous recipe, we have created a blank solution and a class library that uses the full .NET Framework. In this recipe, let's create a classic Windows Forms application that uses the class library created in the previous recipe. We are going to build a Windows form that takes a name using a text box and a button, and that triggers the public method we have created in the class library.

Getting ready

For this recipe, you will require the solution and the class you built in the previous recipe. Open Visual Studio 2017 and prepare for the project. Click **Build** | **Build Solution**, or press *Ctrl* + *Shift* + *B*, and the solution should build successfully. Everything's ready for testing our class library.

How to do it...

1. Open Visual Studio 2017.
2. Now open the solution from the previous recipe. Click **File** | **Open** | **Project/Solution**, or press *Ctrl* + *Shift* + *O*, and select the `Chapter1.Library` solution.
3. Now click on the `Chapter1.Library` solution label. Click **File** | **Add** | **New Project....**
4. In the **Add New Project** template dialog box, expand the **Visual C#** node in the left-hand pane.
5. Select **Windows Classic Desktop** and select **Windows Forms App (.NET Framework)** in the right template pane:

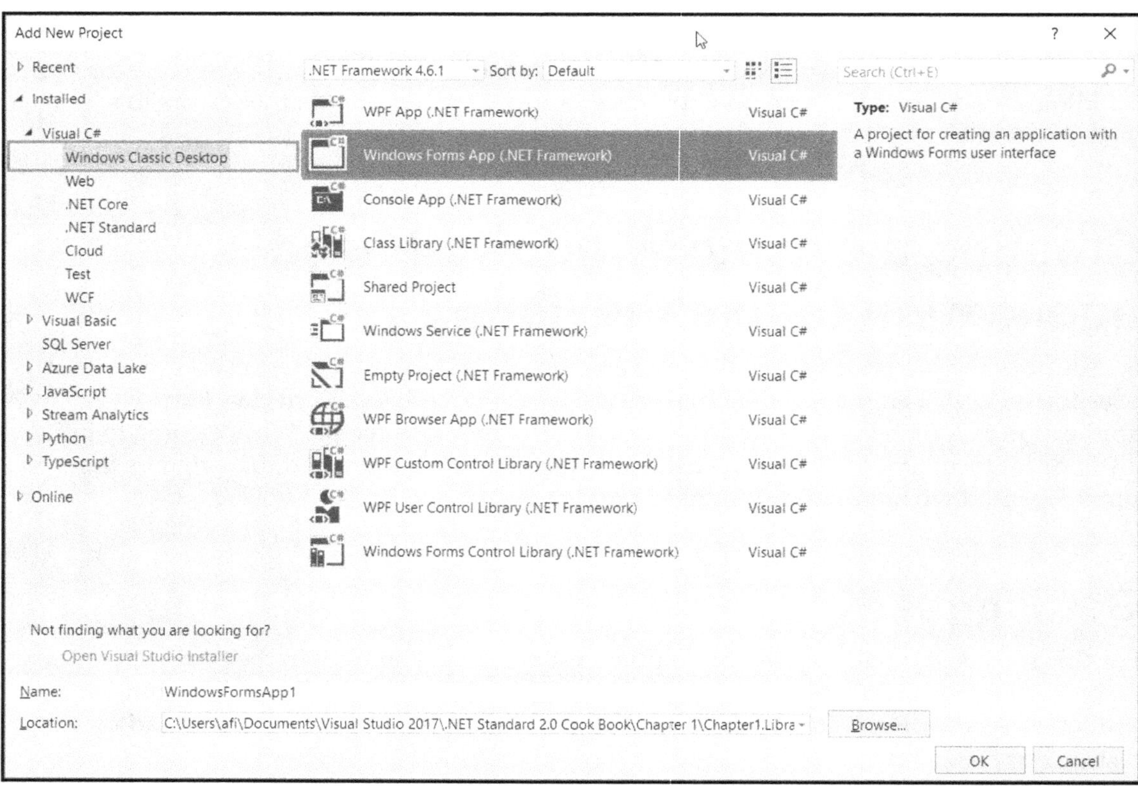

6. Now, in the **Name:** textbox, type a name for the new project. Let's type `Chapter1.Library.HelloWindowsForms` and leave the **Location:** textbox as it is and the defaults as well. Click **OK** to create the new project.

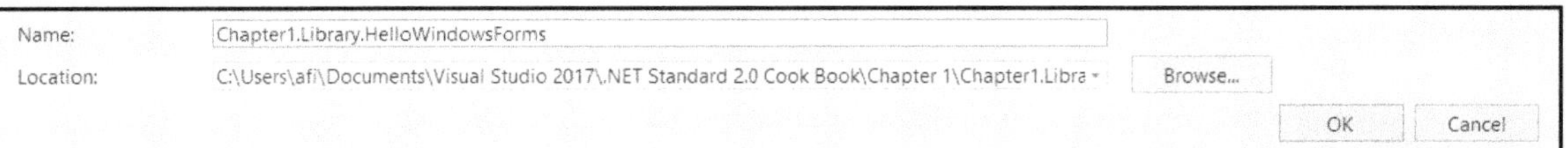

7. The new project will be added to the **Solution Explorer** and it should look like this:

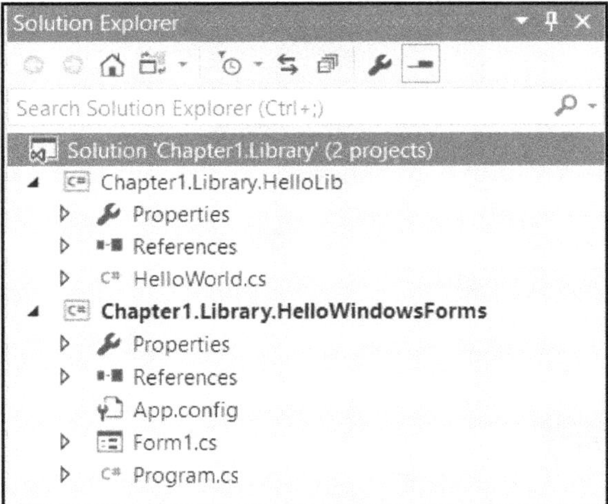

8. Now let's do some cleaning of the names. Change `Form1.cs` to `MainForm.cs`. Remember, giving a meaningful name to your files is very important and a very good practice.
9. Select the Form in the **MainForm [Design]** tab and go to the **Properties** window (or press *F4*). Now change the **Text** property to `Hello World`.

10. Let's add some UI components to the form. Go to the tool box window (or press *Ctrl* + *Alt* + *X*) and drag and drop a **Label**, a **TextBox**, and a **Button** to the form. Arrange them as per the following screenshot:

11. Let's change some properties of the components we just dropped on the form. Go to the **Properties** window and change the defaults to the following:

Component	**Property**	**Value**
Label	**Name**	`NameLabel`
Label	**Text**	`Type your name`
TextBox	**Name**	`NameTextBox`
Button	**Name**	`HelloButton`
Button	**Text**	`Say Hello`

After the changes, the Windows form designer should look like this:

12. Let's add our library to the Windows Forms project. To do this, expand **References** under the `Chaper1.Library.HelloWindowsForms` project. Right-click on the **References** label and select **Add Reference...**.
13. Under the **Reference Manager** dialog box, click on the **Projects** label in the left-hand pane. In the middle pane, check the `Chapter1.Library.HelloLib` project:

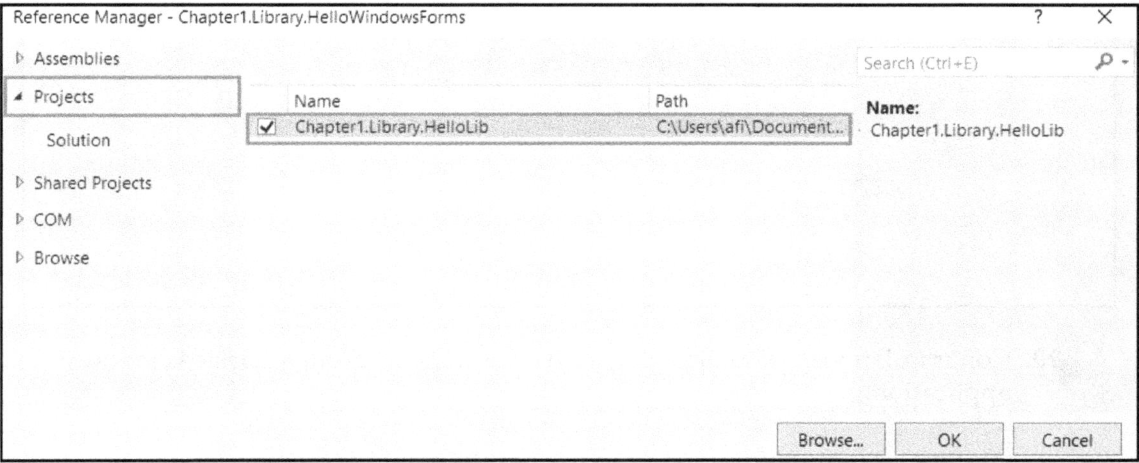

14. Click **OK**.
15. Now double-click on the **Say Hello** button to open the code window.
16. In the code window, scroll to the top and type the following code, at the end of the very last line of `using` directive:

```
using Chapter1.Library.HelloLib;
```

17. Now scroll down to the `HelloButton_Click` method. In between the curly brackets, type the following code:

```
var helloMessage = new HelloWorld();
var yourName = NameTextBox.Text;
MessageBox.Show(helloMessage.SayHello(yourName));
```

18. Time to test our classic Windows application with the class library created in the previous recipe. Hit *F5* to debug the code. Now you should see the Windows form created.

19. Type your name in the text box and hit the **Say Hello** button. A message box will appear with a message from the class library:

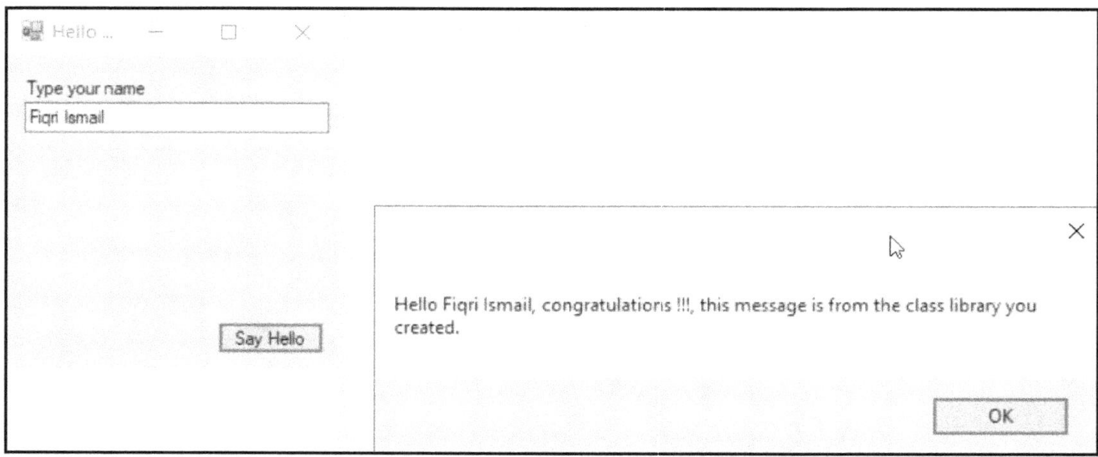

20. Congratulations!!! You have just used a class library from a classic Windows application.

How it works...

If you have a closer look at the recipe we just completed, we have used a solution created from a previous recipe. In a real-world application, this is a day-to-day process. From steps 1 to 7, we opened an existing solution that contained the class library from the previous recipe and added a Classic Windows Forms application to the solution.

In steps 8 to 11, we prepared the Windows Form projects. Proper naming of the components and files is good practice. Even though this is a small application, proper naming is a good discipline. Steps 12 to 14 are the most important steps in this recipe. In these steps, we have added our class library to the Windows project as a reference. Now you can access all the public methods given by the class library from your Windows application.

In steps 15 to 17, we have added code to the button click event of `HelloButton`. Double-clicking on a component will get you to the C# code of the Windows form. Visual Studio will generate the code for you. In this case, it's the button click event. The default event of a component will vary depending on the component you have selected. In step 17, we created a variable to hold the instance of the `HelloWorld` class from the class library created. Then, we created another variable to hold the user input to the text box. The last line of code will call the `HelloWorld.SayHello(string name)` method with the string parameter supplied from the variable created in the previous line of code. Finally, a default message box will display the `string` returned from the `SayHello(string name)` method from the `HelloWorld` class.

Step 19 will execute the default project, in this case, our Windows-based application. Sometimes, if the class library project is selected as the default project, Visual Studio will complain that you cannot execute this sort of project. So make sure you have selected the Windows project as the default startup project.

Creating a WPF-based application to use the library

Now, in this recipe, let's add a **Windows Presentation Foundation** (**WPF**)-based application to the solution and use the class library created in a previous recipe. WPF is the shortened name for Windows Presentation Foundation. The purpose of this recipe is to demonstrate how to share a library within the different .NET-based applications.

Getting ready

For this recipe, you will require the solution and the class library you built in the previous recipe. Open Visual Studio 2017 and prepare for the project. Click **Build** | **Build Solution**, or press *Ctrl* + *Shift* + *B*, and the solution should build successfully. Everything's ready for testing our class library.

How to do it...

1. Open Visual Studio 2017.
2. Now open the solution from the previous recipe. Click **File** | **Open** | **Open Project/Solution**, or press *Ctrl* + *Shift* + *O*, and select the `Chapter1.Library` solution.
3. Now click on the `Chapter1.Library` solution label. Click **File** | **Add** | **New Project**.
4. In the **Add New Project** template dialog box, expand the Visual C# node in the left-hand pane.
5. Select **Windows Classic Desktop** and select **WPF App (.NET Framework)** in the right template pane.

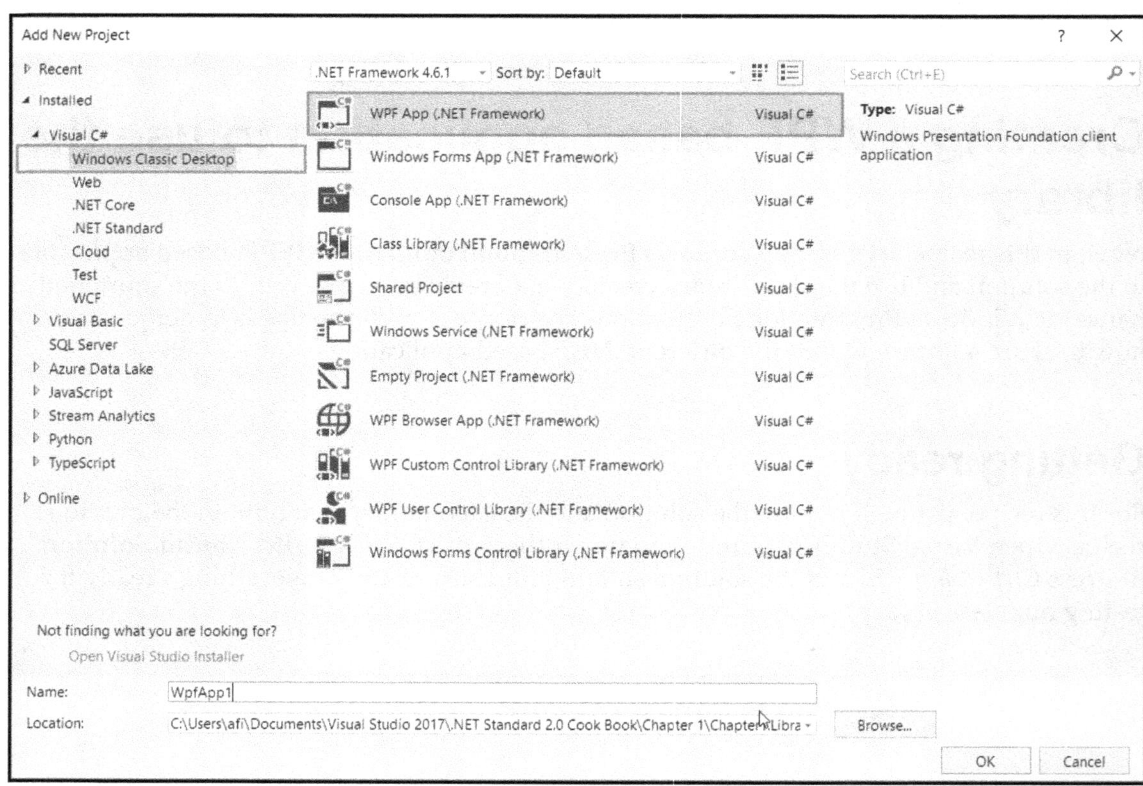

6. Now, in the **Name:** text box, type a name for the new project. Let's type `Chapter1.Library.HelloWPF` and leave the **Location:** as it is and the defaults as well. Click **OK** to create the new project.

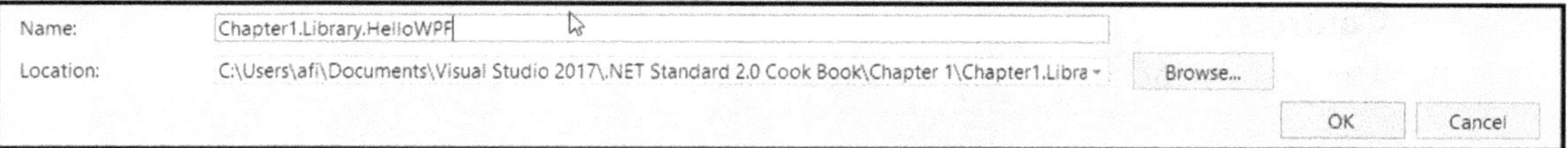

7. Now the **Solution Explorer** (if it's not visible, press *Ctrl* + *Alt* + *L*) should look like this:

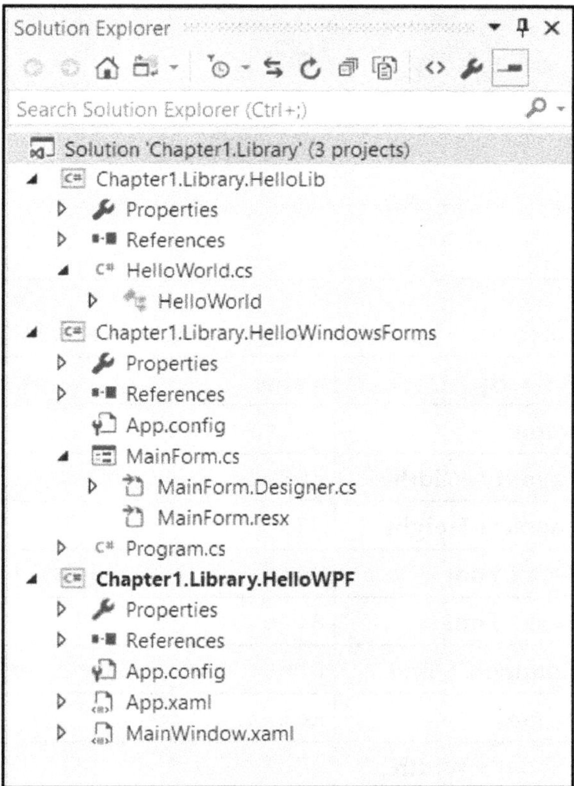

8. Now click on the `MainWindow.xaml` tab and make sure you are in the Design mode.
9. Now, drag and drop a **Button** and a **TextBlock** from the tool box (to view the tool box, press *Ctrl* + *Alt* + *X*). You can find these components under **Common WPF Controls**.
10. The main window should look like this:

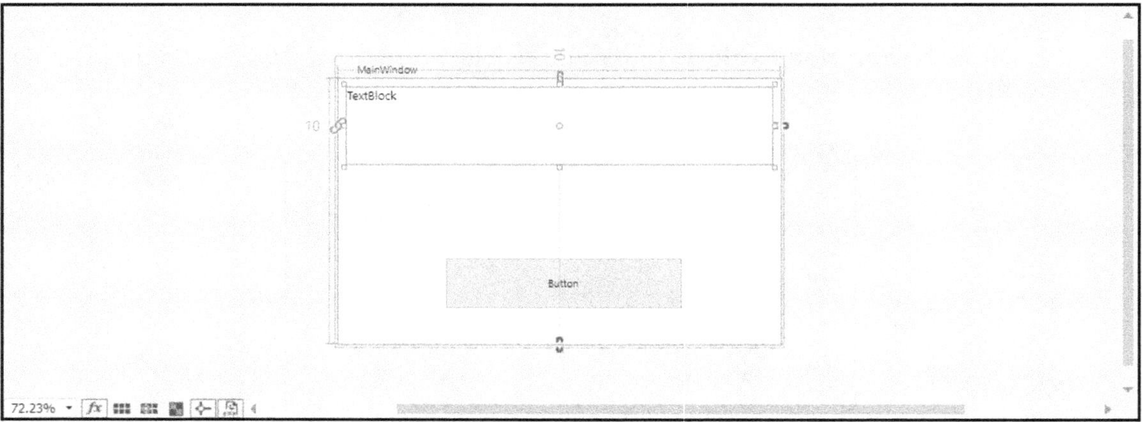

11. Let's name our controls and change some properties as follows:

Control	Property	Value
TextBlock	**Name**	`MessageLabel`
TextBlock	**Layout | Width**	`498`
TextBlock	**Layout | Height**	`93`
TextBlock	**Text | Font**	`Bold`
TextBlock	**Text | Font**	`Size 14`
TextBlock	**Common | Text**	`Press the button to see the message`
Button	**Name**	`HelloButton`
Button	**Layout | Width**	`276`
Button	**Layout | Height**	`60`
Button	**Common | Content**	`Say Hello`

12. Let's add our class library as a reference to the WPF project we have just created. Expand the `Chapter1.Library.HelloWPF` project node and expand the **References** node in the **Solution Explorer** (if you don't see the **Solution Explorer** press *Ctrl* + *Alt* + *L*).
13. Right-click on the **References** label and select **Add Reference...**.
14. Under the **Reference Manager** dialog box, click on the **Projects** label in the left-hand pane. In the middle pane, check the `Chapter1.Library.HelloLib` project:

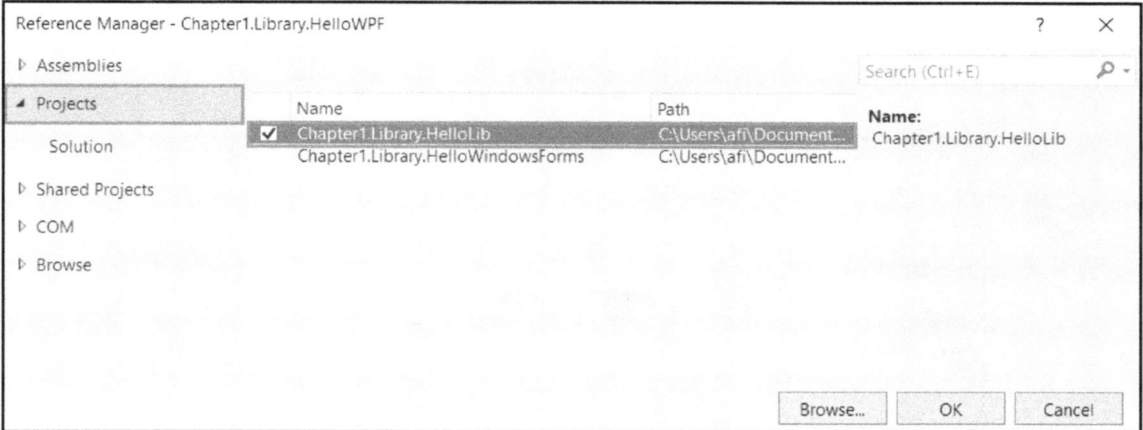

15. Click **OK**.
16. In the `MainWindow.xaml` tab, double-click on the `SayHello` button.
17. In the `MainWindow.xamal.cs` tab, scroll up till you see the `using` code block. Add this code as the last line of the `using` code block:

```
using Chapter1.Library.HelloLib;
```

18. Now scroll down till you reach the `HelloButton_Click` method. Type the following code block in between the curly brackets of the `HelloButton_Click` method:

```
var yourName = "Fiqri Ismail";
var helloMessage = new HelloWorld();

MessageLabel.Text = helloMessage.SayHello(yourName);
```

19. Now we are ready to test. Press *F5* to debug our code:

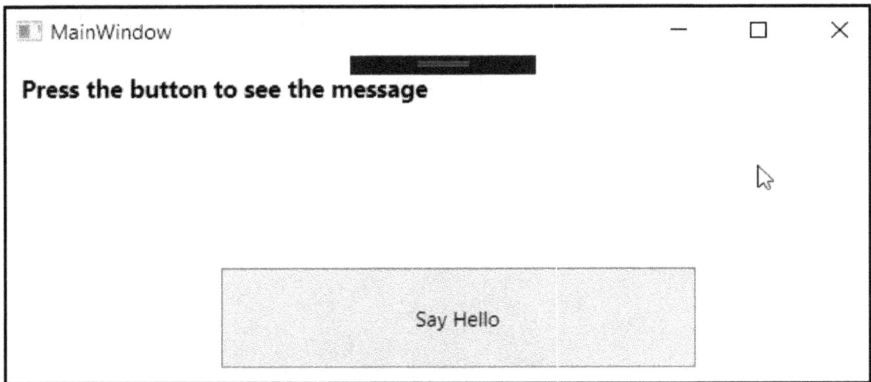

20. Click on the **Say Hello** button to see the message from the class library:

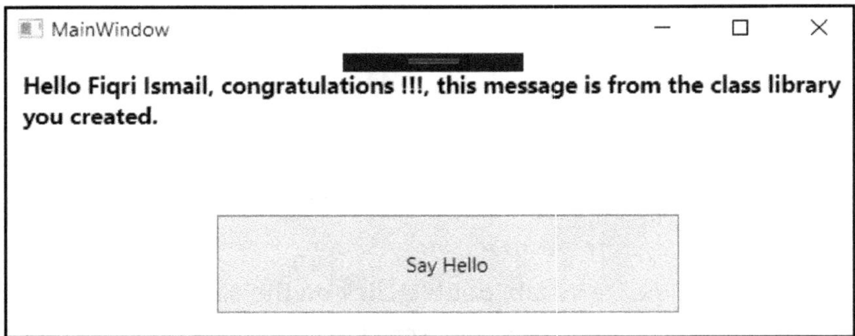

21. Congratulations!!! You have just used a library created with a WPF application.

How it works...

Let's have a look at the bits and pieces and how they are bound together. From steps 1 to 7, we have opened an existing solution and added a WPF project to that solution. In steps 8 to 10, we added a control to the WPF main form, from the toolbox. Since this is a WPF application, we went through an additional element; setting up the UI. In step 11, we have set up the UI elements using the properties window.

In steps 12 to 15, we added a reference to the WPF project. Referencing the library we have created is the most important part. Without referencing, the WPF project is totally unaware of the library. After referencing the library only, it will available to the WPF project. Step 17 tells the compiler to use the namespace of the library. Now we don't have to call the full namespace of the class inside the library. In step 18, we created a simple variable and stored a name. The next line creates an instance of the `HelloWorld` class inside the library. Finally, we used the **Text** property of the WPF **TextBlock** control to store the value from the `SayHello(string name)` method.

In the final steps – 19 to 20, we have executed the code and tested it.

Hello Universe – My first .NET Standard class library

Now it's time to move on and take a look at the Microsoft .NET Standard. In this recipe, we will be looking at version 2.0 of the .NET Standard library. At the start, we will be building a small .NET Standard class library and using it with different .NET-based applications.

Getting ready

Let's make sure we have downloaded and installed one of the flavors of Visual Studio 2017. If you are running on Windows, you have the option of choosing Visual Studio 2017 Community Edition, Professional Edition, or Enterprise Edition. If you are running on a mac, you have the choice of Visual Studio 2017 for macOS. Also, Visual Studio Code is available for all Windows, Mac, and Linux platforms. Visit `http://www.visualstudio.com` and follow the instructions to download the Visual Studio of your choosing.

In the next step, we will be required to download and install .NET Core 2.0. Again, simply visit `http://www.dot.net/core` and download the latest version, in this case, version 2.0 of .NET Core. The site has a very simple and informative set of instructions on how to install .NET Core 2.0 on your system.

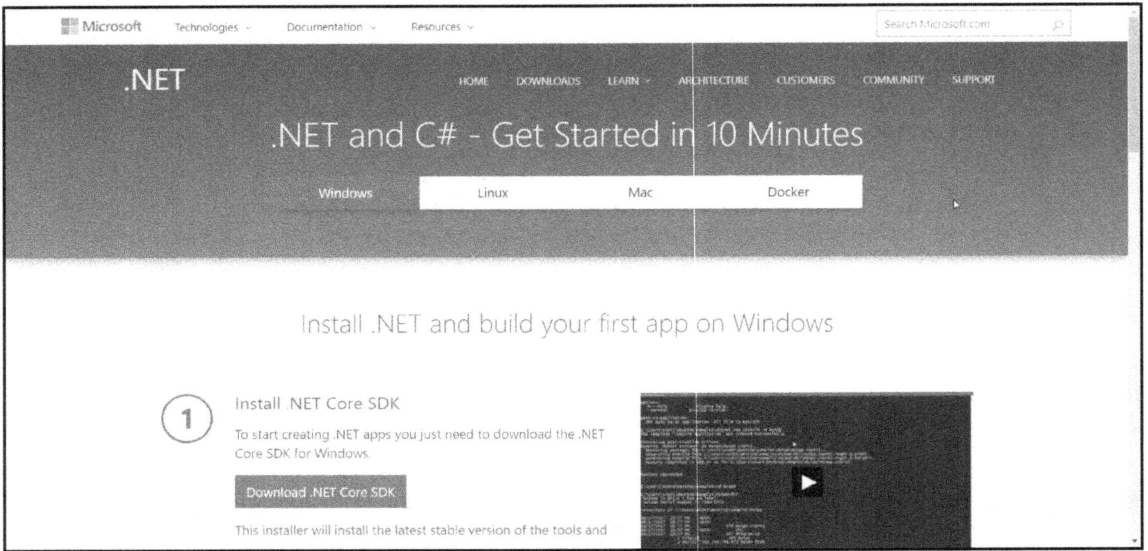

How to do it...

1. Open Visual Studio 2017.
2. Click **File** | **New** | **Project**.
3. Now, in the **New Project** dialog box, expand the **Visual C#** node in the left-hand pane and select **Class Library .NET Standard**, and in the right-hand pane, select **Class Library (.NET Standard)**:

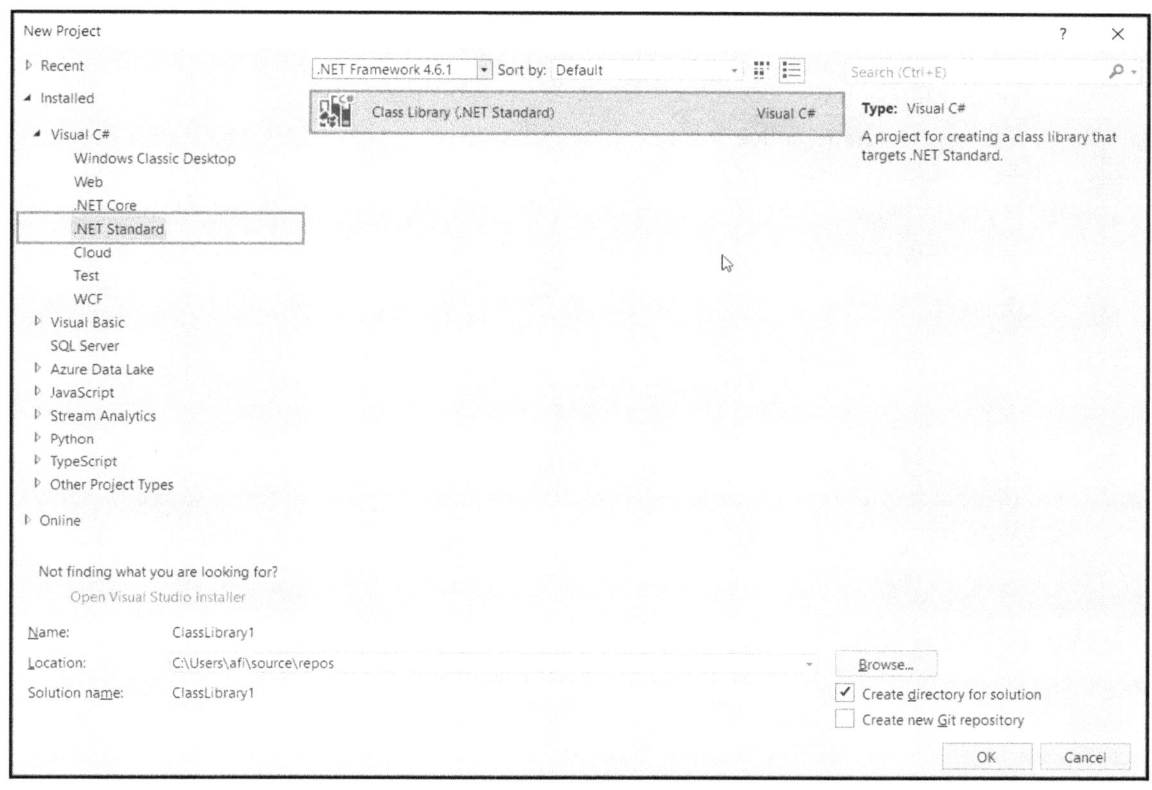

4. In the **Name:** text box, type a name for your class library. Let's type `Chapter1.StandardLib.HelloUniverse` and select a preferred location under the **Location:** drop-down list, or click the **Browse...** button and select a location. Leave the defaults as they are. Finally, in the **Solution name:** text box, type `Chapter1.StandardLib`.

Name: Chapter1.StandardLib.HelloUniverse
Location: C:\Users\afi\Documents\Visual Studio 2017\.NET Standard 2.0 Cook Book\Chapter 1\
Solution name: Chapter1.StandardLib
Browse...
Create directory for solution
Create new Git repository
OK
Cancel

5. Click **OK**.

6. In the **Solution Explorer** (press *Ctrl* + *Alt* + *L*) , click on **Class1.cs**, press *F2*, and rename it `HelloUniverse.cs`. Confirm the renaming by selecting Yes in the confirmation box.
7. Change the namespace from `Chapter1.StandardLib.HelloUniverse` to `Chapter1.StandardLib`.
8. Now, in between the curly brackets of the `HelloUniverse` class, type the following code:

```
public string SayHello(string name)
{
    return $"Hello {name},
    welcome to a whole new Universe of .NET Standard 2.0";
}
```

9. Press *Ctrl* + *S* to save the changes and press *Ctrl* + *Shift* + *B* to build the code. If the build completes without any errors, we are good to go with the next recipe on how to use this class library.

How it works...

.NET Standard 2.0 is the latest release of its kind. .NET Standard is all about sharing code. Unlike .NET Framework class libraries, .NET Standard class library code can be shared across almost all of the .NET ecosystem. The latest version of .NET Standard is 2.0. At the time of writing, it can be shared across NET Framework 4.6.1, .NET Core 2.0, Mono 5.4, Xamarin.iOS 10.14, Xamarin.Mac 3.8, Xamarin.Android 7.5, and the upcoming version of **Universal Windows Platform** (**UWP**). It also replaces **Portable Class Libraries** (**PCLs**) as the tool for building .NET libraries that work everywhere.

In steps 1 to 5, we have created a new .NET Standard 2.0-based class library project. In step 4, we have given a proper name to the class library as well as to the solution. It is good practice to give a meaningful name to the project and to the solution. In step 6, we have changed the name of the default class to `HelloUniverse.cs`, and it automatically changed the class name thanks to refactoring features in Visual Studio. If you look at the layout of the .NET Standard 2.0 library template, you will see a **Dependencies** node. In a normal .NET Framework class library, we had **References**. The **Dependencies** node will list all the dependent components for that class library.

In step 8, we added a simple public method that takes a string parameter and returns a message with the parameter sent to the method. Finally, we checked for syntax errors and typos by building the solution.

Creating a Windows console-based application to use the library

We have created a .NET Standard 2.0-based class library in the previous recipe. In this recipe, we will be creating a Windows console-based application to use the library. The console-based application will be using the full .NET Framework under Windows, the current version of .NET Framework is 4.6.1.

Getting ready

Let's get ready to create the Windows console application to use the .NET Standard library we have built in the previous recipe. If you haven't followed the previous recipe, make sure you have completed it. We are going to use that solution and add the Windows console application to it. Open Visual Studio 2017 and open the solution we saved from the previous recipe. Click **Build** | **Build Solution**, or press *Ctrl* + *Shift* + *B*, and the solution should build successfully. Everything's ready for testing our class library.

How to do it...

1. Open Visual Studio 2017.
2. Now, open the solution from the previous recipe. Click **File** | **Open** | **Open Project/Solution**, or press *Ctrl* + *Shift* + *O*, and select the `Chapter1.StandardLib` solution.
3. Now, click on the `Chapter1.Library` solution label. Click **File** | **Add** | **New Project**.

4. In the **Add New Project** template dialog box, expand the **Visual C#** node in the left-hand pane. Select **Windows Classic Desktop** and select **Console App (.NET Framework)** from the right-hand pane.

Add New Project
Recent
Installed
Visual C#
Windows Classic Desktop
Web
.NET Core
.NET Standard
Cloud
Test
WCF
Visual Basic
SQL Server
Azure Data Lake
JavaScript
Stream Analytics
Python
TypeScript
Online
.NET Framework 4.6.1 Sort by: Default
WPF App (.NET Framework) Visual C#
Windows Forms App (.NET Framework) Visual C#
Console App (.NET Framework) Visual C#
Class Library (.NET Framework) Visual C#
Shared Project Visual C#
Windows Service (.NET Framework) Visual C#
Empty Project (.NET Framework) Visual C#
WPF Browser App (.NET Framework) Visual C#
WPF Custom Control Library (.NET Framework) Visual C#
WPF User Control Library (.NET Framework) Visual C#
Windows Forms Control Library (.NET Framework) Visual C#
Search (Ctrl+E)
Type: Visual C#
A project for creating a command-line application
Not finding what you are looking for?
Open Visual Studio Installer
Name: ConsoleApp1
Location: C:\Users\afi\Documents\Visual Studio 2017\.NET Standard 2.0 Cook Book\Chapter 1\Chapter1.Stan
Browse...
OK Cancel

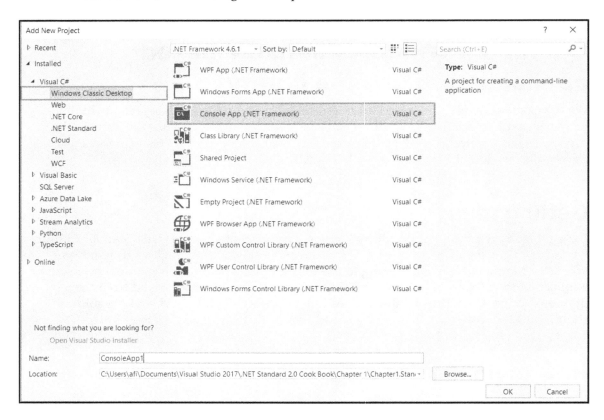

5. Now, in the **Name:** text box, type `Chapter1.Standard.HelloConsole` and leave the **Location:** text box as it is.

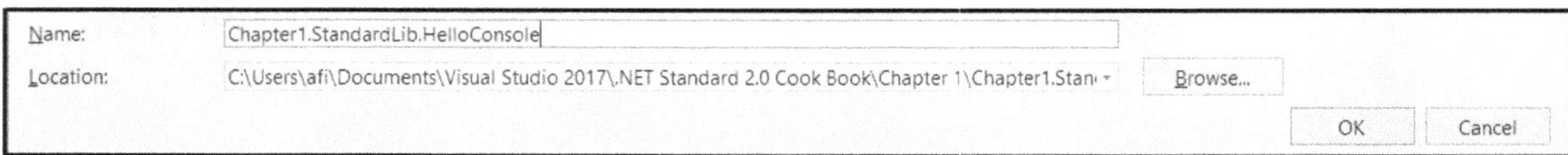

6. Click **OK**.
7. Now, the **Solution Explorer** (if not visible, press *Ctrl* + *Alt* + *L*) should look like this:

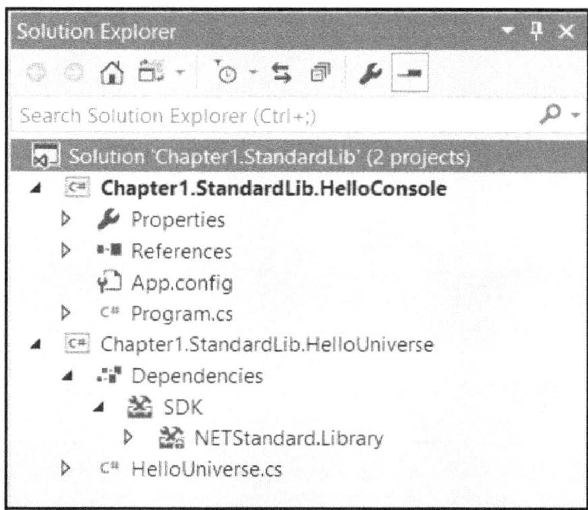

8. In the `Chapter1.StandardLib.HelloConsole` project tree, right-click on the **References** label and select **Add Reference...**.
9. Under the **Reference Manager** dialog box, click on the **Projects** label in the left-hand pane. In the middle pane, check the `Chapter1.StandardLib.HelloUniverse` project.

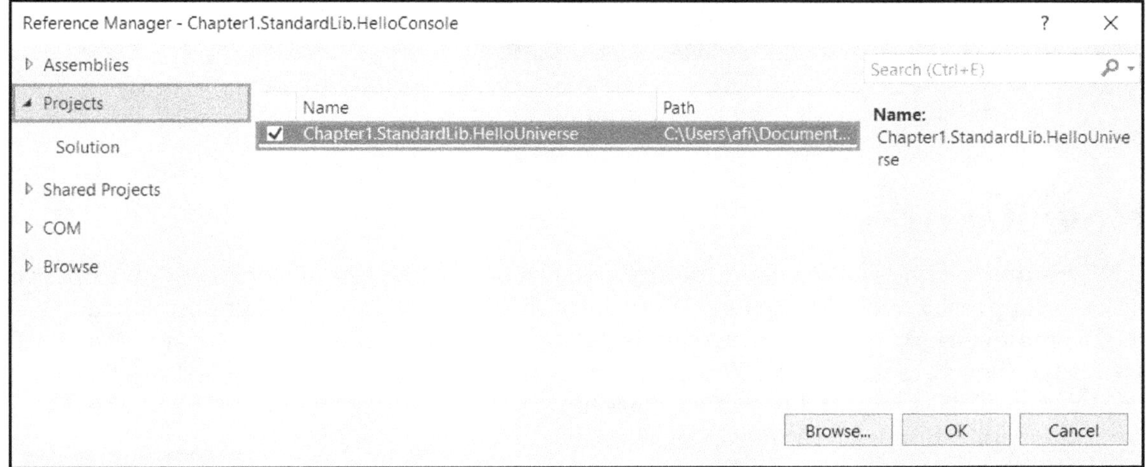

10. Click **OK**.
11. In the **Solution Explorer**, double-click on the `Program.cs` filename under the `Chapter1.StandardLib.HelloConsole` project.
12. Scroll up till you reach the `using` directive part of the code and add the following code as the last line of that section:

```
using Chapter1.StandardLib;
```

13. Now, in between the curly brackets of the `Main()` method, type the following code:

```
var myName = "Fiqri Ismail";
var helloMessage = new HelloUniverse();
Console.WriteLine(helloMessage.SayHello(myName));
Console.ReadLine();
```

14. Hit *F5* and see the code running:

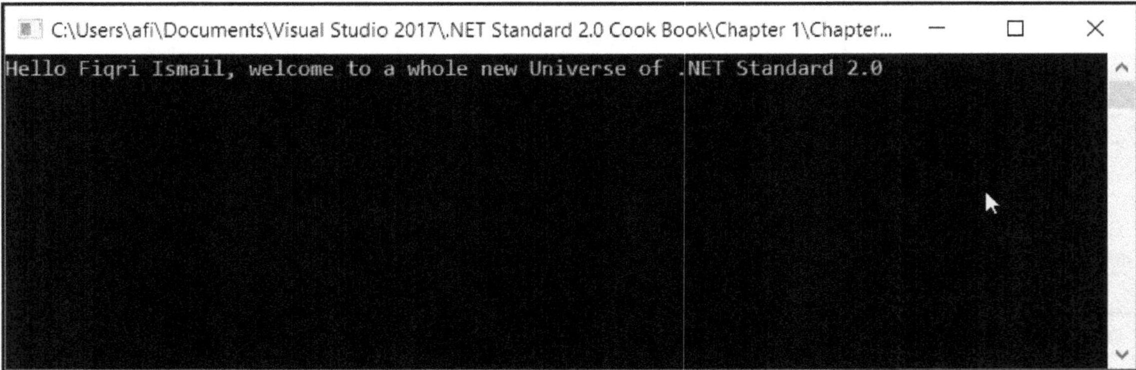

15. Press *Enter* to exit from the **Command Prompt**.

How it works...

OK, let's dive behind the scenes of the stuff we just completed. From steps 1 to 7, we opened an existing project and added a new Windows console application. This project is a full .NET Framework project and its version is .NET Framework version 4.6.1. In steps 9 and 10, we added the reference to a .NET Standard class library project from the Windows console application. This is required to test the class library. Then, we can reference it and use it from the application, as we did in step 12.

In step 13, we created a variable to store the name (keep in mind, hardcoding is not a good practice). And then we have created an instance of the `HelloUniverse` class that we created in the .NET Standard 2.0 class library. To display the output of the `SayHello()` method to the console window, we have directly used the `Console.WriteLine()` method. Finally, we waited until the user presses a key to exit from the console by using the `Console.ReadLine()` method, or else the end user wouldn't be able to see any output in the console.

Creating an ASP.NET Core-based web application to use the library

So far, we have tested the .NET Standard 2.0 class library with a Windows console application that runs under full .NET Framework version 4.6.1. In this recipe, we are going to create an ASP.NET Core 2.0 application. ASP.NET Core uses .NET Core, which is an open source, cross-platform supported .NET flavor.

Getting ready

Let's get ready to create the ASP.NET Core application to use the .NET Standard library we have built in the previous recipe when we created the .NET Standard library. If you haven't followed that recipe, make sure you have completed it. We are going to use that solution and add the ASP.NET Core application to it. Also, make sure you have downloaded and installed the latest version of .NET Core Framework, which is available at `http://www.dot.net/core`.

Open Visual Studio 2017 and open the solution we saved from the previous recipe. Click **Build** | **Build Solution**, or press *Ctrl* + *Shift* + *B*, and the solution should build successfully. Everything's ready for testing our class library.

How to do it...

1. Open Visual Studio 2017.
2. Now, open the solution from the previous recipe. Click **File** | **Open** | **Open Project/Solution**, or press *Ctrl* + *Shift* + *O*, and select the `Chapter1.StandardLib` solution.

3. Now click on the `Chapter1.Library` solution label. Click **File** | **Add** | **New Project**.
4. In the **Add New Project** template dialog box, expand the **Visual C#** node in the left-hand pane. Select **Web** and select **ASP.NET Core Web Application** from the right-hand pane:

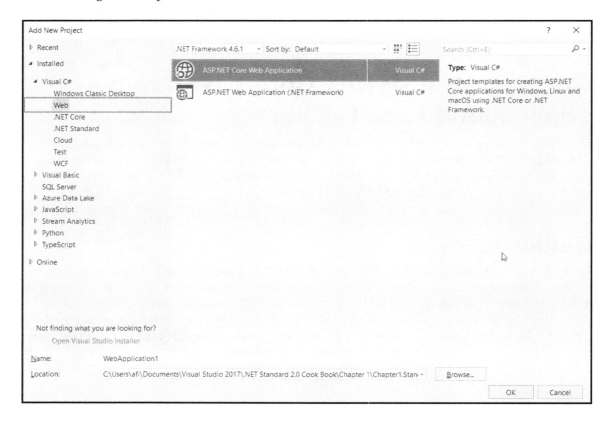

5. In the **Name:** text box, type `Chapter1.StandardLib.AspNetCore` as the name of the project and leave the **Location:** as it is:

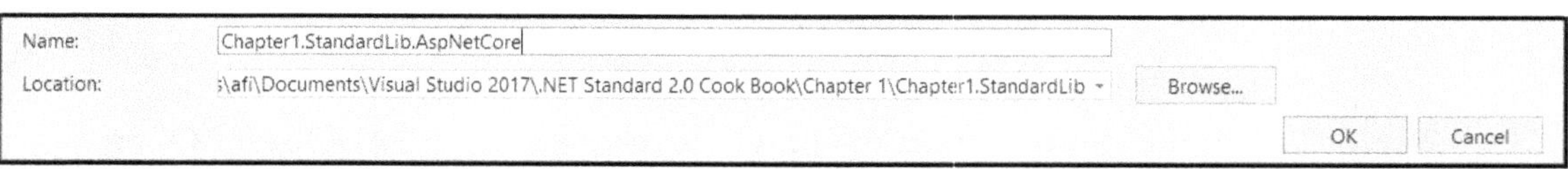

6. Click **OK**.

7. Now, in the **New ASP.NET Core Web Application** dialog box, select **.NET Core** from the first drop-down list and **ASP.NET Core 2.0** from the second drop-down list. Finally, select **Web Application (Model-View-Controller)** from the templates list:

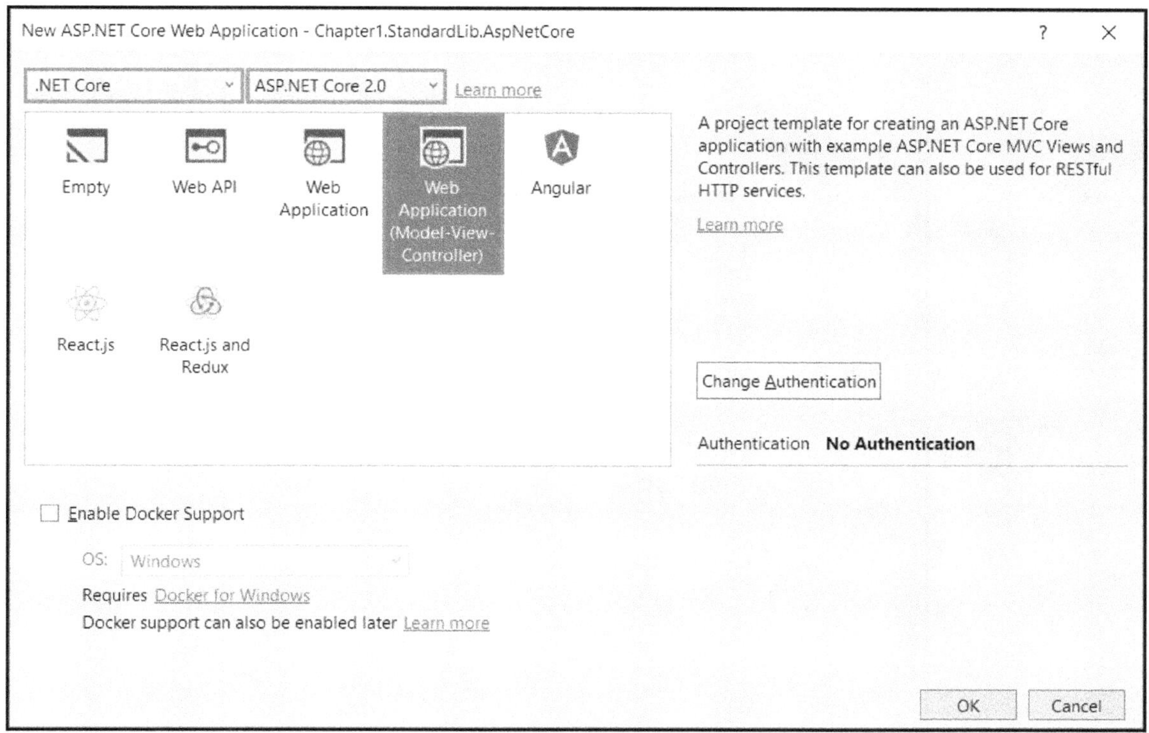

8. Leave the defaults as they are and Click **OK**.
9. Now, the **Solution Explorer** should look like this:

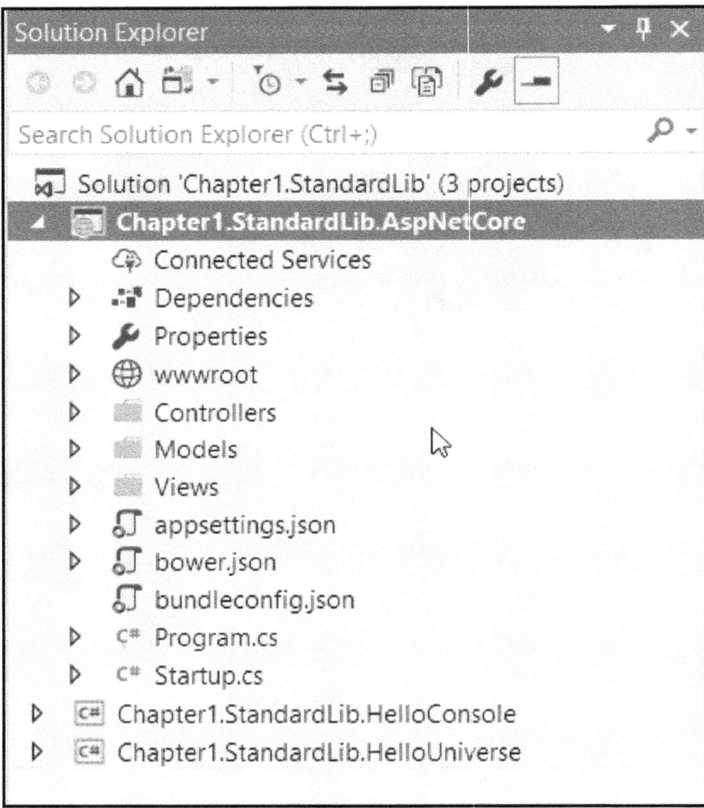

10. Select the `Chapter1.StandardLib.AspNetCore` project, right-click, and select **Set as Startup Project**.

11. Now hit *F5* for a test run. If everything is running smoothly, you should see this default ASP.NET Core template running on your default browser:

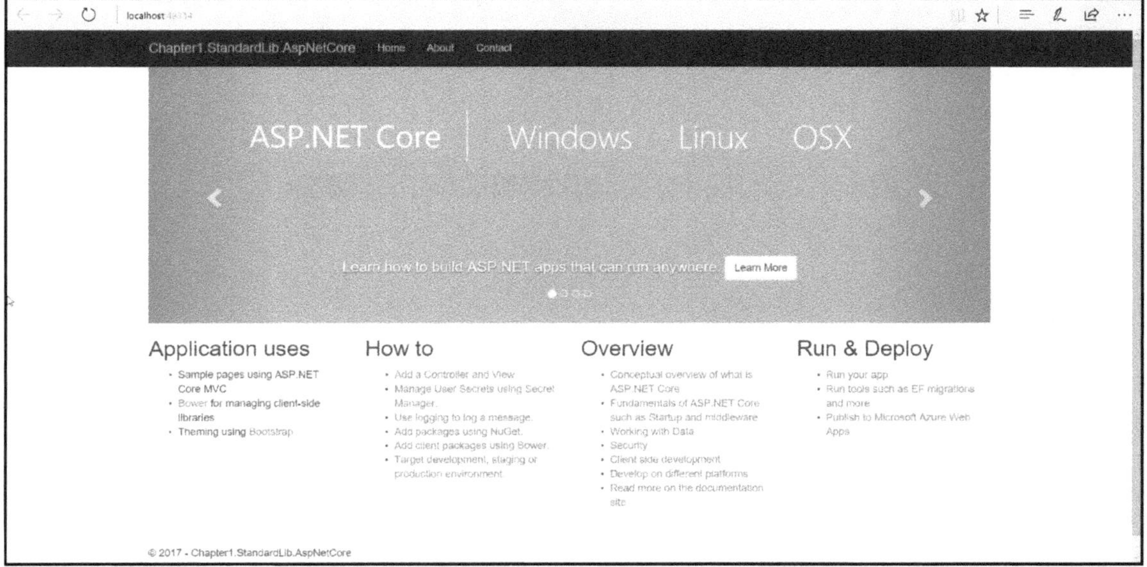

Default ASP.NET Core template running on your default browser

12. Let's close the browser and add our .NET Standard class library as a reference. To do this, expand the `Chapter1.StandardLib.AspNetCore` project tree and select **Dependencies**.
13. Right-click on the **Dependencies** label and select **Add Reference**.

14. Under the **Reference Manager** dialog box, click on the **Projects** label in the left-hand pane. In the middle pane, check the `Chapter1.StandardLib.HelloUniverse` project and click **OK**.

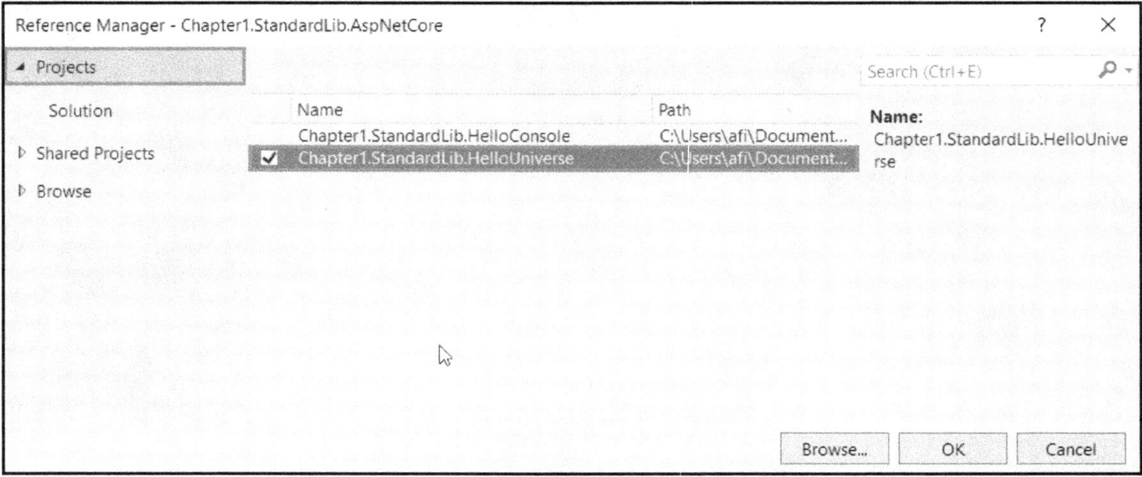

15. Let's expand the **Controllers** folder and double-click `HomeController.cs`.
16. In `HomeController.cs`, add this code right next to the last line of the `using` directive block:

```
using Chapter1.StandardLib;
```

17. Now, inside the `About()` action, add the following code block after the `ViewData["Message"]` line (by default, this is after line 21 in the default template):

```
var myName = "Fiqri Ismail";
var helloMessage = new HelloUniverse();
ViewData["HelloMessage"] = helloMessage.SayHello(myName);
```

18. Now expand the `Views` folder. Again, expand the `Home` folder as well.
19. Double-click on `About.cshtml`.
20. At the end of `About.cshtml`, add the following code:

```
<p>@ViewData["HelloMessage"]</p>
```

21. Now press *F5* to see it in action.

22. You will see the default ASP.NET Core template in the browser. Now click **About** to view the `About.cshtml` page:

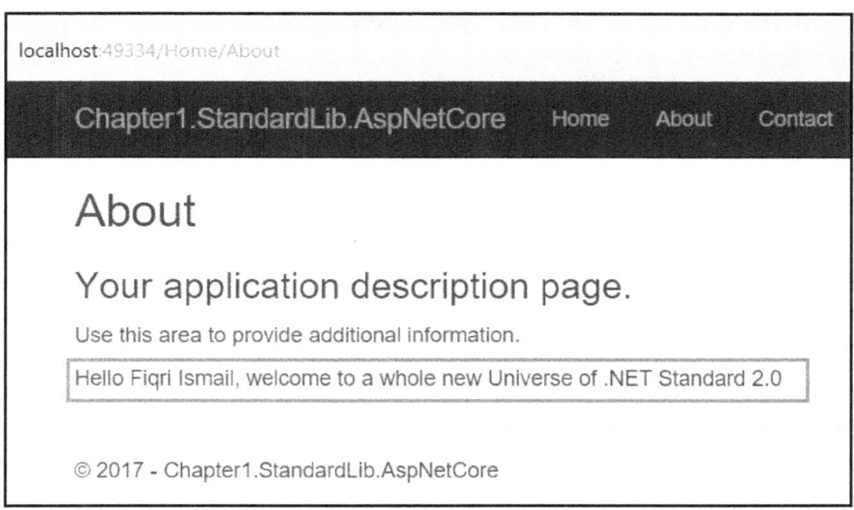

About.cshtml page

23. Excellent, now you have used a .NET Standard 2.0 library with an ASP.NET Core 2.0 web application.

How it works...

Let's have a look what we did just now. From steps 1 to 9, we opened and previously built an existing solution containing .NET Standard 2.0 library code. Then, we added an ASP.NET Core project to that solution. In step 10, we told Visual Studio to execute the ASP.NET Core project when we hit F5 or started debugging. In step 11, we tested the default template of ASP.NET Core in a default browser.

In steps 12 to 14, we added the reference to our ASP.NET Core application from the .NET Standard 2.0 class library. This allows you to access the library from an ASP.NET Core 2.0 web application. In step 16, we referenced the class library using the `using` directive. In step 17, we created a variable to hold the name and created an instance of the `HelloUniverse` class.

Finally, we have stored the message from the `SayHello()` method in the `ViewData` collection. The `ViewData` collection allows you to transfer data from Controllers to Views. In steps 19 and 20, we opened the relevant view for the `About()` action, which is `About.cshtml`. Finally, in step 20, we added simple HTML code to display the stored value in `ViewData` in the `HomeController` class. As a last step, we executed the web application and tested it.

2
Primitives, Collections, LINQ, and More

In this chapter, we will be covering the following recipes:

- Building a .NET Standard 2.0 library that uses primitives
- Building a .NET console application to use the library
- Creating collections
- Building a WPF application to use the library
- Describing our library with Reflections
- Building a .NET Core console application to use the library
- Building a .NET Standard 2.0 library that uses LINQ
- Building an ASP.NET MVC application to use the library

Technical requirements

Readers should have a basic knowledge of C#. They should also have a basic knowledge of using Visual Studio, installing packages using NuGet, and referencing libraries within projects from other projects.

The code files for this chapter can be found on GitHub:
`https://github.com/PacktPublishing/DotNET-Standard-2-Cookbook/tree/master/Chapter02`

Check out the following video to see the code in action:
`https://goo.gl/BiXiAM`

Introduction

When you look at C# as a language, there are things we need to look at first: what C# can do, how it supports our day-to-day programming requirements, and how it helps us to solve a problem. In this chapter, we will be mainly looking at primitive data types, collections, and LINQ features supported in C#. In the full .NET Framework, using these features is not a problem, but when it comes to cross-platform and code shared across flavors of the .NET Framework, it does becomes a concern.

Each recipe will go through building a .NET Standard 2.0 library and how to use it with an application that uses a flavor of the .NET Framework.

Building a .NET Standard 2.0 library that uses primitives

In this recipe, we will have a look at C# primitives and their usage in a .NET Standard 2.0 library. Primitives are one of the core parts of the framework. These types are defined in the .NET Framework itself and not in the C# language specification.

We will be building a .NET Standard 2.0 library that uses primitives in the .NET Framework and use it in the next recipe.

Getting ready

As mentioned, primitive data types are defined under .NET Framework itself and it's not language specific. It means you can use these data types across all languages supported under .NET Framework. It doesn't mean you can use these primitives under different flavors of .NET Framework. For example, if a data type is defined under .NET Framework version 4.6.1, and it's not defined under .NET Core 2.0, your code will fail under .NET Core 2.0.

Also, make sure you have the latest version of Visual Studio, which is 2017 at the time of writing.

How to do it...

1. Open Visual Studio 2017.
2. Click **File** | **New** | **Project** and, in the **New Project** template dialog box, select **Visual Studio Solutions** under the **Other Project Types** node in the left-hand pane and select **Blank Solution** in the right-hand pane.
3. In the **Name:** text box, type `Chapter2.Primitives` as the name of the solution. Select a preferred location under the **Location:** drop-down list or click the **Browse...** button and select a location. Leave the defaults as they are.

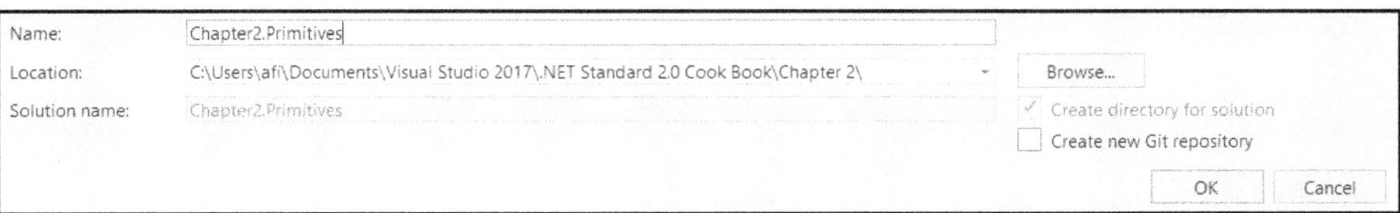

4. Click **OK**.
5. Now, in the **Solution Explorer** (or press *Ctrl* + *Alt* + *L*), select **Chapter2.Primitives**. Right-click and, select **Add** | **New Project.**
6. In the **Add New Project** dialog box, expand the **Visual C#** node and select **.NET Standard** in the left-hand pane.

7. In the right-hand pane, select **Class Library (.NET Standard)**:

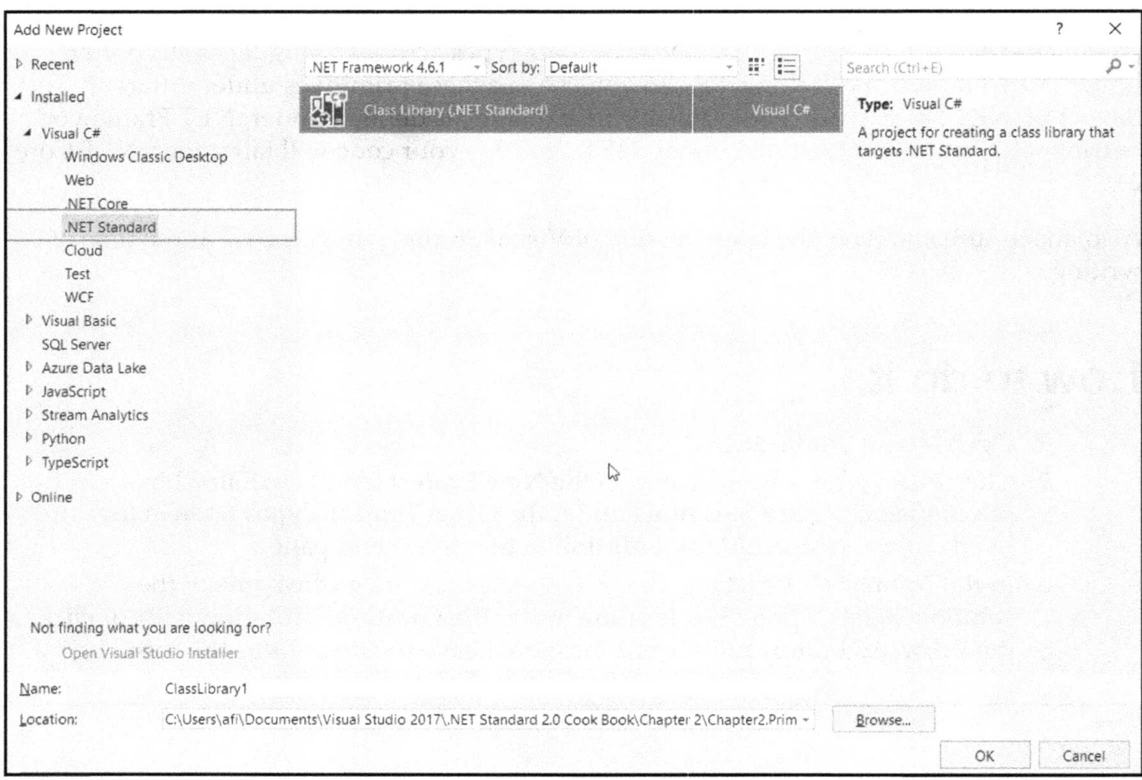

8. Now, in the **Name:** text box, type `Chapter2.Primitives.PrimitiveLib` and leave the **Location:** text box as it is:

Name: Chapter2.Primitives.PrimitiveLib
Location: C:\Users\afi\Documents\Visual Studio 2017\.NET Standard 2.0 Cook Book\Chapter 2\Chapter2.Prim
Browse...
OK
Cancel

9. Click **OK**.

10. Now, the **Solution Explorer** should look like this:

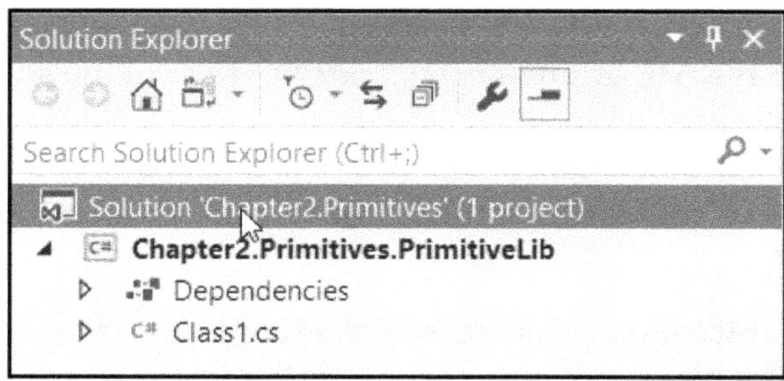

11. Click on **Class1.cs** and press *F2* to rename it. Type `Helpers.cs` as the new name.
12. Select **Yes** in the confirmation dialog box for renaming.
13. Now, double-click on `Helpers.cs` to open its code window.
14. Type the following code in between the curly brackets of the `Helpers` class:

```
public char WhatIsMyGrade(int yourMarks)
{
    var grade = 'F';
    if (yourMarks >= 85)
        grade = 'A';
    else if (yourMarks >= 65)
         grade = 'B';
    else if (yourMarks >= 55)
         grade = 'C';
    else if (yourMarks >= 35)
         grade = 'S';

    return grade;
}
```

15. Press *Ctrl* + *Shift* + *B* to build your code.
16. Again, type the following code next to the ending curly bracket from step 14:

```
public double CmToInches(double cm)
{
    var oneCmToInches = 0.393700787;
    return oneCmToInches * cm;
}
```

17. Let's build our code to check that everything is fine. Click **Build** | **Build Solution** or press *Ctrl* + *Shift* + *B* and the solution should build successfully. Let's test our class library in the next recipe.
18. Click **File** | **Save All**, or press *Ctrl* + *Shift* + *S*, to save the solution and the class library project.

How it works...

Let's have a look at what we have achieved so far. From steps 1 to 4, we opened Visual Studio 2017 and created a blank solution. Blank solutions are a very good foundation for a project that has multiple projects. In steps 5 to 10, we added a new project to the blank solution. In step 7, we used an existing base .NET Standard 2.0 project template and gave it a proper name in step 8.

In steps 11 and 12, we changed the default `Class1.cs` to a meaningful name. These names are very important and it helps a developer to understand what the code is for inside that file. In this case, we chose `Chapter2.Primitives.PrimitiveLib` as the project name. The first two sections provide the solution name and, at the end, there is the actual project name.

In step 14, we created code that includes a public method. The method takes an `int` type variable as the parameter. `int` is a primitive data type that is supported in the framework itself, so we have used it inside a .NET Standard library. It means the code can be shared across .NET Framework, .NET Core, and Mono running applications.

The data type `int` is an alias for `System.Int32` and these are the primitive types supported under .NET that can be used and shared in a .NET Standard 2.0 library:

- `Boolean`
- `Byte`
- `SByte`
- `Int16`
- `UInt16`
- `Int32`
- `UInt32`
- `Int64`
- `UInt64`
- `IntPtr`

- `UIntPtr`
- `Char`
- `Double`
- `Single`

The code takes a `char` variable and each `if` statement validates the marks sent through the `yourMarks` parameter in the method. Finally, the method returns a `char` value as the grade and then we confirmed all the syntax was correct and built successfully in step 15. In step 16, we created another method that converts centimeters to inches. The input parameter is another primitive type called `double`, which is also an alias for `System.Double`. This is because C# represents all primitives as objects. Inside the code, one variable already converts centimeters into inches and is stored as `oneCmToInches`. In the last line, we return the inches as `double`, converted from centimeters given in the parameter of the method.

In step 17, we did another build to check all code for syntax and finally did a save all.

A .NET console application to use the library

In this recipe we are going to do two things. First, we will be opening Visual Studio and doing a quick build of the previously built solution for the .NET Standard 2.0 library. Finally, we will be adding a .NET console application to use the library. This console application will be using .NET Framework 4.6.1 as the base framework under Windows.

Getting ready

Make sure you have completed the previous recipe that builds the .NET Standard 2.0 library. We will be using it in this recipe. Open Visual Studio 2017 and prepare for the project. Click **Build** | **Build Solution**, or press *Ctrl* + *Shift* + *B*, and the solution should build successfully. Everything's ready for testing our class library.

How to do it...

1. Open Visual Studio 2017.
2. Now open the solution from the previous recipe. Click **File** | **Open** | **Open Project/Solution**, or press *Ctrl* + *Shift* + *O*, and select the **Chapter2.Primitives** solution.

3. Now click on the **Chapter2.Library** solution label. Click **File** | **Add** | **New Project**.
4. In the **Add New Project** template dialog box, expand the **Visual C#** node in the left-hand pane.
5. Select **Windows Classic Desktop** and then **Console App (.NET Framework)** in the right-hand pane:

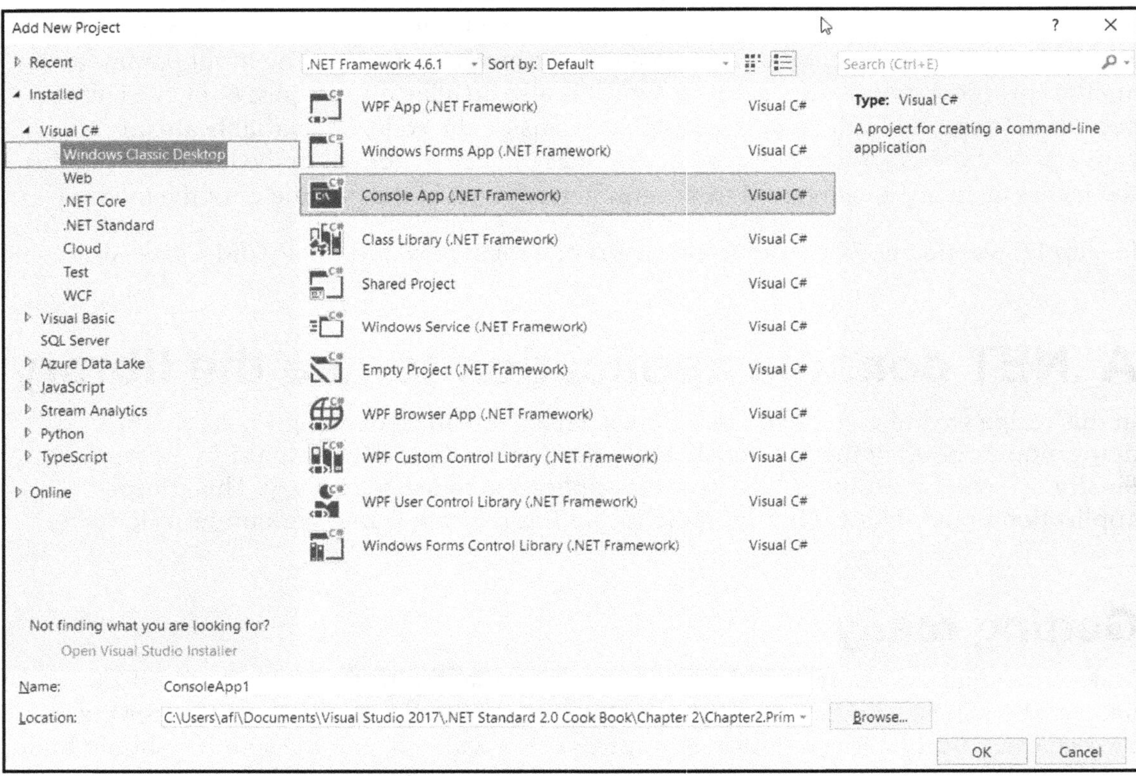

6. Now, in the **Name:** text box, type `Chapter2.Primitives.PrimitivesConsole` and leave the **Location:** text box as it is.

7. Click **OK**.
8. After adding the new project, the **Solution Explorer** (*Ctrl* + *Alt* + *L*) should look like this:

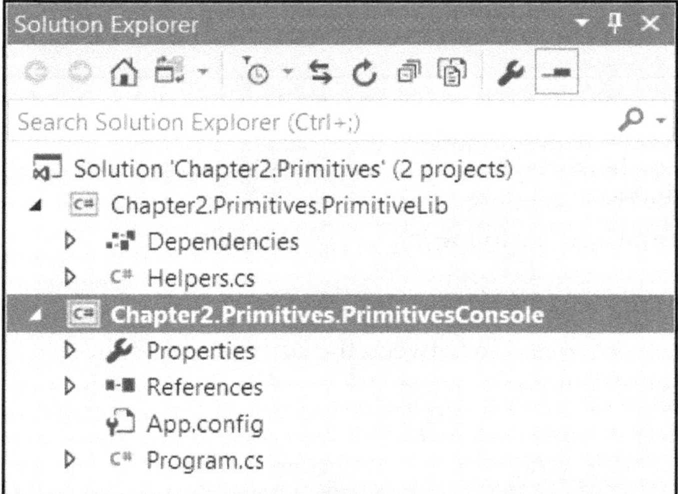

9. Click on the **References** label in the **Chapter2.Primitives.PrimitivesConsole** project node. Right-click and select **Add** | **Add Reference**.

10. In the **Reference Manager**, select **Projects** in the left-hand pane and check the **Chapter2.Primitives.PrimitiveLib** in the right-hand pane:

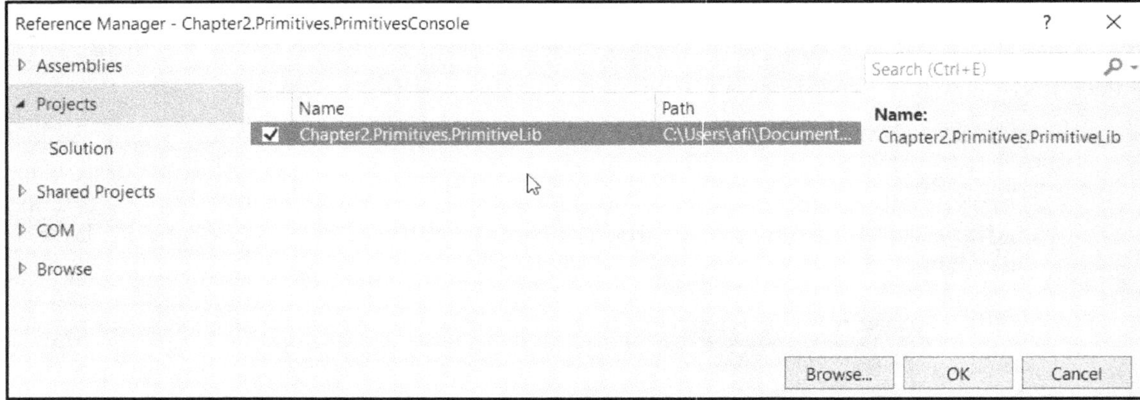

11. Click **OK** to add the reference to the selected project.
12. Now, in the newly added console application project, double-click on **Program.cs** to open the code window.
13. Scroll up and add the following `using` directive:

```
using Chapter2.Primitives.PrimitiveLib;
```

14. Now, scroll down and in between the curly braces of the `Main()` method, type the following code:

```
var myHelper = new Helpers();
var myGrade = myHelper.WhatIsMyGrade(65);
Console.WriteLine($"You are current grade is {myGrade}");

Console.ReadLine();
```

15. Now press *F5* to debug the code.

16. You should see output like this:

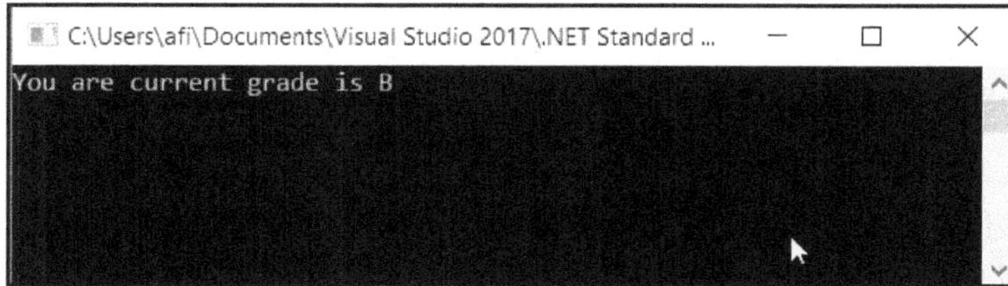

17. Now, press any key to exit the console, click just before the `Console.ReadLine()` line, and press *Enter* to add some new code.
18. Let's type the following code now:

```
var cm = 15;
var inches = myHelper.CmToInches(cm);
Console.WriteLine($"{cm} centimeters in inches are {inches}");
```

19. Press *F5* to see the output and you should see the following:

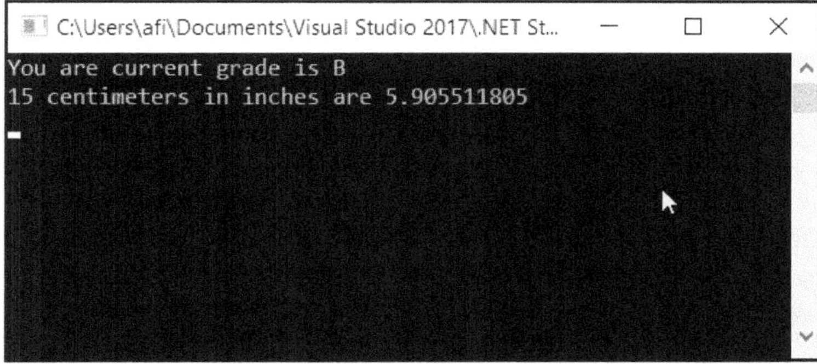

20. Now that we have successfully tested the library, change some values and see how it works.

How it works...

In steps 1 to 7, we opened an existing Visual Studio solution and added a new project to it. The newly added project is a .NET-based console application. In steps 9 to 11, we added the reference to the .NET Standard 2.0 library project. This is an important step. To use the functionality in the library, you must add the project as a reference.

In step 13, we added code to use the libraries' first method. The first line of code will define a variable to hold the instance of the `Helpers()` class. The `var` keyword helps you to create a local variable without giving an explicit type. It simply tells the compiler to get the type of variable from the expression on the right-hand side of the initialization statement. For example, see the following:

```
var myInteger = 10;
```

This is the same as the following:

```
int myInteger = 10;
```

The second line of code saves the return value from the `WhatIsMyGrade()` method. The next line will display the output to the console window. The last line will tell the console to wait till a key is pressed. In steps 14 and 15, we see the output of the code we wrote.

In step 17, we are testing the second method inside the `Helpers()` class inside the .NET Standard 2.0 library we created. In the first line, we created a variable that stores a default value that needs to be converted. In the second line, it stores the converted output in a variable. Again, we have used the `var` keyword to store the variable, which will automatically store the value with the type returned from the method, in this case to a `System.Double`. The third line will display the output to the console window. In steps 18 and 19, we executed the console application.

Creating collections

There are three kind of collections supported inside the .NET Framework. In this recipe, we will be focusing on using these collections inside a .NET Standard 2.0 library. In general, collections are used to manage groups of related objects. Creating arrays of objects is a way of grouping related objects. But our focus is on using these collections, which is the second method of grouping related objects.

Getting ready

These are the three kinds of collections we have in .NET Framework:

- `System.Collections.Generic` Classes
- `System.Collections.Concurrent` Classes
- `System.Collections` Classes

Let's have a look at these and their usage inside a .NET Standard 2.0 library.

How to do it...

1. Open Visual Studio 2017.
2. Click **File** | **New** | **Project** and, in the **New Project** template dialog box, select **Visual Studio Solutions** under the **Other Project Types** node in the left-hand pane, and then **Blank Solution** in the right-hand pane.
3. In the **Name:** text box, type `Chapter2.Collections` as the name of the solution. Select a preferred location under the **Location:** drop-down list or click the **Browse...** button and select a location. Leave the defaults as is they are:

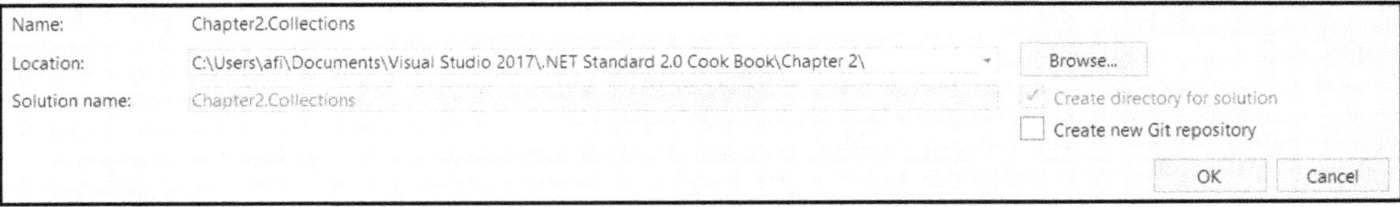

4. Click **OK**.
5. Now, in the **Solution Explorer** (or press *Ctrl* + *Alt* + *L*), select **Chapter2.Collections**. Right-click and select **Add** | **New Project**.
6. In the **Add New Project** dialog box, expand the **Visual C#** node and select **.NET Standard** in the left-hand pane.

7. In the right-hand pane, select **Class Library (.NET Standard)**:

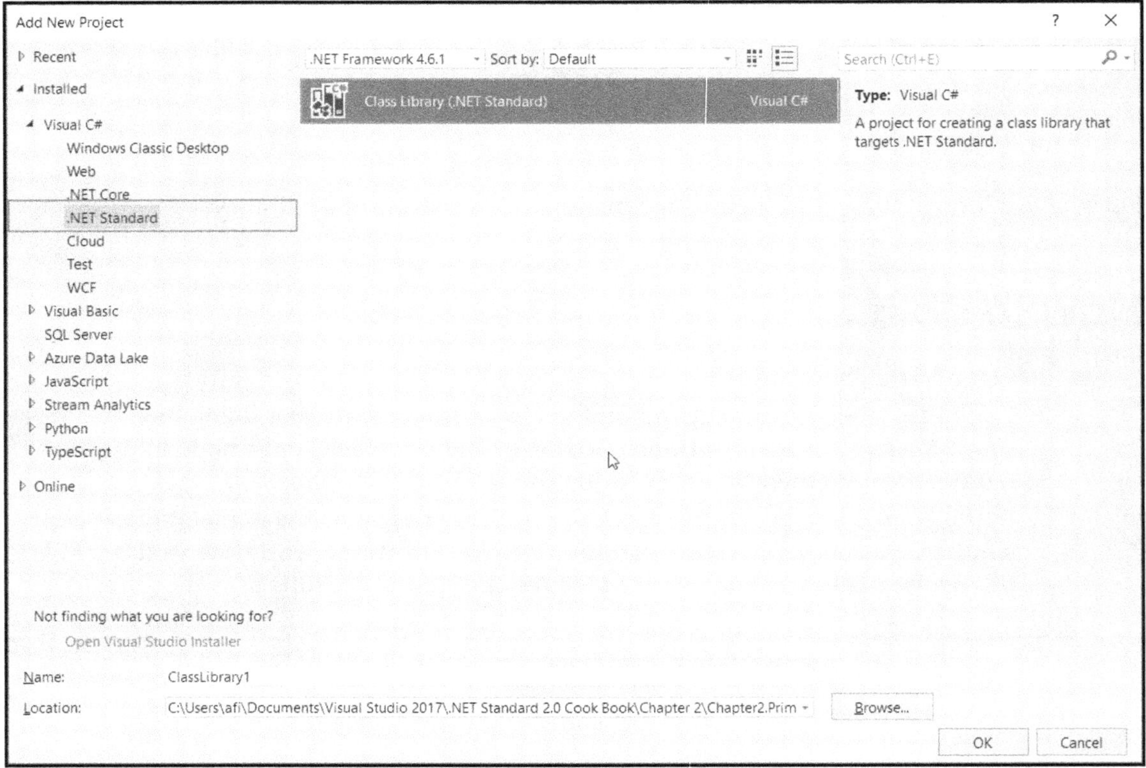

8. Now, in the **Name:** text box type `Chapter2.Collections.CollectionsLib` and leave the **Location:** text box, as it is:

Name: Chapter2.Collections.CollectionsLib
Location: C:\Projects\Chapter 2\Chapter2.Collections
Browse...
OK Cancel

9. Click **OK**.

10. Now, the **Solution Explorer** should look like this:

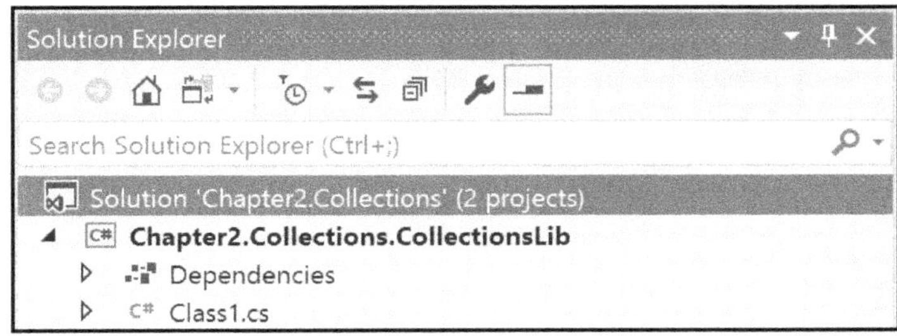

11. Click on the **Class1.cs** and press *F2* to rename it. Type `LittleShop.cs` as the new name.
12. Select **Yes** in the confirmation dialog box for renaming.
13. Now double-click on `LittleShop.cs` to open its code window.
14. At the top of the code window, move the cursor (or click the mouse) at the last line of the `using` directives and add the following `using` directive:

```
using System.Collections.Generic;
```

15. Type the following code in between the curly brackets of the `LittleShop` class:

```
public List<string> GetFruitsList()
{
    var fruitsList = new List<string>();
    fruitsList.Add("Apples");
    fruitsList.Add("Grapes");
    fruitsList.Add("Mangoes");
    fruitsList.Add("Oranges");
    fruitsList.Add("Pineapples");

    return fruitsList;
}
```

16. Let's press *Ctrl* + *Shift* + *B* for a quick build and check for any syntax errors.
17. Now type the following code at the end of the `using` directives at the top of your code window:

```
using System.Collections;
```

18. At the end of the `GetFruitsList()` method, add the following code:

```
public ArrayList GetShopItems()
{
    var shopItems = new ArrayList();
    shopItems.Add("Fruits");
    shopItems.Add("Vegetables");
    shopItems.Add("Chocolates");

    return shopItems;
}
```

19. Let's quickly hit a quick *Ctrl* + B to debug and check for syntax errors.
20. Now we are good to go and test the library.

How it works...

Let's see what's going on behind the scenes. From steps 1 to 4, we created the base for the project. This base will help you to create the .NET Standard 2.0 library and the project that will be using that library. A blank solution is always a good starting point for any sort of project. In steps 5 to 10, we added the .NET Standard 2.0 library project to the blank solution and gave it a meaningful name. In steps 11 to 13, we changed the default class template name to a meaningful name.

In step 14, we created a reference to the `System.Collections.Generics` namespace. This will give you access to all the collections available under this namespace. In step 15, we used one generic collection object known as `List<T>`. In the next few lines, we added some string objects to the variable created. Finally, we returned the list collection, which is the same return type as the `GetFruitsList()` method. Then, in step 16, we did a quick build, and this will help us to check the syntax of the code. It's good practice to do a quick build for syntax checking.

Again, in step 17, we added another reference to the `System.Collections` namespace. Then, in step 18, we added a `public` method that returns an `ArrayList()`, which contains in `System.Collections` namespace. In the first line of the `GetShopItems()` method, we are creating an instance of the `ArrayList()` object, and, in the next few lines, we are adding a string object to the `ArrayList()` using its `Add()` method. Finally, in the last line, we are returning the array list stored in the variable. Then, in step 19, we did a quick build, and this will help us to check the syntax of the code. It's good practice to do a quick build for syntax checking.

The last kind is the `System.Collections.Concurrent` namespace. This namespace contains collections that are thread safe. It means multiple threads can safely add or remove items from these collections.

A WPF application to use the library

In this recipe, we will be creating a Windows Presentation Foundation application to use the .NET Standard 2.0 library we created in the previous recipe. We will be continuing to build the application from the previous solution we created. Windows Presentation Foundation is a UI framework that works under .NET Framework and runs in a Windows OS.

Getting ready

Open Visual Studio 2017 and prepare for the project. Make sure you have completed building the .NET Standard 2.0 library in the preview build. Open that project if it's not already open and click **Build** | **Build Solution**, or press *Ctrl* + *Shift* + *B*, and the solution should build successfully. Everything's ready for testing our class library.

How to do it...

1. Open Visual Studio 2017.
2. Now open the solution from the previous recipe. Click **File** | **Open** | **Open Project/Solution**, or press *Ctrl* + *Shift* + *O*, and select the **Chapter2.Collections** solution.
3. Now, click on the **Chapter2.Collections** solution label. Click **File** | **Add** | **New Project**.
4. In the **Add New Project** template dialog box, expand the **Visual C#** node in the left-hand pane.

5. Select **Windows Classic Desktop** and then **WPF App (.NET Framework)** in the right-hand pane:

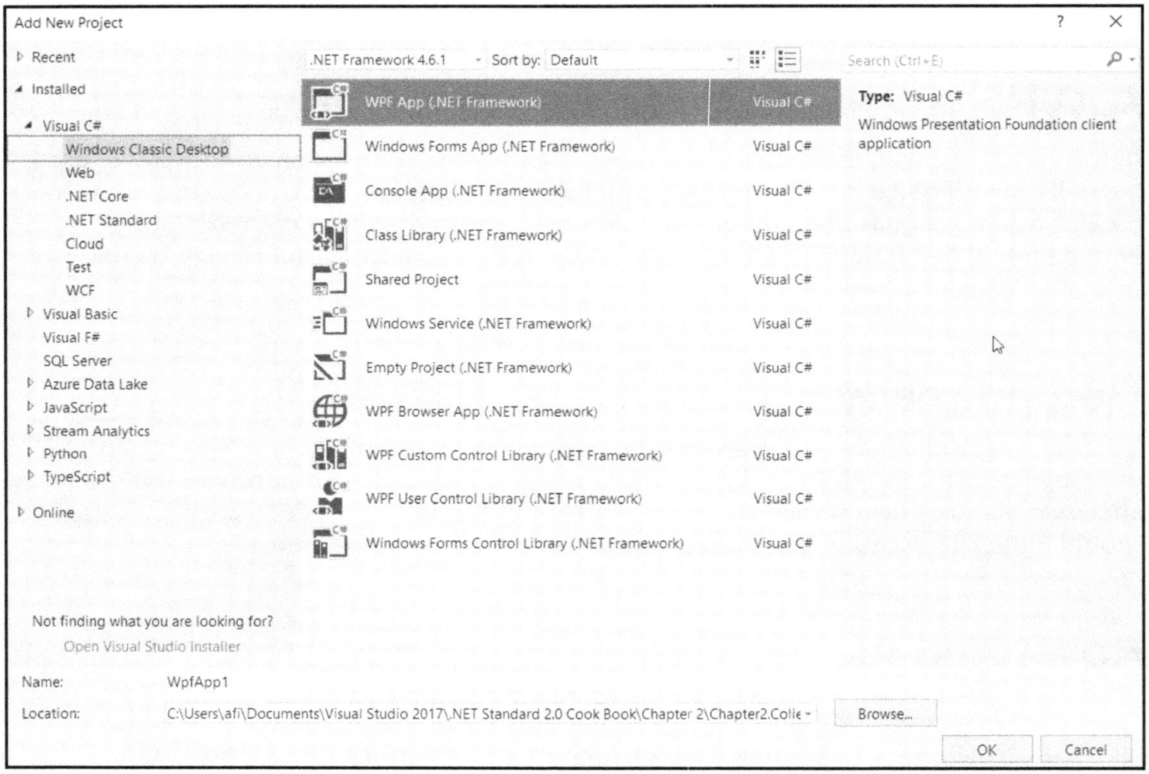

Add New Project
Recent
Installed
Visual C#
Windows Classic Desktop
Web
.NET Core
.NET Standard
Cloud
Test
WCF
Visual Basic
Visual F#
SQL Server
Azure Data Lake
JavaScript
Stream Analytics
Python
TypeScript
Online
.NET Framework 4.6.1
Sort by: Default
Search (Ctrl+E)
WPF App (.NET Framework) Visual C#
Windows Forms App (.NET Framework) Visual C#
Console App (.NET Framework) Visual C#
Class Library (.NET Framework) Visual C#
Shared Project Visual C#
Windows Service (.NET Framework) Visual C#
Empty Project (.NET Framework) Visual C#
WPF Browser App (.NET Framework) Visual C#
WPF Custom Control Library (.NET Framework) Visual C#
WPF User Control Library (.NET Framework) Visual C#
Windows Forms Control Library (.NET Framework) Visual C#
Type: Visual C#
Windows Presentation Foundation client application
Not finding what you are looking for?
Open Visual Studio Installer
Name: WpfApp1
Location: C:\Users\afi\Documents\Visual Studio 2017\.NET Standard 2.0 Cook Book\Chapter 2\Chapter2.Colle
Browse...
OK
Cancel

6. In the **Name:** text box, type `Chapter2.Collections.WPFLittleShop` as the name of the project and leave the **Location:** text box as it is:

Name: Chapter2.Collections.WPFLittleShop
Location: C:\Users\afi\Documents\Visual Studio 2017\.NET Standard 2.0 Cook Book\Chapter 2\Chapter2.Colle
Browse...
OK
Cancel

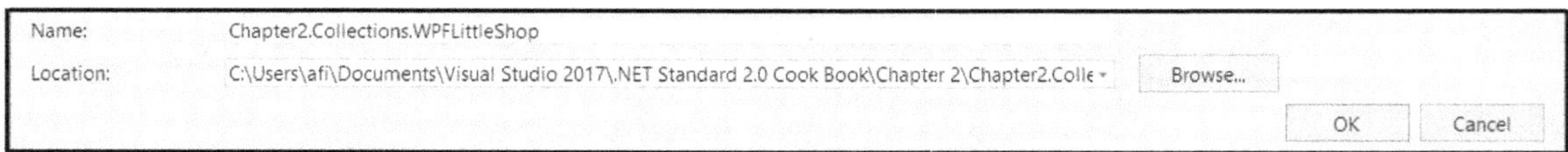

7. Click **OK**.
8. Now, the **Solution Explorer** (press *Ctrl* + *Alt* + *L* to open) should look like this:

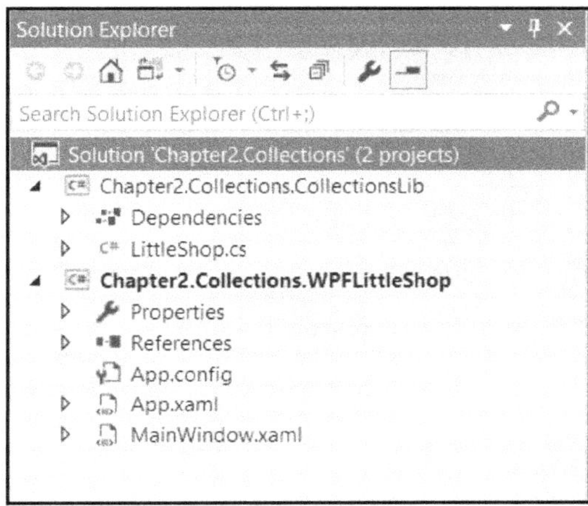

9. Now, double-click on the **MainWindow.xaml** to open the designer view.
10. Open the **Tool Box** by pressing *Ctrl* + *Alt* + *X* and drag and drop two **Buttons** and two **List Boxes** to the main window.
11. Place them as shown:

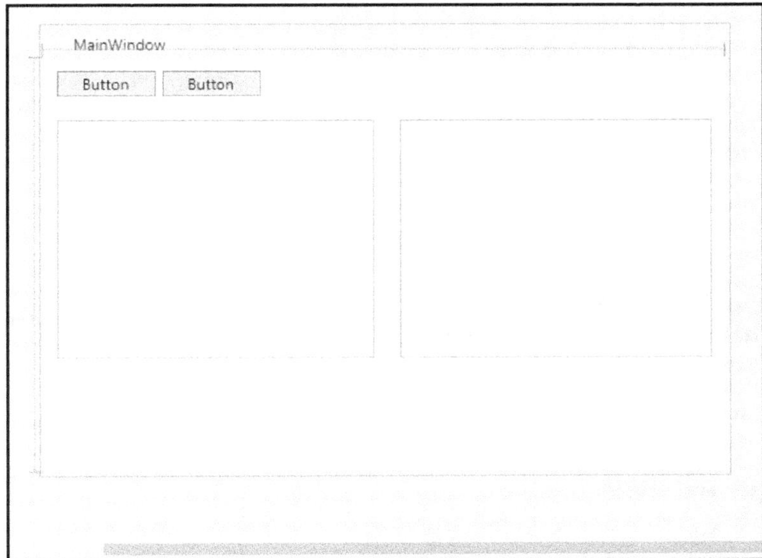

12. Now, open the **Properties** window, or press *F4*, and change the following properties:

Controler	**Property**	**Value**
Button *(first from the left)*	**Name**	`FruitsButton`
Button *(first from the left)*	**Content**	`Get Fruits`
Button *(second from the left)*	**Name**	`ItemsButton`
Button *(second from the left)*	**Content**	`Get Items`
ListBox (first from the left)	**Name**	`FruitsList`
ListBox (second from the left)	**Name**	`ItemsList`

13. After applying the previous properties, the **MainWindow** should look like this:

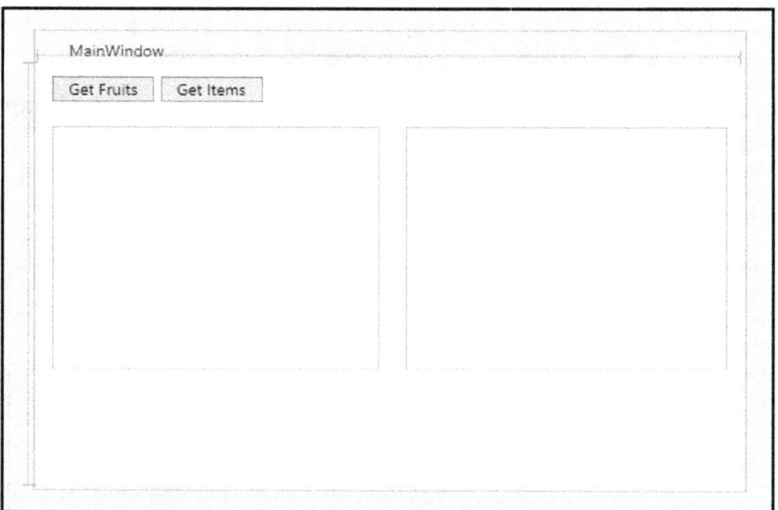

14. Now, in the **Solution Explorer** (or press *Ctrl* + *Alt* + *L*), expand the **Chapter2.Collections.WPFLittleShop** project tree.
15. Right-click on the **References** label and select **Add Reference**.
16. In the **Reference Manager** dialog box, expand the **Projects** node in the left-hand pane.
17. Click on **Solution**.

18. Now, check **Chapter2.Collections.CollectionsLib** in the right-hand pane:

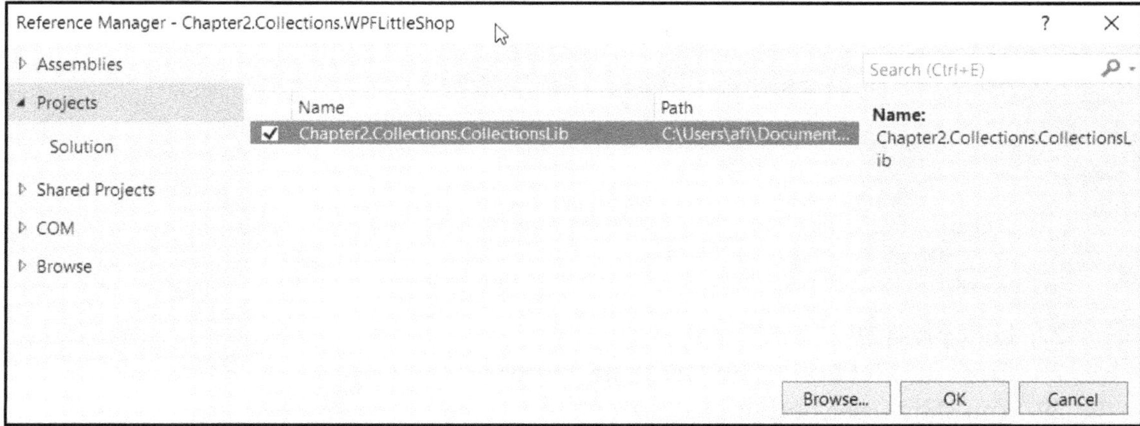

19. Click **OK**.
20. Double-click on the **Get Fruits** button.
21. You will see the `FruitsButton_Click()` method.
22. Scroll up the code window and add the following `using` directive at the end of all the `using` directives:

```
using Chapter2.Collections.CollectionsLib;
```

23. Again, scroll down and inside the `FruitsButton_Click()` method, write the following code:

```
var littleShop = new LittleShop();
var fruits = littleShop.GetFruitsList();
foreach (var fruit in fruits)
{
    FruitsList.Items.Add(fruit);
}

FruitsList.Items.Add("--------");
FruitsList.Items.Add($"Item Count: {fruits.Count}");
FruitsList.Items.Add($"Capacity: {fruits.Capacity}");
```

24. Switch back to the `MainWindow.xaml` design view by clicking on its tab or just double-clicking on the `MainWindow.xaml` label in the **Solution Explorer**.
25. Select the **Get Items** button and double-click on it.

26. Now type the following code inside the `ItemsButton_Click()` event method:

```
var littleShop = new LittleShop();
var items = littleShop.GetShopItems();

for (int i=0; i<items.Count; i++)
{
    ItemsList.Items.Add(items[i]);
}

ItemsList.Items.Add("--------");
ItemsList.Items.Add($"Item Count: {items.Count}");
ItemsList.Items.Add($"Capacity: {items.Capacity}");
```

27. Let's press *F5* and debug the code.
28. Press the **Get Fruits** and **Get Items** buttons.
29. You should see output like this:

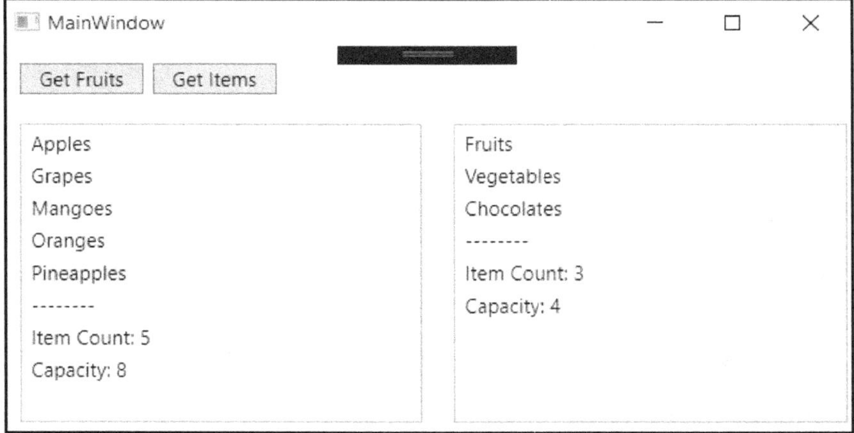

How it works...

Now we have a working WPF application that uses a .NET Standard 2.0 library as its source. Let's have a look at the steps we followed. In steps 1 to 7, we opened the previously built .NET Standard 2.0 library project and the solution. After that, we added a Windows Presentation Foundation project to the solution. As you know, WPF is a UI framework that runs on top of the .NET Framework.

From steps 9 to 13, we just created the user interface for our application. Then, in step 12, we changed some default properties of the controls we added. Giving meaningful names is a very good practice as it helps you to build readable code. In step 20, we just double-clicked on a control, in this case the button, to open the code windows. By default, Visual Studio chooses an event for us. Mainly, it chooses a commonly used event and, in this case, it's the click event of the button.

In step 22, we referenced the .NET Standard 2.0 library to the code. This will allow you to access its available methods in the WPF application. In step 23, we have the actual running code for the button click event. In the first line, we created an instance of `LittleShop()` and stored it in a variable. Then we used the `GetFruitsList()` method to get the list of fruits and stored it in a variable. Then we looped through all the available items in the `fruits` variable.

```
foreach (var fruit in fruits)
{
    FruitsList.Items.Add(fruit);
}
```

In the previous code for the `fruits` variable, there is a `List` collection. `foreach` will loop through each item inside the `List` collection stored in the `fruits` variable. And inside the loop, a `FruitsList` list box control adds each item in the `fruits` collection, which is stored in the `fruit` variable.

```
FruitsList.Items.Add("--------");
FruitsList.Items.Add($"Item Count: {fruits.Count}");
FruitsList.Items.Add($"Capacity: {fruits.Capacity}");
```

After we have added each item to the list box (`FruitsList`), we have added a string that displays the number of items in the `List` collection. We have used the `Count` property in the `List` collection to get that information. And, in the last line of code, we picked the `Capacity` of the `List` collection. The capacity property gets or sets the total number of elements the internal data structure can hold without resizing.

In step 26, we created an instance of the `LittleShop()` class and used the `GetShopItems()` method to get the items returned as an `ArrayList()`. Then we used a `for` loop to get the items inside the second list box. The rest is the same as we did with the `List` collection.

Describing our library with Reflections

In this recipe, we will be building a class object that will have two public methods. After using a console application, we will be describing this class object using Reflections. A Reflection gives you the ability to read its own metadata of finding assemblies, type, and module information at runtime.

Getting ready

Make sure we have Visual Studio 2017 and all the updates installed. We will be starting with a blank solution. A blank solution is a very good starting point for any scale of project. Let's build our .NET Standard 2.0 library.

How to do it...

1. Open Visual Studio 2017.
2. Click **File** | **New** | **Project** and, in the **New Project** template dialog box, select **Visual Studio Solutions** under the **Other Project Types** node in the left-hand pane and then **Blank Solution** in the right-hand pane.
3. In the **Name:** text box, type `Chapter2.Reflections` as the name of the solution. Select a preferred location under the **Location:** drop-down list or click **Browse...** button and select a location. Leave the defaults as they are:

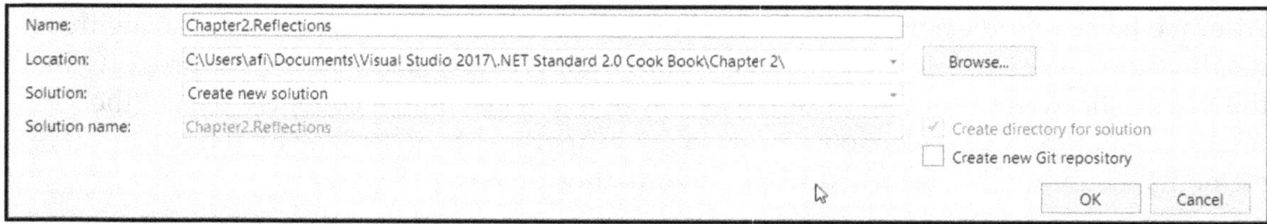

4. Click **OK**.
5. Now, in the **Solution Explorer** (or press *Ctrl* + *Alt* + *L*), select **Chapter2.Reflections**. Right-click and select **Add** | **New Project**.
6. In the **Add New Project** dialog box, expand the **Visual C#** node and select **.NET Standard** in the left-hand pane.

7. In the right-hand pane, select **Class Library (.NET Standard)**:

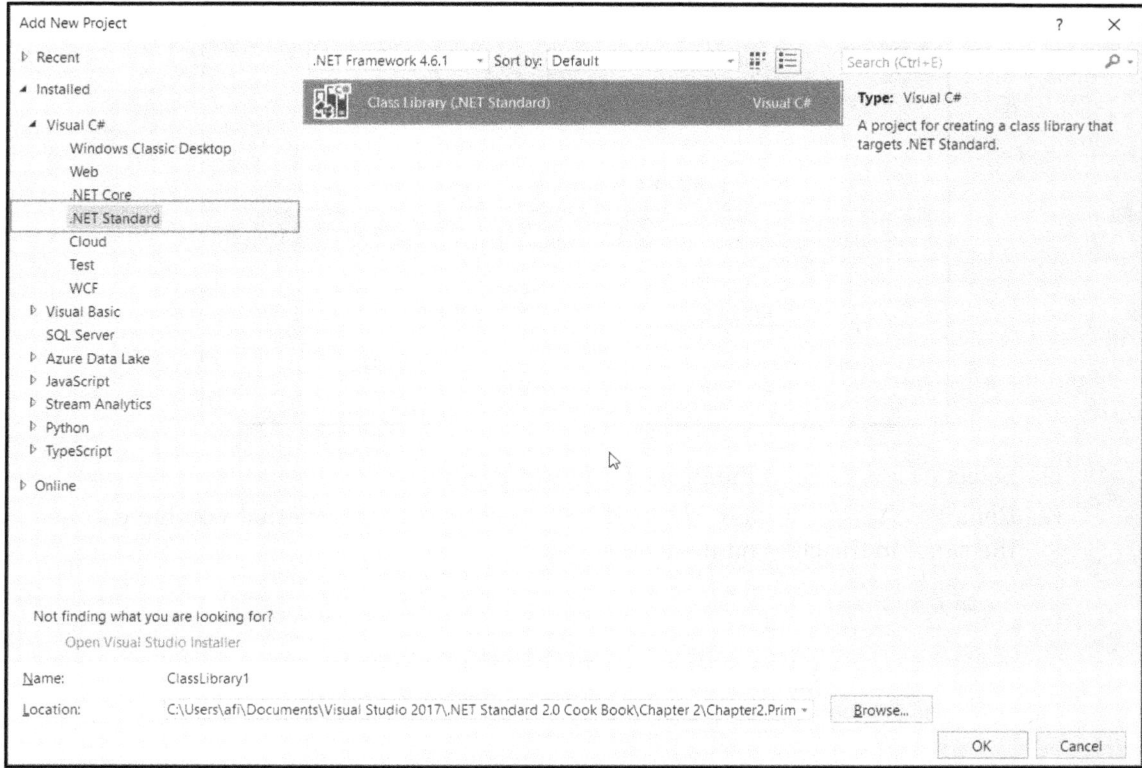

8. Now, in the **Name:** text box, type `Chapter2.Reflections.CalculatorLib` and leave the **Location:** text box as it is:

Name: Chapter2.Reflections.CalculatorLib
Location: C:\Users\afi\Documents\Visual Studio 2017\.NET Standard 2.0 Cook Book\Chapter 2\Chapter2.Refle
Browse...
OK Cancel

9. Click **OK**.

10. Now, the **Solution Explorer** (press *Ctrl* + *Alt* + *L* to open) should look like this:

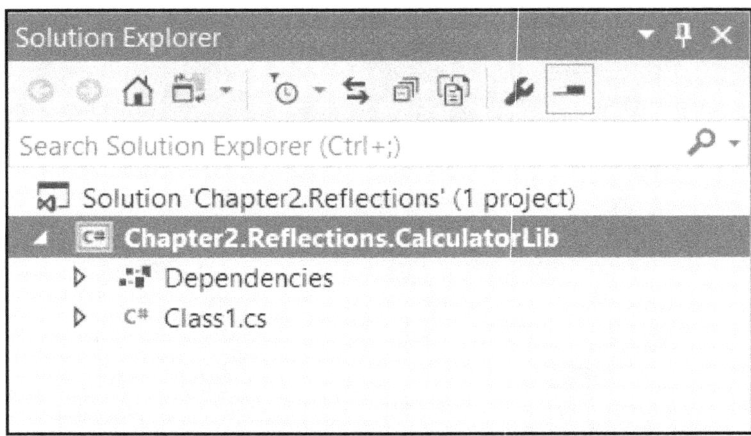

11. Select `Class1.cs` in the project tree and press *F2*.
12. Rename `Class1.cs` as `Calculator.cs`, also making sure that you have done the same to the class name itself:

```
using System;

namespace Chapter2.Reflections.CalculatorLib
{
    public class Calculator
    {
    }
}
```

13. Now, the **Solution Explorer** should look like this:

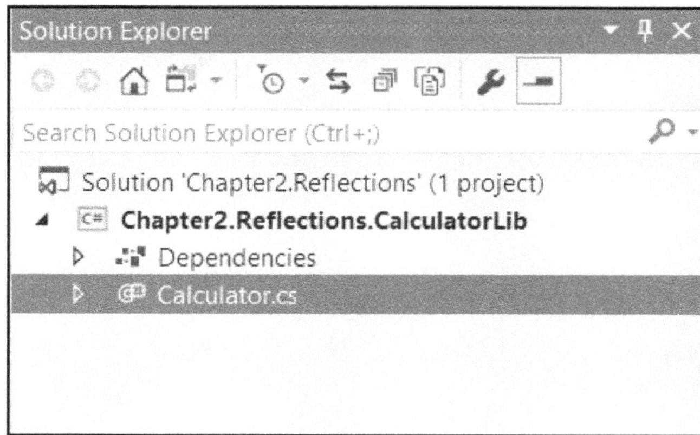

14. In the code window, and in between the curly brackets of the `Calculator` class, write the following code:

```
public int Add(int number1, int number2)
{
    return number1 + number2;
}

public int Subtract(int number1, int number2)
{
    return number1 - number2;
}
```

15. Let's do a quick build by pressing *Ctrl* + *Shift* + *B*.

How it works...

From steps 1 to 4, we created a blank solution. Then, from steps 5 to 9, we added a .NET Standard 2.0 library to the blank solution. In step 12, we renamed the existing `Class1.cs` that came with the template to something more meaningful. We also renamed the class name to match the filename. This is good practice and is also the default behavior of Visual Studio when you create a brand new class. We changed the name to `Calculator.cs` and the class name to `Calculator`.

In step 14, we added two simple methods to the `Calculator` class. The first method adds the given integers and the second method subtracts one integer from another. Finally, we did a quick build to check for syntax errors.

A .NET Core console application to use the library

Let's have a look at using Reflections in this recipe. We have built a small .NET Standard 2.0 library in the last recipe. Now we will be creating a .NET Core-based console application and use reflections to describe our library. We will be using the `System.Reflection` namespace and a few of its classes

Getting ready

Let's make sure you have completed the previous recipe and, if not, complete it and come back to this one. Open Visual Studio 2017 and locate and open the previously built .NET Standard library.

How to do it...

1. Open Visual Studio 2017.
2. Now open the solution from the previous recipe. Click **File** | **Open** | **Open Project/Solution**, or press *Ctrl* + *Shift* + *O*, and select the `Chapter2.Reflections` solution.
3. Press *Ctrl* + *Shift* + *B* for a quick build to check that everything is fine.
4. Now click on the **Chapter2.Reflections** solution label. Click **File** | **Add** | **New Project**.
5. In the **Add New Project** template dialog box, expand the **Visual C#** node in the left-hand pane.

6. Select **.NET Core** and then **Console App (.NET Core)** in the right-hand pane:

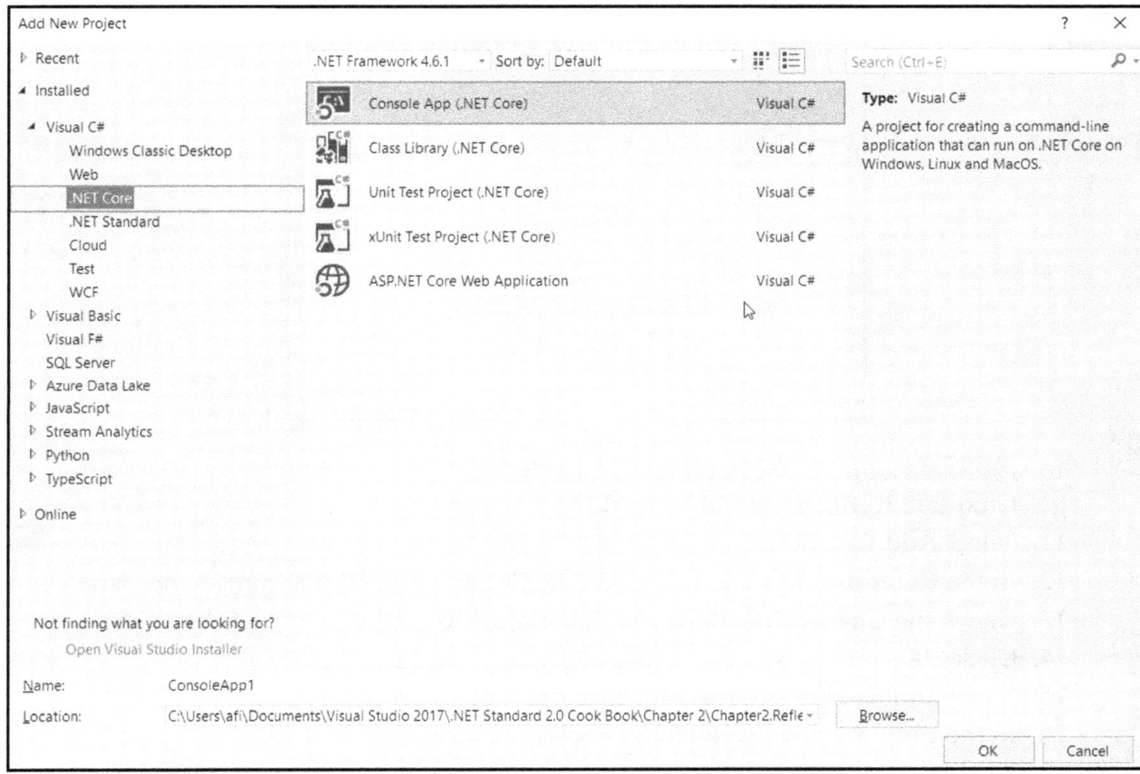

7. Now, in the **Name:** text box, type `Chapter2.Reflections.ReflectCore` as the name of the project. The rest of the fields should be left as defaults:

Name: Chapter2.Reflections.ReflectCore
Location: C:\Users\afi\Documents\Visual Studio 2017\.NET Standard 2.0 Cook Book\Chapter 2\Chapter2.Refle
Browse...
OK Cancel

8. Click **OK**.

9. Now, the **Solution Explorer** (press *Ctrl* + *Alt* + *L*) should look like this:

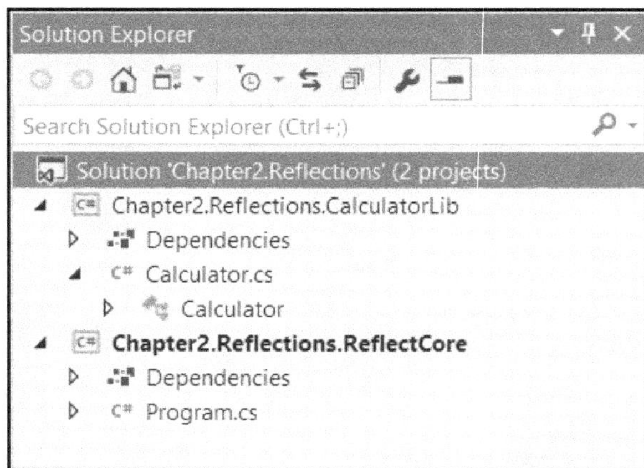

10. Right-click on the **Dependencies** label in the **Chapter2.Reflections.CalculatorLib**.
11. Select **Add Reference**.
12. In the **Reference Manager**, click on the **Projects** label in the right-hand pane.
13. Check the **Chapter2.Reflections.CalculatorLib** project in the left-hand pane.
14. Click **OK**.
15. Now, double-click on **Program.cs** to open the code window.
16. In the code window, scroll to the top of the screen.
17. Next to the last line of the `using` directives, add this `using` directive:

```
using System.Reflection;
using Chapter2.Reflections.CalculatorLib;
```

18. Again, scroll down until you reach the `Main()` method and write the following code in between the curly brackets of the `Main()` method:

```
MemberInfo info = typeof(Calculator);
Console.WriteLine($"Assembly Name: {info.Name}");
Console.WriteLine($"Module Name: {info.Module.Name}");
Console.WriteLine();

var calculator = new Calculator();
var typeObject = calculator.GetType();
var methods = typeObject.GetRuntimeMethods();

foreach (var method in methods)
```

```
    {
        Console.WriteLine($"Method name : {method.Name},
        ---> Return type : {method.ReturnType}");
    }

    Console.ReadLine();
```

19. Let's hit *F5* and see the output:

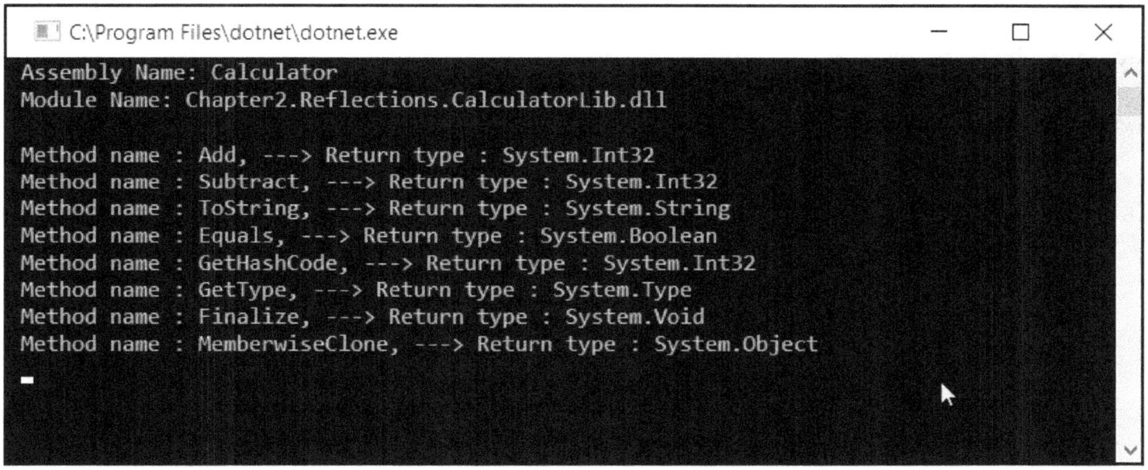

```
C:\Program Files\dotnet\dotnet.exe
Assembly Name: Calculator
Module Name: Chapter2.Reflections.CalculatorLib.dll

Method name : Add, ---> Return type : System.Int32
Method name : Subtract, ---> Return type : System.Int32
Method name : ToString, ---> Return type : System.String
Method name : Equals, ---> Return type : System.Boolean
Method name : GetHashCode, ---> Return type : System.Int32
Method name : GetType, ---> Return type : System.Type
Method name : Finalize, ---> Return type : System.Void
Method name : MemberwiseClone, ---> Return type : System.Object
```

20. Press any key to exit.

How it works...

Let's have a look at the steps and try to understand. In steps 1 to 3, we opened an existing solution that contained the .NET Standard 2.0 library. We did a quick build to check that all the syntax was OK and the project is compiling without any issues. In steps 4 to 8, we added a .NET Core console-based application to the project and gave it a proper name.

In steps 10 to 14, we added a reference to the .NET Standard 2.0 library project from our .NET Core console application. In step 17, we added two namespaces to the `Program.cs` code. One is for accessing reflection classes, which are contained in the `System.Reflection` namespace. The other one is the .NET Standard 2.0 library itself.

In step 18, we added code to the `Program.cs`, `Main()` method:

```
MemberInfo info = typeof(Calculator);
Console.WriteLine($"Assembly Name: {info.Name}");
Console.WriteLine($"Module Name: {info.Module.Name}");
Console.WriteLine();
```

In the first line of code we have stored a `Calculator` class type into a variable named `info`, which is a type of `System.Reflections.MemberInfo()`. In the second line of code, we have accessed the of the assembly class name using a `Name` property, while again we have accessed the module name using a `Module.Name` property. The `Member Info()` class allows you to get information about the attributes of a member and provides access to member metadata:

```
var calculator = new Calculator();
var typeObject = calculator.GetType();
var methods = typeObject.GetRuntimeMethods();

foreach (var method in methods)
{
    Console.WriteLine($"Method name : {method.Name},
    ---> Return type : {method.ReturnType}");
}

Console.ReadLine();
```

In the preceding few lines of code, we have created an instance of the `Calculator()` class established inside the .NET Standard 2.0 library. In the second line, we stored the type of class. In the third line, we have a variable named methods to store all the available runtime methods inside that class. Since `GetRuntimeMethods()` is a collection, we can easily use a `foreach` statement to iterate through the collections. And finally, inside the `foreach()` statement we have output the name and the return type of each method available inside the `Calculator()` class.

At the end, we waited for the user to press any key to exit the console application.

In step *19*, in the output, you might have noticed that apart from the two public methods we have created, there are several more methods. These are coming from the base `Object` class itself.

Building a .NET Standard 2.0 library that uses LINQ

In this recipe, we will be using LINQ inside our .NET Standard 2.0 library. LINQ stands for .NET Language-Integrated Query. LINQ defines a set of general purpose standard query operators: list, select, sort, and projection operators in any .NET-based programming language. The standard query operators allow queries to be applied to any IEnumerable<T>—based information source.

We will be building a .NET Standard 2.0 library that utilizes LINQ and use the library in the next recipe.

Getting ready

Let's get prepared by opening Visual Studio 2017 and creating a .NET Standard 2.0 library-based project. We can start with a blank solution and later on add the library project.

How to do it...

1. Open Visual Studio 2017.
2. Click **File** | **New** | **Project** and, in the New Project template dialog box, select **Visual Studio Solutions** under the **Other Project Types** node in the left-hand pane and then **Blank Solution** in the right-hand pane.
3. In the **Name:** text box, type `Chapter2.Linq` as the name of the solution. Select a preferred location under the **Location:** drop-down list or click the **Browse...** button and select a location. Leave the defaults as they are:

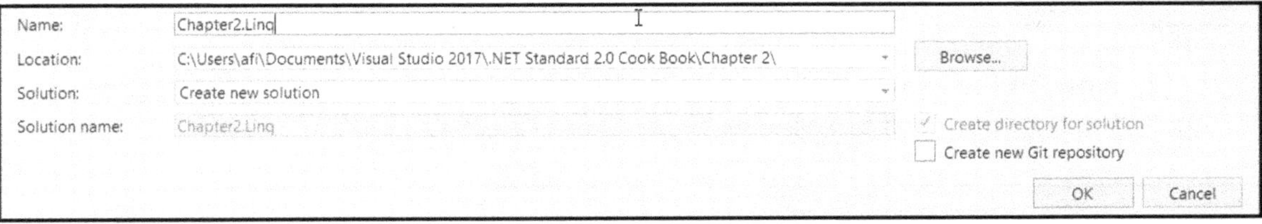

4. Click **OK**.
5. Now, in the **Solution Explorer** (or press *Ctrl* + *Alt* + *L*), select **Chapter2.Linq**. Right-click and select **Add** | **New Project**.
6. In the **Add New Project** dialog box, expand the **Visual C#** node and select **.NET Standard** in the left-hand pane.
7. In the right-hand pane, select **Class Library (.NET Standard)**.

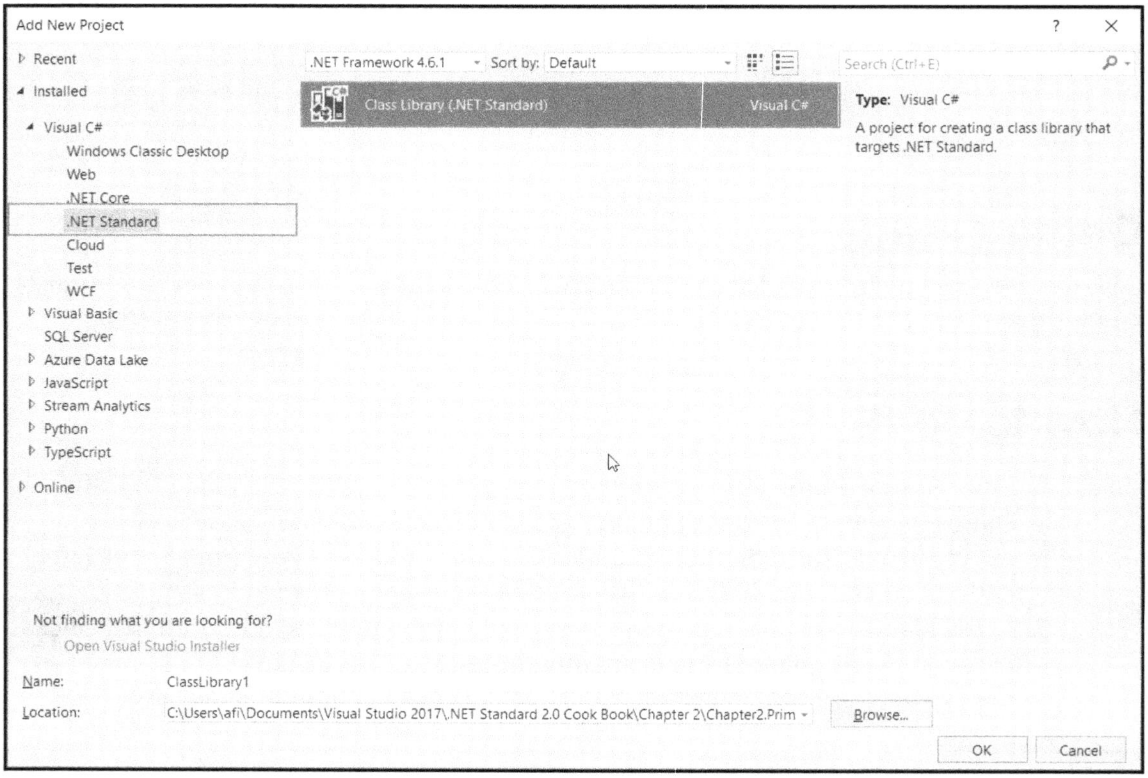

8. Now, in the **Name:** text box, type `Chapter2.Linq.QueriesLib` and leave the **Location:** text box as it is:

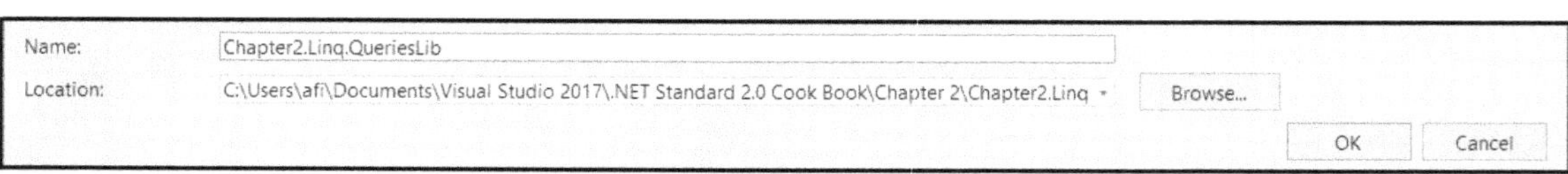

9. Click **OK**.

10. Now, the **Solution Explorer** (press *Ctrl* + *Alt* + *L* to open) should look like this:

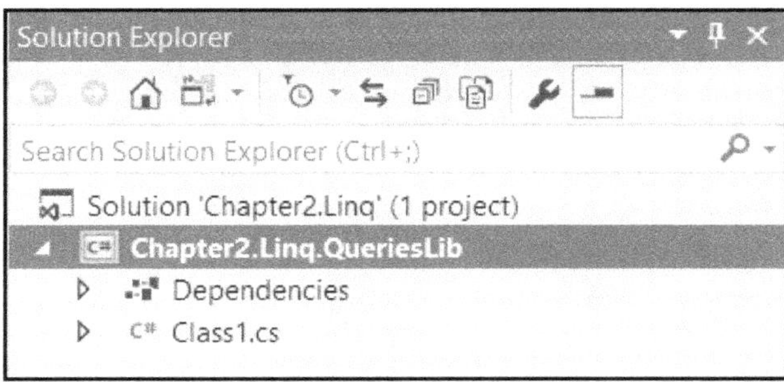

11. Select **Class1.cs** in the project tree and press *F2*.
12. Rename `Class1.cs` as `TelephoneBook.cs`, also making sure that you have done the same to the class name itself.
13. Answer **Yes** in the confirmation dialog box for renaming.
14. Now, the **Solution Explorer** should look like this:

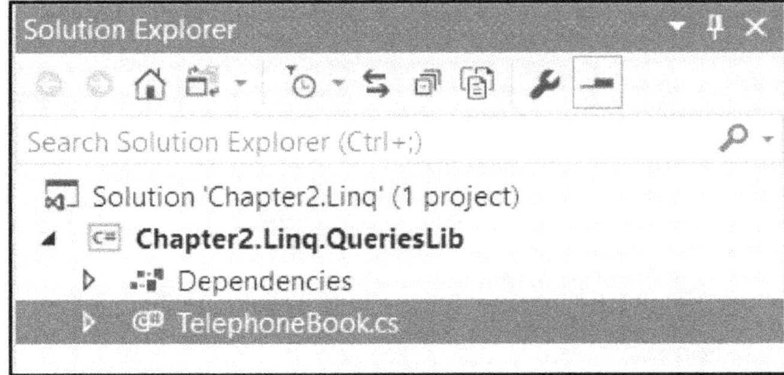

15. Double-click the **TelephoneBook.cs** file to open the code window.
16. Now, scroll up to the top of the code window and add the following code next to the last line of the `using` directives:

```
using System.Collections.Generic;
using System.Linq;
```

17. Again, scroll down till you reach the open curly bracket of the `TelephoneBook` class and add the following code:

    ```
    private List<string> _contactList;
    ```

18. Now, in the next line, add the following code as the `constructor` method:

    ```
    public TelephoneBook()
    {

        _contactList = new List<string>();

        _contactList.Add("Lenna Paprocki");
        _contactList.Add("Donette Foller");
        _contactList.Add("Simona Morasca");
        _contactList.Add("Mitsue Tollner");
        _contactList.Add("Leota Dilliard");
        _contactList.Add("Sage Wieser");
        _contactList.Add("Kris Marrier");
        _contactList.Add("Minna Amigon");
        _contactList.Add("Abel Maclead");
        _contactList.Add("Kiley Caldarera");
        _contactList.Add("Graciela Ruta");
    }
    ```

19. Next to the constructor, add the following code:

    ```
    public List<string> GetContacts()
    {
        return _contactList;
    }
    ```

20. Again, add this code block at the end of the `GetContacts()` method:

    ```
    public List<string> GetContactsByLastName(string lastName)
    {
        var contacts = _contactList.Where(
        c => c.Contains(lastName)).ToList();
        return contacts;
    }
    ```

21. Finally, add the following code block at the end of the `GetContactsByLastName()` method:

```
public List<string> GetSortedContacts(bool ascending = true)
{
    var sorted = _contactList.OrderBy(c => c).ToList();

    if (!ascending)
    {
        sorted = _contactList.OrderByDescending(c => c).ToList();
    }

    return sorted;
}
```

22. Now that we are done with adding code to the .NET Standard 2.0 library, let's hit *Ctrl* + *Shift* + *B* for a quick build and check for syntax errors.

How it works...

From steps 1 to 4, we created a blank solution using Visual Studio 2017 and gave it a location and a proper meaningful name. Then, from steps 5 to 9, we added a new .NET Standard 2.0 library to the blank solution. As usual, we gave it a proper and meaningful name.

In steps 12 and 13, we renamed the default `Class1.cs` template to `TelephoneBook.cs`. It's a good practice to keep both the class and filename the same. This is more readable and understandable when you come back to your code. In step 16, we added two namespaces to the code. `System.Collections.Generic` will get you the `List<T>` class used in the code and `System.Linq` gives you more control over those generic collections by allowing the LINQ functionality.

In step 17, we introduced a private variable type of `List<string>`. In step 18, we initiated the variable and added some data to the list. Everything is done inside the constructor of the `TelephoneBook()` class. In step 19, we created a method that returns the list of contacts. It has one line of code that returns the populated list.

Again, in step 20, we created a method that takes a string as a parameter. The parameter is the last name and we have used LINQ queries in this line:

```
var contacts = _contactList.Where(c => c.Contains(lastName)).ToList();
```

We have used a `Where` clause to filter down the list and used an inline function to pass the `lastName` parameter to the operation. Finally, we output the result as a list and returned the result at the end of the method.

In step 21, we created a method that ordered the list using LINQ.
The `GetSortedContacts()` takes one Boolean parameter and it is optional. C# has supported optional parameters since C# 4.0.

```
var sorted = _contactList.OrderBy(c => c).ToList();
```

The previous line of code uses the `OrderBy()` method in the list to order the list in ascending order and pass it as a list. If we need it in descending order, just pass the method parameter as `false`.

An ASP.NET MVC application to use the library

In this recipe, we will be creating an ASP.NET MVC application to use the .NET Standard 2.0 library. This was created in the previous recipe. ASP.NET MVC applications run in Windows-based systems under IIS and use the full .NET Framework. We will be starting with an empty ASP.NET MVC project, before moving to its components and use of the library.

Getting ready

Locate the previously built .NET Standard 2.0 library and make sure it builds without any errors. It is also assumed you have basic knowledge of MVC-based ASP.NET applications and are familiar with the terms Models, Views, and Controllers.

How to do it...

1. Open Visual Studio 2017.
2. Now, open the solution from the previous recipe. Click **File** | **Open** | **Open Project/Solution**, or press *Ctrl* + *Shift* + *O*, and select the **Chapter2.Linq** solution.
3. Press *Ctrl* + *Shift* + *B* for a quick build to check that everything is fine.
4. Now, click on the **Chapter2.Linq** solution label. Click **File** | **Add** | **New Project**.

5. In the **Add New Project** template dialog box, expand the **Visual C#** node in the left-hand pane.
6. Select **Web** and then **ASP.NET Web Application (.NET Framework)** in the right-hand pane:

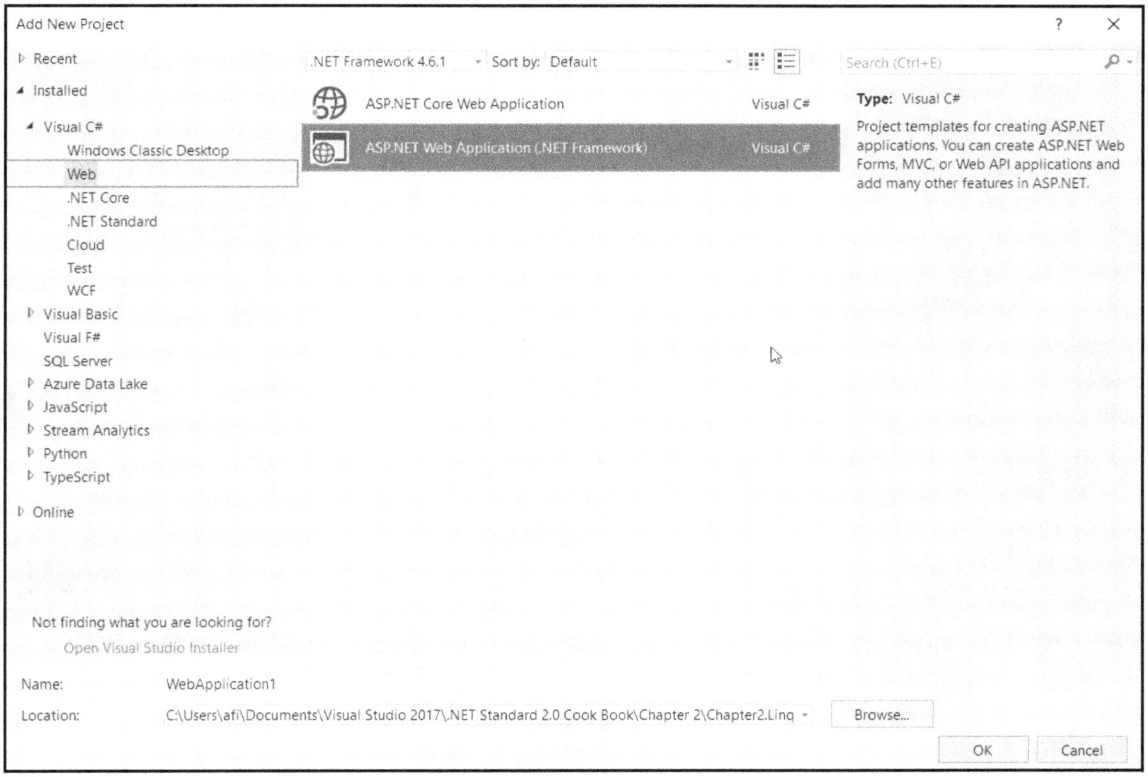

7. Now, in the **Name:** text box, type `Chapter2.Linq.QueriesMVC` as the name and leave the **Location:** text box at its default value:

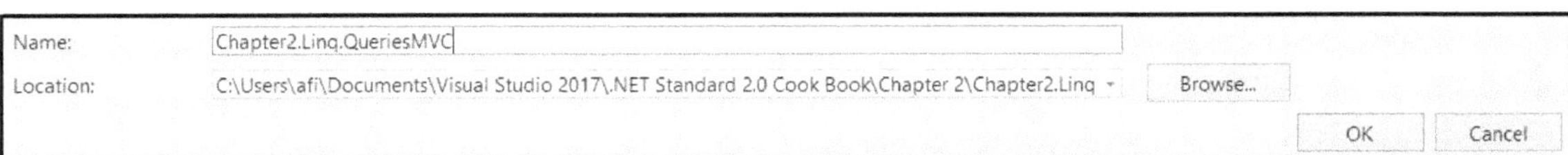

8. In the **New ASP.NET Web Application** dialog box, select **Empty** from the template list.

9. Select **MVC** as the **Add folders and core references for:** option:

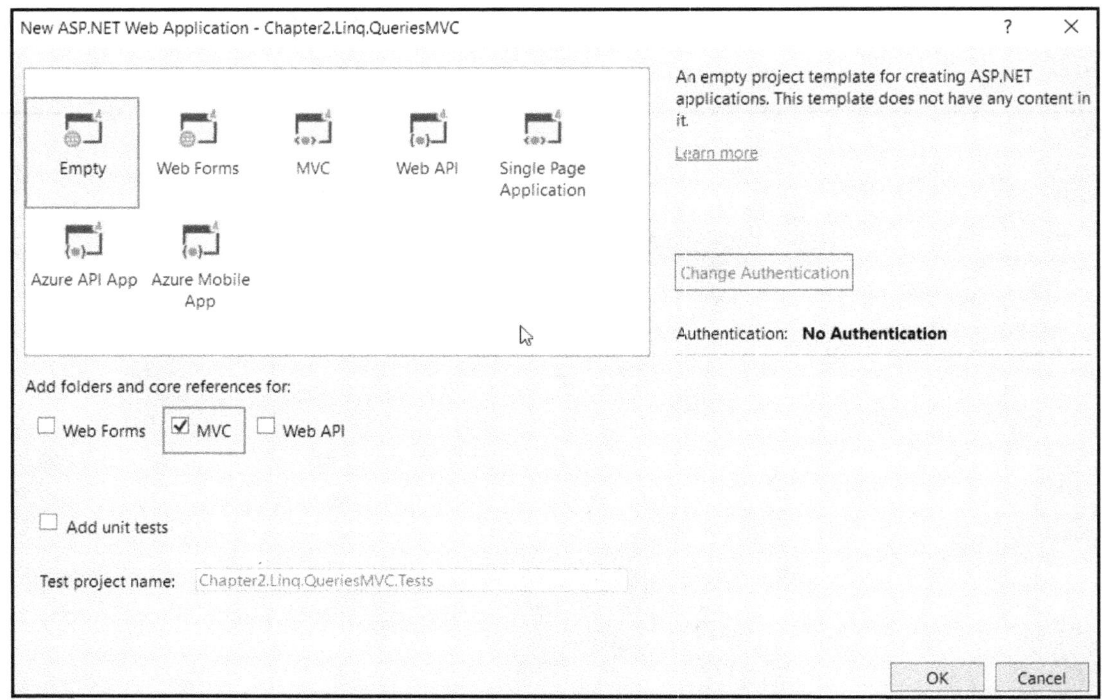

10. Leave the rest as it is and click **OK** to create the default **ASP.NET MVC Web Application** template.

11. Now, **Solution Explorer** should look like this:

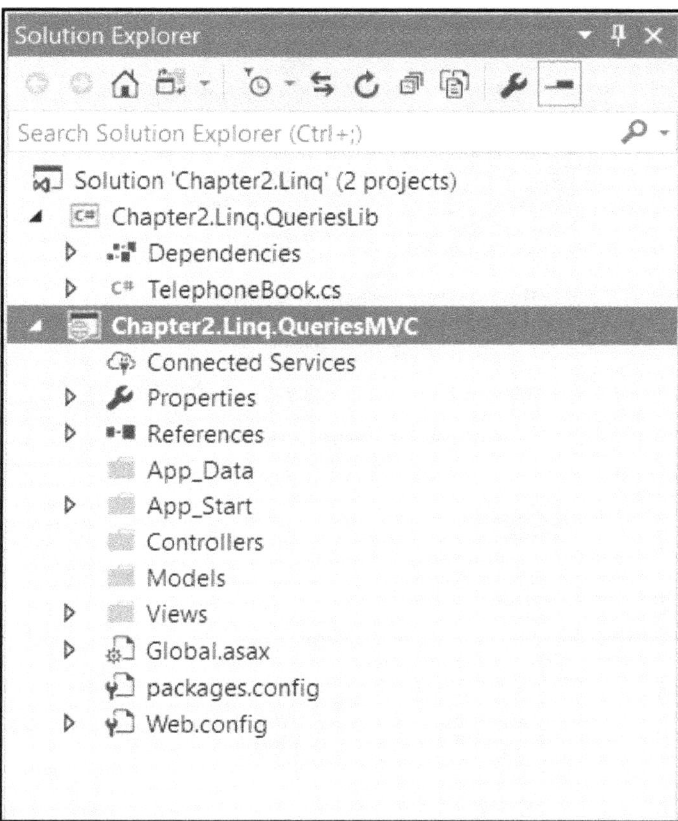

12. Now, right-click on the **Controllers** folder inside the **Chapter2.Linq.QueriesMVC** project.
13. Select **Add** | **Controller**.

14. In the **Add Scaffold** dialog box, select **MVC 5 Controller - Empty**:

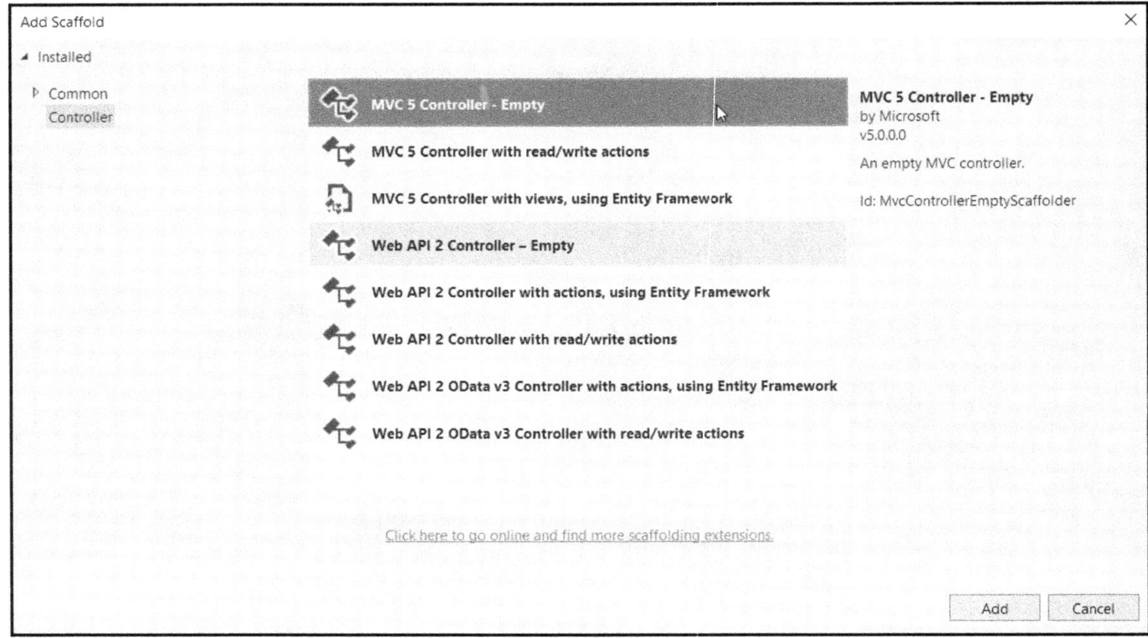

15. Click **Add**.

16. In the **Add Controller** dialog box, type `HomeController` as the name of the controller:

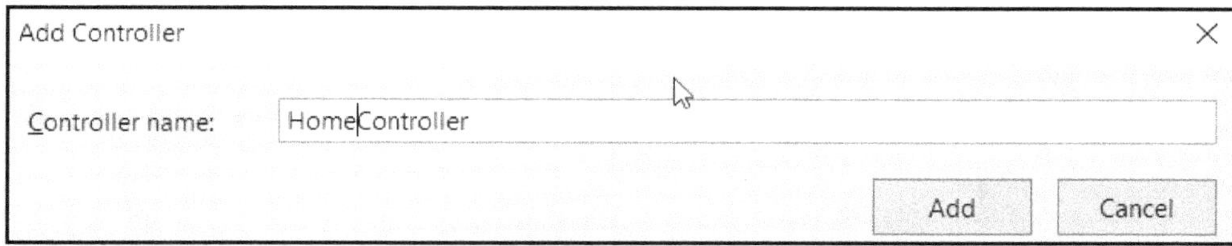

17. Click **Add**.
18. Now, the **Solution Explorer** (press *Ctrl* + *Alt* + *L*) should look like this:

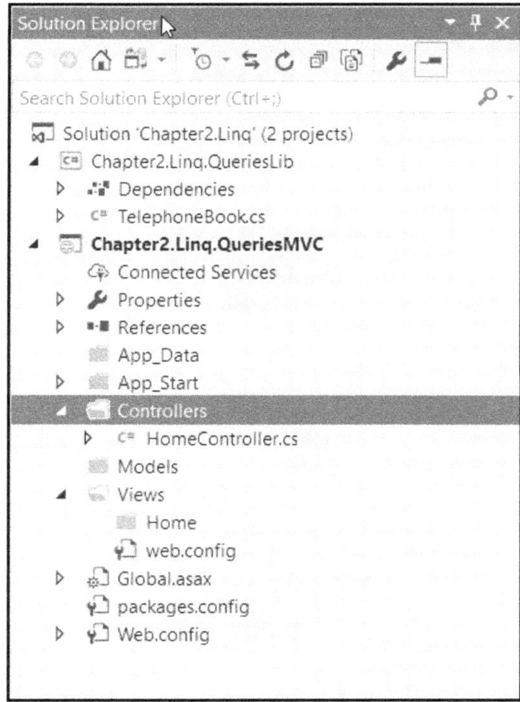

19. Now, right-click on the **References** label and select **Add Reference**.
20. In the **Reference Manager**, select **Projects** and check **Chapter2.Linq.QueriesLib** from the list:

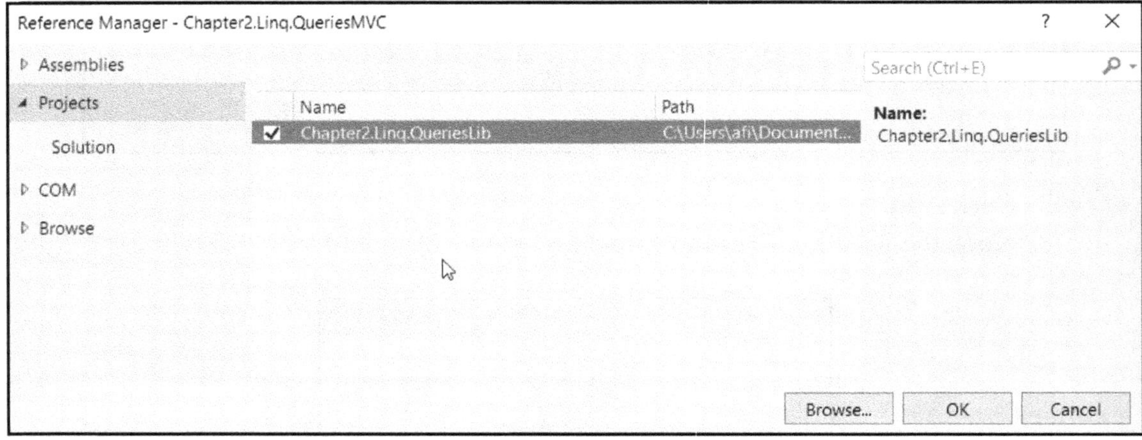

21. Click **OK**.
22. Now, double-click on **HomeController.cs** in the **Controllers** folder.
23. In the code window for **HomeController.cs**, scroll up and add the following code at the last line of the `using` directives:

```
using Chapter2.Linq.QueriesLib;
```

24. Inside the `Index()` action, before the `return` keyword, add the following code:

```
var telephoneBook = new TelephoneBook();

ViewBag.Contacts = telephoneBook.GetContacts();
```

25. Right-click on the method name of the `Index()` method and select **Add View**:

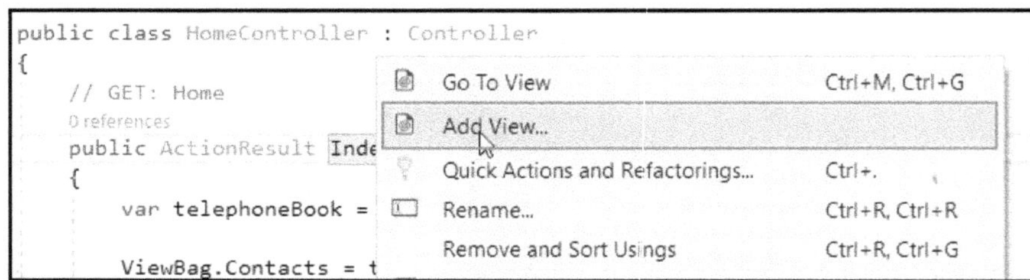

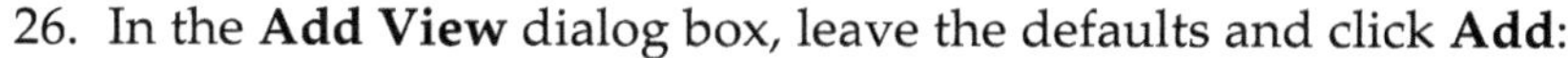

26. In the **Add View** dialog box, leave the defaults and click **Add**:

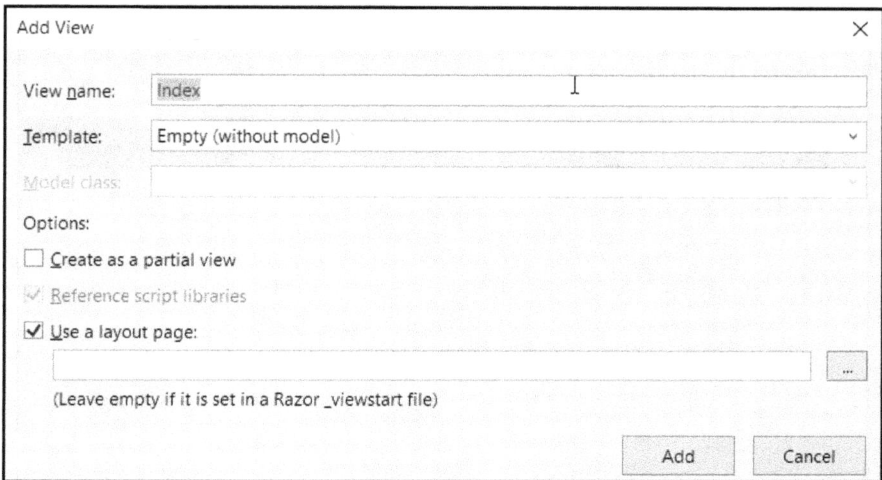

27. You will be presented with an Index.cshtml code window with the default template.
28. Change the code <h2>Index</h2> as follows:

```
<h2>Contacts</h2>
```

29. Now move the cursor to the bottom of the code window and add this code:

```
<ul>
    @foreach(var contact in ViewBag.Contacts as List<string>)
    {
        <li>@contact</li>
    }
</ul>
```

30. Let's press *F5* and test the code.

31. By default, the browser will load `http://localhost:portnumber/Home/` and here is the output:

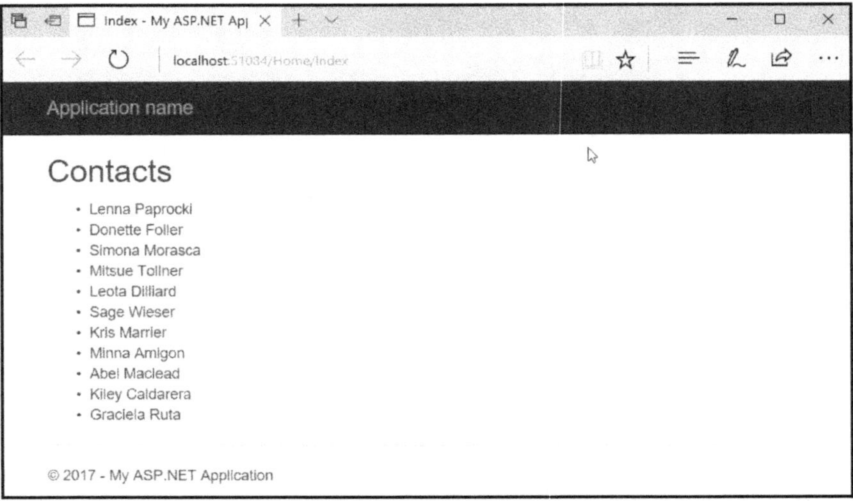

32. Now let's close the browser and switch back to the `HomeController.cs` code window.
33. Right after the end curly bracket of the `Index()` action method, add the following code:

```
public ActionResult Search(string ln)
{

    var telephoneBook = new TelephoneBook();

    if (string.IsNullOrEmpty(ln))
    {
        ViewBag.Contacts = telephoneBook.GetContacts();
    }
    else
    {
        ViewBag.Contacts =
        telephoneBook.GetContactsByLastName(ln);
    }

    return View();
}
```

34. Right-click on the method name of the `Search()` action and select **Add View**.
35. Follow steps *26* and *27* to add the `Search.chtml` view.
36. In the `Search.chtml` code window, change the code `<h2>Search</h2>` to the following :

```
<h2>Search Results - Contacts</h2>
```

37. Add the following code to `Search.chtml` after the `<h2>` tags:

```
<ul>
    @foreach (var contact in ViewBag.Contacts as List<string>)
    {
        <li>@contact</li>
    }
</ul>
```

38. Let's press *F5* and debug the current code.
39. Type `http://localhost:portnumber/Home/Search` in the browser address bar and press *Enter*:

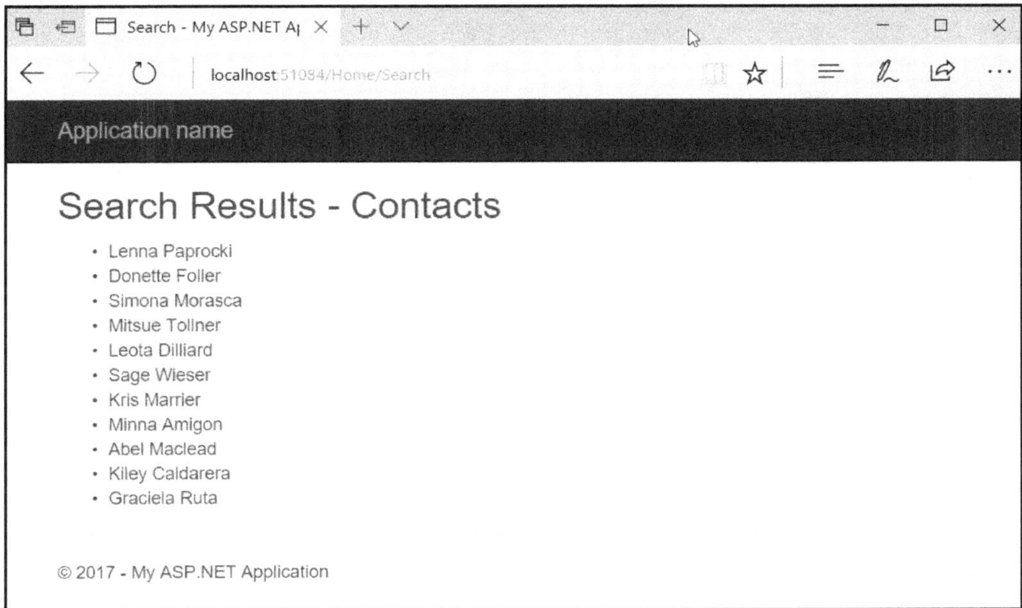

40. Now again, type `http://localhost:portnumber/Home/Search?ln=Marrier` in the address bar and press *Enter*:

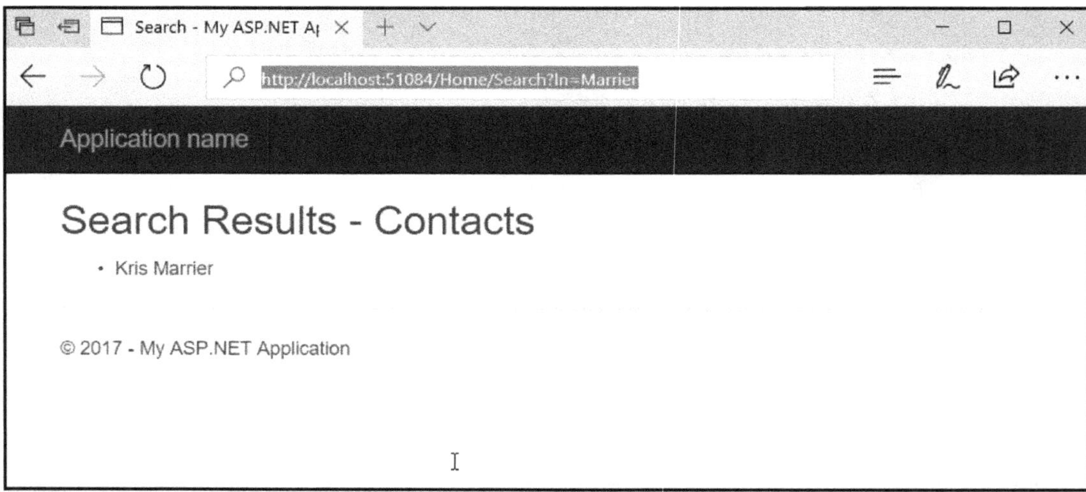

41. Close the browser and switch back to the `HomeController.cs` code window.
42. Add the following code after the `Search()` action method:

```
public ActionResult SortedContacts(bool asc = true)
{
    var telephoneBook = new TelephoneBook();
    ViewBag.Contacts = telephoneBook.GetSortedContacts(asc);

    return View();
}
```

43. Right-click on the method name of the `SortedContacts()` action and select **Add View**.
44. Follow steps *26* and *27* to add the `SortedContacts.chtml` view.

45. Now, in the `SortedContacts.chtml`, change `<h2>SortedContacts</h2>` to `<h2>Sorted Contacts</h2>`.
46. At the end of the `<h2>` tags add the following code.

```
<ul>
    @foreach (var contact in ViewBag.Contacts as List<string>)
    {
        <li>@contact</li>
    }
</ul>
```

47. Press *F5* to debug the current code.
48. Type `http://localhost:portnumber/Home/SortedContacts` in the address bar of the browser and press *Enter*:

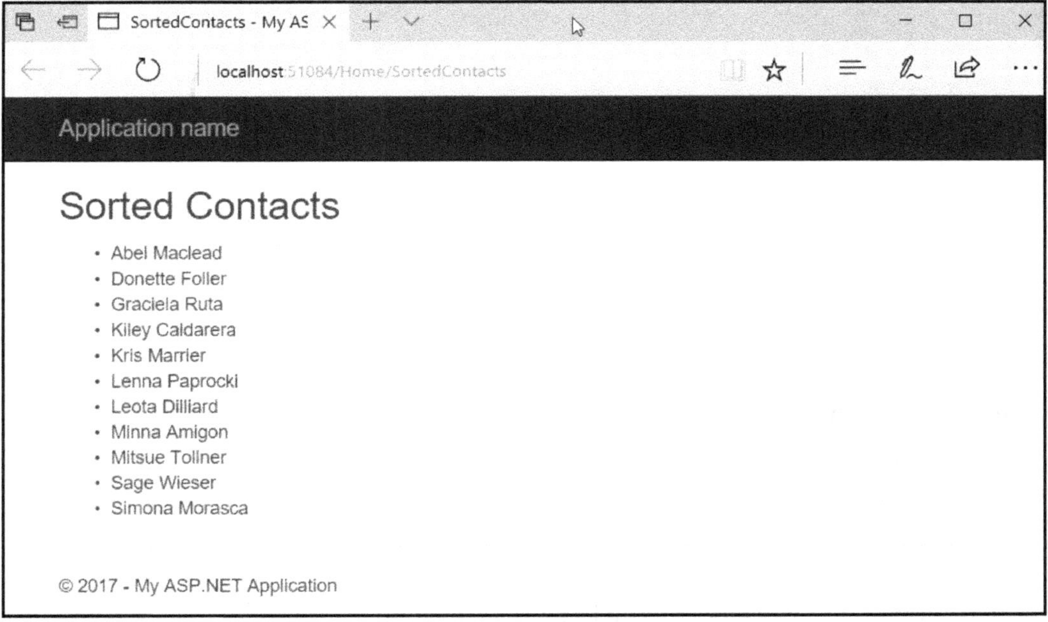

49. Again, type `http://localhost:51084/Home/SortedContacts?asc=false` in the address bar and press *Enter*:

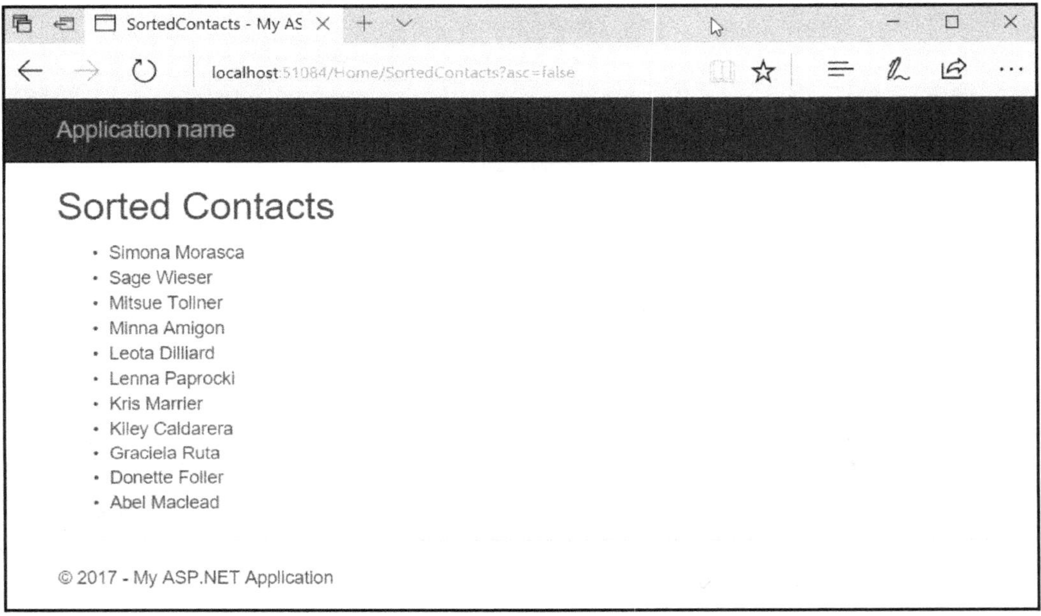

50. Close the browser.

How it works...

Let's have a look at the completed steps. From steps 1 to 3, we opened an existing solution, which was completed in the previous recipe. Then we did a quick build for syntax checking. From steps 4 to 6, we have added an ASP.NET Web Application project to the existing solution. In step 7, we gave it a proper name.

Later on, in steps 8 and 9, we decided what sort of ASP.NET Web Application it should be. In this case, we have selected MVC empty template. In steps 13 to 15, we have added a Controller to the MVC application. We have selected an empty MVC 5 Controller.

In steps 19 to 21, we added the reference from the .NET Standard 2.0 library. In step 23, we referenced it at the code level. In step 24, in the first line of code, we created an instance of the `TelephoneBook()` class. In the second line, we invoked the `GetContacts()` method and stored it in `ViewBag.Contacts`. `ViewBag` is used to send data from the Controller to the View.

From steps 25 to 27, we added a View to the Controllers action method. In step 28, we changed existing code in the `View` template created for us by Visual Studio. Then, we looped through the contacts using Razor syntax. In steps 30 and 31, we tested the code in the browser.

From steps 31 to 50, we created views and tested other methods found in the `TelephoneBook()` class.

3
Working with Files

In this chapter, we will be looking at these recipes:

- Setting up .NET Core in Ubuntu
- Creating a log as text
- Creating an ASP.NET Core application in Ubuntu to use the library
- Setting up .NET Core in macOS
- Reading from a comma separated (CSV) text file
- Creating a .NET Core console application in macOS to use the library
- Compressing? Why not?
- Creating a classic Windows application to use the library
- Encrypting and Decrypting content in a text file
- Creating a classic Windows application to use the library

Technical requirements

Readers should have a basic knowledge of C#. They should also have a basic knowledge of using Visual Studio, installing packages using NuGet, and referencing libraries within projects from other projects.

The code files for this chapter can be found on GitHub:
`https://github.com/PacktPublishing/DotNET-Standard-2-Cookbook/tree/master/Chapter03`

Check out the following video to see the code in action:
`https://goo.gl/82FCEP`

Introduction

As a developer, at some point, we will have to write some data to the disk or read data from the disk. This may be a simple text file, or may be a log file in a system you have written. .NET Framework offers great support for working with files. Mainly, we will be looking at the `System.IO` namespace and its usage of it.

In this chapter, we will be looking at some cross-platform applications as well. Each recipe will go through setting up new environments, such as Ubuntu and macOS, as well as building a .NET Standard 2.0 library and an accompanying application that uses the library.

Setting up .NET Core in Ubuntu

In this recipe, we will be going through how to set up .NET Core 2.x in an Ubuntu system. Ubuntu is a widely used Debian-based Linux environment. By visiting `https://www.ubuntu.com/desktop`, you can easily download and install Ubuntu on your system. You may have to use a virtual PC to do this. There are two great free tools that you can use:

1. VMWare Workstation Player for Windows: `https://www.vmware.com/products/workstation-player.html`
2. Oracle Virtual Box for Windows, Linux, and macOS: `https://www.virtualbox.org/wiki/Downloads`

This chapter assumes you have already set up and installed the required operating systems.

Getting ready

You will have to download a virtual PC and install the latest version of Ubuntu. If you haven't got a virtual PC that runs Ubuntu, make sure you have before continuing this recipe done it yet. I am using Ubuntu version 16.04 here. To find out which version you have, simply type the following command in the terminal:

```
$ lsb_release -a
```

You should get the following output:

```
fiqriismail@ubuntu: ~
fiqriismail@ubuntu:~$ lsb_release -a
No LSB modules are available.
Distributor ID: Ubuntu
Description:    Ubuntu 16.04.3 LTS
Release:        16.04
Codename:       xenial
fiqriismail@ubuntu:~$
```

How to do it...

1. Open your favorite browser, type the following URL, and press *Enter*: `https://www.microsoft.com/net/download/linux`

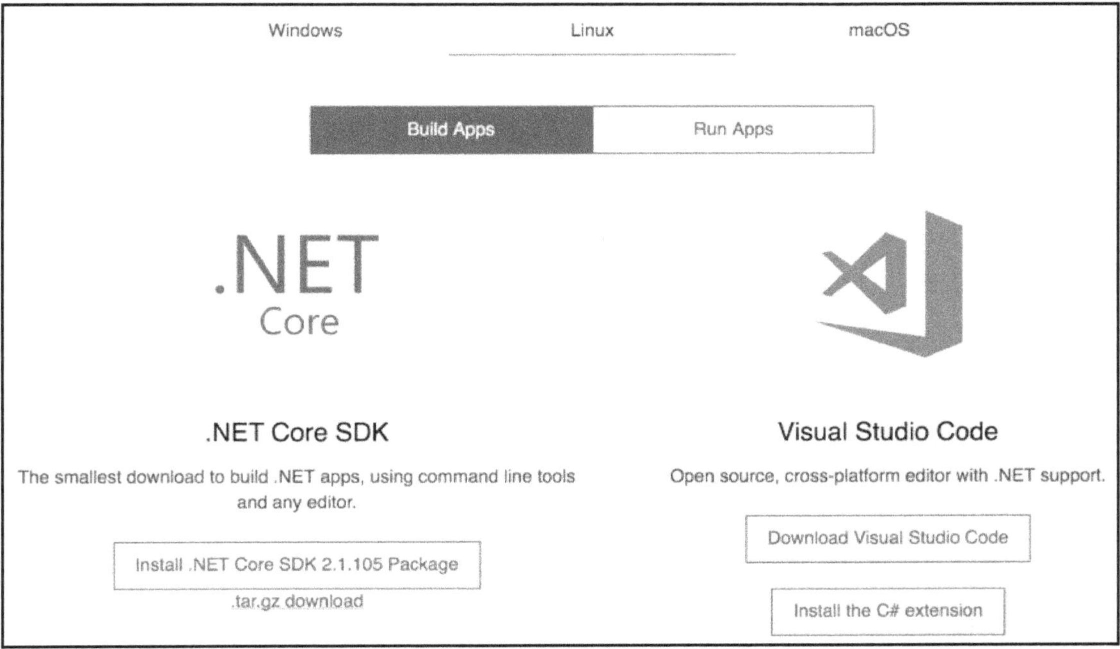

2. Select the Install .NET Core SDK 2.x Package button.

3. From the **Linux Distribution** drop-down list, select **Ubuntu 16.04.**

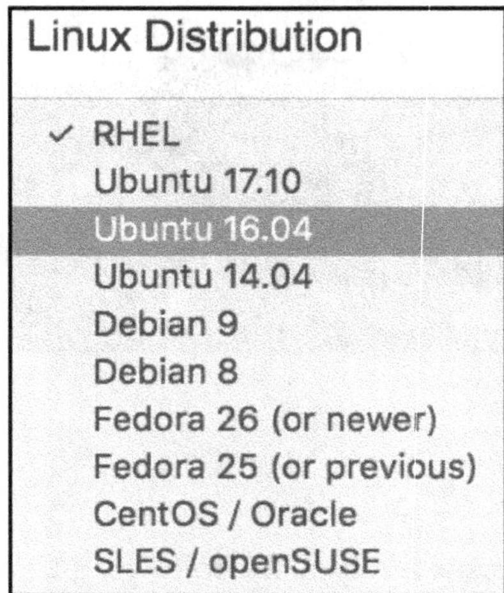

4. Follow the instructions on the page to install the current SDK or perform the following steps to install.
5. Now open the terminal, type the following command, and press *Enter*:

```
$ curl https://packages.microsoft.com/keys/microsoft.asc |
gpg --dearmor > microsoft.gpg
```

6. If you have a fresh installation of Ubuntu you might not have curl installed. If not use the following command to install curl:

```
$ sudo apt-get install curl
```

7. Now, again in the terminal type the following command and press *Enter* to get the list of files:

```
$ sudo mv microsoft.gpg /etc/apt/trusted.gpg.d/microsoft.gpg
```

8. Type the following command and press *Enter* in the terminal:

```
$ sudo sh -c 'echo "deb [arch=amd64]
https://packages.microsoft.com/repos/
microsoft-ubuntu-xenial-prod xenial main" >
/etc/apt/sources.list.d/dotnetdev.list'
```

9. Let's update the package list using this command:

```
$ sudo apt-get update
```

10. Finally, let's install the SDK using this command:

```
$ sudo apt-get install dotnet-sdk-2.0.2
```

11. Now we are done with installing the SDK, let's test it using the following command:

```
$ dotnet --version
```

12. If it's all OK, you should get the following output:

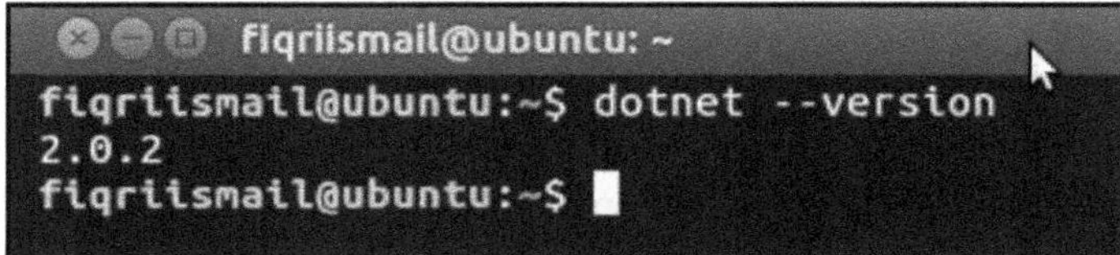

How it works...

In steps 1 to 3, we navigated through to find the required SDK version for our Ubuntu installation. These commands are straightforward. I have used Ubuntu 16.04 as my operating system. In steps 4 and 5, we used `curl` to download the security key to the system and to tell Ubuntu that we will be downloading the SDKs from a trusted source. In a fresh Ubuntu installation, we might not have the `curl` command. So, if you ran into a `command not found` problem, you can just simply install `curl` first as in step 4.

In step 6, we used an Ubuntu command to update its package list with Microsoft repositories. Then, in step 7, we updated the source list using the `apt-get` command. Finally, in step 8, we did the actual installation of .NET Core 2.0 SDK.

In steps 9 and 10, we checked that our installation was all OK to move on.

Creating a log as text

In this recipe, we will be creating a .NET Standard 2.0 library that writes a text file as a log file. This log file will contain simple text entries of operations we do in an application. It will also demonstrate the use of command-line tools that come under the .NET Core SDK to create a solution and add projects as we move on.

Getting ready

Make sure you have installed Ubuntu 16.04 and .NET Core 2.0 SDK. If not, please follow the previous recipe to do so. Assuming everything is installed and .NET Core 2.0 is up and running, let's get started on creating the library that writes logs as text.

Make sure you have downloaded and installed Visual Studio Code from `https://code.visualstudio.com`. It's a straightforward installation of a `.deb` file from the site.

How to do it...

1. Open the terminal.
2. Now in your home directory or any other directory type the following command and press *Enter*:

```
$ dotnet new sln -o Chapter3 -n Chapter3.LogFile
```

3. Now, change to the newly created directory, using the following command:

```
$ cd Chapter3
```

4. Now you are inside the root of your solution. Let's create the .NET Standard library project using the following command:

```
$ dotnet new classlib -o Chapter3.LogFile.LogLib
```

5. Now that we have created our `Class Library Project`, let's open the whole solution using Visual Studio Code.
6. Type the following command in the terminal and press *Enter*:

```
$ code .
```

7. The previous command will open Visual Studio Code in the current directory and the IDE should look like this:

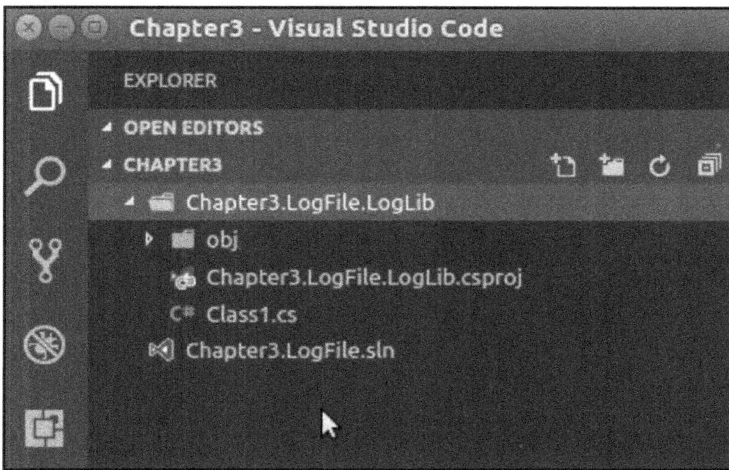

8. Now, in the code tree, select `Class1.cs`, press *F2*, and change the name to `TextLog.cs` and press *Enter*.
9. Also in the code window, change the class name from `Class1` to `TextLog`.
10. Now your code should look like this:

```
using System;

namespace Chapter3.LogFile.LogLib
{
    public class TextLog
    {
    }
}
```

11. Let's add our new project to the solution. Make sure you are in the root of the project directory. Type the `ls` command and the output should look like this:

```
fiqriismail@ubuntu: ~/Projects/Chapter3
fiqriismail@ubuntu:~/Projects/Chapter3$ ls
Chapter3.LogFile.LogLib  Chapter3.LogFile.sln
fiqriismail@ubuntu:~/Projects/Chapter3$
```

12. Type the following command in the terminal and press *Enter*:

```
$ dotnet sln Chapter3.LogFile.sln
add Chapter3.LogFile.LogLib/Chapter3.LogFile.LogLib.csproj
```

13. Now, in the root directory of the solution, type the following command to build the solution and its attached projects:

```
$ dotnet build
```

14. The output window should look like this:

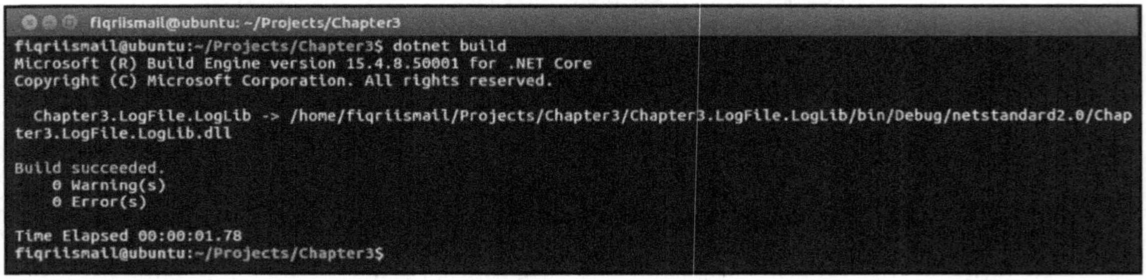

```
fiqriismail@ubuntu: ~/Projects/Chapter3
fiqriismail@ubuntu:~/Projects/Chapter3$ dotnet build
Microsoft (R) Build Engine version 15.4.8.50001 for .NET Core
Copyright (C) Microsoft Corporation. All rights reserved.

  Chapter3.LogFile.LogLib -> /home/fiqriismail/Projects/Chapter3/Chapter3.LogFile.LogLib/bin/Debug/netstandard2.0/Chap
ter3.LogFile.LogLib.dll

Build succeeded.
    0 Warning(s)
    0 Error(s)

Time Elapsed 00:00:01.78
fiqriismail@ubuntu:~/Projects/Chapter3$
```

15. Let's add some code to our library. At the top of the `using` directives, add the following code:

```
using System.IO;
```

16. At the top of the class, next to the open curly bracket, add the following code:

```
private string logFileName = "server_log.txt";
private StreamWriter logFile;
```

17. Let's add a constructor. Add the following code next to the variables we have created:

```
public TextLog()
{
    if (!File.Exists(logFileName))
    {
        logFile = File.CreateText(logFileName);
    }
    else
    {
        logFile = File.AppendText(logFileName);
    }
}
```

18. Next to the constructor code, add the method to write the log file:

```
public void WriteLog(string message)
{
    logFile.WriteLine($"{DateTime.Now} Log Message: {message} ");
}
```

19. Let's add the last method to the code:

```
public void CloseLog()
{
    logFile.Close();
}
```

20. Now that we have added all our code to the library, let's go back to the terminal window and perform a build using the following command:

```
$ dontnet build
```

How it works...

In the first step, we opened the terminal window in the Ubuntu system. This terminal is similar to the command window you use in Windows operating systems. A terminal helps you to execute shell commands supported by the .NET Core 2.0. In step 2, we created a blank solution. The `dotnet new` command creates a new solution file containing directories. In step 3, we changed the directory to the root of the solution file. From this point onwards, we will be adding the projects to the solution.

In step 4, we used the same `dotnet new` command to create the class library. By default, this class library will use the .NET Standard 2.0 library, so we don't have to tell the command-line tool to create the .NET Standard 2.0 library. We can confirm this by expanding the `Chapter3.LogFile.LogLib` node in Visual Studio Code, then clicking on the `Chapter3.LogFile.LogLib.csproj` label. In the right-hand pane of Visual Studio Code, you will be able to see this XML code:

```
<Project Sdk="Microsoft.NET.Sdk">
    <PropertyGroup>
        <TargetFramework>netstandard2.0</TargetFramework>
    </PropertyGroup>
</Project>
```

In this code, `<TargetFramwork>` markup says it's `netstandard2.0` and it's confirmed, we have a .NET Standard 2.0 library on our hands. In steps 6 to 10, we used Visual Studio Code to open the current directory and make changes to the existing class. In step 11, we made sure we were in the root directory of the solution. In step 12, we added the Class Library project to the solution using the command-line tool. You will be able to list all the projects in the solution by executing the following command in the terminal:

```
$ dotnet sln list
```

The command will list all the available projects in the current solution file. In step 13, we performed a `build` command to make sure everything was intact and working fine. In step 15, we added the namespace for handing inputs and outputs to the system. The `System.IO` namespace contains all the file handling classes inside it.

In step 16, we created two `private` variables to hold the filename and `StreamWriter` class that helps you to write to text files. In step 17, we created a constructor method that checks whether the file, exists. If it doesn't exist, it will create a whole new text file and, if there is a file already, we will open the file to append text to it. This is a very good practice when you handle files for these sort of tasks.

In step 18, we created a method that takes a `string` parameter as the message and writes that message to the file. In step 19, we created a method to close the opened file. Finally, step 20 verified that the syntax is OK and builds correctly using a `build` command.

Creating an ASP.NET Core application in Ubuntu to use the library

We will be creating an ASP.NET Core application to use the library in this recipe. ASP.NET Core will be using the MVC design pattern, as well as working in Linux, macOS, and, of course, in Windows. We will be using Ubuntu as the operating system for building this small app to demonstrate the cross-platform capabilities of .NET Core.

Getting ready

Make sure you have completed the previous recipe that includes setting up the environment and building of the .NET Standard 2.0 library that creates a text file as a log. This recipe assumes you have basic knowledge of MVC architecture. In simple terms, MVC is a software architectural pattern that separates data models, controlling code, and user interfaces. Let's have a look at how to build this application and use our library.

How to do it..

1. Open the terminal and navigate to the root of your application built in the previous recipe.
2. The directory structure should look like this:

```
fiqriismail@ubuntu: ~/Projects/Chapter3
File Edit View Search Terminal Help
fiqriismail@ubuntu:~/Projects/Chapter3$ ls
Chapter3.LogFile.LogLib  Chapter3.LogFile.sln
fiqriismail@ubuntu:~/Projects/Chapter3$
```

3. Now type the following command and press *Enter* in the terminal to create the new ASP.NET Core MVC application:

```
$ dotnet new mvc -o Chapter3.LogFile.LogAppMvc
```

4. Let's add this new project to the solution:

```
$ dotnet sln add
Chapter3.LogFile.LogAppMvc/Chapter3.LogFile.LogAppMvc.csproj
```

5. Now let's perform a build to check that everything is working fine:

```
$ dotnet build
```

6. Now, navigate to the app we just created:

```
$ cd Chapter3.LogFile.LogAppMvc/
```

7. Execute the application with the following command:

```
$ dotnet run
```

8. If everything is fine, open your browser and type `http://localhost:5000` in the address bar and hit *Enter*. The browser output should look like this:

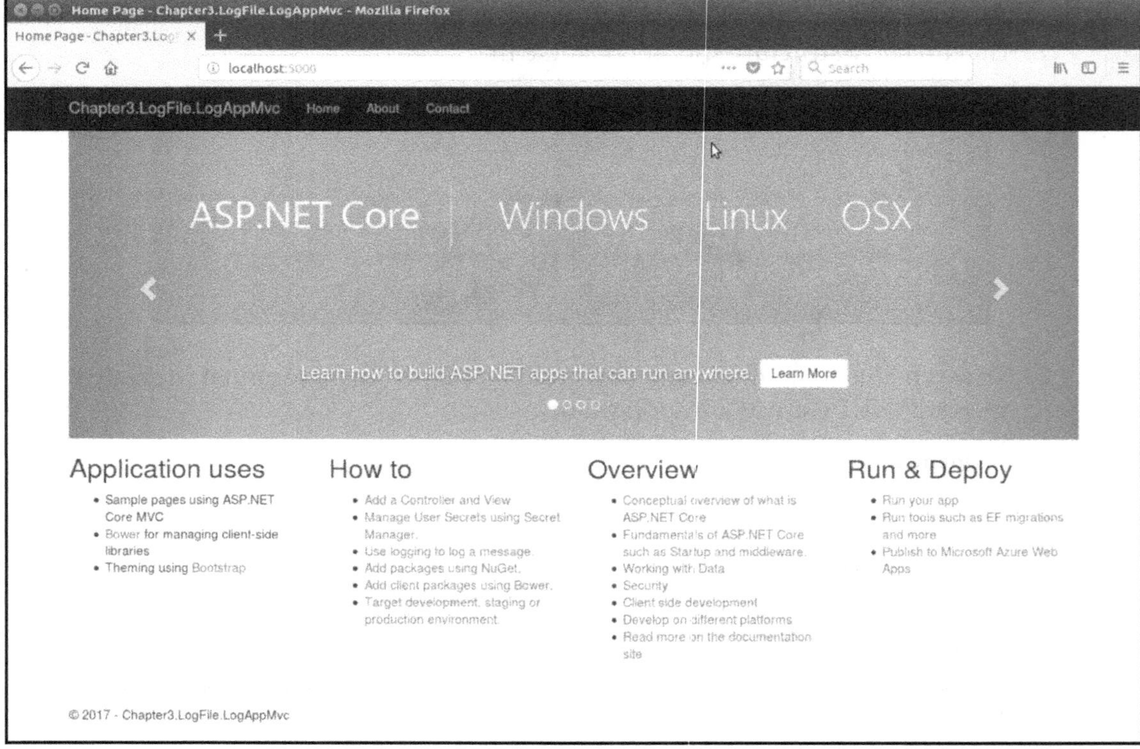

9. Let's close the browser and, in the terminal window, hit *Ctrl* + *C* to stop the web server.
10. We need to add the reference to our .NET Standard 2.0 library we built before. Let's add it now using this command in the terminal:

```
$ dotnet add reference
../Chapter3.LogFile.LogLib/Chapter3.LogFile.LogLib.csproj
```

11. Let's get back to the root folder by typing the following command:

```
$ cd ..
```

12. Now, in the root of the solution directory, type the following command to open Visual Studio Code using the current directory:

```
$ code .
```

13. In Visual Studio Code, expand the `Chapter3` label and expand `Chapter3.LogFile.LogAppMvc`.
14. Again, expand the `Controllers` folder and click on `HomeController.cs`:

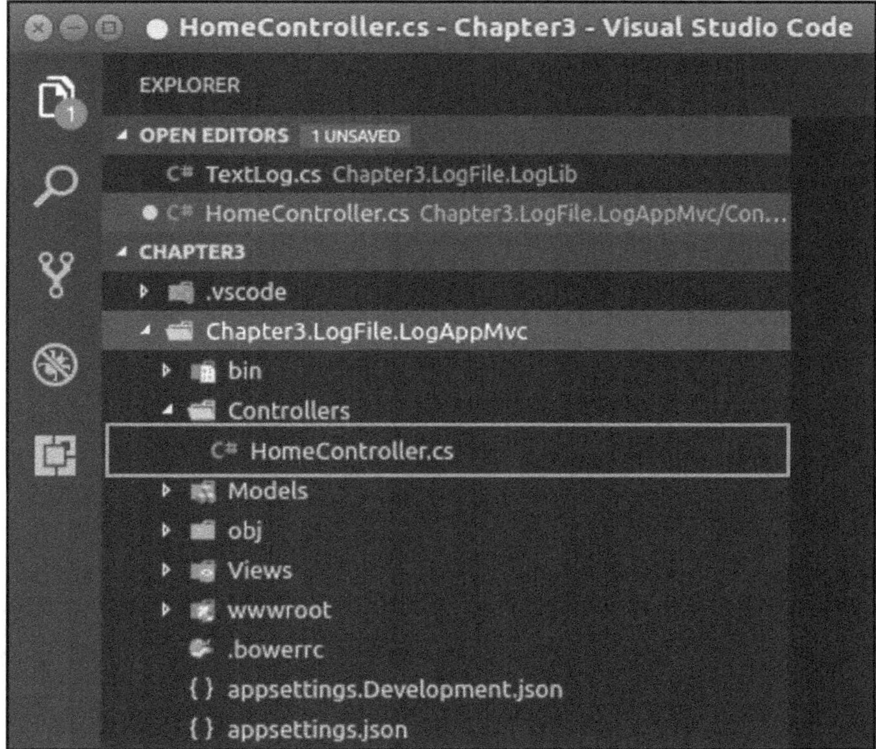

15. In `HomeController.cs`, add the following `using` directive to the last line of the `using` directives block:

```
using Chapter3.LogFile.LogLib;
```

16. Now, next to the starting curly bracket of the `Index` method of the `HomeController` class, add the following code:

```
TextLog logFile = new TextLog();
logFile.WriteLog("You are in the Index action.");
logFile.CloseLog();
```

17. Let's add more code inside the `About` method too:

```
TextLog logFile = new TextLog();
logFile.WriteLog("You are in the About action.");
logFile.CloseLog();
```

18. Do the same to the `Contact` method as well:

```
TextLog logFile = new TextLog();
logFile.WriteLog("You are in the Contact action.");
logFile.CloseLog();
```

19. Now we are done with adding code, let's navigate to `Chapter3.LogFile.LogAppMvc`:

```
$ cd Chapter3.LogFile.LogAppMvc/
```

20. Let's run the application:

```
$ dotnet run
```

21. Open your favorite browser, type `localhost:5000` in the address bar, and press *Enter*. Click on the navigation links for **Home**, **About**, and **Contact** a few times.
22. Close the browser.

23. Now go to Visual Studio Code, expand the `Chapter3` label, and expand `Chapter3.LogFile.LogAppMvc`. You should see a file named `server_log.txt` in the root:

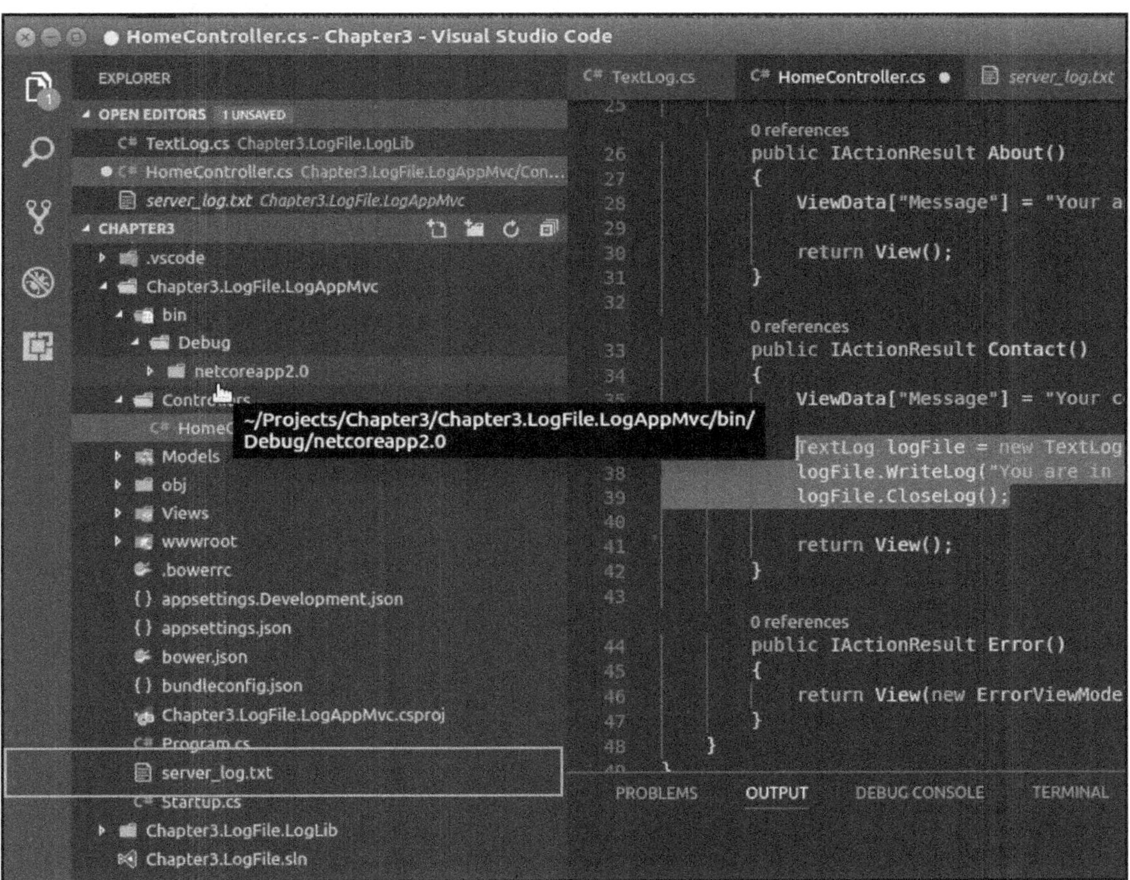

24. Now click on the `server_log.txt` filename to see the output:

```
12/24/17 2:01:49 PM Log Message: You are in the Index action.
12/24/17 2:33:30 PM Log Message: You are in the Index action.
12/24/17 2:33:37 PM Log Message: You are in the About action.
12/24/17 2:33:39 PM Log Message: You are in the Index action.
12/24/17 2:33:41 PM Log Message: You are in the About action.
12/24/17 2:34:53 PM Log Message: You are in the Index action.
12/24/17 2:34:54 PM Log Message: You are in the Index action.
12/24/17 2:34:57 PM Log Message: You are in the Contact action.
12/24/17 2:34:59 PM Log Message: You are in the Contact action.
12/24/17 2:35:00 PM Log Message: You are in the Index action.
12/24/17 2:35:01 PM Log Message: You are in the Contact action.
12/24/17 2:35:01 PM Log Message: You are in the Contact action.
```

How it works...

In steps 1 and 2, we opened the terminal and made sure we are in the correct directory, which is the root of the solution. After that, in step 3, we created the ASP.NET Core 2.0 MVC application. In step 4, we added that project to the solution. After this step, we have two projects in the solution and you will be able to see all projects in the solution by giving this command in the root of the solution directory:

```
dotnet sln list
```

In steps 5, 6, and 7, we built the project from the root to check that everything was fine. Then, we navigated to the newly created project folder and executed the project to test whether everything was OK. In step 8, we opened the default browser and gave the URL to test the ASP.NET Core 2.0 application. As you can see, the URL looked like `http://localhost:5000`. By default, the web server (which is kestrel) runs on port 5000.

Kestrel is a cross-platform web server for ASP.NET Core and is built using a cross-platform asynchronous I/O library called **libuv.**

So, we didn't change anything and kept the defaults as they are. In step 11, we navigated back to the root solution directory and then, in step 12, we opened Visual Studio Code using that directory.

In step 14, we navigated to `HomeController.cs` and, in step 15, we added the first `using` statement to access the classes that allow you to use the file operations. In step 16, we created the `TextLog` class and used it in the `WriteLog()` method. Finally, we used the `CloseLog()` method to close the opened file. We did the same in steps 17 and 18. In steps 19 and 20, we navigated to the ASP.NET Core 2.0 application directory and executed the application.

In steps 21 and 22, we opened the browser and used the application to write some text to the disk. Then we closed the browser. Finally, in steps 23 and 24, we witnessed the file that was written to the disk while we were using the application.

Setting up .NET Core in macOS

In this recipe, we will be looking at how to set up things on macOS to run .NET Core 2.0 applications. At the time of writing, the macOS version is macOS High Sierra 10.13.2. We need a device such as a MacBook or an iMac for running macOS, or else you can skip this recipe.

Getting ready

Make sure you have macOS up and running on a device. Have your favorite browser open. Also, I assume you have experience of downloading and installing applications on a Mac device.

How to do it...

1. Open your favorite browser and navigate to `https://www.microsoft.com/net/download/macos`.

2. Click on the `Download .NET Core 2.1.x SDK` (at the time of writing, the version is 2.1.105) button.

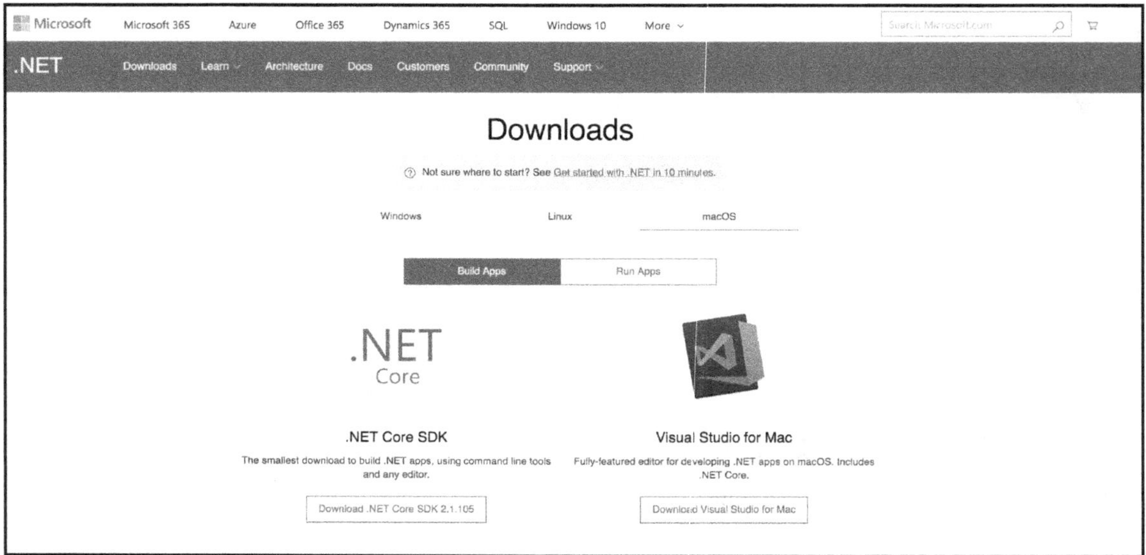

3. Now, in the download dialog box, select **Save**.
4. Now double-click on the file from the downloaded location (typically in the `Downloads` folder) and follow the instructions to install.
5. After installation, you should be good to go. Let's open a terminal and test the installation. (**Applications** | **Utilities** | **Terminal**).
6. Now, in the terminal, type the following command:

```
$ dotnet --version
```

7. If everything is OK, you should see output like this:

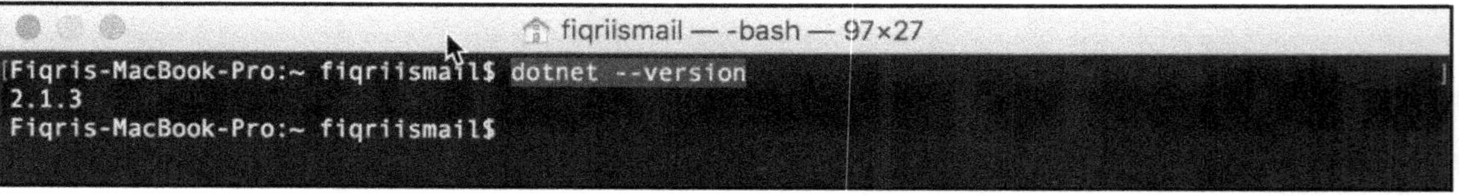

8. Let's download Visual Studio Code for Mac at `https://code.visualstudio.com/`.
9. In the dialog box, choose **Save File** to download.

10. After downloading the file, locate it and double-click on it to extract. Then drag drop the file in the `Applications` folder and you are good to go with Visual Studio Code.

How it works...

Throughout these steps, we have downloaded and installed .NET Core 2.0 and Visual Studio Code. Each step is self-explanatory. After opening Visual Studio Code, you might have to install a few extensions such as C# to make things easier.

Reading from a comma separated (CSV) text file

In this recipe, will be using .NET Core 2.0 under macOS. I assume you are familiar with using a terminal and typing a few commands in it. We will be looking at command-line tools supplied with .NET Core 2.0 to create our .NET Standard 2.0 library that reads a **Comma Separated Values** (**CSV**) file and returns its data.

Getting ready

If you have not already completed the previous recipe, make sure you have done it. It will help you to download .NET Core 2.0 and Visual Studio Code as an IDE. Let's fire up the terminal and get started.

How to do it...

1. Open a terminal window (**Applications** | **Utilities** | **Terminal**).
2. Now, in your `home` directory, type the following command (you might have to create a separate directory for your projects and do the following command):

```
$ dotnet new sln -o Chapter3.CsvFile
```

3. Now, type the following command to navigate to the newly created solution:

```
$ cd Chapter3.CsvFile
```

4. Again, type this command to create the .NET Standard 2.0 library project:

```
$ dotnet new classlib -o Chapter3.CsvFile.CsvReader
```

5. Now let's add this project to our solution by typing this command:

```
$ dotnet sln add
Chapter3.CsvFile.CsvReader/Chapter3.CsvFile.CsvReader.csproj
```

6. Let's open Visual Studio Code and open the current solution directory (**File** | **Open**). (**Visual Studio Code** should normally list it under the **Applications** directory).
7. Visual Studio Code should look like this:

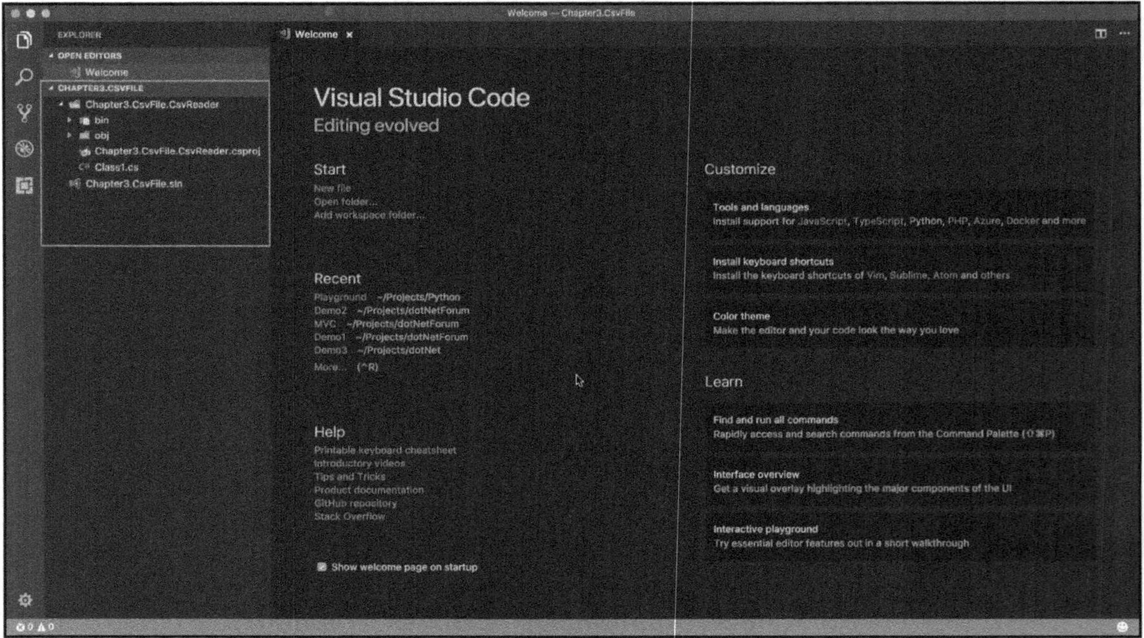

Visual Studio Code

8. Now, select the `Class1.cs` label in the file tree.
9. Press the *Enter* key and rename the `Class1.cs` to `CsvFileLib.cs` and press *Enter* again.
10. Now, in the code editor, change the `Class1` class name to match the filename `CsvFileLib`.

11. Let's click on the **CsvFileLib.cs** tab and add some code. Add the `using` directive on the top of the code window next to the last line of the `using` directives:

```
using System.IO;
using System.Collections.Generics;
```

12. At the top of the class, after the open curly bracket of the `CsvFileLib`, class add the following code:

```
private string _fileName;
```

13. Now, next to the preceding line, add the following constructor code for the class:

```
public CsvFileLib(string csvFile)
{
    _fileName = csvFile;
}
```

14. Finally, let's add the method to read all the lines in a CSV file:

```
public List<string> ReadCsvFile()
{
    var fileContents = new List<string>();

    using (var csvFile = File.OpenRead(_fileName))
    {
        var fileStream = new StreamReader(csvFile);

        while(!fileStream.EndOfStream)
        {
            fileContents.Add(fileStream.ReadLine());
        }
        fileStream.Close();
    }

    return fileContents;
}
```

15. Now, type the following command in the terminal to build the solution (make sure you are in the root of the solutions directory):

```
$ dotnet build
```

16. This will build and check the code for any syntax errors.

How it works...

In steps 1 to 5, we used .NET Core command-line tools to create a solution and then create a project. Then, we added the project to the solution. In steps 6 and 7, we opened Visual Studio Code for macOS and opened the directory we just created. Visual Studio Code for macOS allows you to work with .NET-based applications on macOS. Also, by installing extensions, it allows you to work with other popular technologies as well.

In steps 9 and 10, we renamed the default `Class1.cs` generated from the template and we renamed the file and the class to a meaningful name. In step 11, we added the necessary namespaces to work with files and collections. In step 12, we created a private variable to hold the filename. In step 13, we created a constructor that takes a filename with a path as a `string` parameter and then populated the variable we created in step 12.

In step 14, we created a method that reads the entire file and stores each line of the text to a List collection. This collection stores its items as `string`, In the first line of the `ReadCsvFile()` method, we created a local variable to hold the handler of the CSV text file. The following part of the code opens the given text file and, in the next line, stores all the content in a variable as a stream. The third line loops through till the end of the file and stores each line on the previous list. Finally, it closes the stream and returns the list of content from the `ReadCsvFile()` Method:

```
using (var csvFile = File.OpenRead(_fileName))
{
    var fileStream = new StreamReader(csvFile);

    while(!fileStream.EndOfStream)
    {
        fileContents.Add(fileStream.ReadLine());
    }
    fileStream.Close();
}
```

Creating a .NET Core console application in macOS to use the library

In this recipe, we will be creating a .NET Core console application to use the library built in the previous session. .NET Core is a cross-platform .NET flavor that runs on Windows, Linux, and macOS. This recipe focuses on .NET Core that runs under macOS.

Getting ready

Let's open the terminal and make sure we are in the root of the solution built in the previous recipe. Perform a quick build command as follows to check that everything is working fine:

```
$ dotnet build
```

How to do it...

1. Open the terminal (**Applications** | **Utilities** | **Terminal**).
2. Navigate to the root of the solution we built in the previous recipe and enter the following command:

```
$ dotnet new console -o Chapter3.CsvFile.ConsoleApp
```

3. Again, type this command to see the content of the directory:

```
$ ls
```

4. Your terminal should look like this:

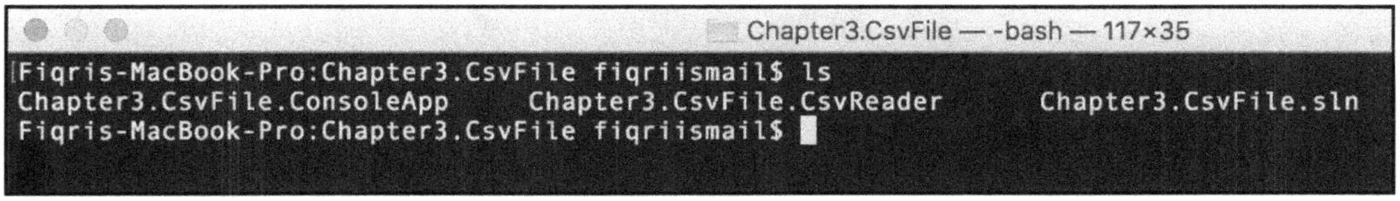

```
Fiqris-MacBook-Pro:Chapter3.CsvFile fiqriismail$ ls
Chapter3.CsvFile.ConsoleApp     Chapter3.CsvFile.CsvReader      Chapter3.CsvFile.sln
Fiqris-MacBook-Pro:Chapter3.CsvFile fiqriismail$
```

5. Execute the following commands to add this project to the solution and to test build:

```
$ dotnet sln add
Chapter3.CsvFile.Console/Chapter3.CsvFile.ConsoleApp.csproj

$ dotnet build
```

6. Let's open Visual Studio Code and open (**File** | **Open**) the full solution.
7. Your Visual Studio Code should look like this:

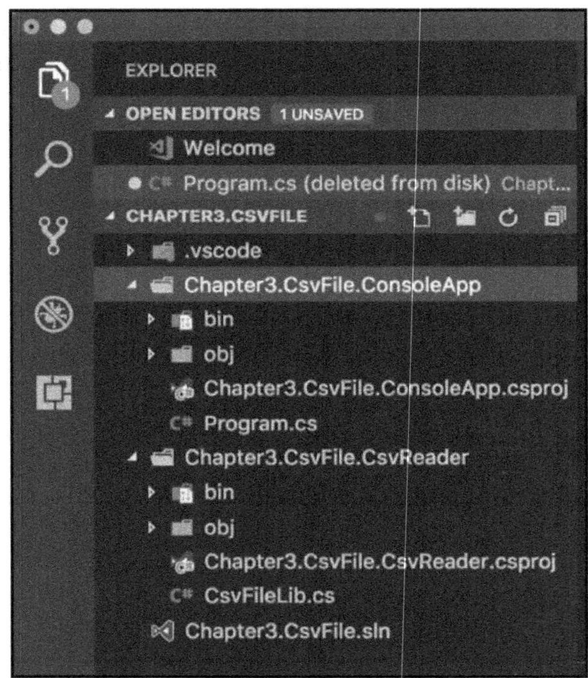

8. Now expand the `Chapter3.CsvFile.Console` node and select the `Chapter3.CsvFile.Console` label.

9. Click on the New File icon in the tab.

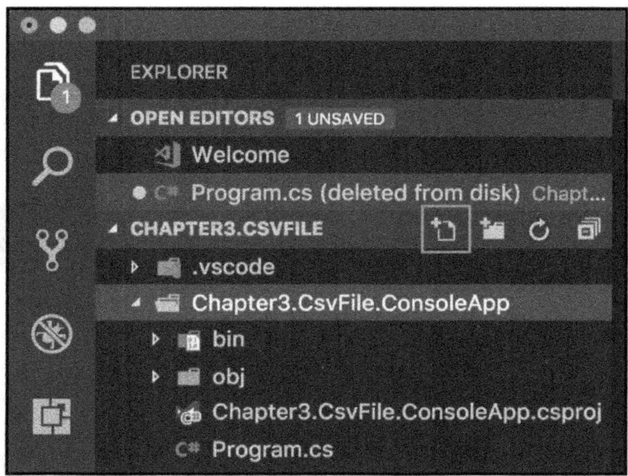

10. Type `movies.txt` as the name and press *Enter*.
11. Now select the `movies.txt` file and add the following content:

```
1,X-Men: Apocalypse,2016
2,The Secret Life of Pets,2016
3,Suicide Squad,2016
4,Independence Day: Resurgence,2016
5,Star Trek 3,2016
6,Batman v Superman: Dawn of Justice,2016
7,The Jungle Book,2016
8,Hail, Caesar!,2016
9,Zoolander 2,2016
10,How to Be Single,2016
```

12. You text file should look like this:

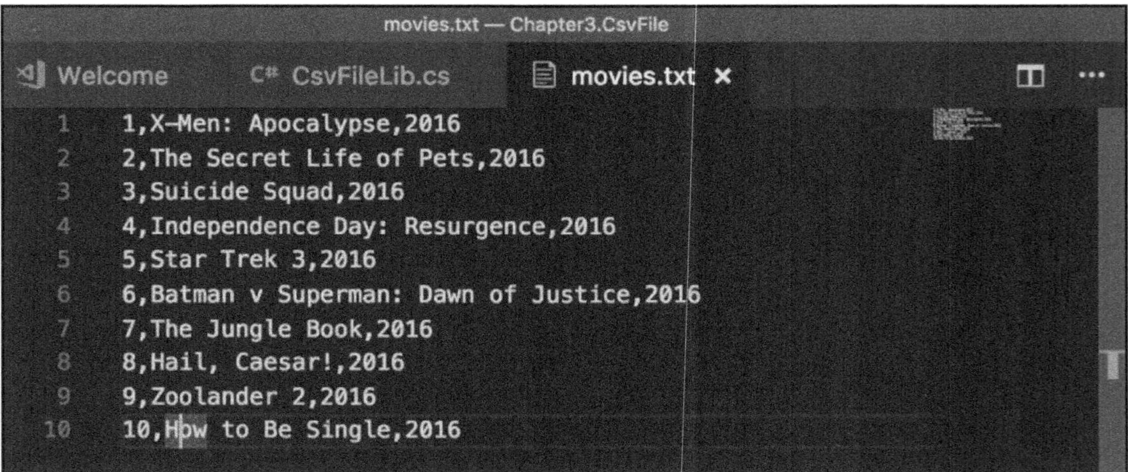

13. Let's open the terminal (**Applications** | **Utilities** | **Terminal**) and navigate to the newly created console project.
14. Type the following command and press *Enter* to add our library to the console application as a reference:

```
$ dotnet add reference
../Chapter3.CsvFile.CsvReader/Chapter3.CsvFile.CsvReader.csproj
```

15. Let's go back to Visual Studio Code, select `Program.cs`, and add this `using` directive after the last line of `using` directives:

```
using Chapter3.CsvFile.CsvReader;
```

16. Now delete any existing code inside the `Main()` method and add this code between the curly brackets:

```
var moviesFile = new CsvFileLib("movies.txt");
var moviesList = moviesFile.ReadCsvFile();

foreach (var movie in moviesList)
{
    var row = movie.Split(',');
    Console.WriteLine($"ID: {row[0]} Title :
        {row[1]} Year : {row[2]}");
}
```

17. Save the current changes and go back to the terminal, type the following command, and press *Enter*:

```
$ dotnet build
```

18. Again, type the following code and press *Enter*:

```
$ dotnet run
```

19. You should see this output in your terminal window:

```
Chapter3.CsvFile.ConsoleApp — -bash — 117×35
Fiqris-MacBook-Pro:Chapter3.CsvFile.ConsoleApp fiqriismail$ dotnet run
ID: 1 Title : X-Men: Apocalypse Year : 2016
ID: 2 Title : The Secret Life of Pets Year : 2016
ID: 3 Title : Suicide Squad Year : 2016
ID: 4 Title : Independence Day: Resurgence Year : 2016
ID: 5 Title : Star Trek 3 Year : 2016
ID: 6 Title : Batman v Superman: Dawn of Justice Year : 2016
ID: 7 Title : The Jungle Book Year : 2016
ID: 8 Title : Hail Year :  Caesar!
ID: 9 Title : Zoolander 2 Year : 2016
ID: 10 Title : How to Be Single Year : 2016
Fiqris-MacBook-Pro:Chapter3.CsvFile.ConsoleApp fiqriismail$
```

How it works...

In steps 1 to 4, we navigated to the previously built .NET Standard 2.0 library. Using the macOS terminal we reached the root of that solution. Also, we have created a new .NET Standard 2.0 library. When you create a library project in .NET Core 2.0, by default it chooses .NET Standard 2.0 as the template. So we don't worry about telling the command-line tool to create the library as .NET Standard 2.0 library.

In step 5, we added the newly created project to our solution and performed a build to check that everything was fine. In steps 6 to 9, we opened the current directory using Visual Studio Code and then, in steps 9 to 12, we created a sample text file with comma separated values for testing purposes. In step 14, we added the library to our console application as a reference.

In step 15, we added the reference for the library project in the `using` statements and then, in step 16, we created an instance of the `CsvFileLib` class and stored the output of the `ReadCsvFile()` method in a variable. Finally, we looped through the list, which is returned by the `ReadCsvFile()` method, and printed the output in the console window.

Compressing? Why not?

In this recipe, we will be looking at file compression capabilities supported on .NET Framework and how to use them in a .NET Standard 2.0 library. File compression classes are supported inside the `System.IO.Compression` namespace. Classes inside this namespace are used to compress the file as well as decompress it. They are also used to read content inside a compressed file. Let's have a look and create a .NET Standard 2.0 library that compresses and decompresses a file.

Getting ready

Make sure you have the latest version of Visual Studio 2017 up and running. As mentioned previously, we will be using classes inside `System.IO.Compression`. Mainly, we will be looking at the `ZipFile` class. Let's get going and build our library that compresses and decompresses a file.

How to do it...

1. Open Visual Studio 2017.
2. Click **File** | **New** | **Project** to create a project.
3. In the **New Project** dialog box, expand the **Other Project Types** node in the left-hand pane, and select **Visual Studio Solutions**. In the right-hand pane, select **Blank Solution.**

4. In the **Name:** textbox, type `Chapter3.Compress` and, in the **Location:** textbox, select path from the drop-down box or click on the **Browse...** button to locate a path.

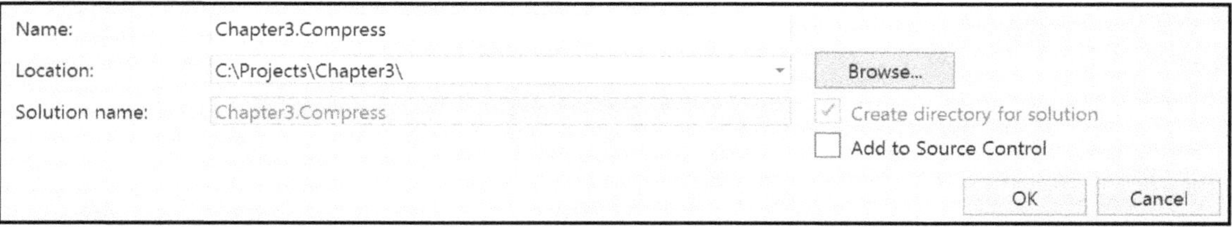

5. Click **OK**.
6. Now, your Solution Explorer (*Ctrl* + *Alt* + *L*) should look like this:

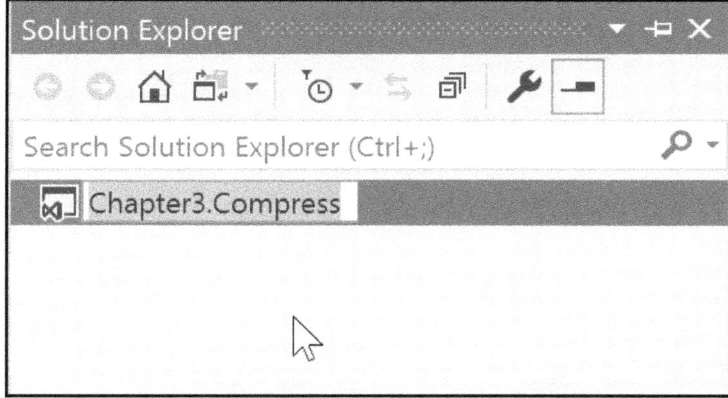

7. Now, right-click on the `Chapter3.Compress` label in the Solution Explorer and select **Add** | **New Project**.
8. In the **New Project** dialog box, expand the **Visual C#** node.

9. Select **.NET Standard** in the left-hand pane and **Class Library (.NET Standard)** in the right-hand pane.

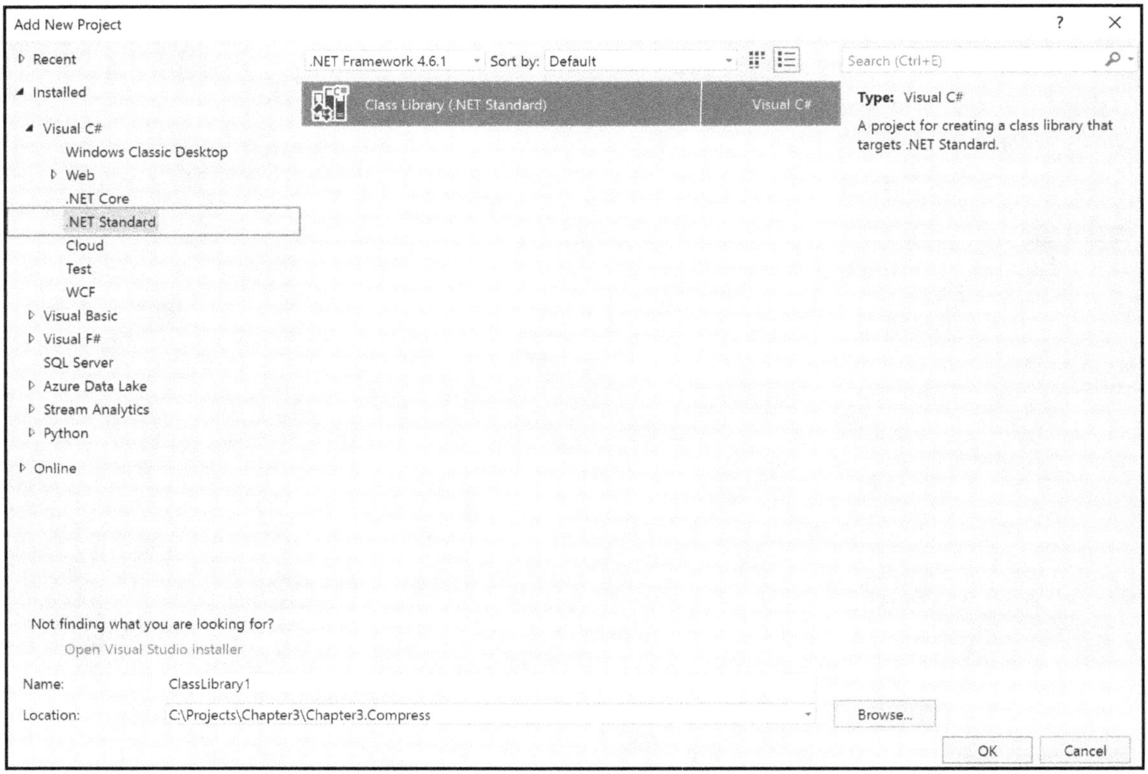

10. Now, in the **Name:** textbox, type `Chapter3.Compress.CompressLib`, leave the other defaults as they are, and click **OK**.

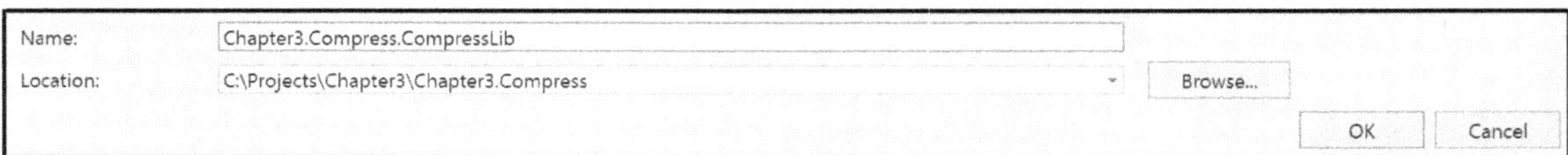

11. Now, the **Solution Explorer** (*Ctrl* + *Alt* + *L*) should look like this:

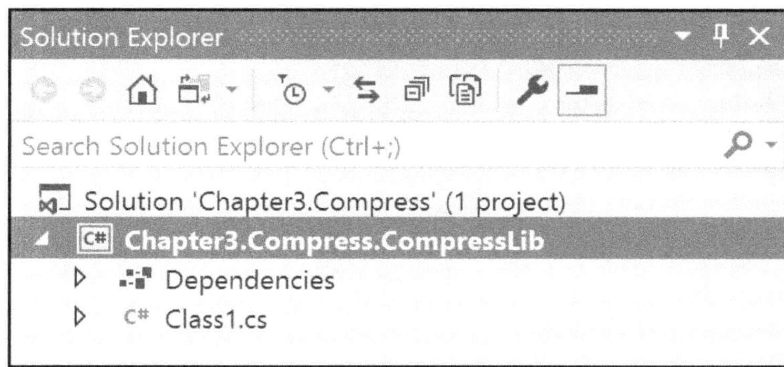

12. Now select `Class1.cs` in the **Solution Explorer** and press *F2* to rename the file `Zipper.cs`.
13. Answer **Yes** in the confirmation dialog box that asks to rename the class name as well.
14. Now, in the `Zipper.cs` code window (double-click on the `Zipper.cs` label in **Solution Explorer** to open), type the following code next to the last line of the `using` directives:

```
using System.Collections.Generic;
using System.IO.Compression;
```

15. Create a `private` class variable at the top of the class code (next to the starting curly bracket of the class):

```
private string _sourcePath;
```

16. Let's add a constructor to our class by adding this code:

```
public Zipper(string sourcePath)
{
    _sourcePath = sourcePath;
}
```

17. Now add this method next to the constructor code:

```
public void CompressFile(string zipPath)
{
    ZipFile.CreateFromDirectory(zipPath, _sourcePath);
}
```

18. Finally, add the following code to list the zipped content:

```
public List<string> ListArchive(string zipFile)
{
    var fileList = new List<string>()
    using (ZipArchive archive = ZipFile.OpenRead(zipFile)
    {
        foreach(var entry in archive.Entries)
        {
            fileList.Add(entry.Name);
        }
    }

    return fileList;
}
```

19. Perform a quick build by pressing *Ctrl* + *Shift* + *B*, for syntax errors.

How it works...

In steps 1 to 5, we created a blank solution using Visual Studio 2017 and gave it a proper, meaningful name. In steps 7 to 10, we added a .NET Standard 2.0 class library to the project. We renamed the default `Class1.cs` generated by the template in step 12. In step 14, we added two namespaces to the code. The `System.IO.Compression` namespace contains all the necessary classes for compressing and decompressing. In step 15, we added a private variable that holds the path to compress. In this case, it is a folder.

Step 16 introduced the constructor with a source path parameter to zip. In step 17, we created a method that uses the `ZipFile` class and its method to compress a given source folder. And then, finally, we created a method that lists the name of a compressed archive. It takes a parameter as the compressed zip files path:

```
var fileList = new List<string>()
    using (ZipArchive archive = ZipFile.OpenRead(zipFile)
    {
        foreach(var entry in archive.Entries)
        {
            fileList.Add(entry.Name);
        }
    }

    return fileList;
```

The first line creates an empty list that populates `strings` as items. Then we created a `ZipArchive` instance. We have used the `using` keyword to wrap around that statement. It's a safe method of programming for this sort of item. The `using` keyword is a very convenient way of using an object that implements the `IDisposable` interface.

The `IDisposable` interface provides a mechanism for releasing unmanaged resources.

And finally, we went through all the entries using a `foreach` and then returned the populated list.

Creating a classic Windows application to use the library

In this recipe, we will be looking at a classic Windows application that compresses a given folder using the library that we built in the previous recipe. Make sure you have completed the previous recipe that creates a .NET Standard 2.0 library.

Getting ready

Let's open the previous solution for the library we built. Make sure you perform a quick build (*Ctrl* + *Shift* + *B*) to check for any syntax errors.

How to do it...

1. Open Visual Studio 2017.
2. Now open the solution that we built from the previous recipe.

3. The **Solution Explorer** should look like this:

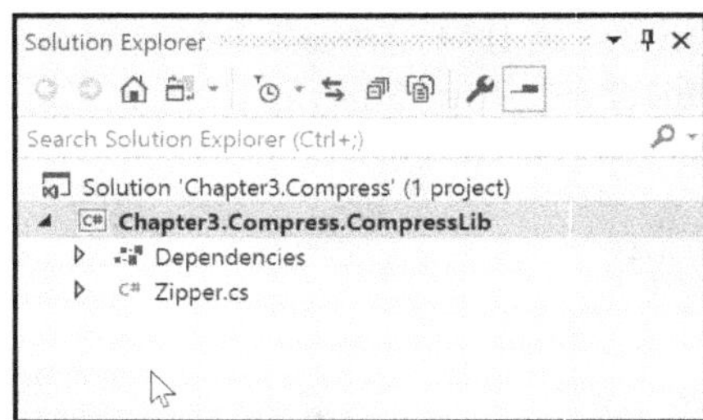

4. Now, let's select the solution name and right-click.
5. From the menu, select **Add** | **New Project**.
6. In the **New Project** dialog box, expand the **Visual C#** node and select **Windows Classic Desktop** in the left-hand pane.
7. In the right-hand pane, select **Windows Forms App (.NET Framework)**:

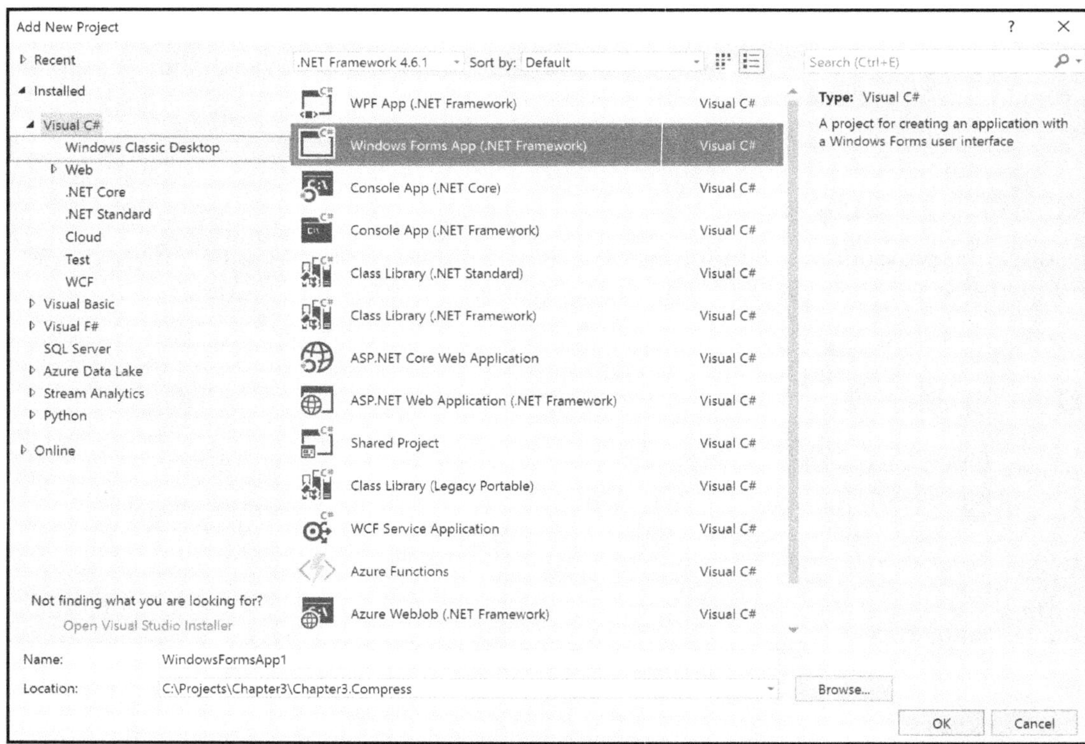

8. Now, in the **Name:** textbox, type `Chapter3.Compress.ZipperWinApp`, leave the **Location:** textbox as it is, and click **OK**.

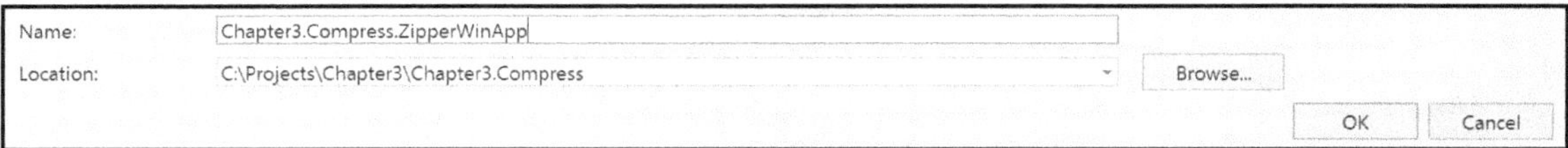

9. Now, the **Solution Explorer** should look like this:

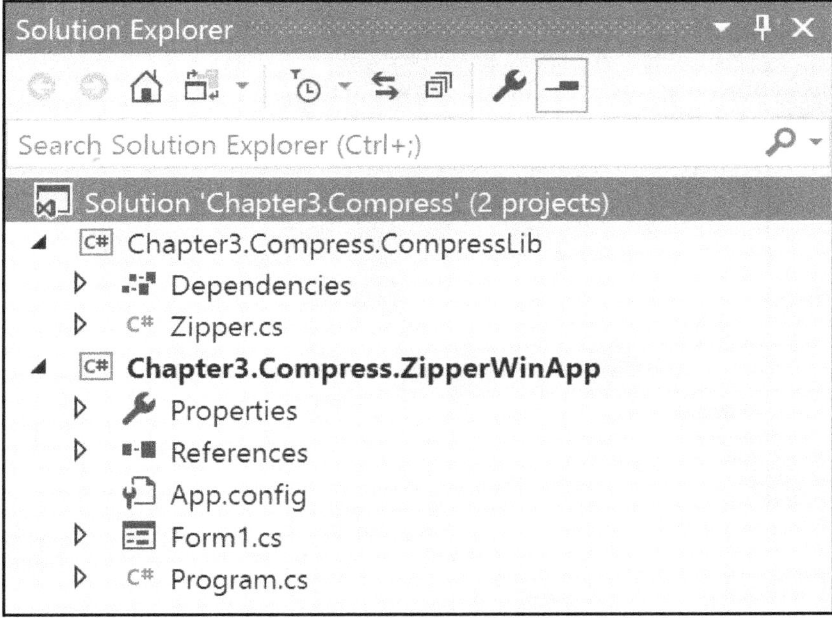

10. Let's rename the `Form1.cs` as `MainForm.cs` by selecting it and pressing *F2*.
11. Answer **Yes** in the confirmation box to confirm the changing of the main class name as well.
12. Now, select the Windows form from the designer window.
13. Drag drop a **TextBox**, a **Button**, and a **ListBox** in the form.
14. Also drag drop a **FolderDialogBox** control in the Windows form.

15. Change the properties of the previous controls as per this table:

Control	Property	Value
TextBox	**Name**	`FolderTextBox`
Button	**Name**	`BrowseButton`
Button	**Text**	`Browse...`
ListBox	**Name**	`FileListBox`
Form	**Text**	`Zipper WinApp`
FolderDialogBox	**Name**	`ZipFolder`

16. Now, your designer area should look like this:

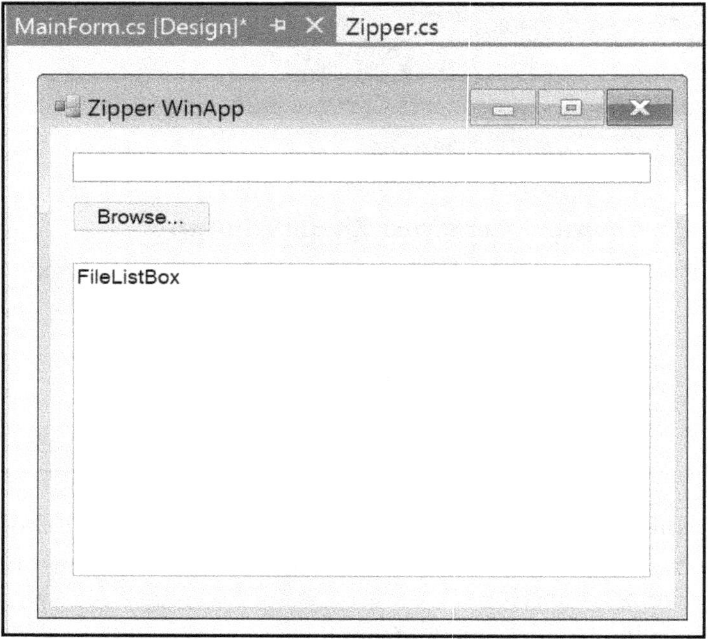

17. Now, select the `Chapter3.Compress.ZipperWinApp` label in the **Solution Explorer** and expand it.
18. Right-click on the **References** label and select **Add Reference**.
19. Click on the **Projects** node in the **Reference Manager** dialog box.
20. Check the checkbox in front of `Chapter3.Compress.CompressLib` from the project list in the right-hand pane.

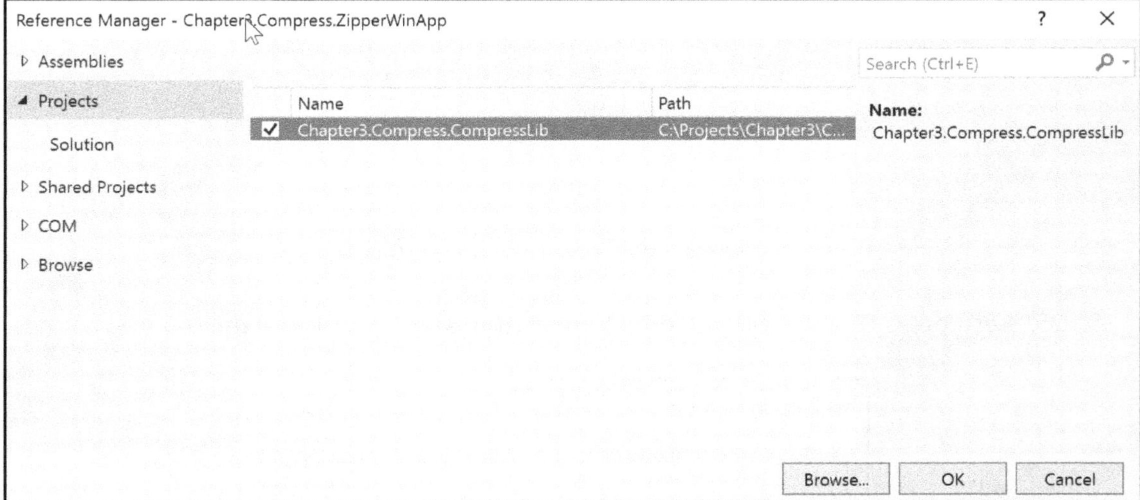

21. Click **OK**.
22. Now double-click on the **Browse...** button to open the code window.
23. Scroll up in the code window and add the following `using` directive to the last line of all the `using` directives, at the top:

```
using Chapter3.Compress.CompressLib;
```

24. Now scroll down till you reach the button click event of the **Browse...** button and add the following code in between the curly brackets:

```
if (ZipFolder.ShowDialog() == DialogResult.OK)
{
    FolderTextBox.Text = ZipFolder.SelectedPath;

    string zipFileName =
        @"C:\Projects\Chapter3\TestFolder\result.zip";
    var zipFile = new Zipper(zipFileName);
    zipFile.CompressFile(FolderTextBox.Text);

    MessageBox.Show("You folder has been zipped.",
        "Information", MessageBoxButtons.OK,
        MessageBoxIcon.Information);

    var fileList = zipFile.ListArchive(zipFileName);

    FileListBox.Items.AddRange(fileList.ToArray());
}
```

25. Let's press *F5* and test our code. Your output should look like this:

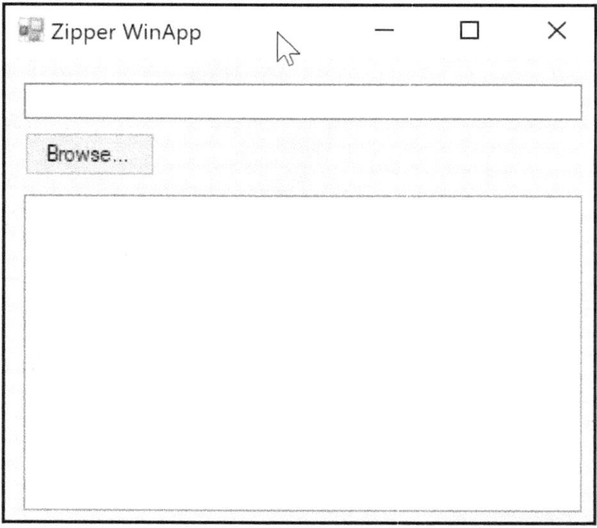

26. Let's click the **Browse...** button and navigate to a folder:

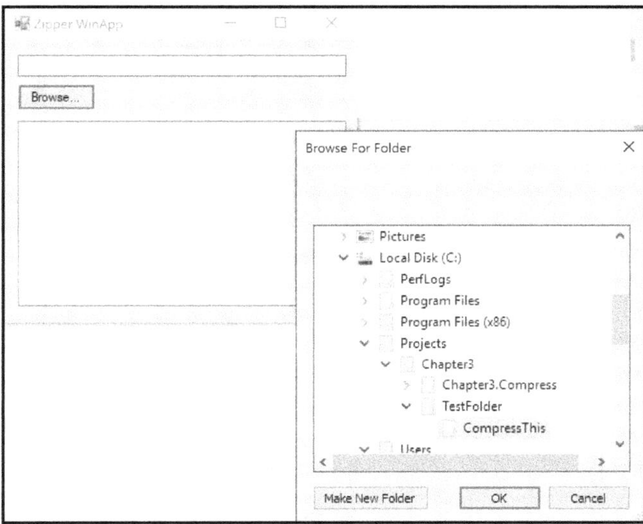

27. Click **OK**. Now, the folder will be compressed and the output file will be `result.zip`.

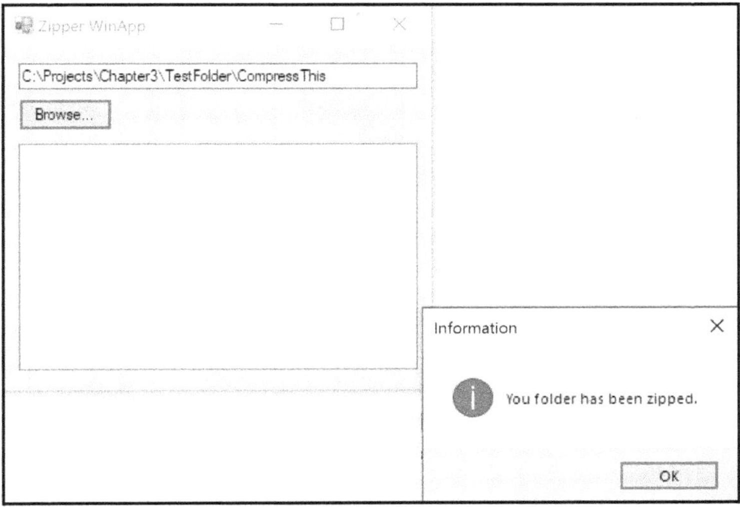

28. Click **OK**.
29. Now you will see the list of files in the compressed ZIP file:

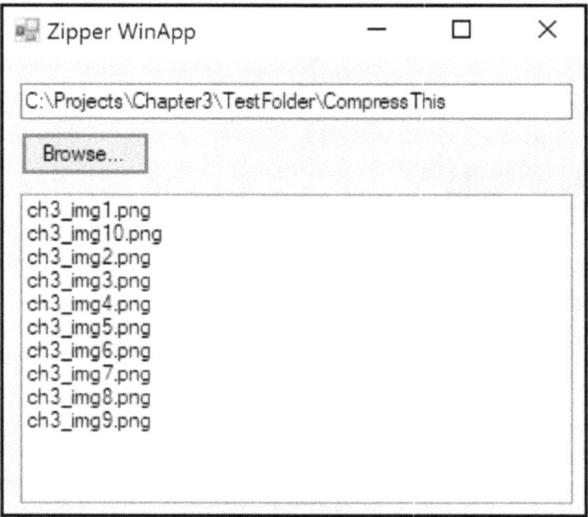

30. Let's browse to the folder selected using Windows Explorer and have a look (you can copy and paste the path from the textbox in the application itself):

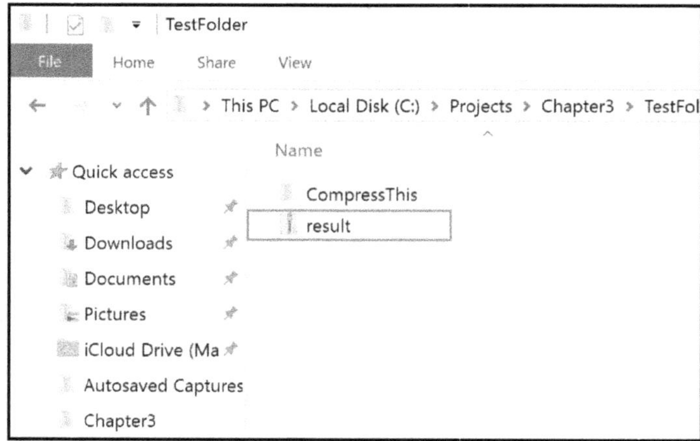

31. Double-click on the file and you will see that the content of the ZIP file matches the list we had in step 29:

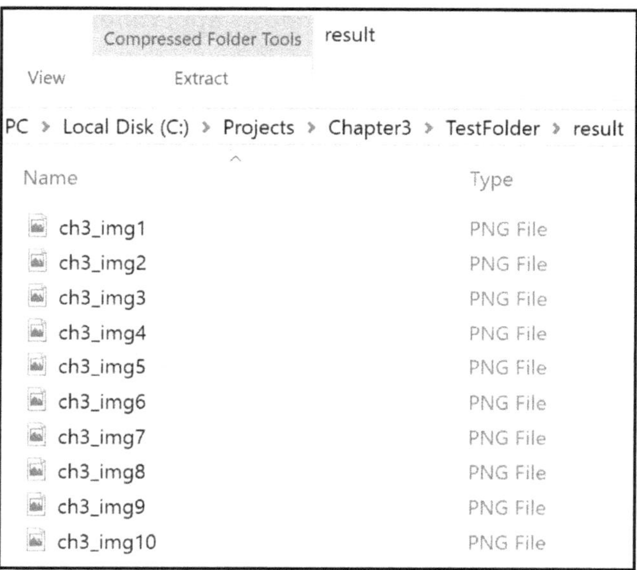

32. Now close the app.

How it works...

In steps 1 to 9, we opened the existing solution with the .NET Standard 2.0 class library built in the previous recipe. Then we added a new Classic Windows Application project to that solution. We also gave it a proper name to match the solution. In steps 10 and 11, we renamed the default Windows form generated by Visual Studio. In steps 12 to 16, we added the necessary controls to build the user interface of our application.

In steps 18 to 21, we added the reference to the .NET Standard 2.0 library from our Classic Windows Application. This is a mandatory step, or else you will not have access to the library and its functionality. In step 23, we added a using statement that will tell the Windows application we have referenced the library and allow us to access its accessible methods.

In step 24, we added code to the button click event of the **Browse...** button. In the first line of that code, we have used an `if` statement to open the folder dialog box and checked whether the **OK** button is pressed in the dialog box. Then, the following two lines of code store the selected path in the textbox of our Windows application:

```
FolderTextBox.Text = ZipFolder.SelectedPath;

string zipFileName = @"C:\Projects\Chapter3\TestFolder\result.zip";
```

Then we have a `string` variable that stores the destination ZIP filename:

```
var zipFile = new Zipper(zipFileName);
zipFile.CompressFile(FolderTextBox.Text);

MessageBox.Show("You folder has been zipped.",
    "Information", MessageBoxButtons.OK, MessageBoxIcon.Information);
```

In the first line, we have an instance of the `Zipper` class and, in the second line, we have used its `CompressFile()` method. Finally, we have displayed a notification to the end user by using the `MessageBox.Show()` method. Finally, in the following two lines of code, we used the `ListArchive()` method to extract the content of the ZIP file and added the output to the list box control:

```
var fileList = zipFile.ListArchive(zipFileName);
FileListBox.Items.AddRange(fileList.ToArray());
```

Encrypting and decrypting content in a text file

In this recipe, we will be looking at another capability of the `System.IO` namespace. We will be creating a .NET Standard 2.0 library that encrypts an existing text file as well as decrypts it.

Getting ready

Encryption is a great way of securing your files. The `System.IO` namespace provides you with great functionality to encrypt and decrypt your content. Let's have a look at how to do it in a .NET Standard 2.0 library.

How to do it...

1. Open Visual Studio 2017.
2. Click **File** | **New** | **Project** to create a project.
3. In the **New Project** dialog box, expand the **Other Project Types** node in the left-hand pane, and select **Visual Studio Solutions**. In the right-hand pane, select **Blank Solution**.
4. In the **Name:** textbox, type `Chapter3.SecureFile` and, in the **Location:** textbox, select the path from the drop-down box or click on the **Browse...** button to locate a path.

5. Click **OK**.
6. Now, your **Solution Explorer** (*Ctrl* + *Alt* + *L*) should look like this:

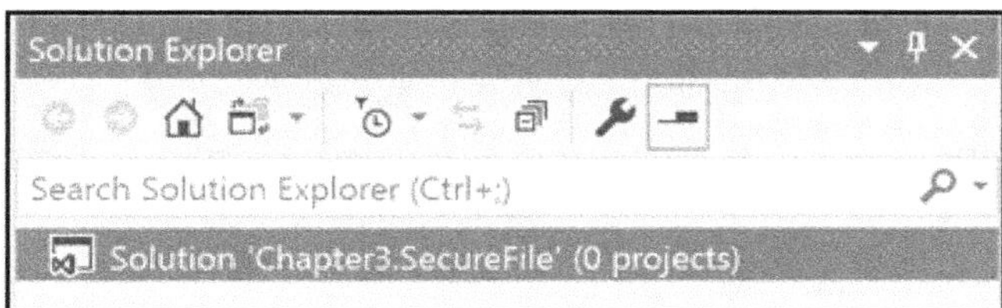

7. Now, right-click on the `Chapter3.SecureFile` label in the **Solution Explorer** and select **Add** | **New Project.**
8. In the **New Project** dialog box, expand the **Visual C#** node.

9. Select **.NET Standard** in the left-hand pane and **Class Library (.NET Standard)** in the right-hand pane.

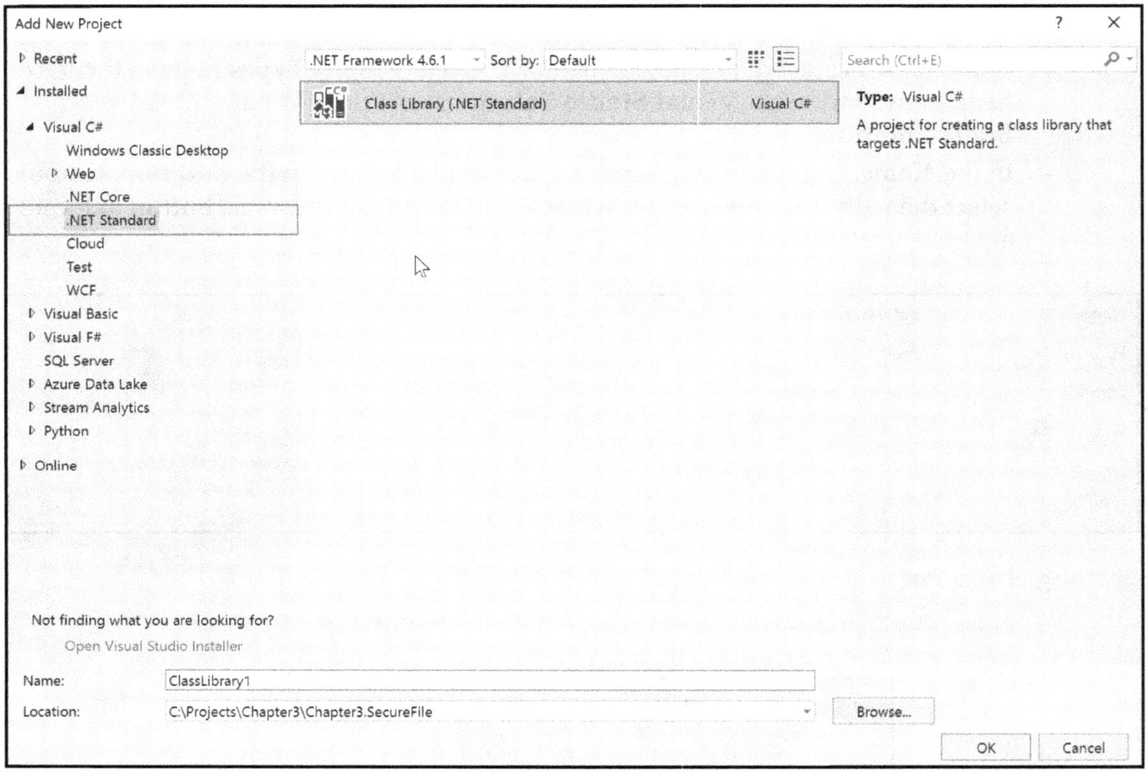

10. Now, in the **Name:** textbox, type `Chapter3.SecureFile.CryptLib`, leave the other defaults as they are, and click **OK**.

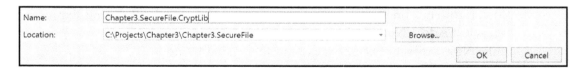

11. Now, the **Solution Explorer** (*Ctrl* + *Alt* + *L*) should look like this:

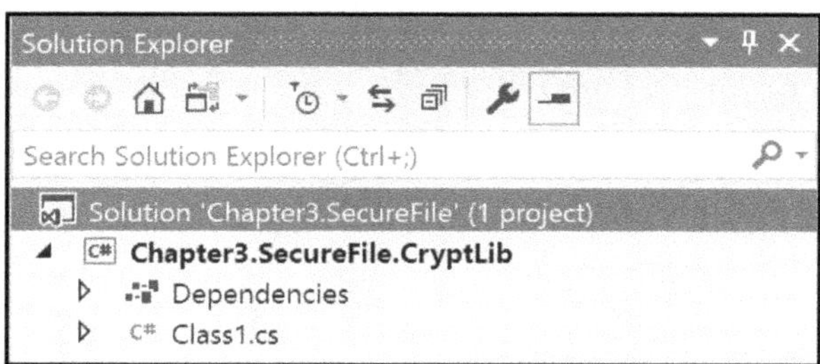

12. Now select `Class1.cs` in the **Solution Explorer** and press *F2* to rename the file to `CryptFile.cs`.
13. Answer **Yes** in the confirmation dialog box that asks to rename the class name as well.
14. Now double-click on`CryptFile.cs` to open the code window.
15. In the code window, scroll up to the top and add the following `using` directive to the last line of the `using` directives:

```
using System.IO;
```

16. Now add the following code next to the start curly bracket of the `CryptFile` class:

```
private string _fileName;
```

17. Let's add the default constructor method as follows:

```
public CryptFile(string fileName)
{
    _fileName = fileName;
}
```

18. Now let's add a method to encrypt the file:

```
public void EncryptFile()
{
    File.Encrypt(_fileName);
}
```

19. Also add this method to decrypt the file:

```
public void DecryptFile()
{
    File.Decrypt(_fileName);
}
```

20. Press *Ctrl* + *Shift* + *B* to perform a quick build to check for the correct syntax.

How it works...

In steps 1 to 5, we opened Visual Studio 2017, created an empty solution, and gave it a proper name. In steps 7 to 11, we added a .NET Standard 2.0 library to the solution. In steps 12 and 13, we changed the default name of the class generated from the template. In step 15, we added the `System.IO` namespace that contains the file encryption and decryption functionality.

In step 16, we added a class-wide private `string` variable to hold the filename to encrypt and decrypt. In step 17, we added the default constructor that populates the private variable to hold the filename. In step 18, we added a method to encrypt the file. We used the `Encrypt()` method of the file class found in the `System.IO` namespace. We did the same in step 19 to decrypt the file.

Finally, we performed a quick build to check that all the syntax was intact.

Creating a classic Windows application to use the library

This recipe will focus on building a classic Windows application to use the .NET Standard 2.0 library that we created in the previous recipe.

Getting ready

Make sure you have completed the previous recipe where we built a .NET Standard 2.0 library. It used the `System.IO` namespace to encrypt and decrypt a file. Open that solution and do a quick *Ctrl* + *Shift* + *B* to check that everything is fine.

How to do it...

1. Open Visual Studio 2017.
2. Now open the solution we built from the previous recipe.
3. The **Solution Explorer** should look like this:

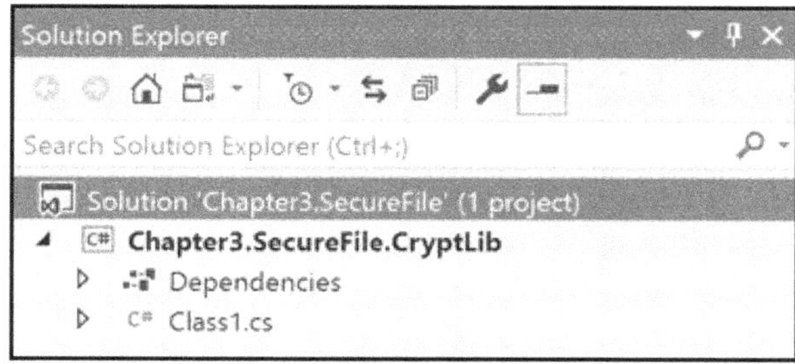

4. Now, let's select the solution name and right-click.
5. From the menu, select **Add** | **New Project**.
6. In the **New Project** dialog box, expand the **Visual C#** node and select **Windows Classic Desktop** in the left-hand pane.

7. In the right-hand pane, select **Windows Forms App (.NET Framework)**:

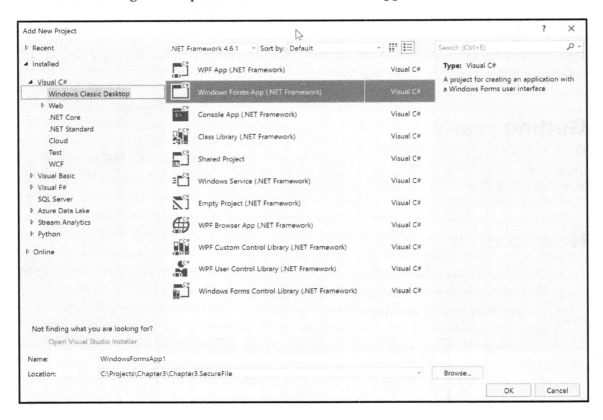

8. Now, in the **Name:** textbox, type `Chapter3.SecureFile.SecureWinApp`, leave the **Location:** textbox as it is, and click **OK**.

9. Now, the **Solution Explorer** should look like this:

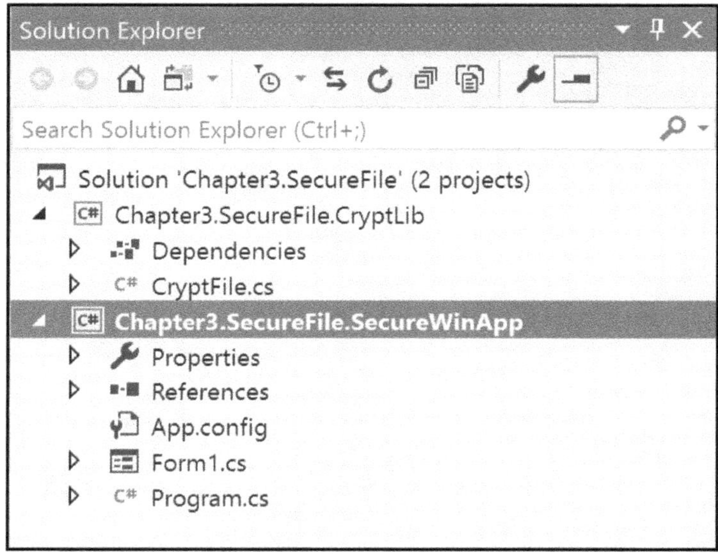

10. Let's rename `Form1.cs` as `MainForm.cs`, by selecting it and pressing *F2*.
11. Answer **Yes** in the confirmation box to confirm the changing of the main class name as well.
12. Now select the Windows form from the designer window.
13. Drag and drop two **Buttons** in the form.
14. Also drag and drop an `OpenFileDialogBox` control in the Windows form.
15. Change the properties of the previous controls as per this table:

Control	Property	Value
Button	**Name**	`EncryptButton`
Button	**Text**	`Encrypt`
Button	**Name**	`DecryptButton`
Button	**Text**	`Decrypt`
OpenFileDialogBox	**Name**	`OpenDialog`
OpenFileDialogBox	**Filter**	`Text Files|*.txt`

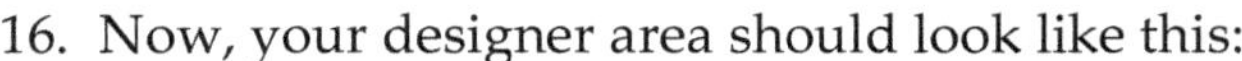

16. Now, your designer area should look like this:

17. Now select the `Chapter3.SecureFile.SecureWinApp` label in the **Solution Explorer** and expand it.
18. Right-click on the **References** label and select **Add Reference**.
19. Click on the **Projects** node in the **Reference Manager** dialog box.

20. Check the check box in front of the `Chapter3.SecureFile.CryptLib` label from the project list in the right-hand pane.

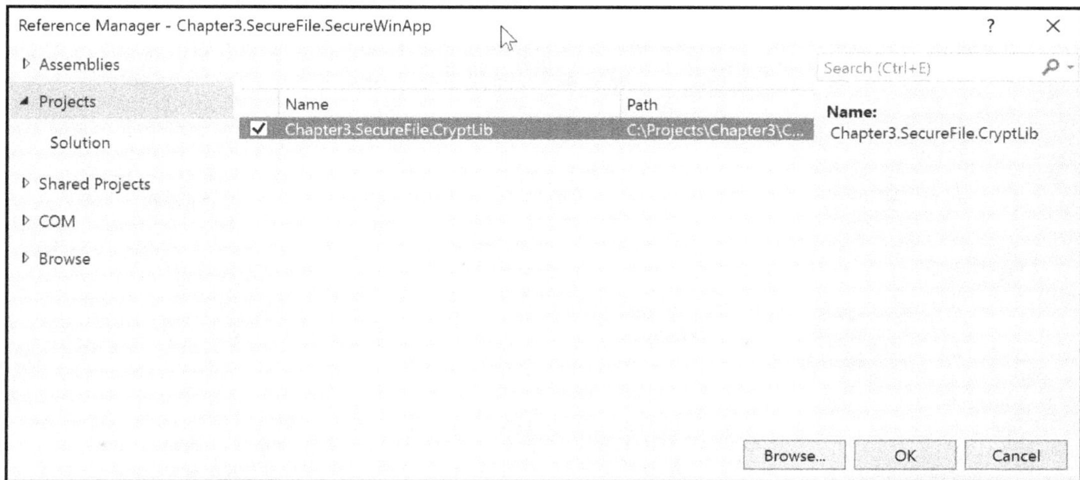

21. Click **OK**.
22. Now switch back to the design window and double-click on the **Encrypt** button to open the code window.
23. In the code window, scroll up to the top and add the following `using` directive as the last line of the `using` block:

```
using Chapter3.SecureFile.CryptLib;
```

24. Now scroll down to the **Encrypt** button, click, and add the following code in between the curly brackets:

```
if (OpenDialog.ShowDialog() == DialogResult.OK)
{
    var textFileName = OpenDialog.FileName;
    var secureFile = new CryptFile(textFileName);

    secureFile.EncryptFile();

    MessageBox.Show("File encrypted", "Information",
        MessageBoxButtons.OK,
        MessageBoxIcon.Information);
}
```

25. Now switch back to the designer window by clicking on the **MainForm.cs [designer]** tab.
26. Double-click on the **Decrypt** button to reach the code for that button click.
27. Add the following code in between the curly brackets of the button click code:

```
if (OpenDialog.ShowDialog() == DialogResult.OK)
{

    var textFileName = OpenDialog.FileName;
    var secureFile = new CryptFile(textFileName);

    secureFile.DecryptFile();

    MessageBox.Show("File decrypted", "Information",
        MessageBoxButtons.OK,
        MessageBoxIcon.Information);
}
```

28. Now press *F5* to execute the code (make sure the classic Windows application project is the default project)
29. Press the **Encrypt** button and select a file:

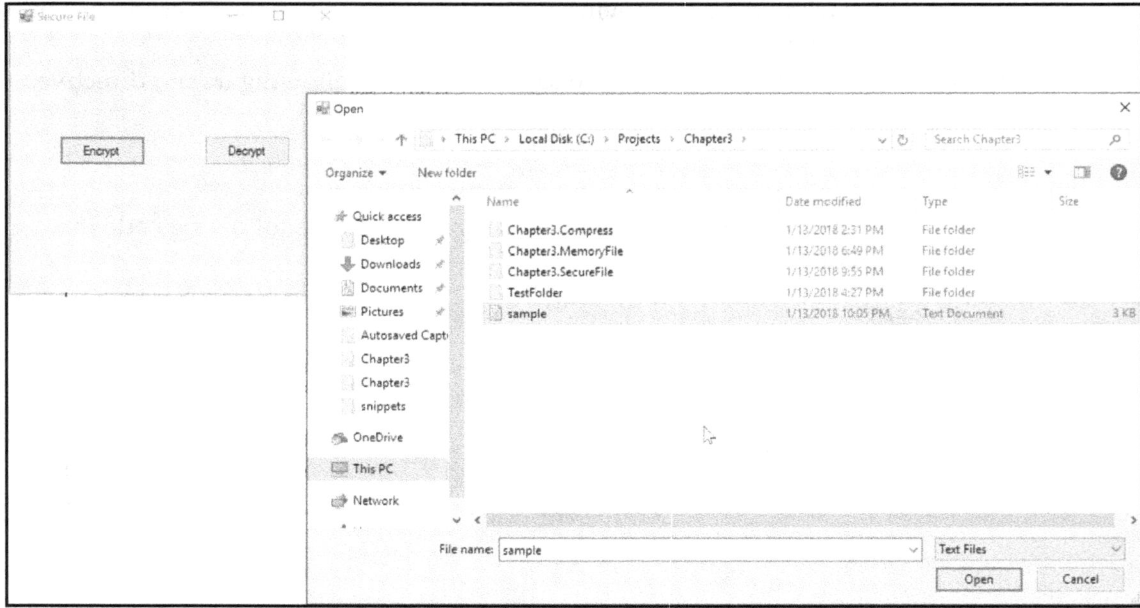

30. Click **Open** and click **OK** in the information box.
31. Now open Windows Explorer and navigate to the location of the file that you just encrypted.
32. You will notice a lock on the file.

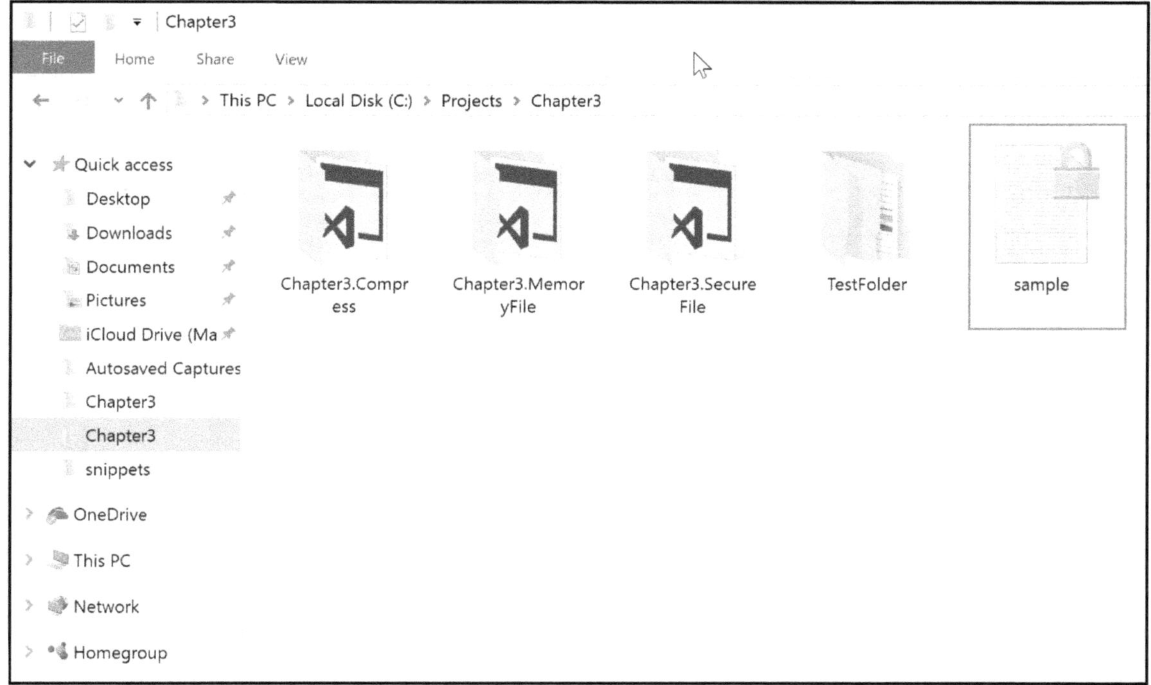

33. Now switch back to your app, click on the **Decrypt** button, and follow the same steps as before.

34. Now the lock is removed from the file.

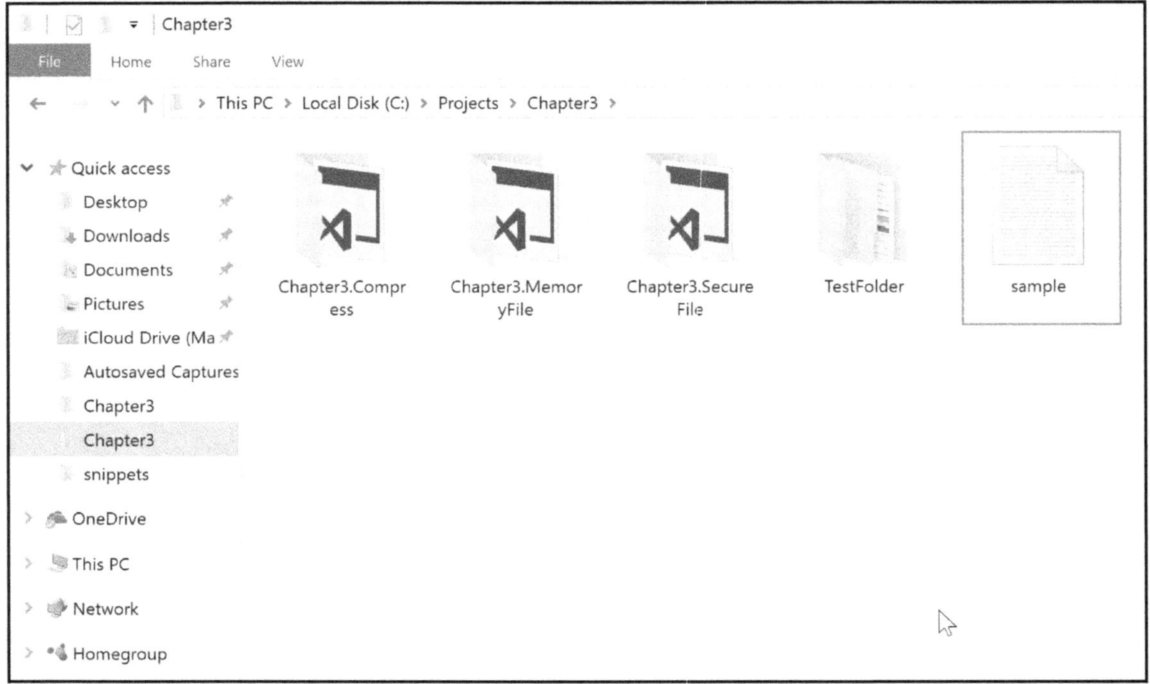

How it works...

In steps 1 to 4, we opened the existing solution with the library we built in the previous recipe. In steps 5 to 9, we added a classic Windows project to the solution. We have assigned proper names to the project to keep consistency and readability. In steps 10 to 15, we changed the name of the Windows form and then added necessary controls to the form. At the end, we changed the properties of those controls.

In steps 18 to 21, we added a reference to the project that contains the library. This is a mandatory step, or else we won't be able to access the library functionality from our Windows application. Now, in step 23, we added the reference to a library project from the code level. This step will allow you to access all the methods available from the code level. In step 24, we used an `if` statement to open the **File Open** dialog box and to check whether the **Open** button is clicked. In the next lines of code, we created an instance of the `CryptFile` class and used the filename with the path as its parameter. Finally, we used the `EncryptFile()` method to start the encryption and `MessageBox.Show()` to display the information to the user. Again, in step 25, we used the Decrypt button of the application to use the other `DecryptFile()` method of the `CryptFile` class.

Finally, in steps 28 to 31, we executed our application and tested it. In steps 32 and 34, we confirmed that encryption and decryption worked.

4
Functional Programming

In this chapter, we will be looking at these recipes:

- Creating a .NET Standard 2.0 library
- Creating a .NET Core console application to use the library
- Creating a .NET Standard 2.0 library that uses tuples
- Creating a Razor Pages web application to use the library
- Creating a .NET Standard 2.0 library that uses delegates and lambda expressions
- Creating a .NET console application to use the library

Technical requirements

Readers should have a basic knowledge of C#. They should also have a basic knowledge of using Visual Studio, installing packages using NuGet, and referencing libraries within projects from other projects.

The code files for this chapter can be found on GitHub:
`https://github.com/PacktPublishing/DotNET-Standard-2-Cookbook/tree/master/Chapter04`

Check out the following video to see the code in action:
`https://goo.gl/yeUdkd`

Introduction

This chapter talks about the functional programming capabilities of C# and how to use them for a .NET Standard 2.0 library. Let's look at a definition of functional programming:

"Functional programming is a style that treats computation as the evaluation of mathematical functions and avoids changing state and mutable data."

Simply put, it means you will be able to use functions as inputs and outputs for other functions. You can also assign them to variables and store them in collections. Have a look at the following code, which explains what we just talked about:

```
Func<int, int> addNumbers = n => n + 1;
var answer = addNumbers(1);

answer // 2

var range = Enumerable.Range(1, 5);
var answers = range.Select(addNumbers);
answers // 2, 3, 4, 5, 6
```

Again, when we follow the functional paradigm, we must avoid state mutation. This means that when an object is created, it never changes; variables should never be reassigned. Functional programming has been around for quite a while and C# supports it very well. Although, if you are looking at functional programming, F# is also a good choice.

Creating a .NET Standard 2.0 library

In this recipe, we will be looking at the basics of functional programming using C# inside a .NET Standard 2.0 library.

Getting ready

Let's get ready and open Visual Studio 2017. You should also check to see whether it's updated to the latest version.

How to do it...

1. Open Visual Studio 2017.
2. Click **File** | **New** | **Project** to create a project.
3. In the **New Project** dialog box, expand the **Other Project Types** node in the left-hand pane and select **Visual Studio Solutions**. In the right-hand pane, select **Blank Solution.**
4. In the **Name:** textbox, type `Chapter4.Functions` and, in the **Location:** textbox, select a path from the drop-down box or click on the **Browse...** button to locate a path:

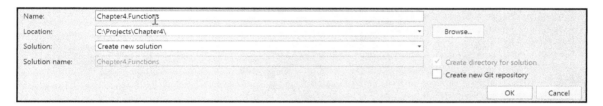

5. Click **OK.**
6. Now, your **Solution Explorer** (*Ctrl* + *Alt* + *L*) should look like this:

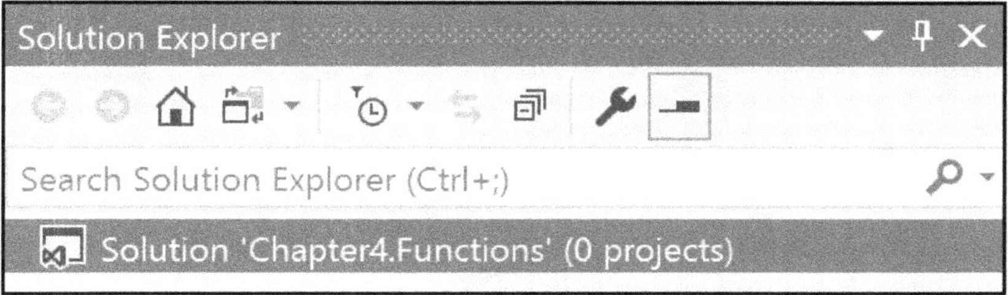

7. Now, right-click on the `Chapter4.Functions` label in the **Solution Explorer** and select **Add** | **New Project.**
8. In the **New Project** dialog box, expand the **Visual C#** node.

9. Select **.NET Standard** in the left-hand pane and **Class Library (.NET Standard)** in the right-hand pane:

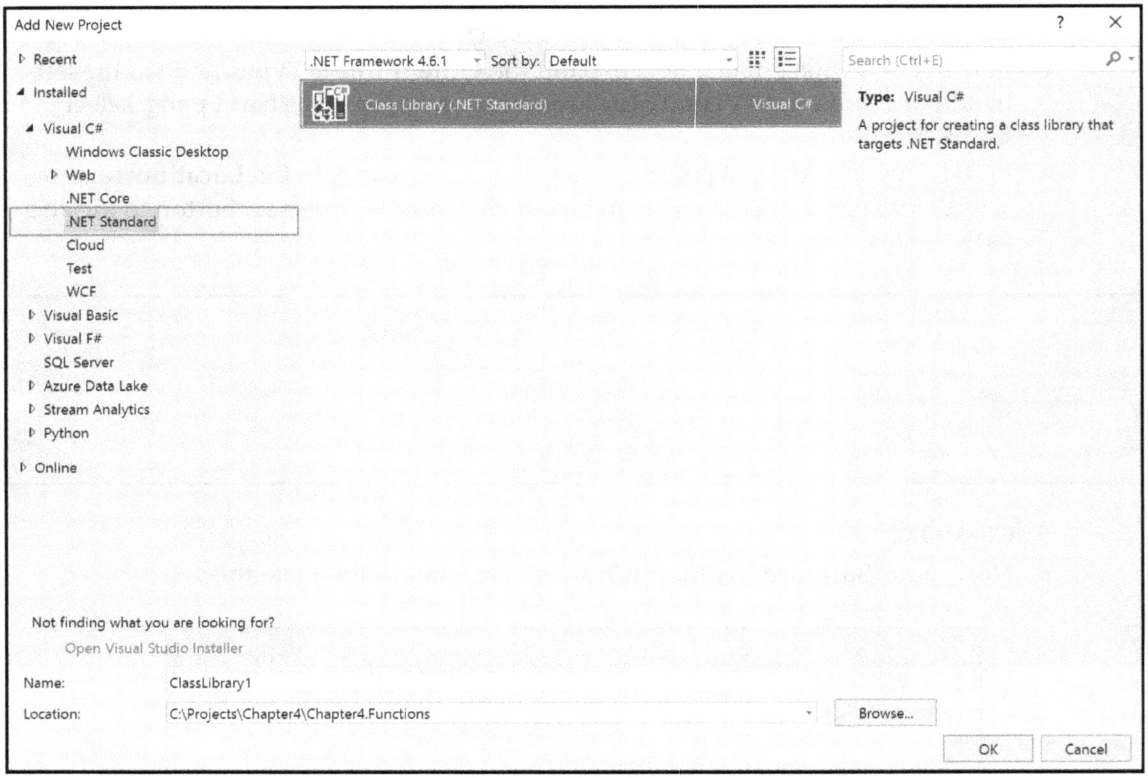

Add New Project
Recent
Installed
Visual C#
Windows Classic Desktop
Web
.NET Core
.NET Standard
Cloud
Test
WCF
Visual Basic
Visual F#
SQL Server
Azure Data Lake
Stream Analytics
Python
Online
.NET Framework 4.6.1
Sort by: Default
Search (Ctrl+E)
Class Library (.NET Standard)
Visual C#
Type: Visual C#
A project for creating a class library that targets .NET Standard.
Not finding what you are looking for?
Open Visual Studio Installer
Name:
ClassLibrary1
Location:
C:\Projects\Chapter4\Chapter4.Functions
Browse...
OK
Cancel

10. Now, in the **Name:** textbox, type `Chapter4.Functions.FuncLib`. Leave the other defaults as they are and click **OK**:

Name:
Chapter4.Functions.FuncLib
Location:
C:\Projects\Chapter4\Chapter4.Functions
Browse...
OK
Cancel

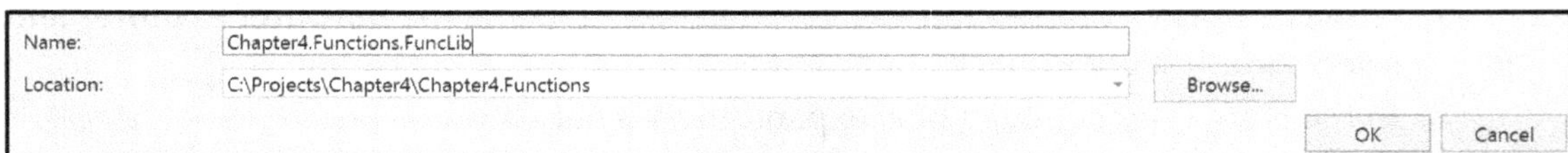

11. Now, the **Solution Explorer** (*Ctrl* + *Alt* + *L*) should look like this:

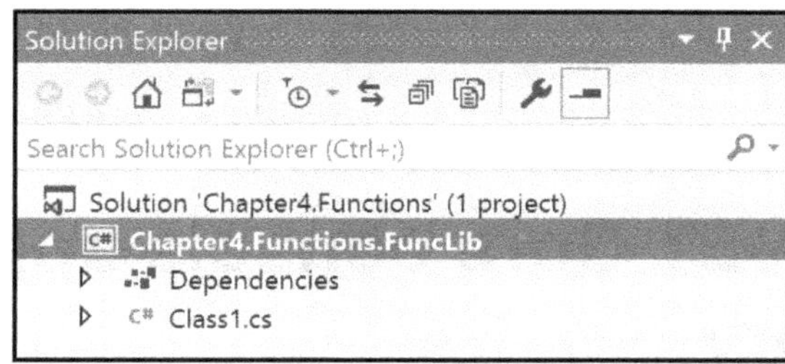

12. Now, select `Class1.cs` in the **Solution Explorer** and press *F2* to rename the file `Helper.cs`.
13. Answer **Yes** in the confirmation dialog box that asks to rename the class name as well.
14. Now, double-click on the `Helper.cs` label in the **Solution Explorer**.
15. In the code window for `Helper.cs`, type the following code in between the curly brackets of the class:

```
public Func<int, int> AddOne = n => n + 1;
public Func<int, bool> IsZero = n => n == 0;
```

16. Let's press *Ctrl* + *Shift* + *B* for a quick build to check that all the syntax is correct.

How it works...

In steps 1 to 5, we added a blank solution. This is the base of the coding we are adding in this recipe and the next. After that, we added a .NET Standard 2.0 library in steps 7 to 11. In steps 12 and 13, we renamed the default class generated by the template. You can always delete this default class template and add a new class to the project with the new name.

In step 15, we added code to the `Helper` class. In the first line, we created a function that takes a number as an integer and returns an integer as the output. Before the output, we added 1 to the input. `Func<>` is used to create the function. The first `int` is taken as the input and the last one as the output. You can add many parameters to this, but the last one is always taken as the output type. For example:

```
Func<string, string, int>
```

The preceding function takes two `string` inputs and returns an `int` as the output. And in the step 15, the second line of code checks whether the input number is zero and returns a Boolean value as the output. If the number is zero, it always returns `true`, or else it returns `false`.

Creating a .NET Core console application to use the library

In this recipe, we will be creating a .NET Core 2.0 console application to use the library we built in the previous recipe.

Getting ready

Make sure you have completed the previous recipe that built the .NET Standard 2.0 library. If you have completed it, locate it, and open it using Visual Studio 2017. Perform a quick build to check for the syntax using *Ctrl* + *Shift* + *B*.

How to do it...

1. Open Visual Studio 2017.
2. Now open the solution that we built from the previous recipe.
3. The **Solution Explorer** should look like this:

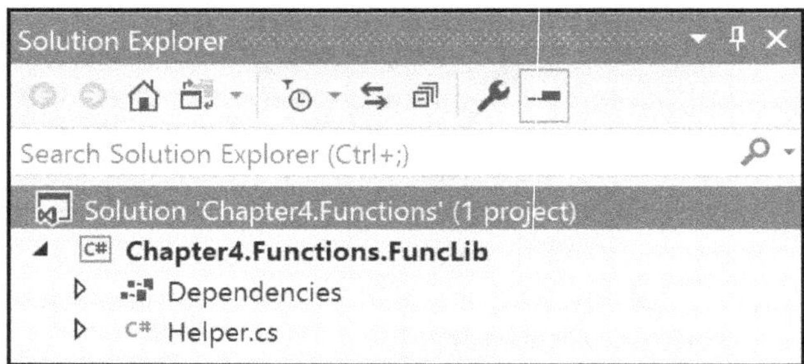

4. Press *Ctrl* + *Shift* + *B* for a quick build to check the syntax.
5. Now, let's select the solution name and right-click.
6. From the menu, select **Add** | **New Project**.
7. In the **New Project** dialog box, expand the **Visual C#** node and select **.NET Core** in the left-hand pane.
8. In the right-hand pane, select **Console App (.NET Core)**:

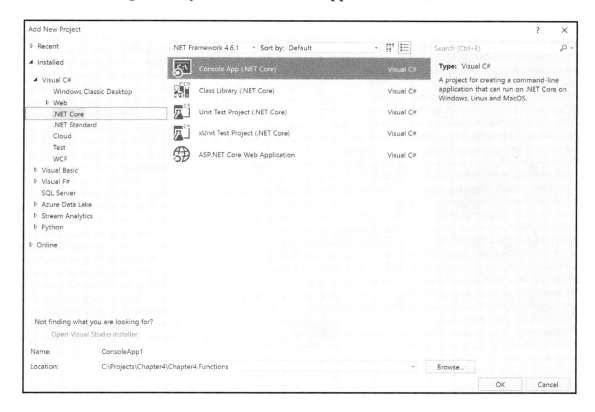

9. In the **Name:** textbox, type `Chapter4.Functions.CoreConsoleApp` and leave the defaults as they are:

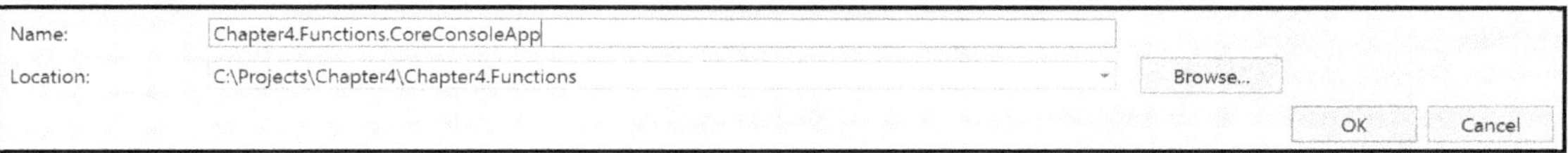

10. Now, the **Solution Explorer** should look like this:

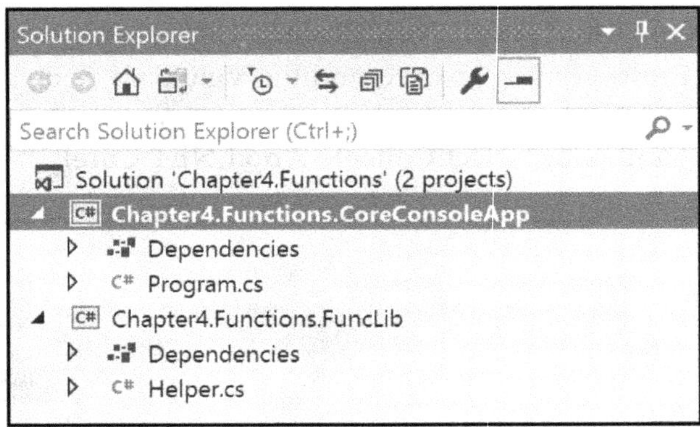

11. Now, select the `Chapter4.Functions.CoreConsoleApp` label in the **Solution Explorer**.
12. Right-click on the **Dependencies** label and select **Add Reference**.
13. In the **Reference Manager** dialog box, in the left-hand pane, select **Projects**.
14. In the right-hand pane, check `Chapter4.Functions.Funclib` in the list:

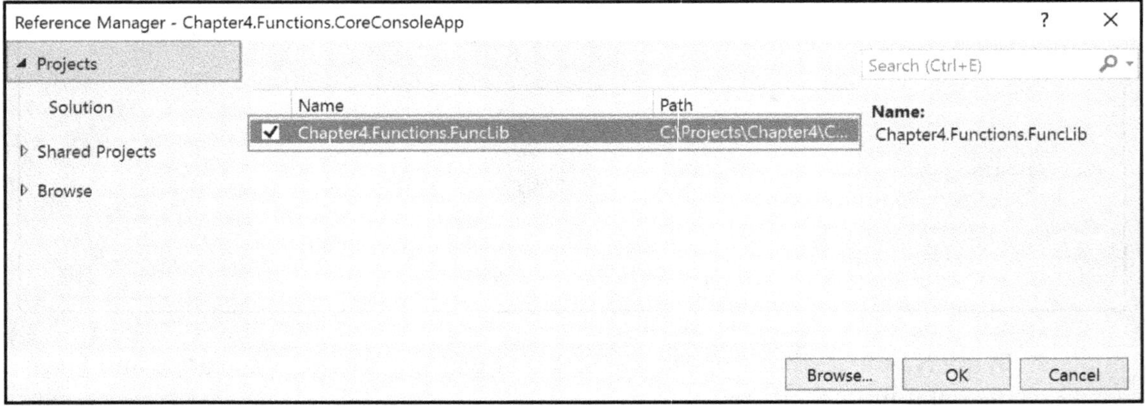

15. Click **OK**.
16. Now, double-click on the `Program.cs` label to open the code window.
17. In the code window, scroll up till you see the `using` directives.

18. Add the following `using` directive at the end of all the `using` directives:

```
using System.Linq;
using Chapter4.Functions.FuncLib;
```

19. Now, scroll down to the main method and replace the default code that was generated from the template with the following:

```
var helper = new Helper();

Console.WriteLine(helper.AddOne(5));

int[] numbers = new int[] { 1, 0, 10, 0, 5, 0 };
Console.WriteLine($"We have found {numbers.Count(helper.IsZero)}
    zeros.");

Console.ReadLine();
```

20. Now, make sure the `Chapter4.Functions.CoreConsoleApp` project is set as the start up project and then press *F5* to execute.
21. You should see output like this:

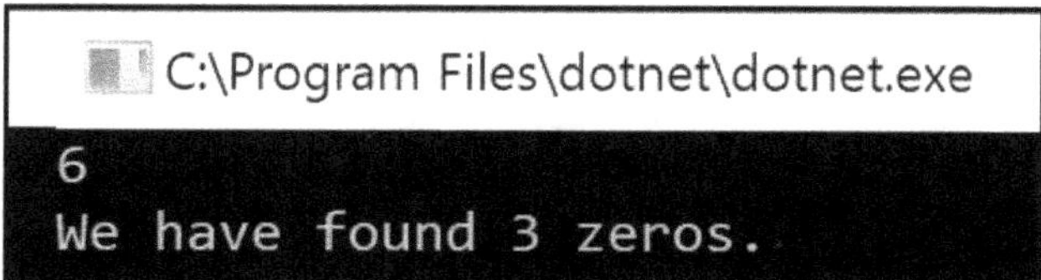

How it works...

In steps 1 to 5, we opened the previous solution from the recipe that built the .NET Standard 2.0 library. Then, we performed a quick build to check for syntax errors. This is very good practice; check for syntax on previously built code before we go further. Then, in steps 6 to 10, we added a .NET Core 2.0 console application to the project. In steps 12 to 14, we added the library we built as a dependency to the .NET Core 2.0 console application.

You must add this reference to use the library's functionality in the console application. Then, we added two `using` statements in step 18. The first one will allow you to use LINQ capabilities in the code and the second one will allow you to use the available methods from the library.

Then, in step 19, we added code to use the methods from the library. In the first line, we created an instance of the `Helper` class and stored it in a variable. Then, we used the `AddOne` function and wrote the output to the console. In the third line, we created an integer array and stored a few numbers. Finally, we used the count function available in LINQ to use the function we created. The count function will go through each number in the array, pass it to our `IsZero` function, and return the output.

At the end, in step 21, we executed the application to see the output.

Creating a .NET Standard 2.0 library that uses tuples

In this recipe, we will be using C# tuples with our library. Tuples allow you to combine the assignment of multiple variables of varying types in a single statement. For example, you can do this in a single line of code:

```
(string firstName, string lastName, int yearsOfExperience) = ("Fiqri",
"Ismail", 15);
```

Let's have a look at using tuples in a .NET Standard 2.0 library.

Getting ready

Let's launch Visual Studio 2017 and make sure it's updated to the latest version. We will require C# 7.0 to complete this recipe.

How to do it...

1. Open Visual Studio 2017.
2. Click **File** | **New** | **Project** to create a project.

3. In the **New Project** dialog box, expand the **Other Project Types** node in the left-hand pane and select **Visual Studio Solutions**. In the right-hand pane, select **Blank Solution.**
4. In the **Name:** textbox, type `Chapter4.Tuples` and, in the **Location:** textbox, select a path from the drop-down box or click on the **Browse...** button to locate a path:

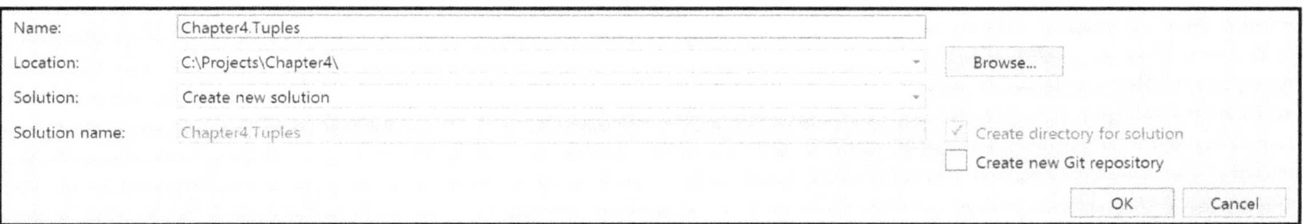

5. Click **OK**.
6. Now, your **Solution Explorer** (*Ctrl* + *Alt* + *L*) should look like this:

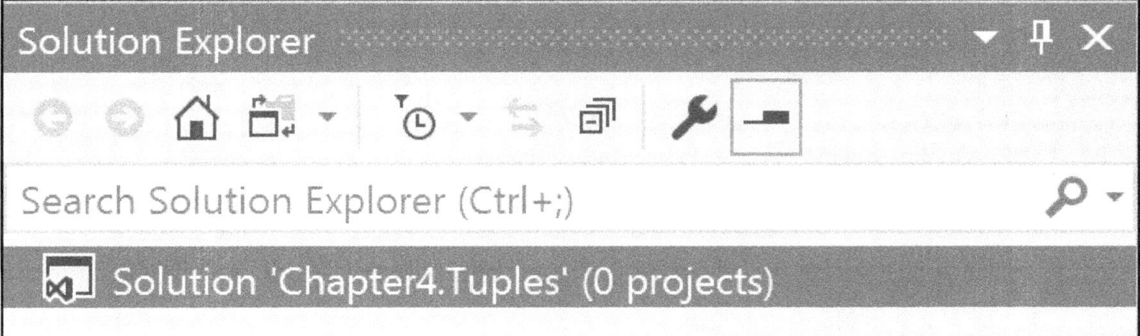

7. Now, right-click on the `Chapter4.Tuples` label in the **Solution Explorer** and select **Add** | **New Project.**
8. In the **New Project** dialog box, expand the **Visual C#** node.

9. Select **.NET Standard** in the left-hand pane and **Class Library (.NET Standard)** in the right-hand pane:

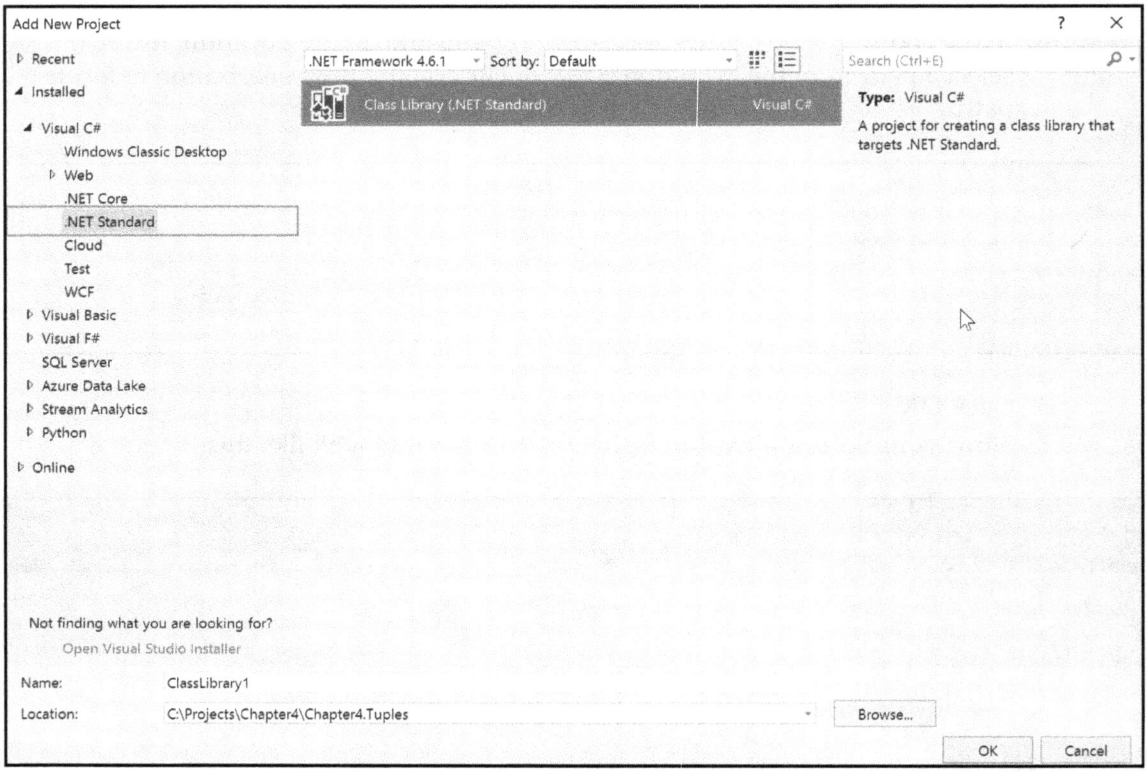

10. Now, in the **Name:** textbox, type `Chapter4.Tuples.TupleLib`, leave the other defaults as they are, and click **OK**:

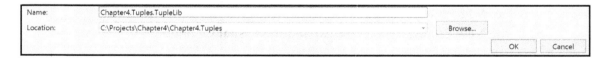

11. Now, the **Solution Explorer** (*Ctrl* + *Alt* + *L*) should look like this:

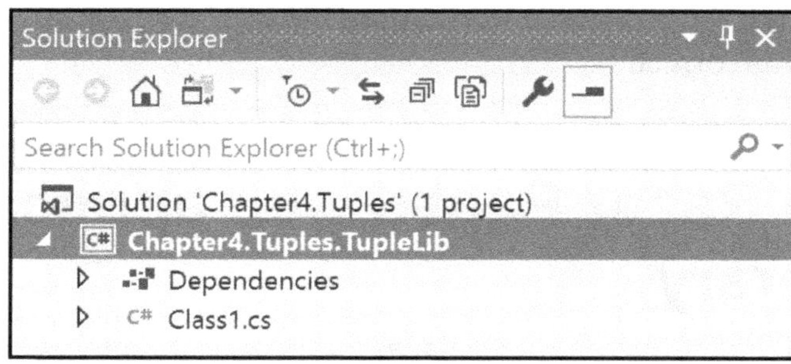

12. Now, select `Class1.cs` in the **Solution Explorer** and press *F2* to rename the file `Employee.cs`.
13. Answer **Yes** in the confirmation dialog box that asks to rename the class name as well.
14. Now, double-click on the `Employee.cs` label in the **Solution Explorer**.
15. In the code window, add the following code in between the curly brackets of the `Employee` class:

```
public (string, string, int) GetBasicDetails()
{

    string firstName = "Fiqri";
    string lastName = "Ismail";
    int experience = 15;

    return (firstName, lastName, experience);
}
```

16. Press *Ctrl* + *Shift* + *B* for a quick build to check syntax.

How it works...

We have created a blank solution in steps 1 to 5 and assigned it a proper name. In steps 6 to 10, we added a new project to the solution. We selected a .NET Standard 2.0 library template as the starting point of the project and then we gave it a proper name. In steps 11 and 12, we renamed the default `Class1.cs` to something more meaningful. This class was generated from the template itself. You can rename it or you can delete that file and add a new one.

In step 15, we created a method that returns two string types and an integer type. This was possible because of tuples. In that method, we assigned the variables and returned them in a sequence to match the return type of the method. Finally, we performed a quick build to confirm the syntax was correct.

Creating a Razor Pages web application to use the library

In this recipe, we will be building a Razor Pages web application to use the .NET Standard 2.0 library created in the previous recipe. A Razor Pages web application is a slimmer version of the MVC framework. You can tell it's the successor to good old `.aspx` web form pages. This was an addition after .NET Core 2.0.

Getting ready

Make sure you have the latest version of Visual Studio 2017 and .NET Core 2.0 installed, and that you have access to the solution we built in the previous recipe. Do a quick *Ctrl* + *Shift* + *B* to check that everything is intact and working.

How to do it...

1. Open Visual Studio 2017.
2. Now open the solution that we built from the previous recipe.
3. The **Solution Explorer** should look like this:

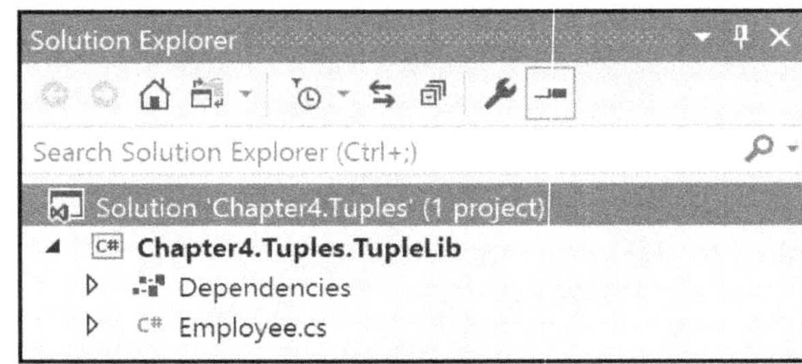

4. Press *Ctrl* + *Shift* + *B* for a quick build to check the syntax.
5. Now, let's select the solution name and right-click.
6. From the menu, select **Add** | **New Project**.
7. In the **New Project** dialog box, expand the **Visual C#** node and select **.NET Core** in the left-hand pane.
8. In the right-hand pane, select **ASP.NET Core Web Application**:

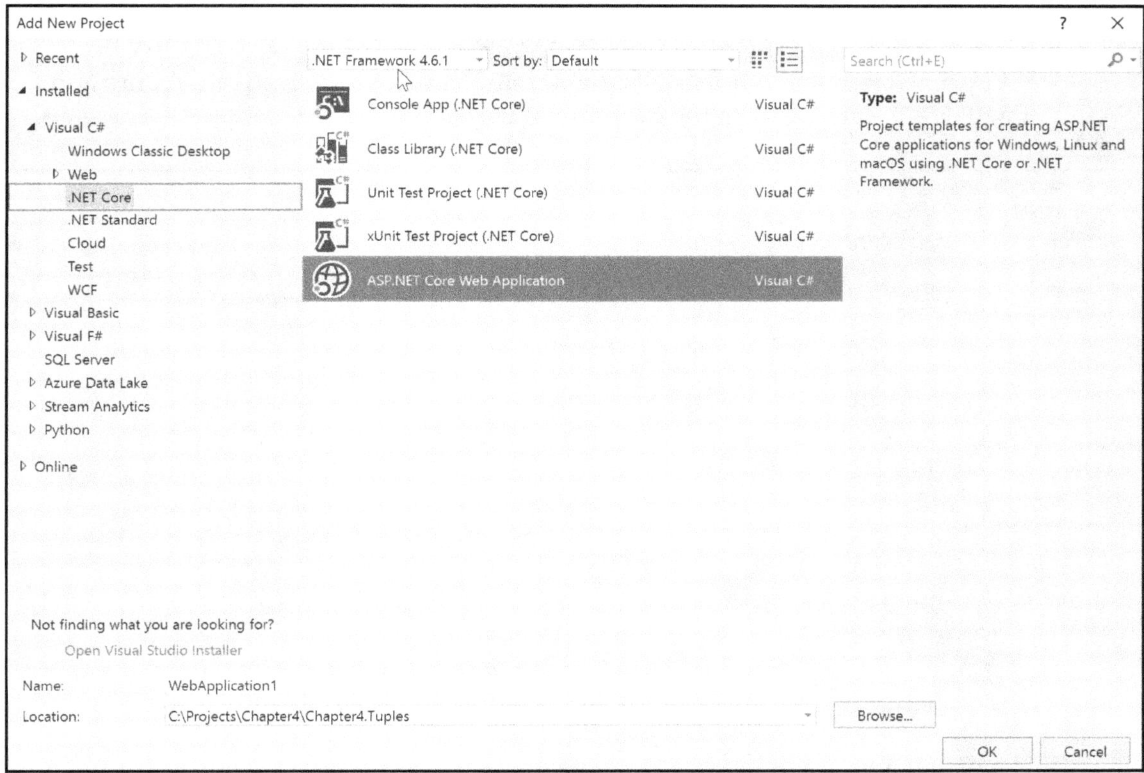

9. In the **Name:** textbox, type `Chapter4.Tuples.CoreRazorWebApp` and leave the defaults as they are:

10. Click **OK**.
11. Now, in the **New ASP.NET Core Web Application** dialog box, select **Web Application** in the templates list (make sure you have selected **.NET Core** and **ASP.NET Core 2.0** from the drop-down lists):

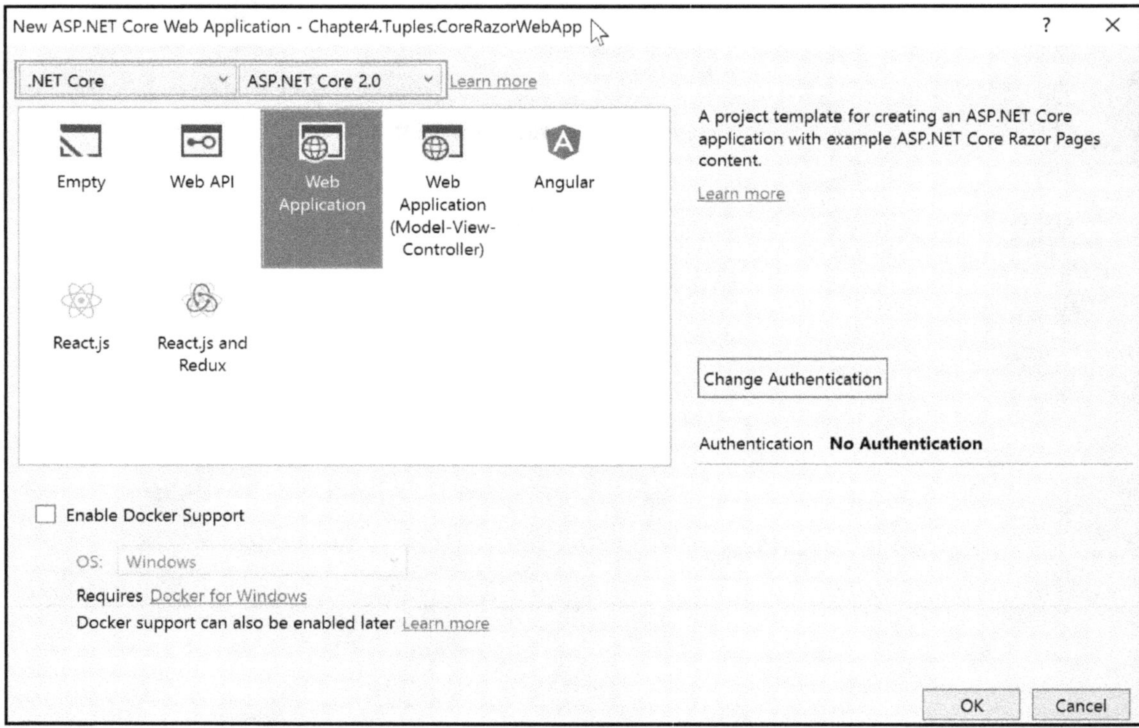

12. Leave the defaults as they are and click **OK**.

13. Now, the **Solution Explorer** should look like this:

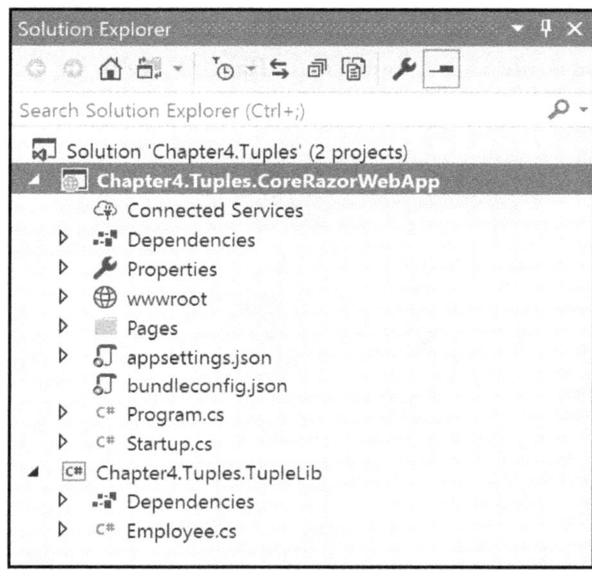

14. Now, select the `Chapter4.Tuples.CoreRazorWebApp` label in the **Solution Explorer**.
15. Right-click on the **Dependencies** label and select **Add Reference**.
16. In the **Reference Manager** dialog box, in the left-hand pane, select **Projects**.
17. In the right-hand pane, check `Chapter4.Tuples.TupleLib` in the list:

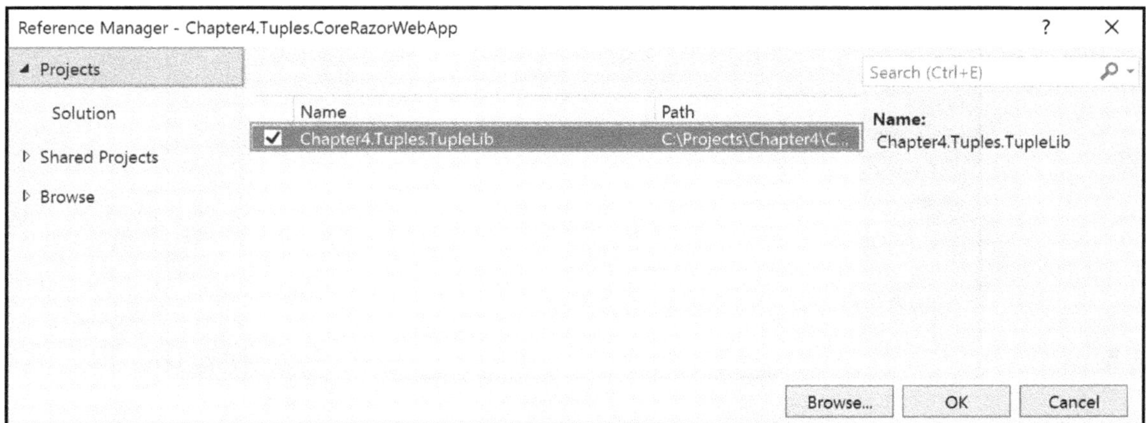

18. Click **OK**.
19. Now expand the **Pages** node.
20. Right-click on the **Pages** label and select **Add** | **Razor Page**.
21. In the **Add Scaffold** dialog box, select **Razor Page** from the template list:

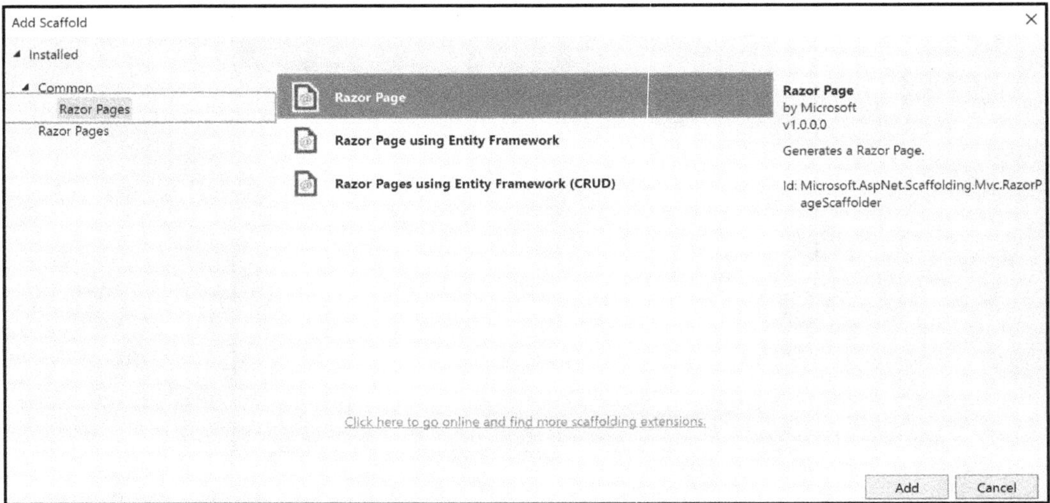

22. Click **Add**.
23. In the **Add Razor Page** dialog box, type `Employee` in the **Razor Page name:** textbox:

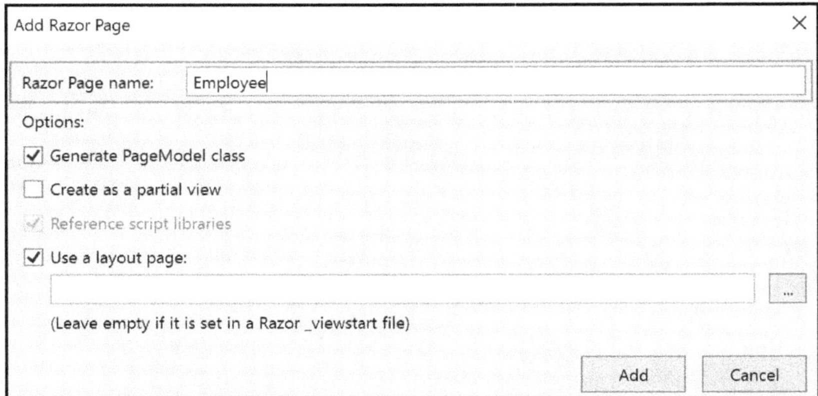

24. Click **Add**.
25. By default, Visual Studio will present you with the `Employee.chtml.cs` file. If not, you can always expand the node for the `Employee.chtml` file and double-click on the `Employee.chtml.cs` label.
26. Now scroll up till you reach the `using` directives.
27. At the end of the `using` directive, add the reference to our library:

```
using Chapter4.Tuples.TupleLib;
```

28. Now scroll down till you reach the `OnGet()` method.
29. Add the following code in between the curly brackets of the `OnGet()` method:

```
var employee = new Employee();

(string FirstName, string LastName, int YearsOfExperience)
    newEmployee = employee.GetBasicDetails();

ViewData["FirstName"] = newEmployee.FirstName;
ViewData["LastName"] = newEmployee.LastName;
ViewData["YearsOfExperience "] = newEmployee.YearsOfExperience;
```

30. Now click on the `Employee.cshtml` tab to enter the **Razor Page**.
31. Add the following code at the end of the page:

```
<p>
    <h2>@ViewData["FirstName"] @ViewData["LastName"]</h2>
    <h3>(@ViewData["YearsOfExperience "] years of experience)
    </h3>
</p>
```

32. Now save your work.
33. Press *F5* to execute the application.

34. The browser will display the default index page as follows:

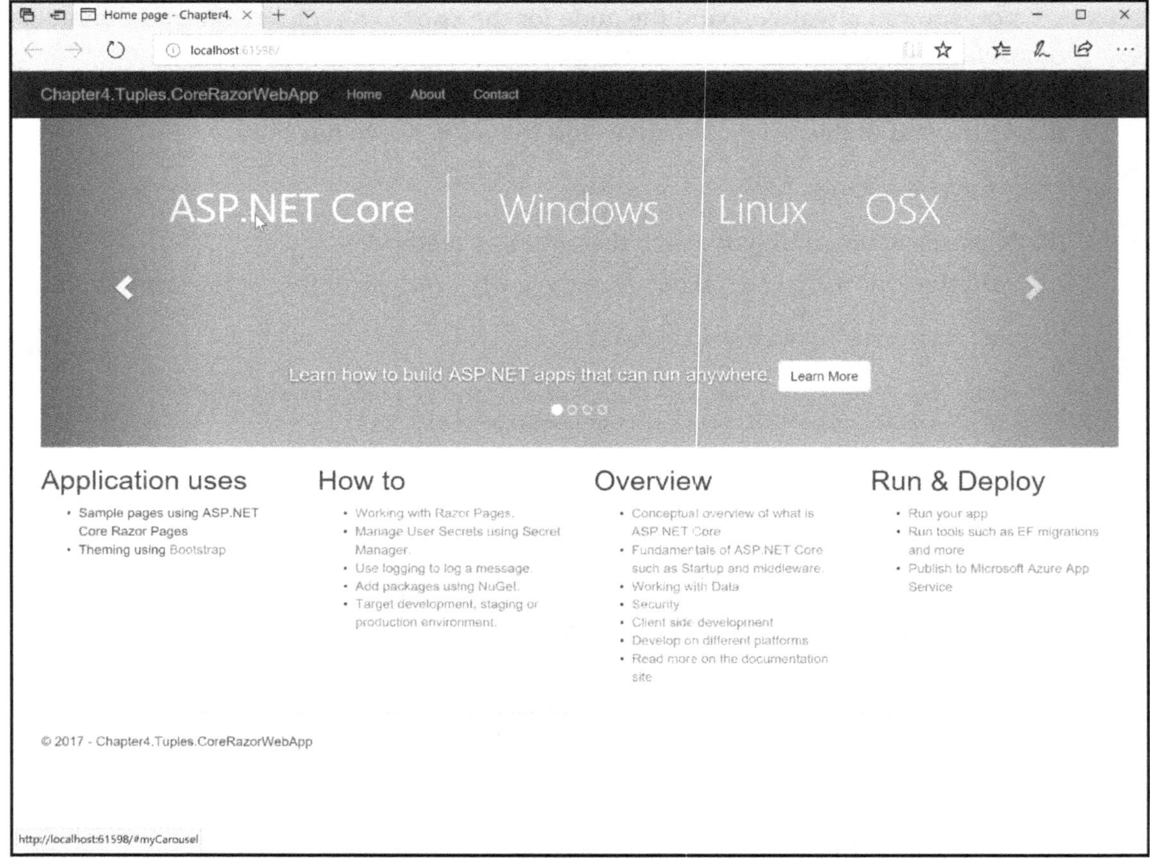

35. Click on the address bar. At the end of the URL, type `Employee` and press *Enter*. (The entire URL should look like this: `localhost:<yourportnumber>/Employee`):

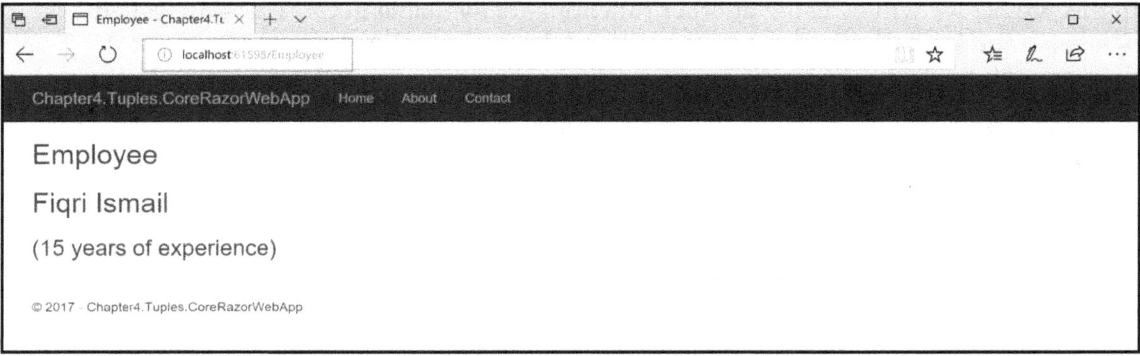

36. Now close the browser.

How it works...

In steps 1 to 5, we opened the solution from the previous recipe. We also performed a quick build to check for syntax. Then, in steps 6 to 13, we added an **ASP.NET Core Web application** to the solution. In steps 14 to 16, we added the reference to the library we built in the previous recipe. This will allow you to use the available functionality from the library in your ASP.NET Core Web application project.

In steps 20 to 24, we added a new **Razor Page** to the project. A **Razor Page** contains two files. One is a `.chtml` file, which contains the look and feel, and the other file contains the code for that Razor file. This is similar to an `.aspx` page and the code behind the file in an **ASP.NET Web Forms application**.

In step 27, we added reference code to our library. Then, in step 29, we added code to use the functionality from the library. In the first line of code, we created an instance of the `Employee` class and stored it in a variable. Then, in the second line, we used the `GetBasicDetails()` method to access employee details using tuples. Finally, we stored those values in the `ViewData` helper class.

In step 31, we used the `ViewData` helper class to display the values to the user. In this step, we used HTML markup and Razor syntax to display the information. Finally, in steps 33 to 36, we executed the application and tested it in the default browser.

Creating a .NET Standard 2.0 library that uses delegates and lambda expressions

In this recipe, we will be using another functionality available in C#. These are called delegates and lambda expressions. What is a delegate in C#? As per the Microsoft documentation, it says:

"A delegate is a type that represents references to methods with a particular parameter list and return type."

Simply put, delegates are used to pass methods as arguments to other methods, and a lambda expression is an anonymous function that you can use to create delegates or expression tree types.

Getting ready

Make sure Visual Studio 2017 is installed and updated to the latest version.

How to do it...

1. Open Visual Studio 2017.
2. Click **File** | **New** | **Project** to create a project.
3. In the **New Project** dialog box, expand the **Other Project Types** node in the left-hand pane and select **Visual Studio Solutions**. In the right-hand pane, select **Blank Solution.**
4. In the **Name:** textbox, type `Chapter4.Delegates` and, in the **Location:** textbox, select a path from the drop-down box or click on the **Browse...** button to locate a path:

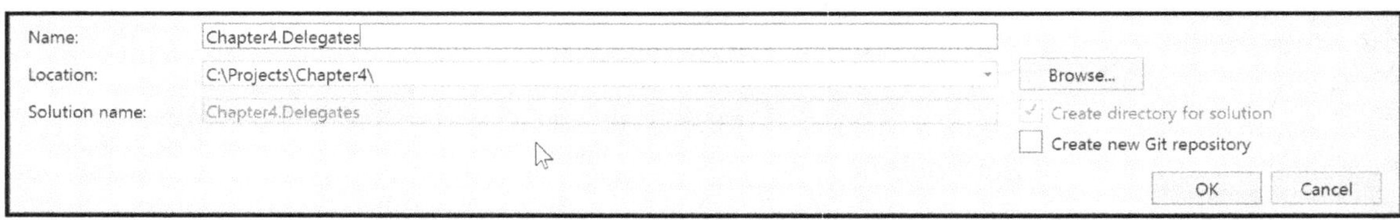

5. Click **OK**.

6. Now, your **Solution Explorer** (*Ctrl* + *Alt* + *L*) should look like this:

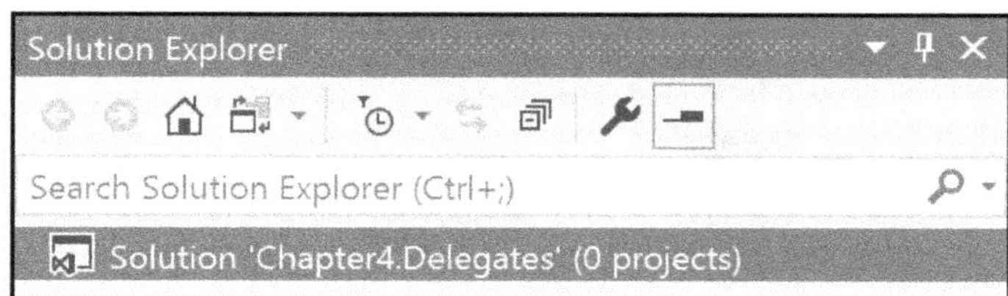

7. Now, right-click on the `Chapter4.Delegates` label in the **Solution Explorer** and select **Add** | **New Project.**
8. In the **New Project** dialog box, expand the **Visual C#** node.
9. Select **.NET Standard** in the left-hand pane and **Class Library (.NET Standard)** in the right-hand pane:

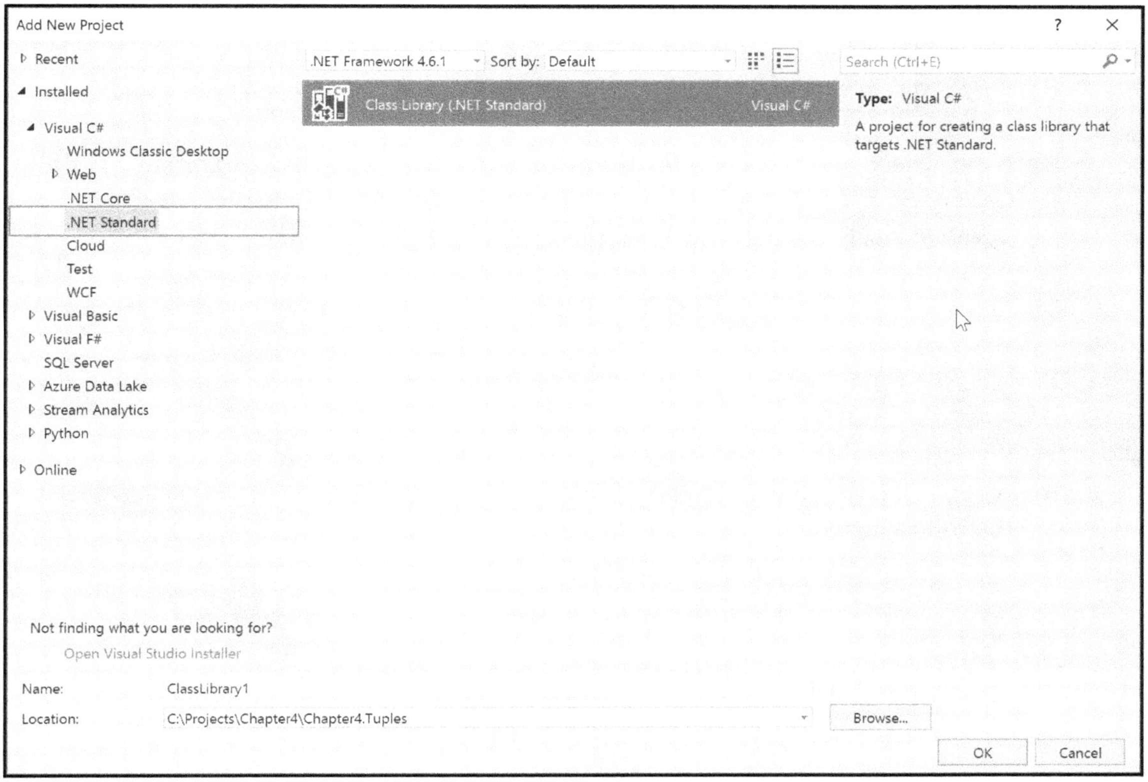

10. Now, in the **Name:** textbox, type `Chapter4.Delegates.DelegateLib`. Leave the other defaults as they are and click **OK**:

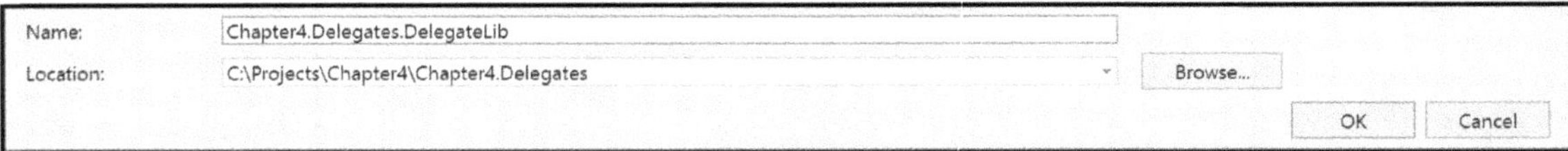

11. Now, the **Solution Explorer** (*Ctrl* + *Alt* + *L*) should look like this:

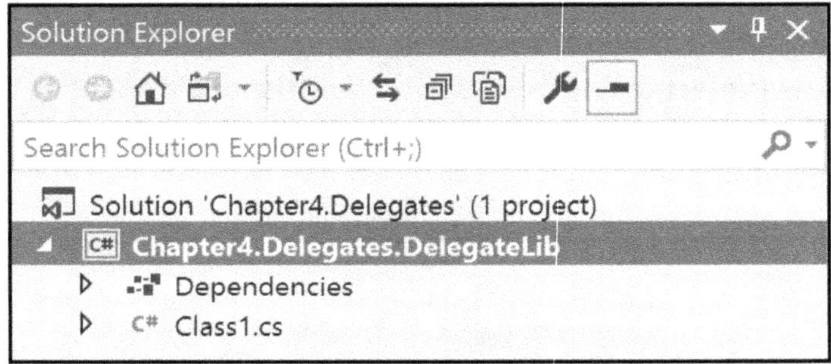

12. Now, select `Class1.cs` in the **Solution Explorer** and press *F2* to rename the file `Calculator.cs`.
13. Answer **Yes** in the confirmation dialog box that asks to rename the class name as well.
14. Now, select the `Calculators.cs` label and double-click on it to open the code window.
15. Add the following `using` directive to the top of the code:

```
using System.Linq;
```

16. Now, scroll down in between the curly brackets of the `Calculator` class and add the following code:

```
public delegate string Message(string msg);
public string AddTwoNumbers(int n1, int n2, Message msg)
{
    return msg($"The answer is : {n1 + n2}");
}
```

17. Now, next to the end curly bracket of the `AddTwoNumbers()` method, add the following code:

```
public string CountScoresMoreThan80(int[] scores)
{
    var count = scores.Where(s => s > 80).Count();

    return $"There are {count} scores more than 80";
}
```

18. Perform a quick build by pressing *Ctrl* + *Shift* + *B* and confirm that all the syntax is correct.

How it works...

We created a blank solution in steps 1 to 5. In steps 7 to 10, we added a .NET Standard 2.0 Class Library project to the solution. We have given a meaningful name to the project in these steps. We renamed the default class name generated from the template in steps 12 and 13. We added a `using` statement for LINQ in step 14. This is necessary to explain the lambda expressions using LINQ.

In step 16, we added code to create a delegate and a method to use that delegate as a parameter. The delegate `Message` takes a parameter as a `string` and returns the output as a `string`. Then, we added a method to add two numbers and return the answer as a string with a message. As you can see, there are three parameters for the `AddTwoNumbers()` method. The first two are integers and the last parameter is the delegate we created.

In step 17, we created another method to count the occurrences of numbers in an array of integers. In the first line of the `CountScoresMoreThan80()` method, we used the `Where()` method that comes with LINQ. Inside the `Where()` method, we used a lambda expression to check for numbers that are greater than `80`. We then used the `Count()` method to count the occurrences filtered with the `Where()` method and returned the answer as a `string`.

Finally, we performed a quick build to confirm the syntax is correct.

Creating a .NET console application to use the library

In this recipe, we will be building a .NET console-based application to test our library. We will be using the full .NET Framework, which is available for Windows only.

Getting ready

Make sure you have located the solution built in the previous recipe and done a quick *Ctrl* + *Shift* + *B* to build the solution. We are all set to test the library, so let's get started.

How to do it...

1. Open Visual Studio 2017.
2. Now, open the solution that we built from the previous recipe.
3. The **Solution Explorer** should look like this:

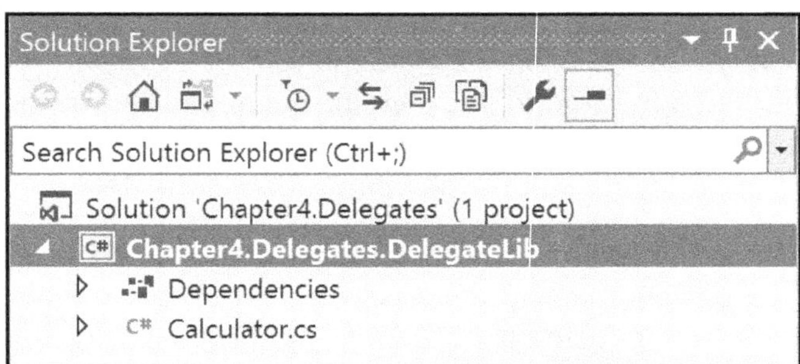

4. Press *Ctrl* + *Shift* + *B* for a quick build to check the syntax.
5. Now, let's select the solution name and right-click.
6. From the menu, select **Add** | **New Project**.
7. In the **New Project** dialog box, expand the **Visual C#** node and select **Windows Classic Desktop** in the left-hand pane.

8. In the right-hand pane, select **Console App (.NET Framework)**:

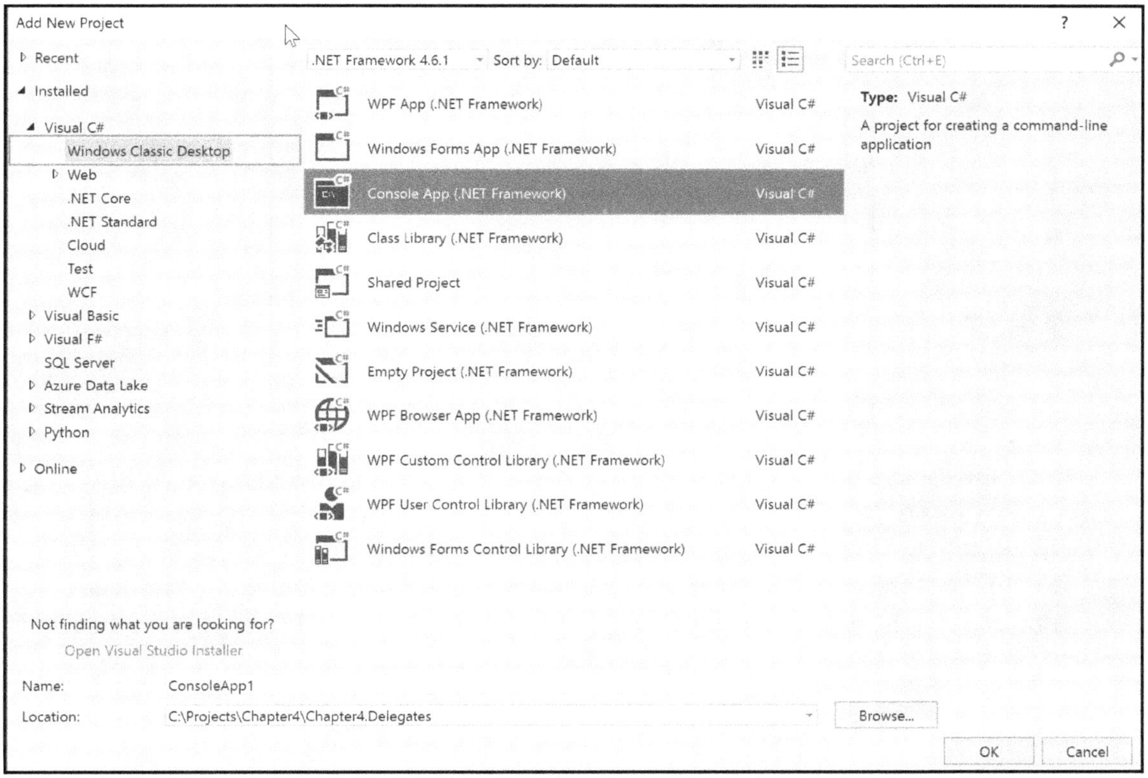

9. In the **Name:** textbox, type `Chapter4.Delegates.ConsoleApp` and leave the defaults as they are:

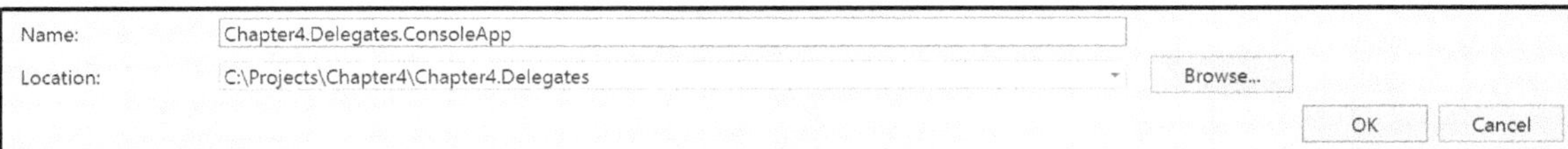

10. Now, the **Solution Explorer** should look like this:

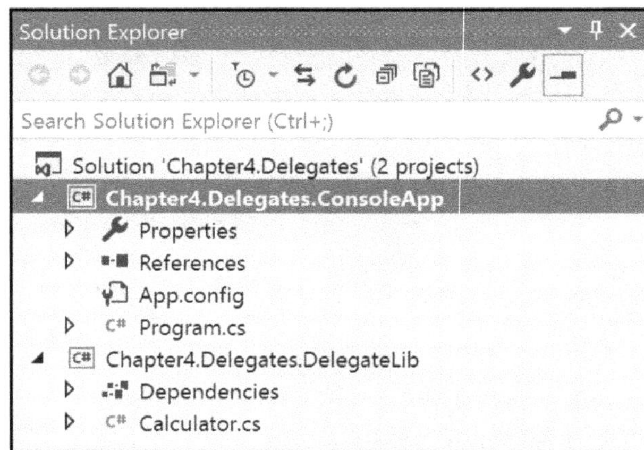

11. Now, select the `Chapter4.Delegates.ConsoleApp` label in the **Solution Explorer**.
12. Right-click on the **References** label and select **Add Reference**.
13. In the **Reference Manager** dialog box, in the left-hand pane, select **Projects**.
14. In the right-hand pane, check `Chapter4.Delegates.DelegateLib` in the list:

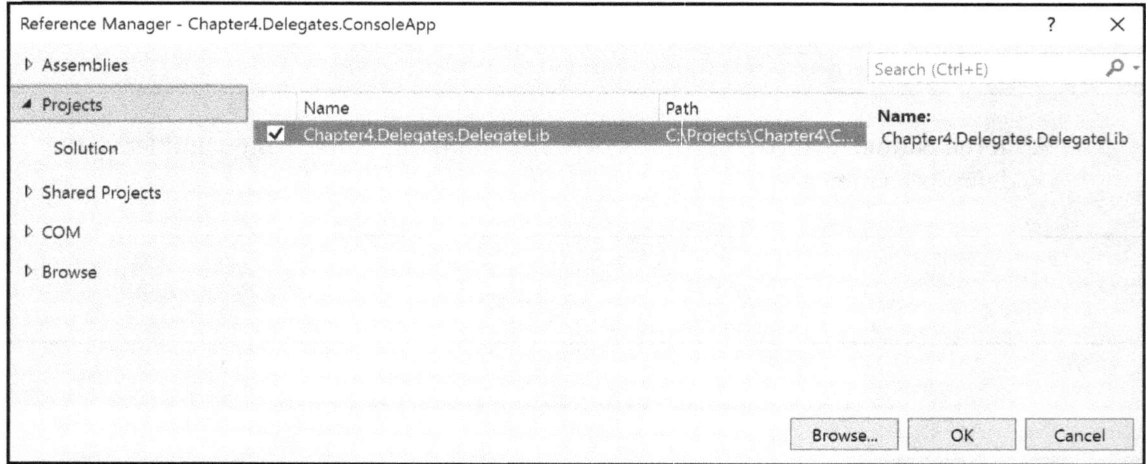

15. Click **OK**.
16. Now double-click on the `Program.cs` label to open the code window.

17. In the code window, scroll up till you see the `using` directives.
18. Add the following `using` directive at the end of all the `using` directives:

```
using Chapter4.Delegates.DelegateLib;
```

19. Now, next to the end curly bracket of the `Main()` method, add the following code:

```
static string DelegateMessage(string msg)
{
    return msg;
}
```

20. Now, scroll down to the `Main()` method and add the following code in between the curly brackets of the `Main()` method:

```
var calculator = new Calculator();

Calculator.Message message = DelegateMessage;
Console.WriteLine(calculator.AddTwoNumbers(10, 20, message));

int[] scores = new int[] { 10, 90, 50, 85, 30, 100, 45, 60 };
Console.WriteLine(calculator.CountScoresMoreThan80(scores));

Console.ReadLine();
```

21. Let's press *F5* to execute the program.
22. You should see output similar to this:

```
C:\Projects\Chapter4\Chapter4.Delegates\Chapter4.Delegates.ConsoleApp\bin\Debug\Chapter4.Delegat
The answer is : 30
There are 3 scores more than 80
```

23. Press *Enter* to close the console console window.

How it works...

In steps 1 to 5, we opened the solution from the previous recipe and perform a quick build. This will make sure the code syntax is correct. If the build fails, you might have to check for any typos and correct them. This is always a good practice to make sure your code builds successfully before you close a solution or send it to source control. In steps 6 to 10, we added a new project to the solution. We have selected a console application template, which supports the full .NET Framework under Windows.

Then, in steps 12 to 15, we added the reference to the .NET Standard 2.0 library from our console application. This will allow you to access all the available functionality in the library for the console application. In step 18, we added the reference to the library. We have used a `using` statement for it. Then, in step 19, we added a method to use with the delegate in the library.

In step 20, in the first line, we created an instance of the Calculator class and stored it in a variable, and then, in the second line, used the delegate inside the class and assigned it from the method created in step 19. Then, we used the `AddTwoNumbers()` method with two integer values and the delegate variable as the parameters and printed the output to the console window. In the fourth line, we created an integer array, stored a few values, used the `CountScoresMoreThan80()` method, passed the integer array as the parameter, and printed the output to the console.

Finally, in steps 21 and 22, we executed the code and checked the output.

5
XML and Data

In this chapter, we will be looking at these recipes:

- Creating a library that reads and writes to an XML file
- Creating an ASP.NET MVC application to use the XMLLib library
- Processing an XML file using LINQ to XML
- Creating a .NET Core console application to use the library

Technical requirements

Readers should have a basic knowledge of C#. They should also have a basic knowledge of using Visual Studio, installing packages using NuGet, and referencing libraries within projects from other projects.

The code files for this chapter can be found on GitHub:
`https://github.com/PacktPublishing/DotNET-Standard-2-Cookbook/tree/master/Chapter05`

Check out the following video to see the code in action:
`https://goo.gl/uQTMeB`

Introduction

XML stands for Extensible Markup Language and is similar to HTML. XML is used to store and read data. Mainly, XML is a data storage system and is also used to transport data. C# supports XML within the language using the `System.XML` namespace. You will be able to read, write, and parse XML data using this namespace. With the support of LINQ, it's much easier to work with XML-based data.

Creating a library that reads and writes to an XML file

In this recipe, we will be using a .NET Standard 2.0 library to create and write to an XML file. We will also be using the same library to write data to an XML file.

Getting ready

Let's fire up Visual Studio 2017 and get things done. Make sure you have the latest version of Visual Studio 2017 installed.

How to do it...

1. Open Visual Studio 2017.
2. Click **File** | **New** | **Project** to create a project.
3. In the **New Project** dialog box, expand the **Other Project Types** node in the left-hand pane and select **Visual Studio Solutions**. In the right-hand pane, select **Blank Solution**.
4. In the **Name:** textbox, type `Chapter5.XmlDoc` and, in the **Location:** textbox, select path from the drop-down box or click on the **Browse...** button to locate a path:

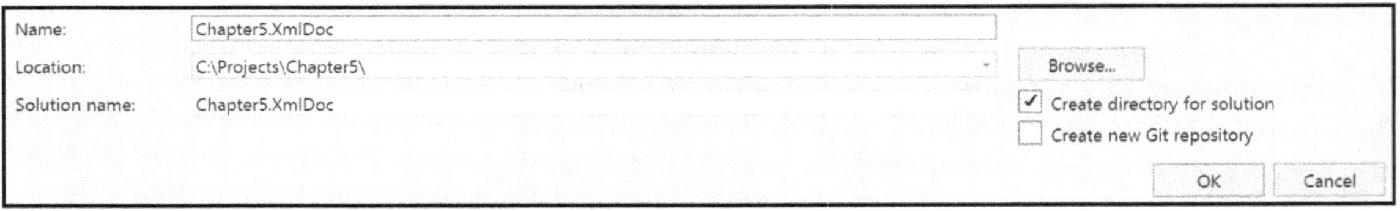

5. Click OK.

6. Now, the **Solution Explorer** (*Ctrl* + *Alt* + *L*) should look like this:

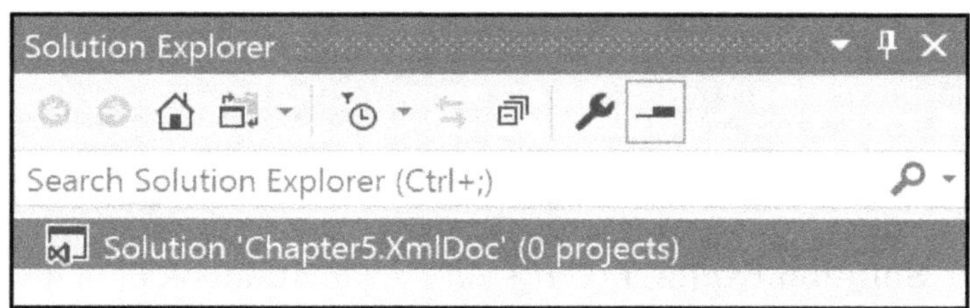

7. Now, right-click on the `Chapter5.XmlDoc` label in the **Solution Explorer** and select **Add** | **New Project**.
8. In the **New Project** dialog box, expand the **Visual C#** node.
9. Select **.NET Standard** in the left-hand pane and **Class Library (.NET Standard)** in the right-hand pane:

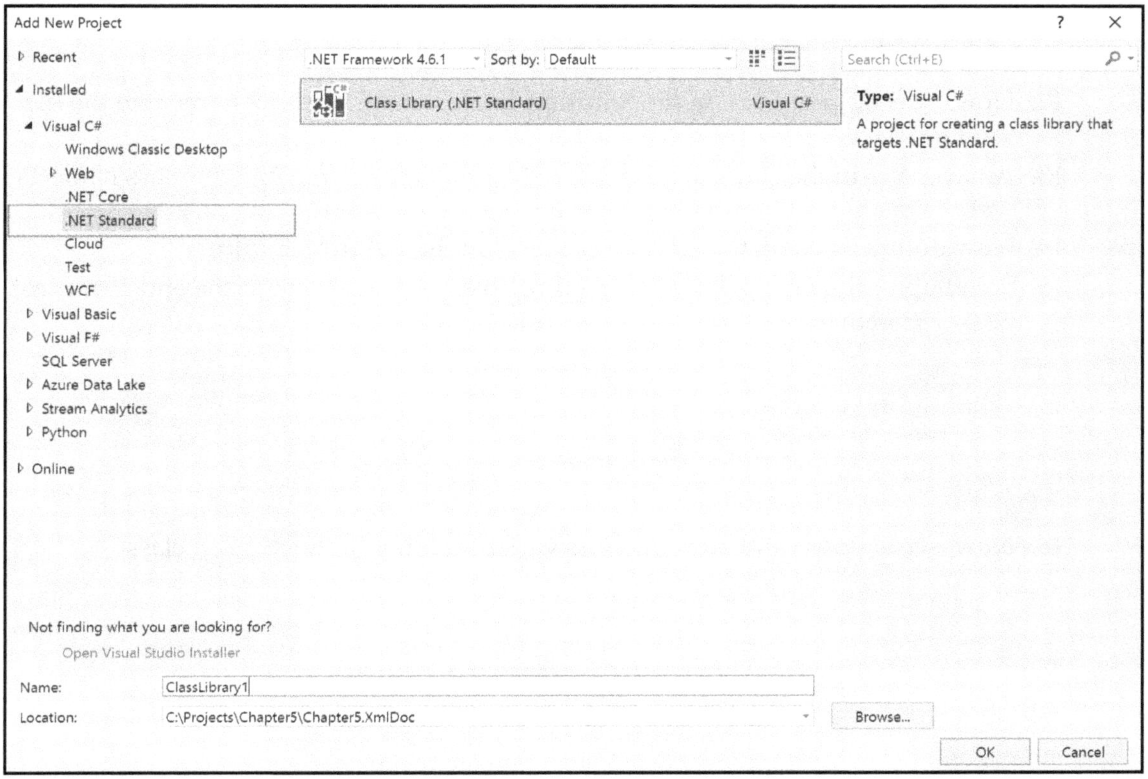

10. Now, in the **Name:** textbox, type `Chapter5.XmlDoc.XmlLib`, leave the other defaults as they are, and click **OK**:

11. Now, the **Solution Explorer** (*Ctrl* + *Alt* + *L*) should look like this:

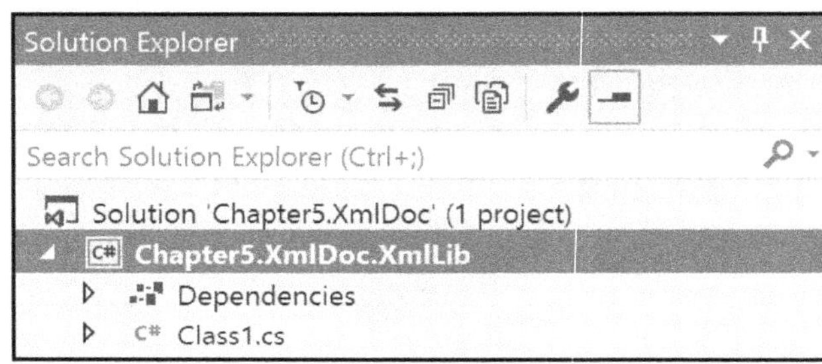

12. Now, select `Class1.cs` in the **Solution Explorer** and press *F2* to rename the file `XMLLog.cs`.
13. Answer **Yes** in the confirmation dialog box that asks to rename the class name as well.
14. Now double-click on the `XMLLog.cs` label in the **Solution Explorer**.
15. Scroll up until you reach the `using` directives and add these at the end of the last `using` directive:

```
using System.Xml;
using System.IO;
using System.Xml.Linq;
using System.Collections.Generic;
using System.Linq;
```

16. Now, scroll down and add this class variable on top of the `XMLLog` class:

```
private string _xmlFile;
```

17. Let's add the constructor for the `XMLLog` class:

```
public XMLLog(string xmlFile)
{
  _xmlFile = xmlFile;
}
```

18. Add the following public method after the constructor of the class:

```
public void WriteToLog(string message)
{

  if (!File.Exists(_xmlFile))
  {
    using (XmlWriter xmlWriter = XmlWriter.Create(_xmlFile))
    {
      xmlWriter.WriteStartDocument();
      xmlWriter.WriteStartElement("Log");
      xmlWriter.WriteStartElement("LogEntry");
      xmlWriter.WriteElementString("LogDate",
DateTime.Now.ToString());
      xmlWriter.WriteElementString("Message", message);
      xmlWriter.WriteEndElement();
      xmlWriter.WriteEndElement();
      xmlWriter.WriteEndDocument();
      xmlWriter.Flush();
      xmlWriter.Close();
    }
  }
  else
  {
    XDocument xDoc = XDocument.Load(_xmlFile);
    XElement root = xDoc.Element("Log");
    IEnumerable<XElement> rows = root.Descendants("LogEntry");
    XElement lastRow = rows.Last();
    lastRow.AddAfterSelf(
      new XElement("LogEntry",
      new XElement("LogDate", DateTime.Now.ToString()),
      new XElement("Message", message)));

    xDoc.Save(_xmlFile);
  }
}
```

19. Now, add this code next to the `WriteToLog()` method:

```
public Dictionary<string, string> ReadLog()
{

  var xmlOutPut = new Dictionary<string, string>();
  var line = 0;

  if (File.Exists(_xmlFile))
  {
    using (XmlReader xmlReader = XmlReader.Create(_xmlFile))
    {
      while(xmlReader.Read())
      {

        if (xmlReader.IsStartElement())
        {

          switch (xmlReader.Name)
          {
            case "LogDate":
              xmlOutPut.Add($"LogDate - {line}",
xmlReader.ReadElementContentAsString());
              break;
            case "Message":
              xmlOutPut.Add($"Message - {line}",
xmlReader.ReadElementContentAsString());
              break;
          }
        }
        line++;
      }
    }

    return xmlOutPut;
  }
}
```

20. Let's press *Ctrl* + *Shift* + *B* for a quick build.

How it works...

We created a blank solution in steps 1 to 5 and gave the solution a proper name. Blank solutions are always a good start for a project of any scale. Then, in steps 6 to 10, we added a .NET Standard 2.0 library project to the solution. In steps 11, 12, and 13, we renamed the default class template generated from Visual Studio.

In step 15, we added all the required namespaces for our library. `System.Xml` and `System.Xml.Linq` are the two namespaces we are going to focus on. `System.Xml` gives you the functionality of creating and maintaining XML documents. `System.Xml.Linq` is a LINQ extension to manipulate XML data.

In step 16, we created a class-level private variable to store the path of the XML file. In step 17, we created the constructor for the class that takes a parameter as a string. This parameter is the filename with the path of the XML file. It also populates the private variable created in step 16. In step 18, we added a public method to write an XML file.

In the first line of code, we check for the existence of the XML file. If it doesn't exist, the following piece of code will take over:

```
using (XmlWriter xmlWriter = XmlWriter.Create(_xmlFile))
{
    xmlWriter.WriteStartDocument();
    xmlWriter.WriteStartElement("Log");
    xmlWriter.WriteStartElement("LogEntry");
    xmlWriter.WriteElementString("LogDate", DateTime.Now.ToString());
    xmlWriter.WriteElementString("Message", message);
    xmlWriter.WriteEndElement();
    xmlWriter.WriteEndElement();
    xmlWriter.WriteEndDocument();
    xmlWriter.Flush();
    xmlWriter.Close();
}
```

We have used the `XmlWriter` class and its `Create` method to create the XML file. In this case, it is wrapped inside a `using` keyword. This is a good practice if the class is implementing an `IDisposable` interface, and when the lifetime is limited to a method. The `using` statement calls the `Dispose` method on the object in the correct way, and it also causes the object itself to go out of scope as soon as `Dispose` is called. Finally, the `XmlWriter` class's `Flush()` method will clear the buffer and the `Close()` method will close the writer stream.

In the next few lines of code, we started writing the document, and finally we cleared things up and closed the `XmlWriter`. If the file exists, we created a few lines of code to handle the existing XML document and append data to it. The code looks like this:

```
XDocument xDoc = XDocument.Load(_xmlFile);
XElement root = xDoc.Element("Log");
IEnumerable<XElement> rows = root.Descendants("LogEntry");
XElement lastRow = rows.Last();
lastRow.AddAfterSelf(
    new XElement("LogEntry",
        new XElement("LogDate", DateTime.Now.ToString()),
            new XElement("Message", message)));

xDoc.Save(_xmlFile);
```

In this part of the code, we created an `XDocument` class to handle the existing XML file. This class is referenced from the `System.Xml.Linq` namespace. In the first line, we loaded the existing XML file. We looked for the root element of the document in the second line. We picked up all the descendants of the root element and picked the last element from that list. This is the point at which we are going to add the new data. We have used the `AddAfterSelf()` method to add the new entry to the XML document and finally, we saved the document.

In step 19, we created a method to read an existing XML document. In the first line, we created a dictionary to store the data we read from the XML document. Then, we checked whether the file is there to read and created code to read the file. We used the `XmlReader()` class this time to read the data and store it in the dictionary:

```
while(xmlReader.Read())
{
    if (xmlReader.IsStartElement())
    {

        switch (xmlReader.Name)
        {
            case "LogDate":
                xmlOutPut.Add($"LogDate - {line}",
xmlReader.ReadElementContentAsString());
                break;
            case "Message":
                xmlOutPut.Add($"Message - {line}",
xmlReader.ReadElementContentAsString());
```

```
                    break;
            }
        }
        line++;
    }
```

We have used a `while` loop to go through each line of the XML document and used a `switch` statement to check for the correct element and store it in the dictionary. As you can see, by using a `counter` (`line`) variable, we have created a unique key for the dictionary as well. Finally, we returned the populated dictionary. In step 20, we performed a quick build to check for correct syntax.

Creating an ASP.NET MVC application to use the XMLLib library

In this recipe, we will be creating an ASP.NET MVC application to use the library. This time, it will be under Windows and will be using the full .NET Framework under Windows.

Getting ready

Let's make sure we have completed the previous recipe. In that recipe, we built a .NET Standard 2.0 library to create and read an XML document. Let's create an ASP.NET MVC application to use the library.

How to do it...

1. Open Visual Studio 2017.
2. Now, open the solution from the previous recipe. Click **File** | **Open** | **Open Project/Solution**, or press *Ctrl* + *Shift* + *O*, and select the `Chapter5.XmlDoc` solution.
3. Press *Ctrl* + *Shift* + *B* for a quick build to check that everything is fine.
4. Now, click on the `Chapter5.XmlDoc` solution label. Click **File** | **Add** | **New Project**.
5. In the **Add New Project** template dialog box, expand the **Visual C#** node in the left-hand pane.

6. Select **Web** and select **ASP.NET Web Application (.NET Framework)** in the right-hand pane:

Add New Project
Recent
Installed
Visual C#
Windows Classic Desktop
Web
.NET Core
.NET Standard
Cloud
Test
WCF
Visual Basic
Visual F#
SQL Server
Azure Data Lake
JavaScript
Stream Analytics
Python
TypeScript
Online
.NET Framework 4.6.1 Sort by: Default
Search (Ctrl+E)
ASP.NET Core Web Application Visual C#
ASP.NET Web Application (.NET Framework) Visual C#
Type: Visual C#
Project templates for creating ASP.NET applications. You can create ASP.NET Web Forms, MVC, or Web API applications and add many other features in ASP.NET.
Not finding what you are looking for?
Open Visual Studio Installer
Name: WebApplication1
Location: C:\Users\afi\Documents\Visual Studio 2017\.NET Standard 2.0 Cook Book\Chapter 2\Chapter2.Linq
Browse...
OK Cancel

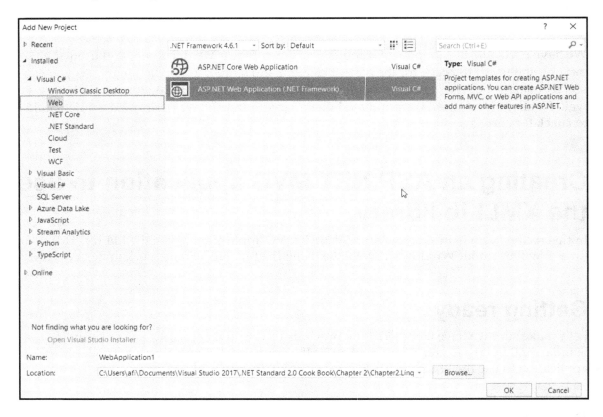

7. Now, in the **Name:** textbox, type `Chapter5.XmlDoc.XmlMVC` as the name and leave the **Location:** textbox at its default value:

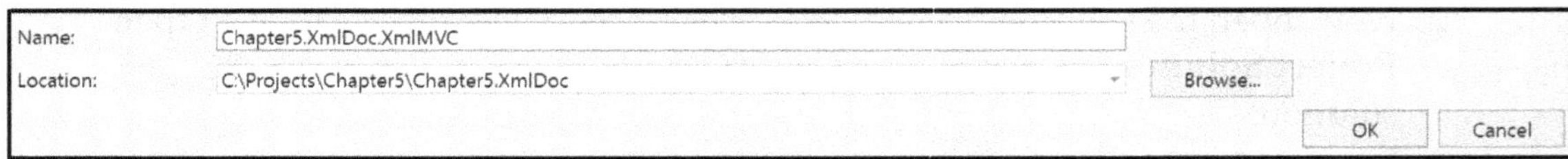

8. In the **New ASP.NET Web Application** dialog box, select **Empty** from the template list.

9. Select **MVC** in the **Add folders and core references for:** option:

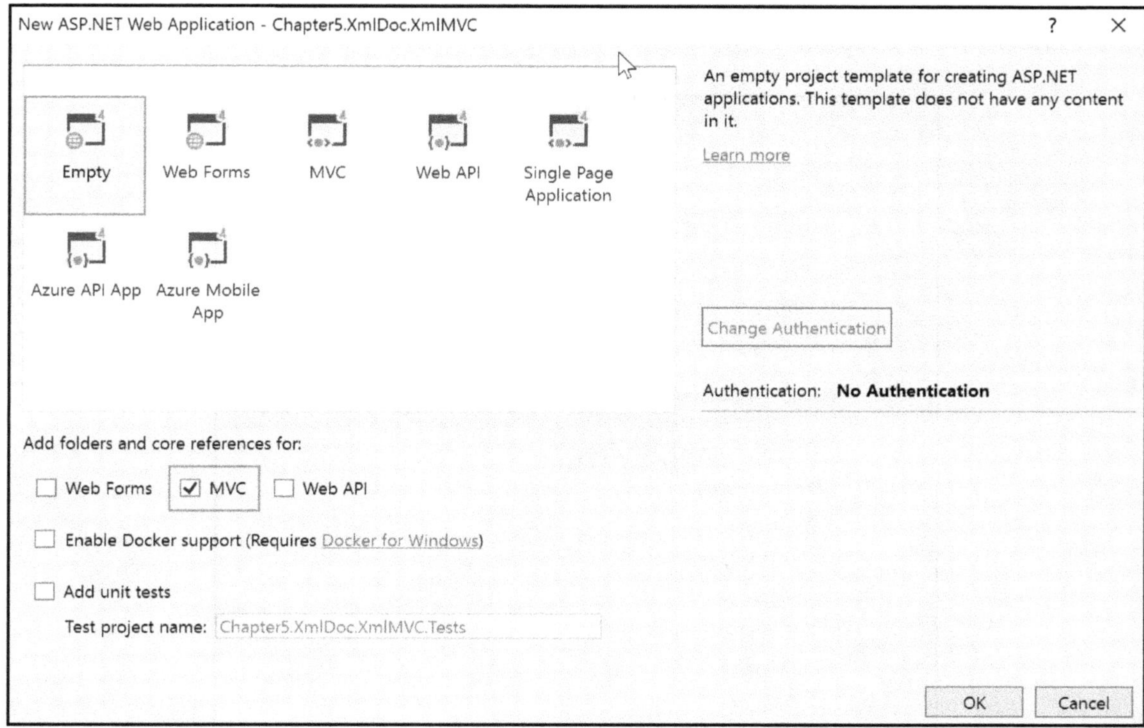

10. Leave the rest as it is and click **OK** to create the default ASP.NET MVC web application template.
11. Now, the **Solution Explorer** should look like this:

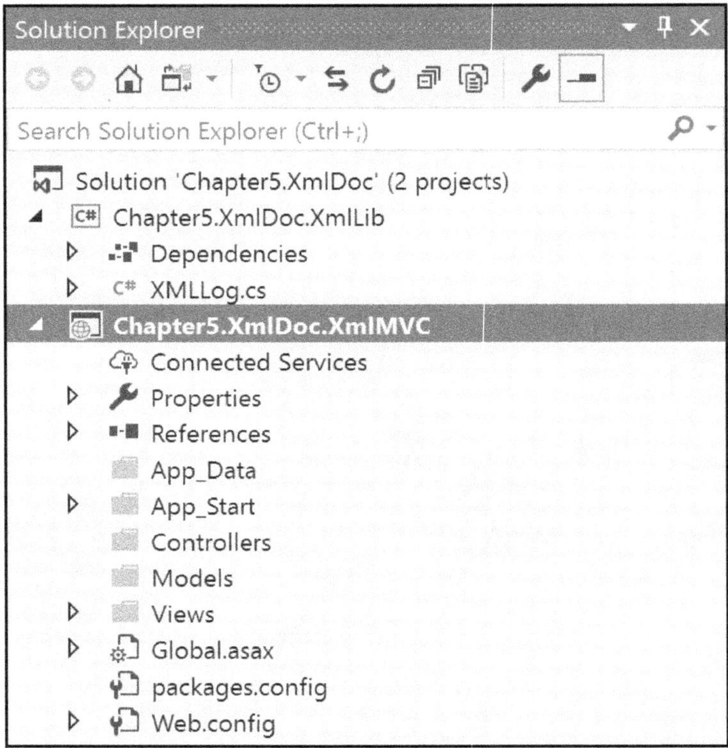

12. Now, right-click on the **References** label under the `Chapter5.XmlDoc.XmlMVC` project and select **Add Reference**.

13. In the **Reference Manager** dialog box, select **Projects** in the left-hand pane and select `Chapter5.XmlDoc.XmlLib` in the right-hand pane:

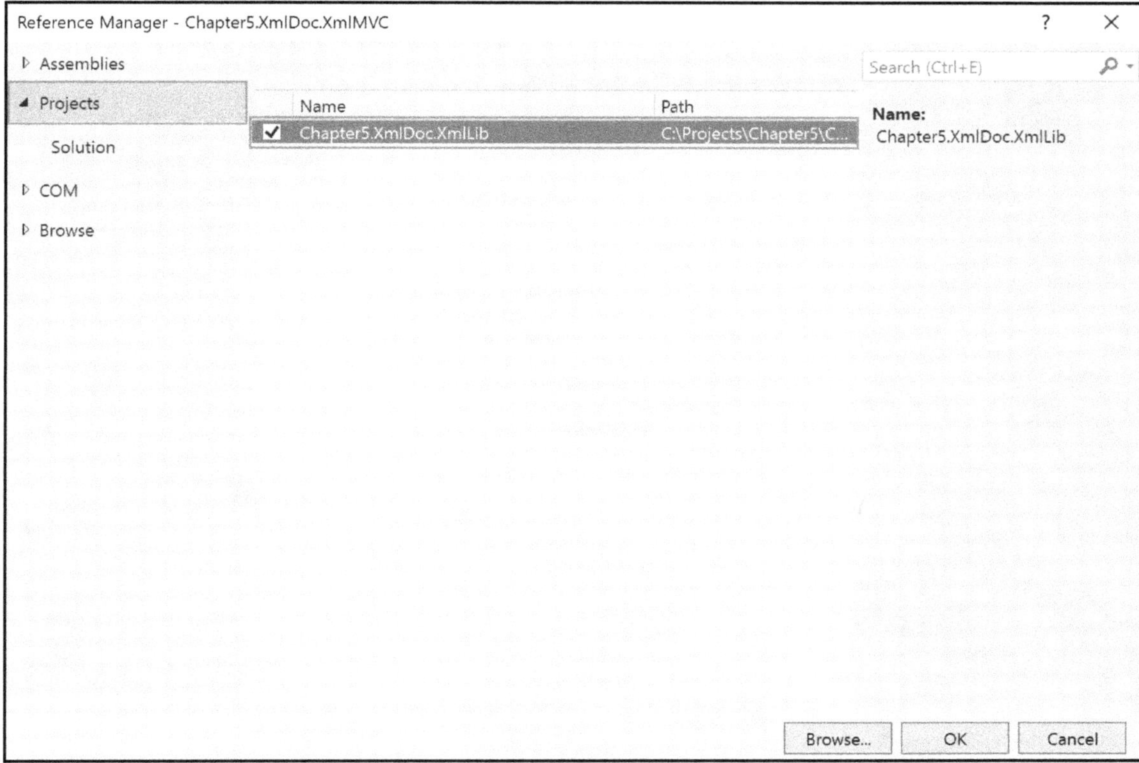

14. Click **OK**.
15. Now, right-click on the `Controllers` folder inside the `Chapter5.XmlDoc.XmlMVC` project.
16. Select **Add** | **Controller**.

17. In the **Add Scaffold** dialog box, select **MVC 5 Controller – Empty** from the template list and click **Add**:

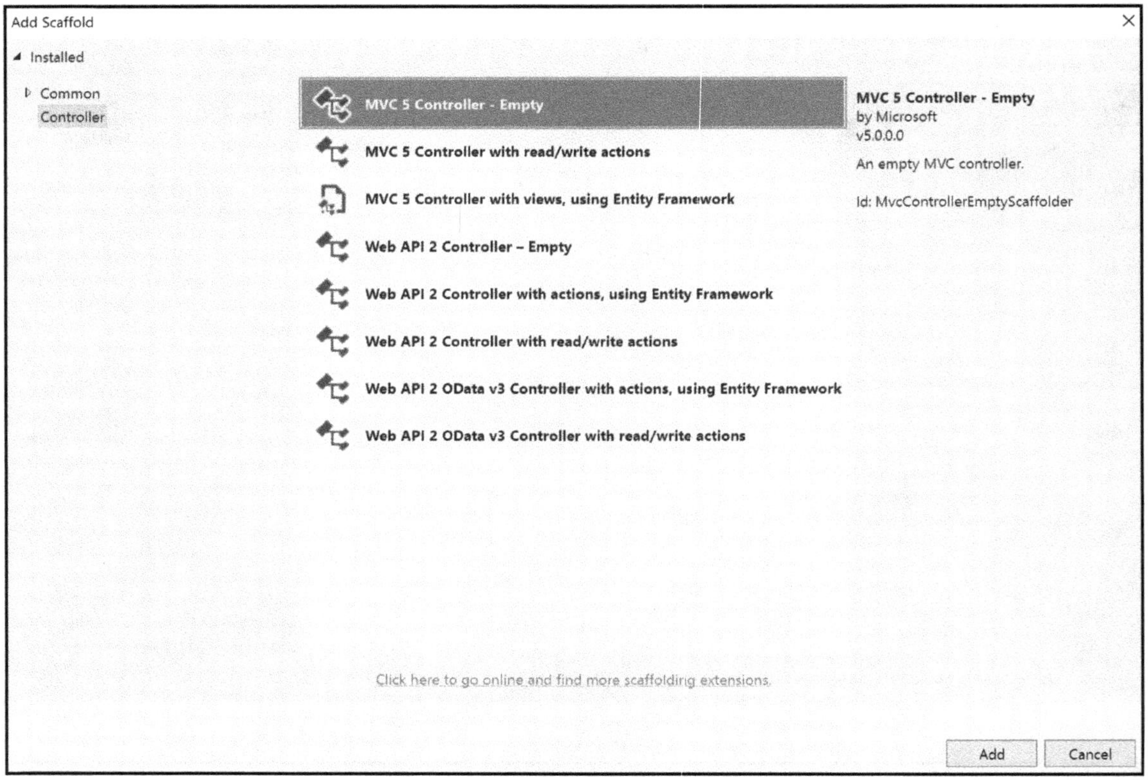

18. Now, in the **Add Controller** dialog box, type `HomeController` in the **Controller name:** textbox:

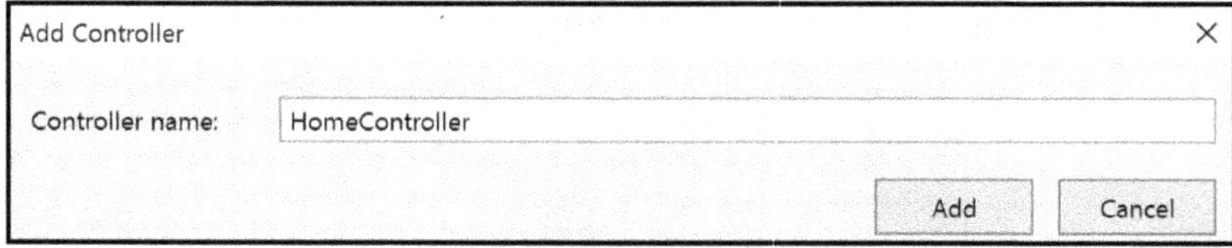

19. Click **Add**.
20. Now double-click on the `HomeController.cs` label under the `Controllers` folder.

21. In the code window, right-click on the `Index()` method name and select **Add View**.
22. Leave the defaults in the **Add View** dialog box and click **Add**:

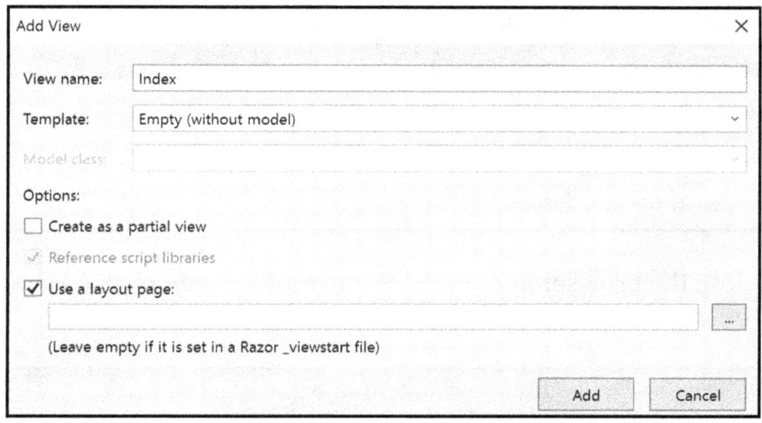

23. Click on the `HomeController.cs` tab in the code window.
24. Add this `using` directive to the top of the code, next to the last line of the directives:

```
using Chapter5.XmlDoc.XmlLib;
```

25. Now, let's add this code inside the `Index()` method and before the `return` statement:

```
var xmlFile = $"{Server.MapPath("~")}/testlog.xml";

var xmlLog = new XMLLog(xmlFile);
xmlLog.WriteToLog("Start at the Index() method");
xmlLog.WriteToLog("Another log entry here");
xmlLog.WriteToLog("Before the return statement");
```

26. Press *F5* to test our code and you should get an output like this:

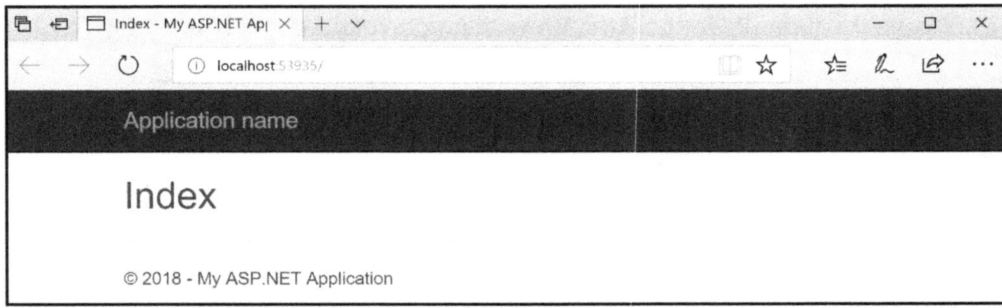

27. Now close the browser and, in the **Solution Explorer**, click on the Show All Files icon:

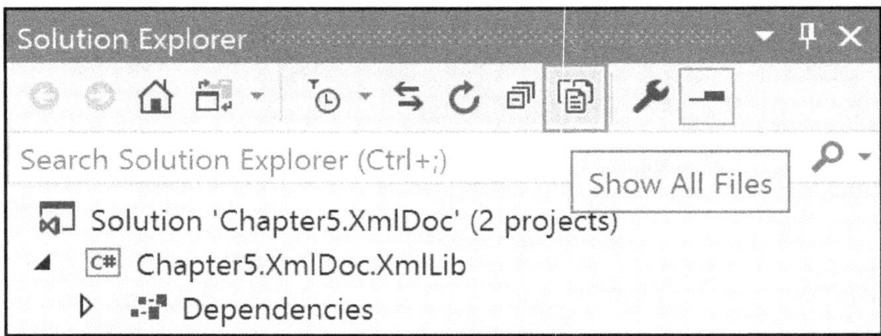

28. Now you should see that the `textlog.xml` label is created and the **Solution Explorer** should look like this:

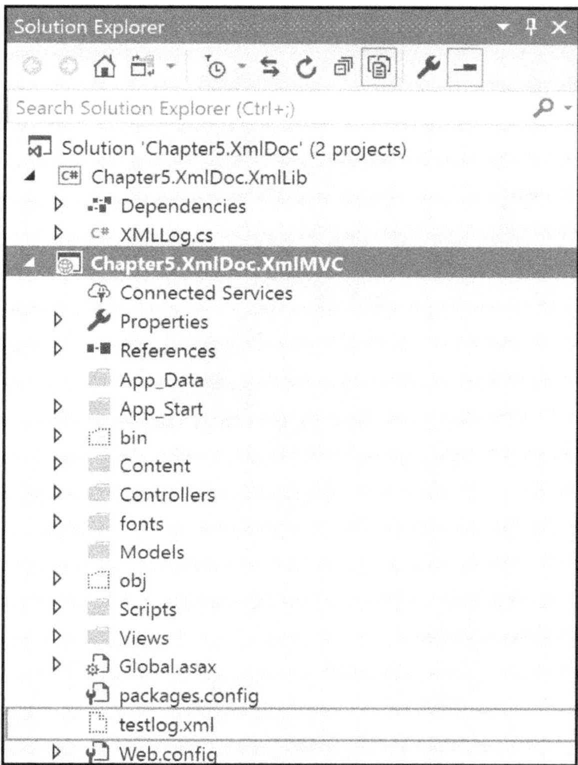

29. Click on the `testlog.xml` label and you should see output similar to this:

Index.cshtml HomeController.cs Chapter5.XmlDoc.XmlMVC XMLLog.cs

```
<?xml version="1.0" encoding="utf-8"?>
<Log>
  <LogEntry>
    <LogDate>2/18/2018 1:03:37 PM</LogDate>
    <Message>Start at the Index() method</Message>
  </LogEntry>
  <LogEntry>
    <LogDate>2/18/2018 1:03:37 PM</LogDate>
    <Message>Another log entry here</Message>
  </LogEntry>
  <LogEntry>
    <LogDate>2/18/2018 1:03:37 PM</LogDate>
    <Message>Before the return statement</Message>
  </LogEntry>
</Log>
```

30. Now, let's click on the `HomeController.cs` tab and add this code next to the `Index()` method:

```
public ActionResult Display()
{

    var xmlFile = $"{Server.MapPath("~")}/testlog.xml";
    var xmlLog = new XMLLog(xmlFile);

    ViewBag.LogDetails = xmlLog.ReadLog();

    return View();
}
```

31. Now, right-click on the `Display()` method name and select **Add View**.
32. Follow step 22 to add the view.
33. Now, in `Display.cshtml`, add the following code next to the `<h2>` tags:

```
@{

    var xmlLogDetails = (Dictionary<string,
string>)ViewBag.LogDetails;

    foreach (var log in xmlLogDetails)
    {
        <p>@log.Key.Split('-')[0]: @log.Value.Split('-')[0]</p>
    }
}
```

34. Now, let's press *F5* to debug the code. By default, this should load `Display.chtml` in the browser; if not, type `http://locahost<portnumber/Home/Display` and press *Enter*.
35. You should see output similar to this:

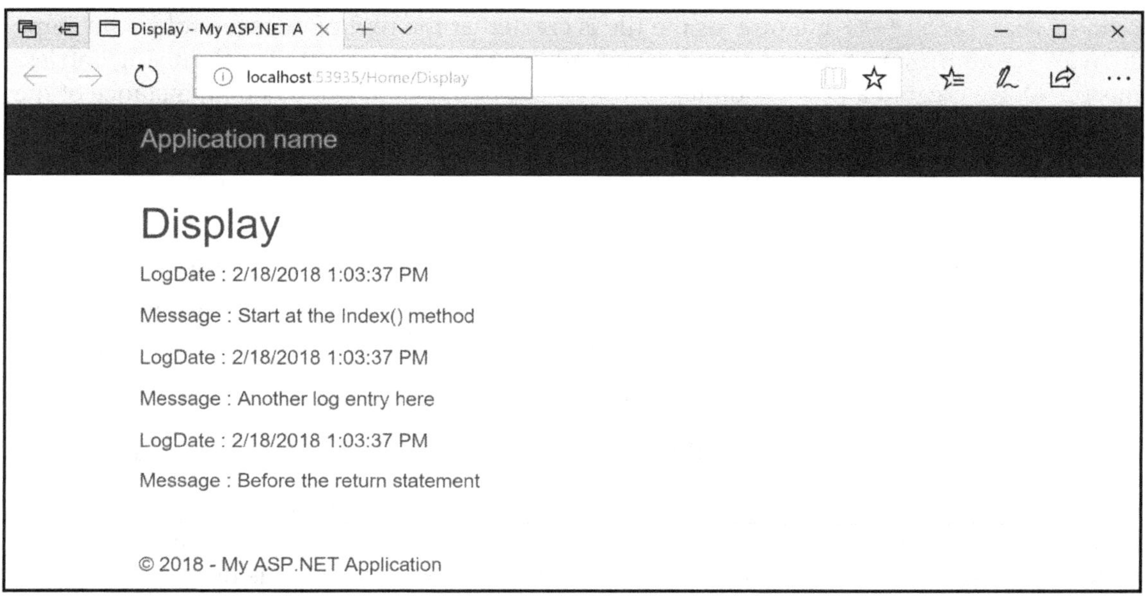

36. Now close your browser and we are done.

How it works...

In steps 1 to 10, we opened an existing solution that contained the library for reading and writing XML files. Then, in these steps, we added an ASP.NET MVC project to that solution. In step 13, we added a reference to our library built in the previous recipe. This will allow you to access available methods from the library.

In steps 16 to 20, we added a controller to the project and named it `HomeController`. In step 24, we added a `using` directive to reference the library. In step 25, we created code to create an instance of the `XMLLog` class and used it in methods to create and write to the XML document. In the following line of code, we are giving the path and name of our XML file:

```
var xmlFile = $"{Server.MapPath("~")}/testlog.xml";
```

`Server.MapPath("~")` guarantees the file is created at the root of our web folder. In steps 26 to 29, we confirmed our code is working and the XML file is created with the log entries. In step 30, we created a new action for our `HomeController`. We created an instance of the `XMLLog` class and used it in methods to read the information from the log file. Then we stored the values in `ViewBag`:

```
ViewBag.LogDetails = xmlLog.ReadLog();
```

In step 32, we created a view for the `Display` action, such as we did in step 22. Then we added code for the view in step 32, which converted `ViewBag` to a dictionary and displayed the content inside it. Finally, we tested the output in steps 34 and 35.

Processing an XML file using LINQ to XML

In this recipe, we will be building a .NET Standard 2.0 library that reads XML data using LINQ to XML. LINQ to XML is a LINQ enabled in-memory programming interface. It enables you to work with XML using your favorite .NET language. C# is used in this book to describe the code. In this recipe, we will mainly be looking at querying an XML document using LINQ to XML. We have used LINQ to XML to write to an XML file in the *A library that reads and writes to an XML file* recipe.

Getting ready

This recipe assumes you have used LINQ. We are focusing on LINQ with XML documents. Let's fire up Visual Studio and get started.

How to do it...

1. Open Visual Studio 2017.
2. Click **File** | **New** | **Project** to create a project.

3. In the **New Project** dialog box, expand the **Other Project Types** node in the left-hand pane and select **Visual Studio Solutions**. In the right-hand pane, select **Blank Solution**.

4. In the **Name:** textbox, type `Chapter5.XmlLinq` and, in the **Location:** textbox, select a path from the drop-down box or click on the **Browse...** button to locate a path:

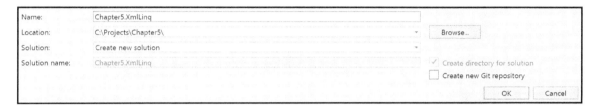

5. Click OK.
6. Now, the **Solution Explorer** (*Ctrl* + *Alt* + *L*) should look like this:

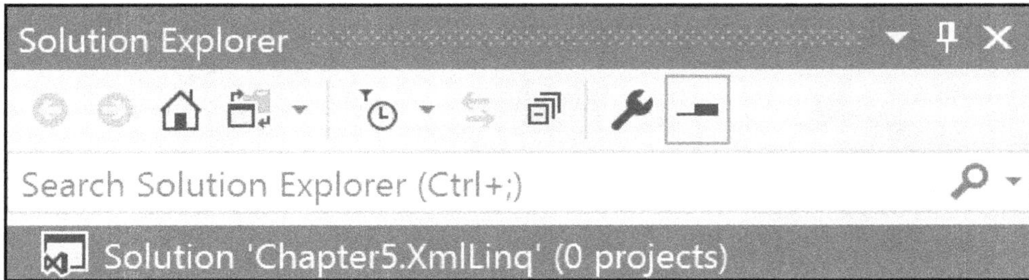

7. Now, right-click on the `Chapter5.XmlLinq` label in the **Solution Explorer** and select **Add** | **New Project**.
8. In the **New Project** dialog box, expand the **Visual C#** node.

9. Select **.NET Standard** in the left-hand pane and **Class Library (.NET Standard)** in the right-hand pane:

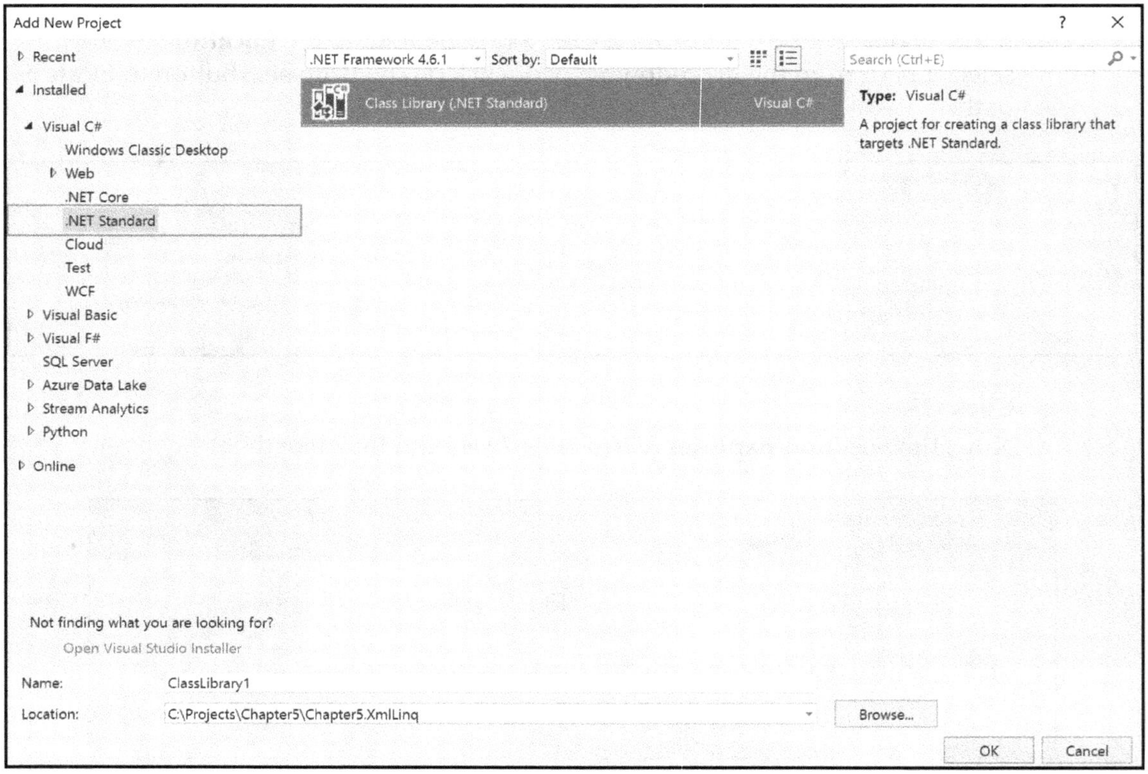

10. Now, in the **Name:** textbox, type `Chapter5.XmlLinq.XmlLinqLib`, leave the other defaults as they are, and click **OK**:

11. Now, the **Solution Explorer** (*Ctrl* + *Alt* + *L*) should look like this:

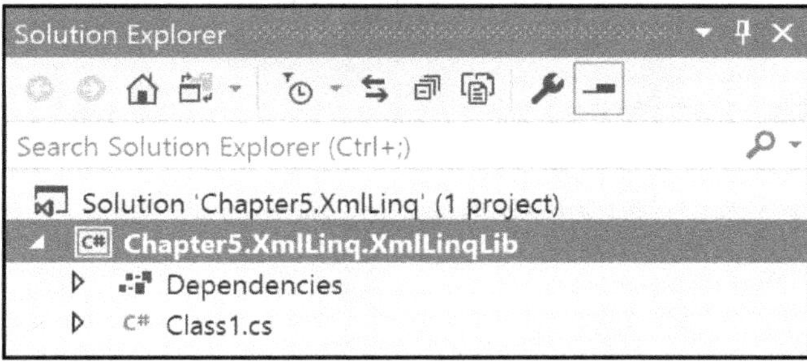

12. Now, select `Class1.cs` in the **Solution Explorer** and press *F2* to rename the file `XmlBooks.cs`.
13. Answer **Yes** in the confirmation dialog box that asks to rename the class name as well.
14. Now double-click on the `XmlBooks.cs` label in the **Solution Explorer**.
15. Add the following `using` directives next to the last directive in the list:

```
using System.Collections.Generic;
using System.Xml;
using System.Xml.Linq;
```

16. Add the following private variable to store the XML filename:

```
private string _xmlFile;
```

17. Create the default constructor as follows:

```
public XmlBooks(string xmlFile)
{
    _xmlFile = xmlFile;
}
```

18. Now add the following method to read the XML file:

```
public List<string> GetBookTitles()
{

    var titles = new List<string>();
    XDocument xDoc = XDocument.Load(_xmlFile);

    var books = xDoc.Descendants("book");
```

```
        foreach (var book in books)
        {
            titles.Add(book.Element("title").Value);
        }

        return titles;
    }
```

19. Now, let's press *Ctrl* + *Shift* + *B* for a quick build to check that all the syntax is intact.

How it works...

In steps 1 to 10, we added a blank solution and a .NET Standard 2.0 class library to the project. We assigned proper names to our solution and the class library project. Then, in step 15, we added using directives. These directives help us to get the functionality we require for generic collections and LINQ support for XML.

In step 16, we added a private variable to store the XML filename. Then, in step 17, we created code to populate this variable using a default constructor for the `XmlBooks` class. In step 18, we created a method to read the titles of the books contained in the XML file. This XML file will be created in the next recipe. In the code, we have used `XDocument` to load the XML file, which was supported by the `System.Xml.Linq` namespace. We stored the decedents in a variable, iterated each element, and stored them in a `List<string>` generic collection.

Finally, we built the code to check the syntax.

Creating a .NET Core console application to use the library

In this recipe, we will be creating a .NET Core console application to use the library created in the previous recipe. You can try this recipe on any platform, such as Linux or macOS, since .NET Core is a cross-platform library. In this recipe, we will be focusing on Windows.

Getting ready

Let's get ready by looking at the previously built .NET Standard 2.0 library that reads an XML file. Make sure you have this XML file created under your project. We will be using this file to read. This sample is from the MSDN library itself:

```
<?xml version="1.0"?>
<catalog>
   <book id="bk101">
      <author>Gambardella, Matthew</author>
      <title>XML Developer's Guide</title>
      <genre>Computer</genre>
      <price>44.95</price>
      <publish_date>2000-10-01</publish_date>
      <description>An in-depth look at creating applications
      with XML.</description>
   </book>
   <book id="bk102">
      <author>Ralls, Kim</author>
      <title>Midnight Rain</title>
      <genre>Fantasy</genre>
      <price>5.95</price>
      <publish_date>2000-12-16</publish_date>
      <description>A former architect battles corporate zombies,
      an evil sorceress, and her own childhood to become queen
      of the world.</description>
   </book>
   <book id="bk103">
      <author>Corets, Eva</author>
      <title>Maeve Ascendant</title>
      <genre>Fantasy</genre>
      <price>5.95</price>
      <publish_date>2000-11-17</publish_date>
      <description>After the collapse of a nanotechnology
      society in England, the young survivors lay the
      foundation for a new society.</description>
   </book>
   <book id="bk104">
      <author>Corets, Eva</author>
      <title>Oberon's Legacy</title>
      <genre>Fantasy</genre>
      <price>5.95</price>
      <publish_date>2001-03-10</publish_date>
      <description>In post-apocalypse England, the mysterious
      agent known only as Oberon helps to create a new life
      for the inhabitants of London. Sequel to Maeve
      Ascendant.</description>
```

```
    </book>
    <book id="bk105">
        <author>Corets, Eva</author>
        <title>The Sundered Grail</title>
        <genre>Fantasy</genre>
        <price>5.95</price>
        <publish_date>2001-09-10</publish_date>
        <description>The two daughters of Maeve, half-sisters,
        battle one another for control of England. Sequel to
        Oberon's Legacy.</description>
    </book>
</catalog>
```

How to do it...

1. Open Visual Studio 2017.
2. Now, open the solution from the previous recipe. Click **File** | **Open** | **Open Project/Solution**, or press *Ctrl* + *Shift* + *O*, and select the `Chapter5.XmlLinq` solution.
3. Press *Ctrl* + *Shift* + *B* for a quick build to check that everything is fine.
4. Now, click on the `Chapter5.XmlLinq` solution label. Click **File** | **Add** | **New Project**.
5. In the **Add New Project** template dialog box, expand the **Visual C#** node in the left-hand pane.
6. Select **.NET Core** and select **Console App (.NET Core)** in the right-hand pane:

Add New Project

- Recent
- Installed
  - Visual C#
    - Windows Classic Desktop
    - Web
    - .NET Core
    - .NET Standard
    - Cloud
    - Test
    - WCF
  - Visual Basic
  - Visual F#
  - SQL Server
  - Azure Data Lake
  - Stream Analytics
  - Python
- Online

.NET Framework 4.6.1 Sort by: Default

Search (Ctrl+E)

Console App (.NET Core)	Visual C#
Class Library (.NET Core)	Visual C#
Unit Test Project (.NET Core)	Visual C#
xUnit Test Project (.NET Core)	Visual C#
ASP.NET Core Web Application	Visual C#

Type: Visual C#

A project for creating a command-line application that can run on .NET Core on Windows, Linux and MacOS.

Not finding what you are looking for?

Open Visual Studio Installer

Name: ConsoleApp1

Location: C:\Projects\Chapter5\Chapter5.XmlLinq

Browse...

OK Cancel

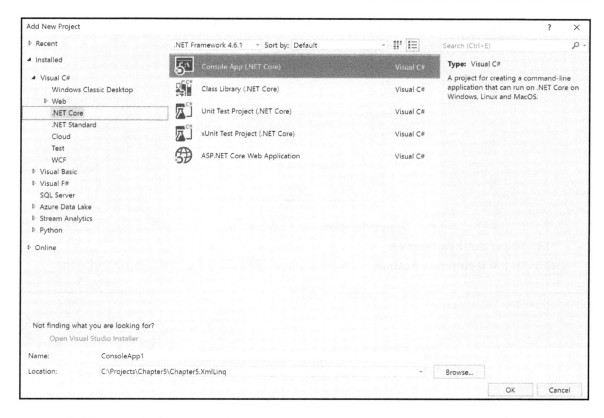

7. Now, in the **Name:** textbox, type `Chapter5.XmlLinq.XmlCore` as the name of the project. The rest of the fields can be left as they are:

8. Click **OK**.

9. Now, the **Solution Explorer** (press *Ctrl* + *Alt* + *L*) should display like this:

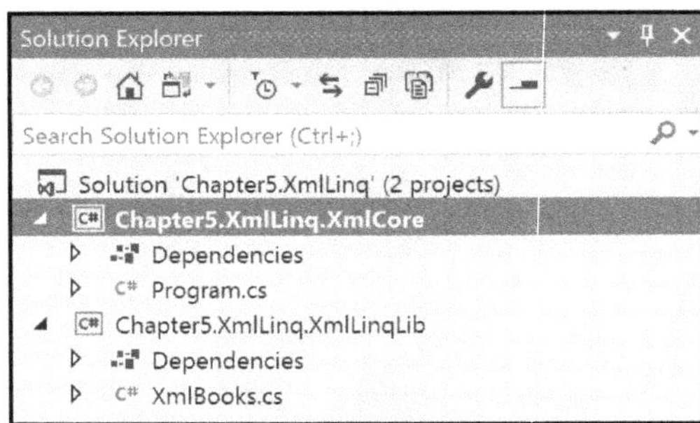

10. Right-click on the **Dependencies** label under `Chapter5.XmlLinq.XmlCore`.
11. Select **Add Reference**.
12. In the **Reference Manager**, click on the **Projects** label in the right-hand pane:

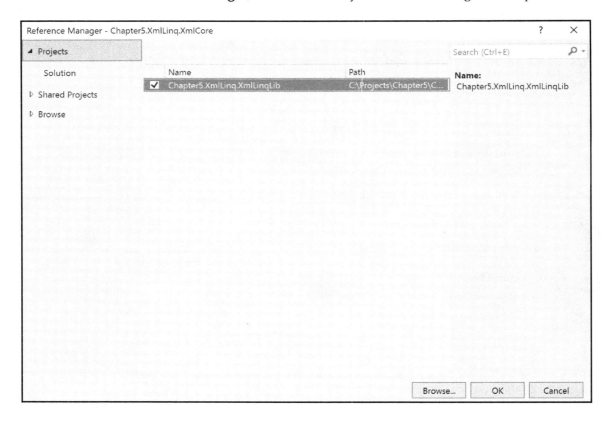

13. Check the `Chapter5.XmlLinq.XmlLinqLib` project in the left-hand pane.
14. Click **OK**.
15. Now click on the project name label of `Chapter5.XmlLinq.XmlCore` and select **Add** | **New Item**.
16. In the **Add New Item** dialog box, in the left-hand pane, select **Data** under **Visual C# Items** and **XML File** in the right-hand pane:

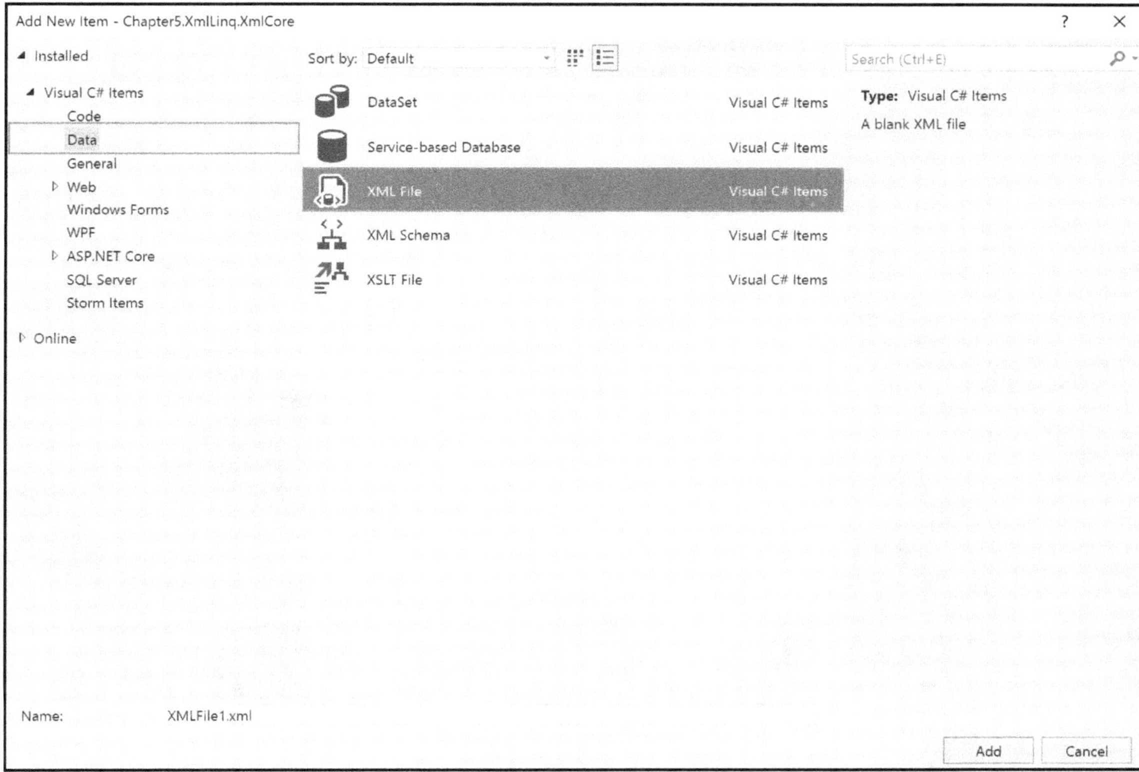

17. Type `books.xml` in the **Name:** textbox and click **Add**.
18. Now replace the existing code with the following:

```
<?xml version="1.0"?>
<catalog>
  <book id="bk101">
      <author>Gambardella, Matthew</author>
      <title>XML Developer's Guide</title>
      <genre>Computer</genre>
```

```
      <price>44.95</price>
      <publish_date>2000-10-01</publish_date>
      <description>An in-depth look at creating applications
      with XML.</description>
   </book>
   <book id="bk102">
      <author>Ralls, Kim</author>
      <title>Midnight Rain</title>
      <genre>Fantasy</genre>
      <price>5.95</price>
      <publish_date>2000-12-16</publish_date>
      <description>A former architect battles corporate zombies,
       an evil sorceress, and her own childhood to become queen
       of the world.</description>
   </book>
   <book id="bk103">
      <author>Corets, Eva</author>
      <title>Maeve Ascendant</title>
      <genre>Fantasy</genre>
      <price>5.95</price>
      <publish_date>2000-11-17</publish_date>
      <description>After the collapse of a nanotechnology
      society in England, the young survivors lay the
      foundation for a new society.</description>
   </book>
   <book id="bk104">
      <author>Corets, Eva</author>
      <title>Oberon's Legacy</title>
      <genre>Fantasy</genre>
      <price>5.95</price>
      <publish_date>2001-03-10</publish_date>
      <description>In post-apocalypse England, the mysterious
      agent known only as Oberon helps to create a new life
      for the inhabitants of London. Sequel to Maeve
      Ascendant.</description>
   </book>
   <book id="bk105">
      <author>Corets, Eva</author>
      <title>The Sundered Grail</title>
      <genre>Fantasy</genre>
      <price>5.95</price>
      <publish_date>2001-09-10</publish_date>
      <description>The two daughters of Maeve, half-sisters,
      battle one another for control of England. Sequel to
      Oberon's Legacy.</description>
   </book>
</catalog>
```

19. Now double-click on `Program.cs` to open the code window.
20. In the code window, scroll to the top of the screen.
21. Next to the last line of the `using` directives, add this `using` directive:

```
using Chapter5.XmlLinq.XmlLinqLib;
```

22. Now replace the existing code in the `Main()` method with this code:

```
        var xmlFile =
@"C:\Projects\Chapter5\Chapter5.XmlLinq\Chapter5.XmlLinq.XmlCore\books.xml"
;

        var books = new XmlBooks(xmlFile);
        var titles = books.GetBookTitles();

        foreach (var title in titles)
        {

            Console.WriteLine(title);
        }

        Console.ReadLine();
```

23. Press *F5* to see the output and it should look like this:

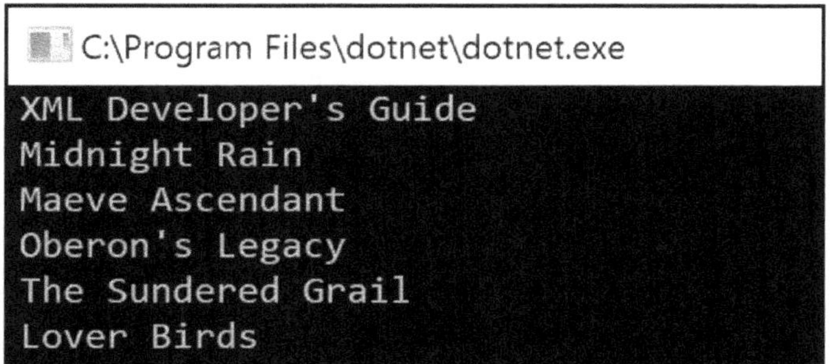

24. Press *Enter* to exit.

How it works...

In steps 1 to 9, we opened an existing solution. Then, we added a .NET Core console application to the solution. During these steps, we assigned a proper name to the project. In steps 10 to 13, we added the project reference to the library we created in the previous recipe. These steps will allow you to use the available methods from the library.

In steps 15 to 18, we added an XML file item to the project and then we populated it with some sample data. In step 21, we referenced our library from the .NET Core console application. In step 22, we added code inside the `Main()` method of the console application. The first line stores the path of our XML file. This might vary in your setup. In the next two lines, we created an instance of the `XmlBooks` class, used its `GetBookTitles()` method, and stored it in a variable. Then, using a `foreach` statement, we iterated through the list returned from the `GetBookTitles()` method. Finally, we executed the code.

6
Exploring Threading

In this chapter, we will be looking at these recipes:

- Creating a library that can perform several things at once
- Creating a .NET Core console application to use the library
- Creating an async method with tasks
- Creating a WPF application to use the library
- Creating a thread pool
- Creating a .NET console application to use the library

Technical requirements

Readers should have a basic knowledge of C#. They should also have a basic knowledge of using Visual Studio, installing packages using NuGet, and referencing libraries within projects from other projects.

The code files for this chapter can be found on GitHub:
`https://github.com/PacktPublishing/DotNET-Standard-2-Cookbook/tree/master/Chapter06`

Check out the following video to see the code in action:
`https://goo.gl/BhsEpf`

Introduction

Threading enables your C# application to do more than one operation at a time. Simply put, you can allow a user to input their personal information and monitor it while doing a background process. As an example, in strategy games, a character might be fetching some wood from a forest. At the same time, another one could be building a wall and another shooting at the enemy. Let's have a look at how threading works inside a .NET Standard 2.0 library.

Creating a library that can perform several things at once

In this recipe, we will be looking at the basics of threading and we will make use of the `System.Threading` namespace inside a .NET Standard 2.0 library.

Getting ready

Let's make sure we have the latest Visual Studio 2017 installed and configured for creating a .NET Standard 2.0 library before we get started building our library.

How to do it...

1. Open Visual Studio 2017.
2. Click **File** | **New** | **Project** to create a project.

3. In the **New Project** dialog box, expand the **Other Project Types** node in the left-hand pane and select **Visual Studio Solutions**. In the right-hand pane, select **Blank Solution.**
4. In the **Name:** textbox, type `Chapter6.Threads` and, in the **Location:** textbox, select a path from the drop-down box or click on the **Browse...** button to locate a path:

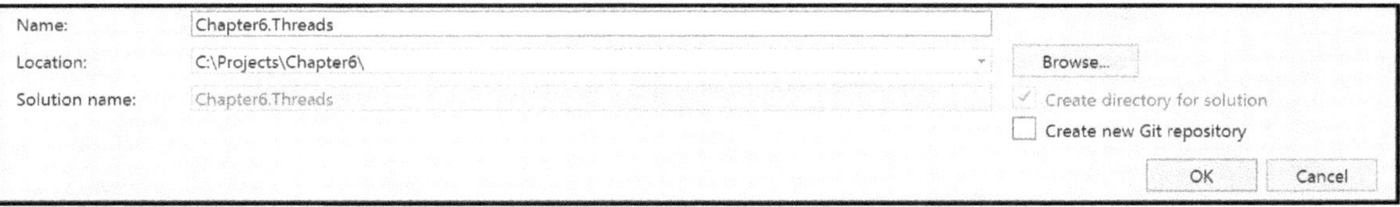

5. Click **OK**.
6. Now, the **Solution Explorer** (*Ctrl* + *Alt* + *L*) should look like this:

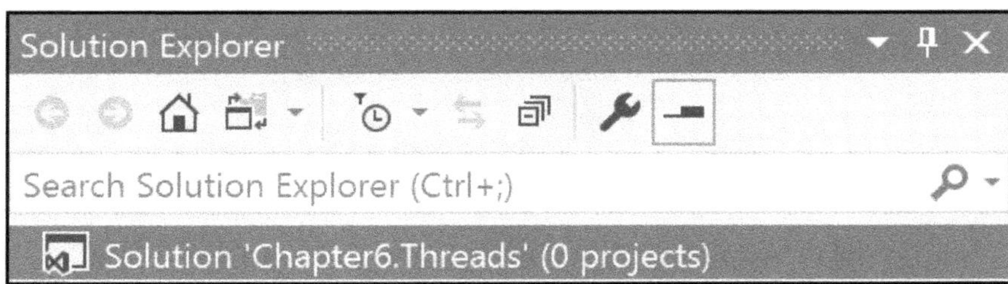

7. Now, right-click on the `Chapter6.Threads` label in the **Solution Explorer** and select **Add** | **New Project.**
8. In the **New Project** dialog box, expand the **Visual C#** node.

9. Select **.NET Standard** in the left-hand pane and **Class Library (.NET Standard)** in the right-hand pane:

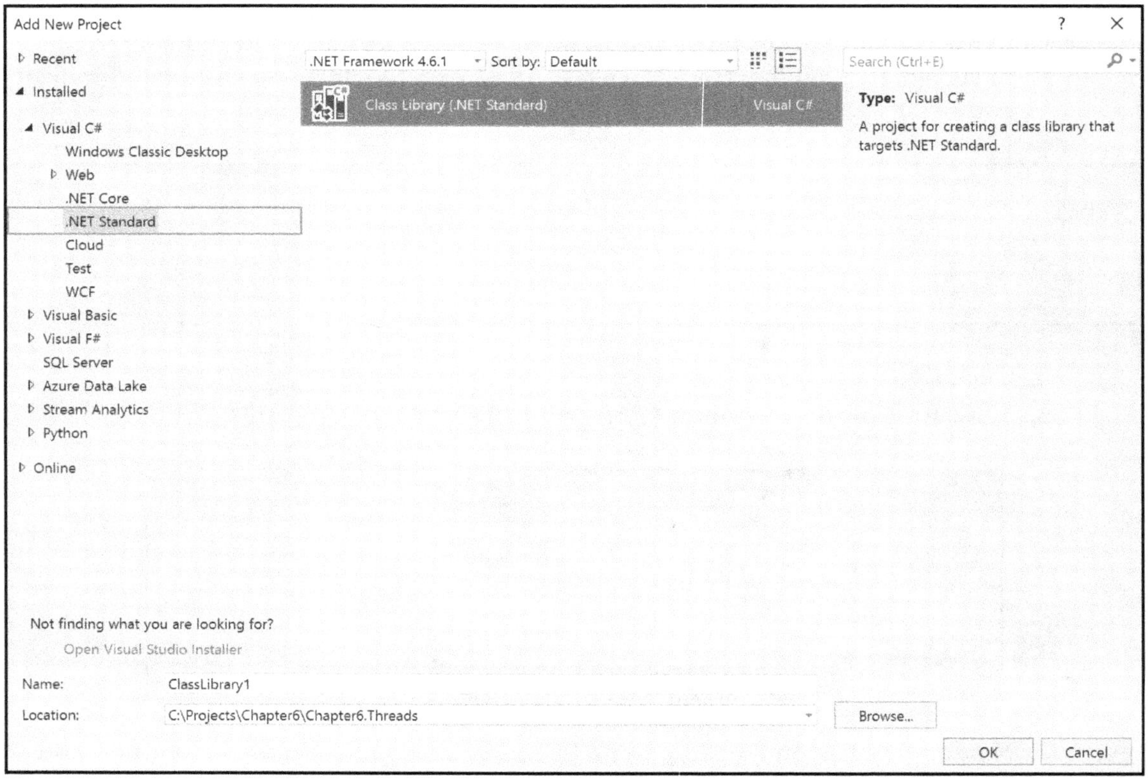

Add New Project
Recent
Installed
Visual C#
Windows Classic Desktop
Web
.NET Core
.NET Standard
Cloud
Test
WCF
Visual Basic
Visual F#
SQL Server
Azure Data Lake
Stream Analytics
Python
Online
.NET Framework 4.6.1
Sort by: Default
Search (Ctrl+E)
Class Library (.NET Standard)
Visual C#
Type: Visual C#
A project for creating a class library that targets .NET Standard.
Not finding what you are looking for?
Open Visual Studio Installer
Name:
ClassLibrary1
Location:
C:\Projects\Chapter6\Chapter6.Threads
Browse...
OK
Cancel

10. Now, in the **Name:** textbox, type `Chapter6.Threads.ThreadLib`. Leave the other defaults as they are and click **OK**:

Name:
Chapter6.Threads.ThreadLib
Location:
C:\Projects\Chapter6\Chapter6.Threads
Browse...
OK
Cancel

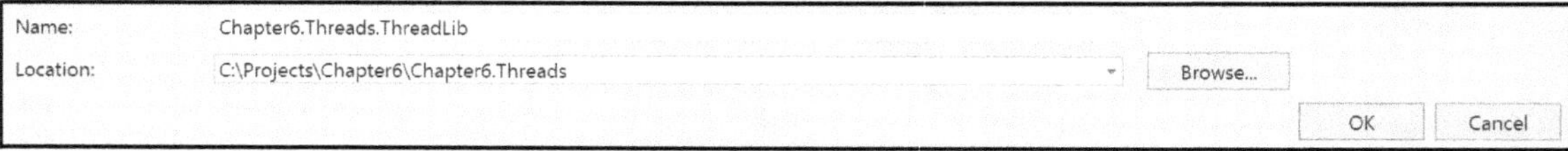

11. Now, the **Solution Explorer** (*Ctrl* + *Alt* + *L*) should look like this:

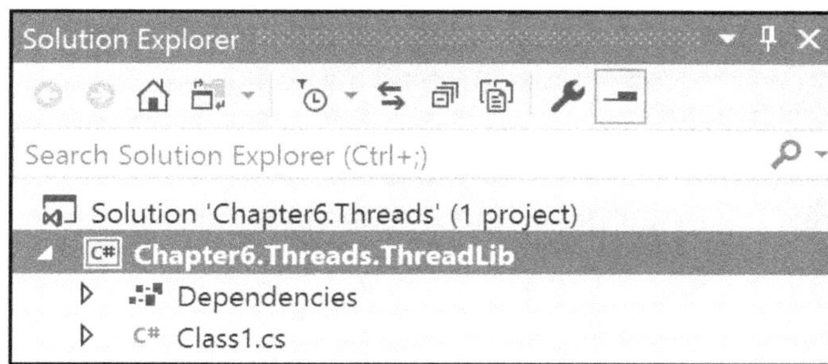

12. Now, select `Class1.cs` in the **Solution Explorer** and press *F2* to rename the file `ThreadGenerator.cs`.
13. Answer **Yes** in the confirmation dialog box that asks to rename the class name as well.
14. Now, double-click on the `ThreadGenerator.cs` label in the **Solution Explorer**.
15. Let's scroll up in the code window and add the following `using` directive:

```
using System.Threading;
using System.Text
```

16. Now, let's add this class-level variable to store our text messages:

```
StringBuilder messages = new StringBuilder();
```

17. Create this method inside the `ThreadGenerator` class:

```
public StringBuilder StartThreads()
{
    var mainThread = Thread.CurrentThread;
    mainThread.Name = "MainThread";

    messages.Append($"This is the {mainThread.Name}\n");

    Thread anotherThread = new Thread(CountTo100);
    messages.Append("Start a new thread\n");
    anotherThread.Start();

    messages.Append($"Now call {mainThread.Name} will count to
50\n");

    for (int j=0; j<50; j++)
    {
```

```
            messages.Append($"MT-{j + 1}\n");
            Thread.Sleep(80);
        }

        messages.Append($"{mainThread.Name} finished\n");
        return messages;
    }
```

18. Finally, create this support method for the main `StartThreads()` method:

```
    private void CountTo100()
    {
        for (int i=0; i<100; i++)
        {
            messages.Append($"Thread 2 counting {i + 1}\n");
            Thread.Sleep(100);
        }
    }
```

19. Let's perform a quick build by pressing *Ctrl* + *Shift* + *B* to check the syntax.

How it works...

In steps 1 to 14, we created a new blank solution and added a .NET Standard 2.0 class library. Then we gave the default template class a proper name. In step 15, we added the `using` directive required for threading support, which is `System.Threading`, and we have used the `System.Text` namespace to get the `StringBuilder` class to store our messages.

We have used `StringBuilder` over `String`. If you are wondering why, it is because `StringBuilder` is mutable. When you perform operations such as insert, replace, or append, a `StringBuilder` object doesn't create a new instance every time. It will update one space in the memory without creating a new space in the memory. However, `String` is immutable, which means that if you create a `String` object, then you cannot modify it and it always creates a new `String` object in the memory.

In step 16, we created an instance of the `StringBuilder` class, which will handle all the messages and store them. Then, we created a method that returns a `StringBuilder`. This `StringBuilder` will contain all the messages generated during execution of the `StartThreads()` methods created in step 17.

In these three lines, we picked up the current running thread, which is the main thread, and gave it a name. Then, we stored a message in the `StringBuilder`:

```
var mainThread = Thread.CurrentThread;
mainThread.Name = "MainThread";

messages.Append($"This is the {mainThread.Name}\n");
```

In these lines, we created another new thread and used the `helper` method created in step 18 to execute the thread. This `private helper` method loops through 100 steps, adds a message to the string builder, and sleeps for 100 milliseconds at each step:

```
private void CountTo100()
{
    for (int i=0; i<100; i++)
    {
        messages.Append($"Thread 2 counting {i + 1}\n");
        Thread.Sleep(100);
    }
}
```

It also stores the relevant message inside the `StringBuilder` as follows:

```
Thread anotherThread = new Thread(CountTo100);
messages.Append("Start a new thread\n");
anotherThread.Start();
```

In the final lines of code, we executed another loop in the main thread and stored messages inside the `StringBuilder` to identify which threads are being executed. Finally, we performed a quick build to check the syntax.

Creating a .NET Core console application to use the library

In this recipe, we will be building a .NET Core console application. This application will use the library we built in the previous recipe.

Getting ready

Make sure you have completed the previous recipe and it builds correctly. Let's get started on the application to use the library.

How to do it...

1. Open Visual Studio 2017.
2. Now, open the solution from the previous recipe. Click **File** | **Open** | **Open Project/Solution**, or press *Ctrl* + *Shift* + *O*, and select the `Chapter6.Threads` solution.
3. Press *Ctrl* + *Shift* + *B* for a quick build to check that everything is fine.
4. Click on the `Chapter6.Threads` solution label. Click **File** | **Add** | **New Project**.
5. In the **Add New Project** template dialog box, expand the **Visual C#** node in the left-hand pane.
6. Select **.NET Core** and select **Console App (.NET Core)** in the right-hand pane:

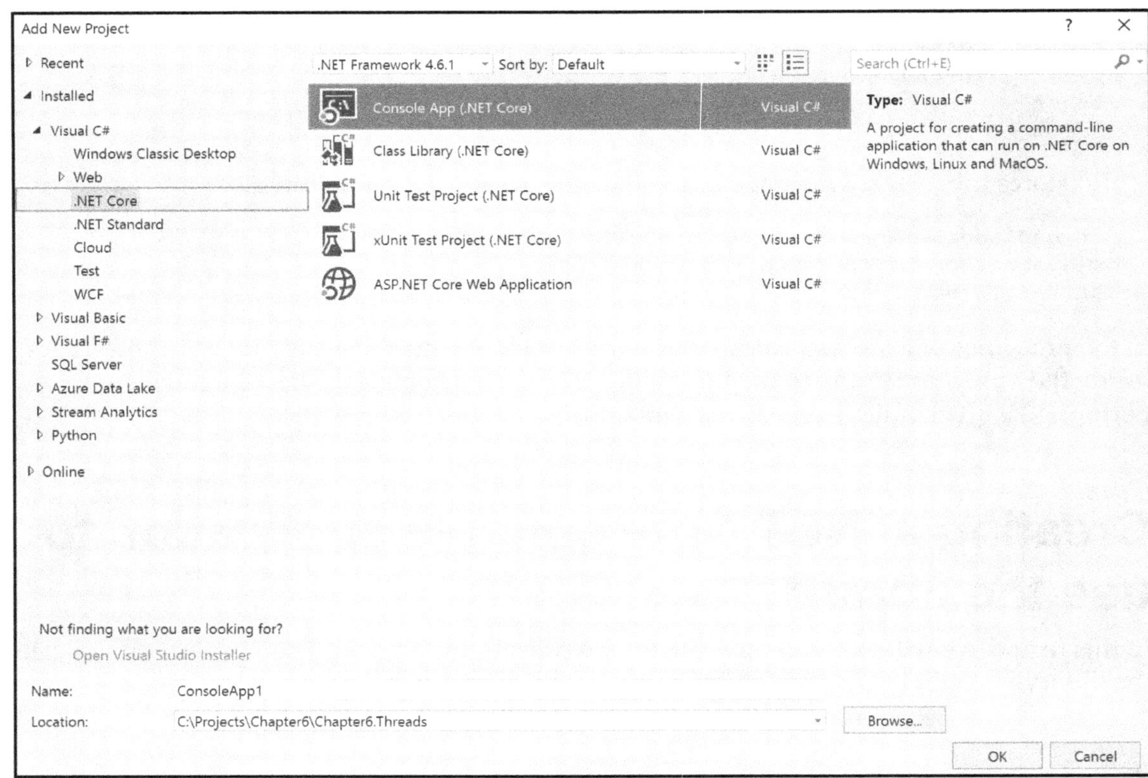

7. Now, in the **Name:** textbox, type `Chapter6.Threads.ThreadsCore` as the name of the project. The rest of the fields should be left as they are:

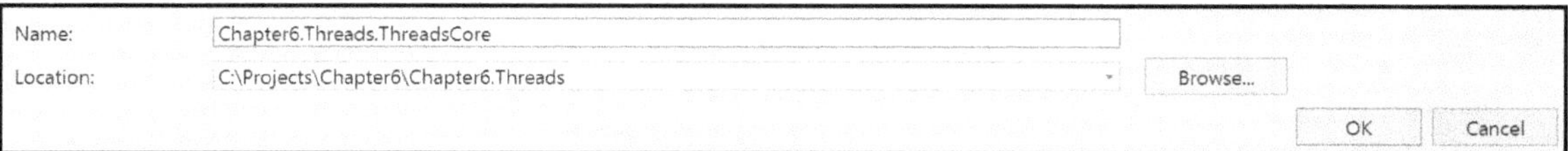

8. Click **OK**.
9. Now, the **Solution Explorer** (press *Ctrl* + *Alt* + *L*) should display like this:

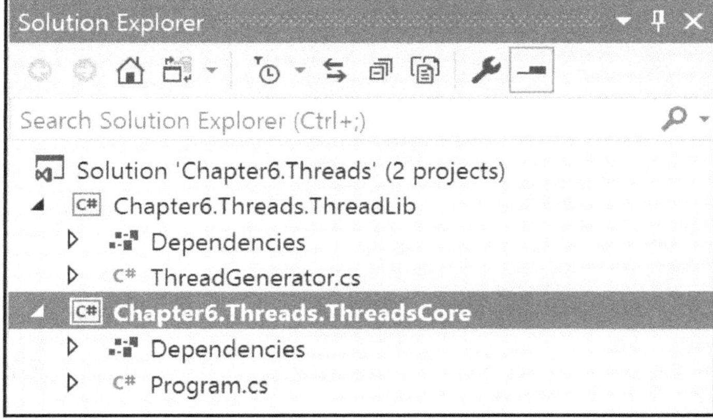

10. Right-click on the **Dependencies** label in the `Chapter6.Threads.ThreadsCore`.
11. Select **Add Reference**.

12. In the **Reference Manager**, click on the **Projects** label in the right-hand pane:

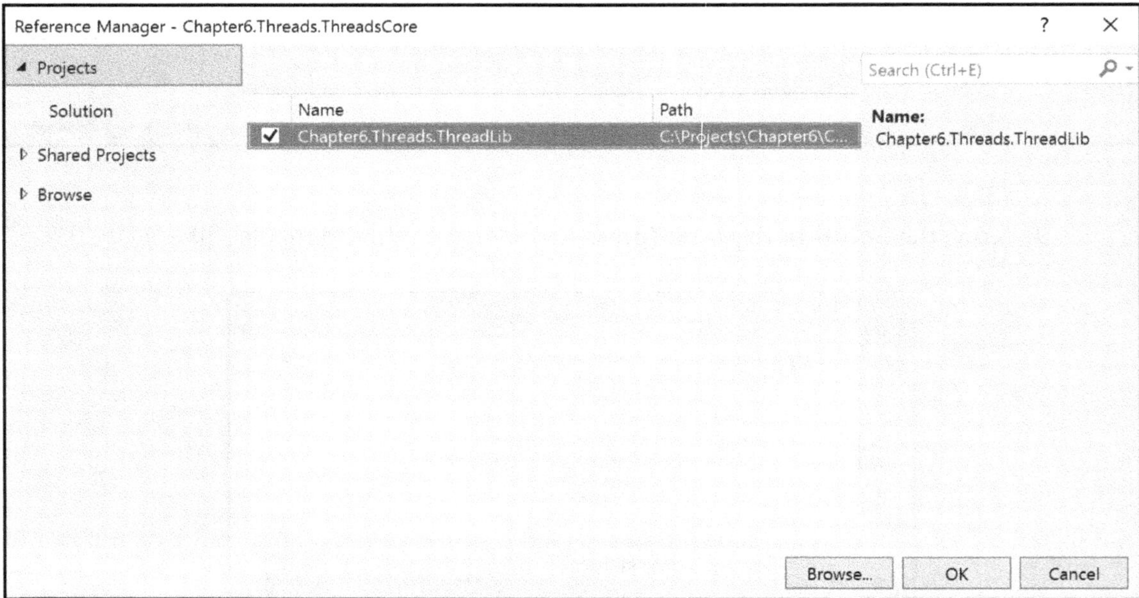

13. Check the `Chapter6.Threads.ThreadLib` project in the left-hand pane.
14. Click **OK**.
15. Now, double-click on the `Program.cs` label in the **Solution Explorer**.
16. Scroll up in the code window and add the following `using` directive:

```
using Chapter6.Threads.ThreadLib;
```

17. Now, delete any existing code generated by Visual Studio in the `Main()` method and add the following code:

```
var threads = new ThreadGenerator();
var output = threads.StartThreads();

Console.WriteLine(output);
Console.ReadLine();
```

18. Press *F5* to execute the app.

19. You should see output like this:

```
C:\Program Files\dotnet\dotnet.exe
This is the MainThread
Start a new thread
Now call MainThread will count to 50
MT-1
Thread 2 counting 1
MT-2
Thread 2 counting 2
MT-3
MT-4
Thread 2 counting 3
MT-5
MT-6
Thread 2 counting 4
MT-7
Thread 2 counting 5
MT-8
MT-9
Thread 2 counting 6
MT-10
MT-11
Thread 2 counting 7
MT-12
MT-13
Thread 2 counting 8
MT-14
Thread 2 counting 9
MT-15
MT-16
Thread 2 counting 10
MT-17
```

20. Press *Enter* to exit.

How it works...

In steps 1 to 9, we opened an existing solution with a .NET Standard 2.0 library project. Then, we added a .NET Core console application to that solution. In steps 10 to 14, we added the .NET Standard 2.0 library project as a dependency to the console application. Then, in step 16, we used the `using` directive to reference the class library. This will allow us to access the available functionality from the library.

In step 17, we created an instance of the `ThreadGenerator` class available in the class library. Then, we used its `StartThreads()` method and stored the returned `StringBuilder` in a variable. Finally, we displayed the output using `Console.WriteLine` and waited for a key press by the user in the last line. In steps 18 to 20, we executed the application and saw the output.

Creating an async method with tasks

In this recipe, we will be looking at the asynchronous programming capabilities found in the C# language. C# has language-level asynchronous capabilities, and therefore you don't have to rely on a third-party library. If you have I/O operations, such as reading data from a network or from a database, you can utilize asynchronous programming. You can also use asynchronous programming for CPU-bound, expensive calculations.

Getting ready

Make sure you have Visual Studio 2017 updated. It is also assumed that you have prior experience in asynchronous programming and what it means.

How to do it...

1. Open Visual Studio 2017.
2. Click **File** | **New** | **Project** to create a project.
3. In the **New Project** dialog box, expand the **Other Project Types** node in the left-hand pane and select **Visual Studio Solutions**. In the right-hand pane, select **Blank Solution.**
4. In the **Name:** textbox, type `Chapter6.AsyncTasks` and, in the **Location:** textbox, select a path from the drop-down box or click on the **Browse...** button to locate a path:

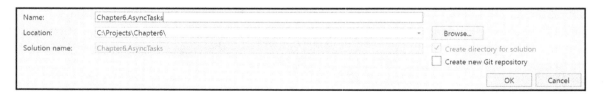

5. Click **OK**.
6. Now, the **Solution Explorer** (*Ctrl* + *Alt* + *L*) should look like this:

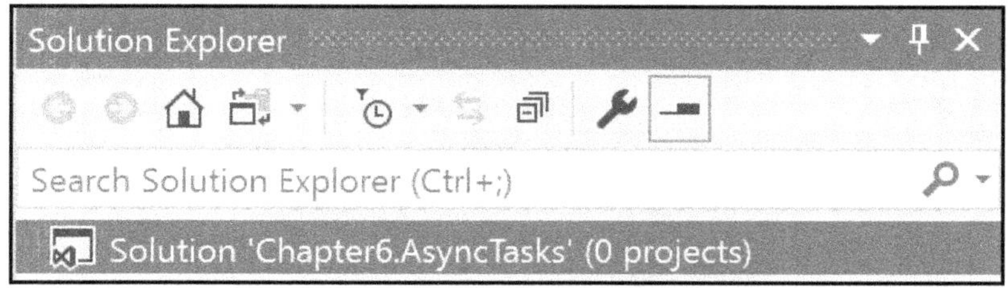

7. Now, right-click on the `Chapter6.AsyncTasks` label in the **Solution Explorer** and select **Add** | **New Project.**
8. In the **New Project** dialog box, expand the **Visual C#** node.
9. Select **.NET Standard** in the left-hand pane and **Class Library (.NET Standard)** in the right-hand pane:

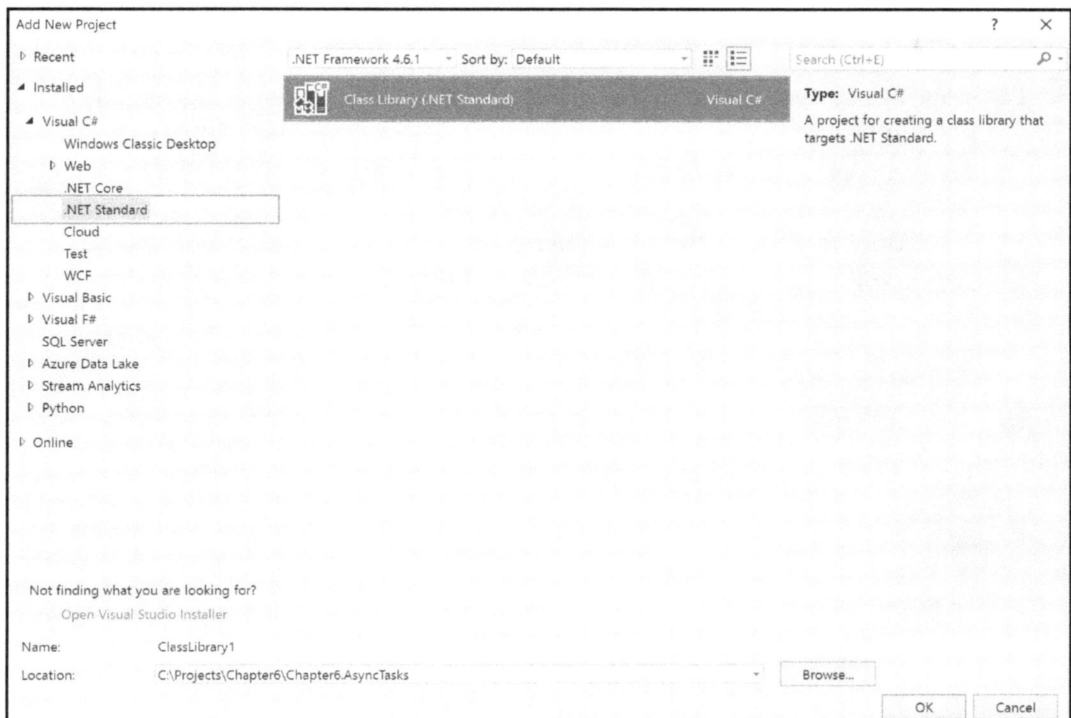

10. Now, in the **Name:** textbox, type `Chapter6.AsyncTasks.AsyncLib`. Leave the other defaults as they are and click **OK**:

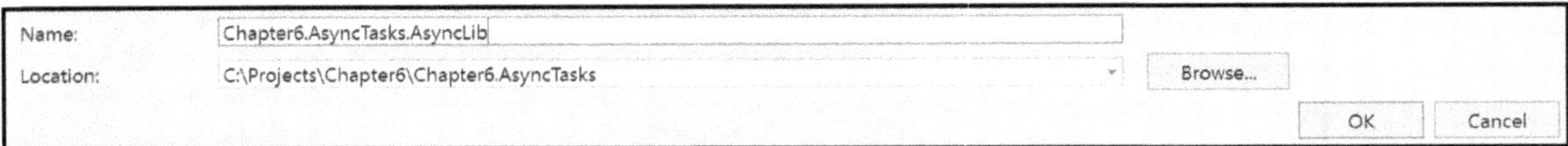

11. Now, the **Solution Explorer** (*Ctrl* + *Alt* + *L*) should look like this:

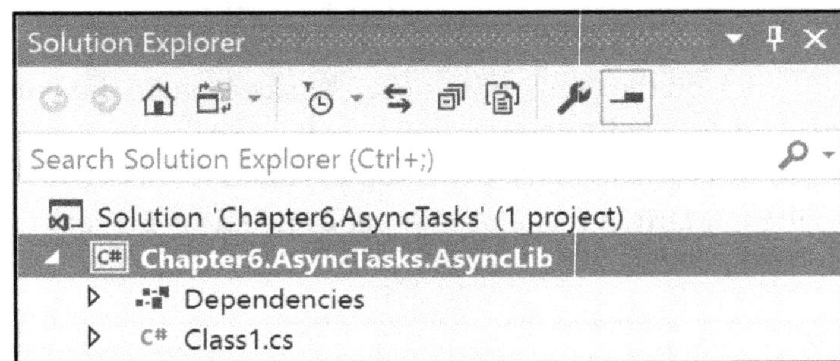

12. Now, select `Class1.cs` in the **Solution Explorer** and press *F2* to rename the file `SiteReader.cs`.
13. Answer **Yes** in the confirmation dialog box that asks to rename the class name as well.
14. Now, double-click on the `SiteReader.cs` label in the **Solution Explorer**.
15. Let's scroll up in the code window and add the following using directive:

```
using System.Net.Http;
using System.Threading.Tasks;
```

16. Now, let's add this class-level variable:

```
private HttpClient _httpClient = new HttpClient();
```

17. Add the following method inside the open and closed curly brackets of the `SiteReader` class:

```
public async Task<string> ReadSiteContent(string url)
{
    var htmlContent = await _httpClient.GetStringAsync(url);

    return htmlContent;
}
```

18. Press *Ctrl* + *Shift* + *B* for a quick build.

How it works...

In steps 1 to 12, we added a blank solution and then we added a .NET Standard 2.0 class library to the solution. In these steps, we assigned proper names to the solution and the project. In steps 13 and 14, we renamed the default class template to something more meaningful. You can also delete this class and create a new one.

In step 15, we added two namespaces to the code. In step 16, we created a class-level variable and created an instance of the `HttpClient` class. In step 17, we created an asynchronous public method that reads the given site content as a `string` and returns the read content.

Finally, we performed a quick build to check the syntax.

Creating a WPF application to use the library

In this recipe, we will be creating a Windows Presentation Foundation application to use the library. A basic user interface will be created to show the content.

Getting ready

Make sure you have opened the .NET Standard 2.0 class library we built in the previous recipe. If not, make sure you complete the previous recipe before we dive into this one.

How to do it...

1. Open Visual Studio 2017.
2. Now, open the solution from the previous recipe. Click **File** | **Open** | **Open Project/Solution**, or press *Ctrl* + *Shift* + *O*, and select the `Chapter6.AsyncTasks` solution.
3. Press *Ctrl* + *Shift* + *B* for a quick build to check that everything is fine.
4. Click on the `Chapter6.AsyncTasks` solution label. Click **File** | **Add** | **New Project**.
5. In the **Add New Project** template dialog box, expand the **Visual C#** node in the left-hand pane.
6. Select **Windows Classic Desktop** and select **WPF App (.NET Framework)** in the right-hand pane:

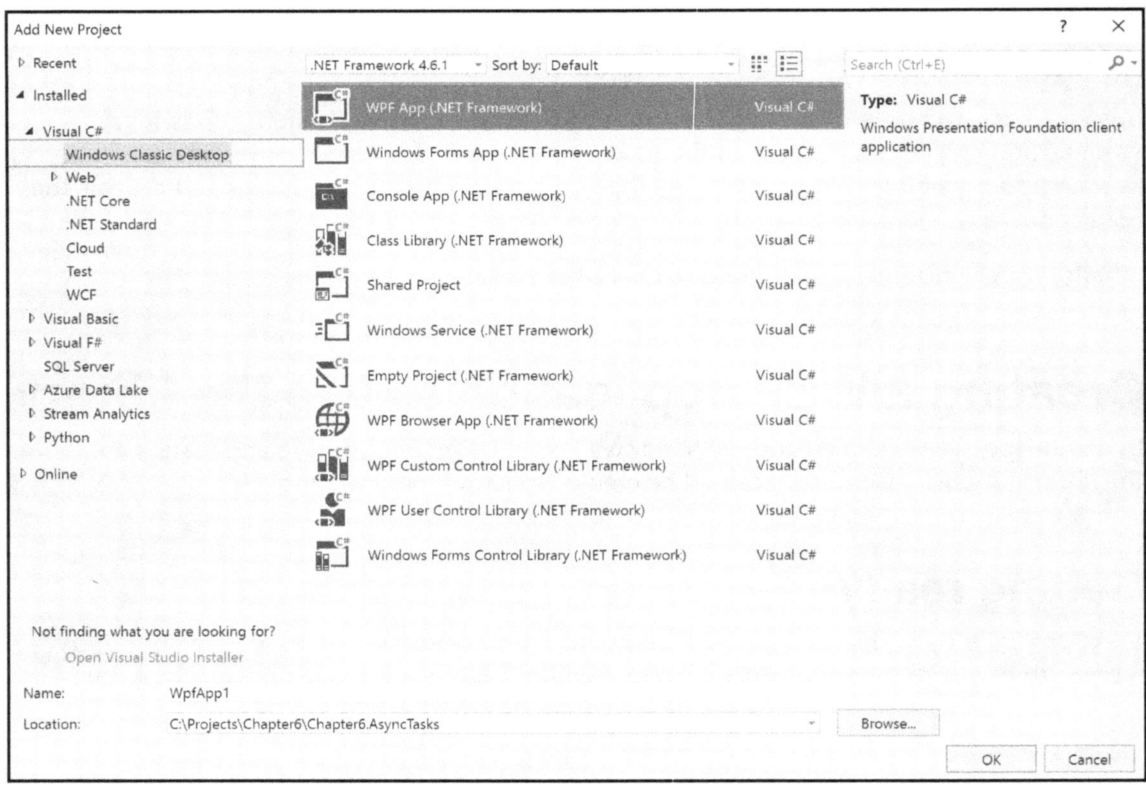

7. Now, in the **Name:** textbox, type `Chapter6.AsyncTasks.WPFSiteContent` as the name of the project. The rest of the fields can be left as they are:

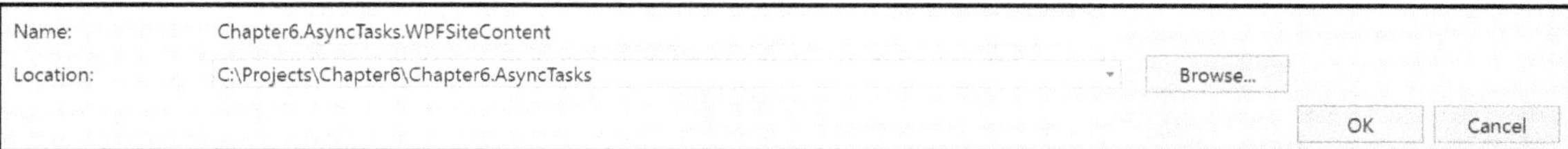

8. Click **OK**.
9. Now, the **Solution Explorer** (press *Ctrl* + *Alt* + *L*) should look like this:

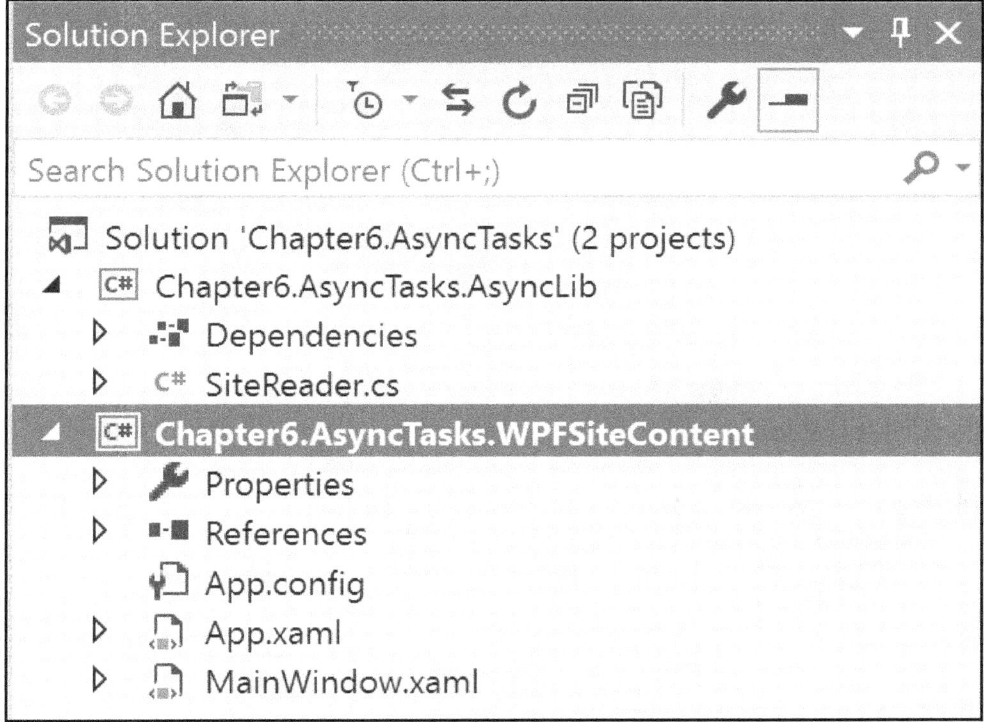

10. Right-click on the **References** label in the `Chapter6.AsyncTasks.WPFSiteContent`.
11. Select **Add Reference**.
12. In the **Reference Manager**, click on the **Projects** label in the right-hand pane:

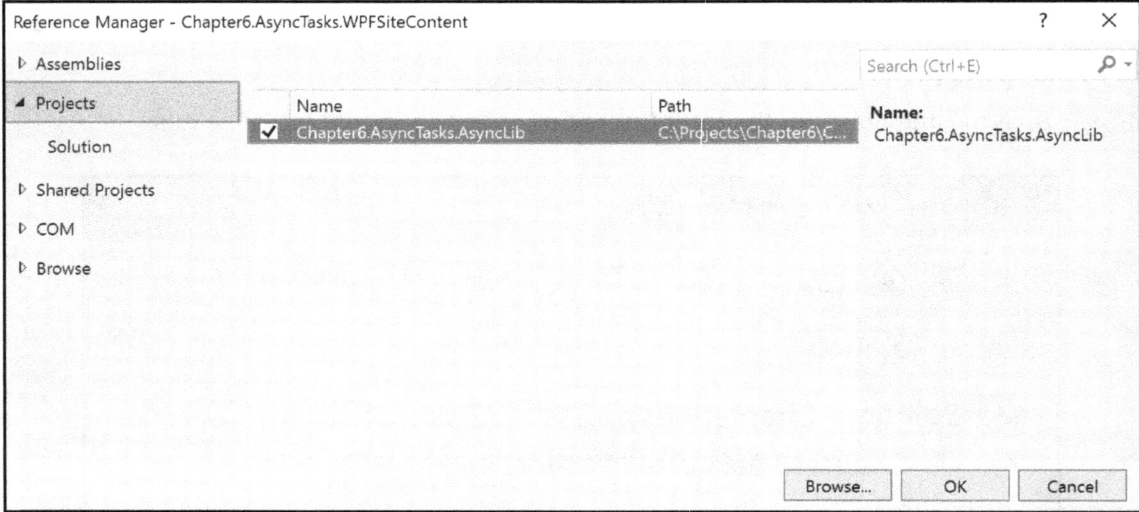

13. Check the `Chapter6.AsyncTasks.AsyncLib` project in the left-hand pane.
14. Click **OK**.
15. Now, click on the `MainWindow.xaml` tab.
16. From the toolbox, add a **TextBox** control, a **Button** control, and a **WebBrowser** control to the **MainWindow** form:

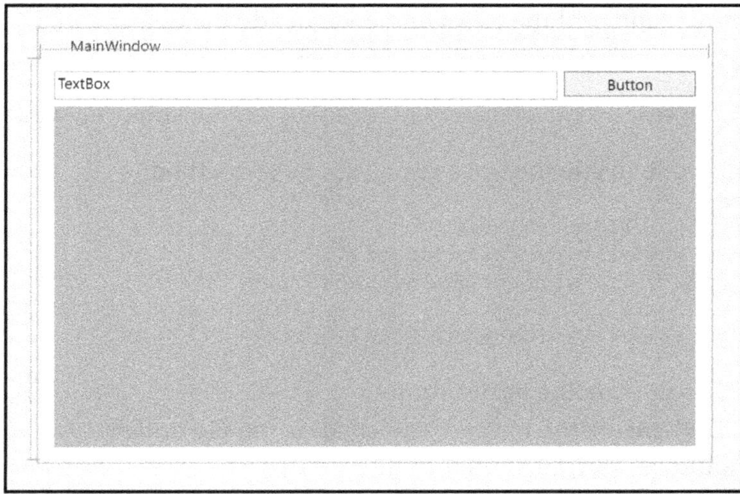

17. Select the **TextBox** and press *F4* to load the **Properties** window.
18. Change the following properties:

Control	Property	Value
TextBox	**Name**	`UrlTextBox`
TextBox	**Text**	`Delete existing text and leave blank`
Button	**Name**	`GoButton`
Button	**Content**	`Go`
WebBrowser	**Name**	`ContentBrowser`

19. Double-click on the **Go** button to reach the code window.
20. Scroll up till you reach the `using` directives.
21. Add the following `using` directive to the last line of the directives:

```
using Chapter6.AsyncTasks.AsyncLib;
```

22. Scroll down and add the following code inside the `GoButton_Click()` event.
23. Change the `GoButton_Click` as follows:

```
private async void GoButton_Click(object sender, RoutedEventArgs e)
```

24. Add this code inside the `GoButton_Click()` method:

```
var url = UrlTextBox.Text;
var siteReader = new SiteReader();
var content = await siteReader.ReadSiteContent(url);

ContentBrowser.NavigateToString(content);
```

25. Press *F5* to execute the application.
26. Type a URL inside the textbox and click on the **Go** button.
27. You should see output similar to this:

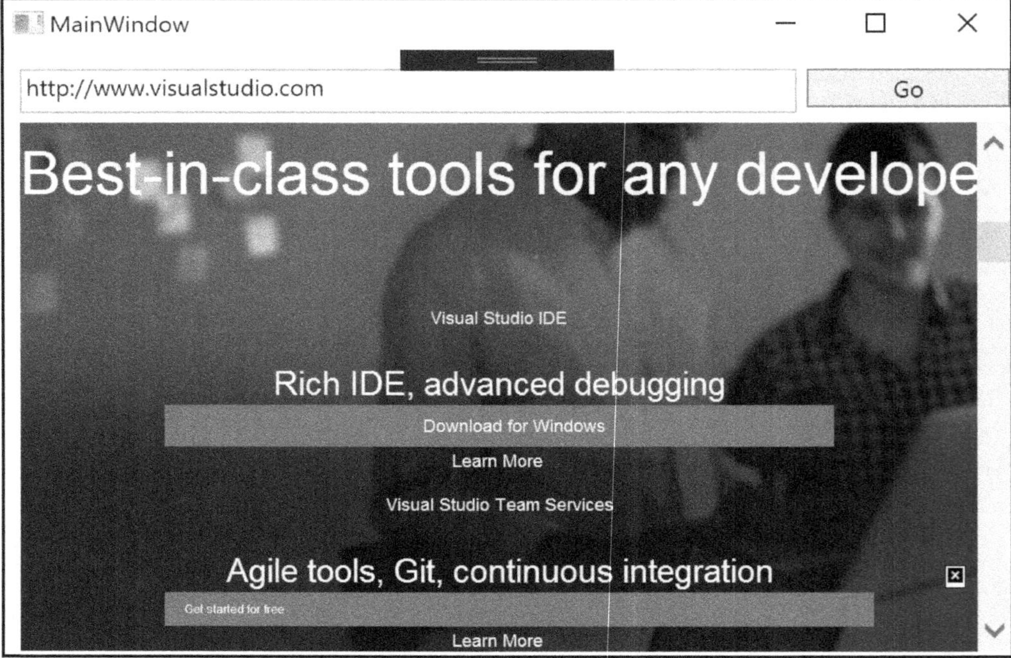

28. Close the application.

How it works...

In steps 1 to 10, we opened the existing solution for the .NET Standard 2.0 library project. Then we added a WPF Project to the solution. In steps 11 to 14, we added a reference to the class library we built in the previous recipe. In steps 16 to 18, we added controls to the `MainWindow` of the WPF application and then we changed a few properties.

In step 21, we referenced the class library using a `using` directive. In step 23, we decorated the `GoButton_Click()` method with an `async` keyword. In step 24, the first three lines of code demonstrate that we have created a variable to store the URL from the **TextBox** after it created an instance of the `SiteReader` class. Then, we used the `ReadSiteConent()` asynchronous method to read the content of a given URL. Finally, we displayed that content in the `WebBrowser` control.

In steps 25 to 27, we tested the application.

Creating a thread pool

In this recipe, we will be looking at thread pools in C#. Basically, a thread pool is a collection of threads that can be used to perform tasks in the background. Once a thread completes its task, then it is sent to a pool of waiting threads, where it can be reused. Let's create a .NET Standard 2.0 library that uses thread pools.

Getting ready

Make sure you have the latest version of Visual Studio 2017 up and running.

How to do it...

1. Open Visual Studio 2017.
2. Click **File** | **New** | **Project** to create a project.
3. In the **New Project** dialog box, expand the **Other Project Types** node in the left-hand pane and select **Visual Studio Solutions**. In the right-hand pane, select **Blank Solution.**

4. In the **Name:** textbox, type `Chapter6.ThreadPools` and, in the **Location:** textbox, select a path from the drop-down box or click on the **Browse...** button to locate a path:

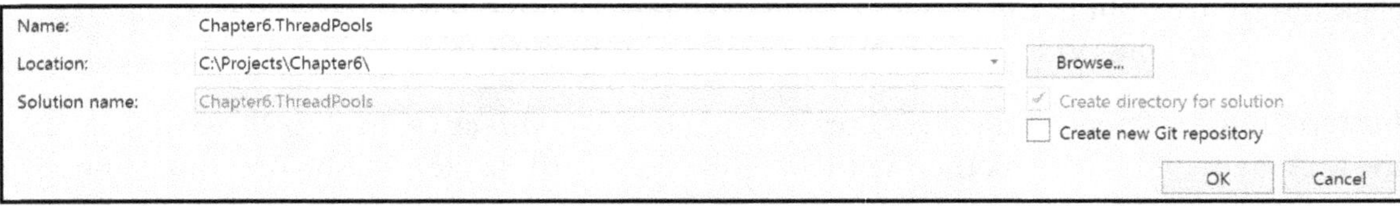

5. Click **OK**.
6. Now, the **Solution Explorer** (*Ctrl* + *Alt* + *L*) should look like this:

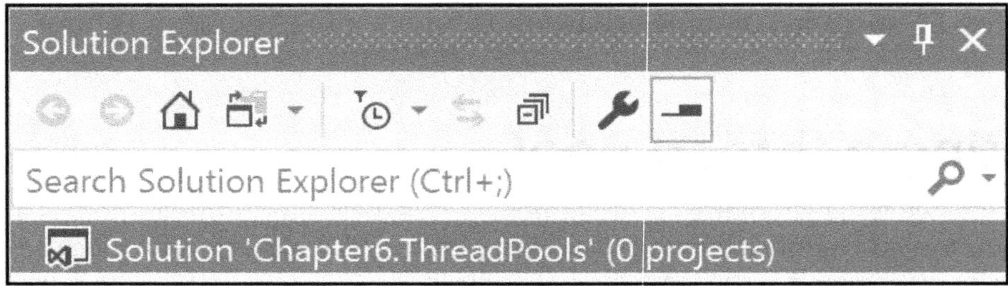

7. Right-click on the `Chapter6.ThreadPools` label in the **Solution Explorer** and select **Add** | **New Project.**
8. In the **New Project** dialog box, expand the **Visual C#** node.
9. Select **.NET Standard** in the left-hand pane and **Class Library (.NET Standard)** in the right-hand pane:

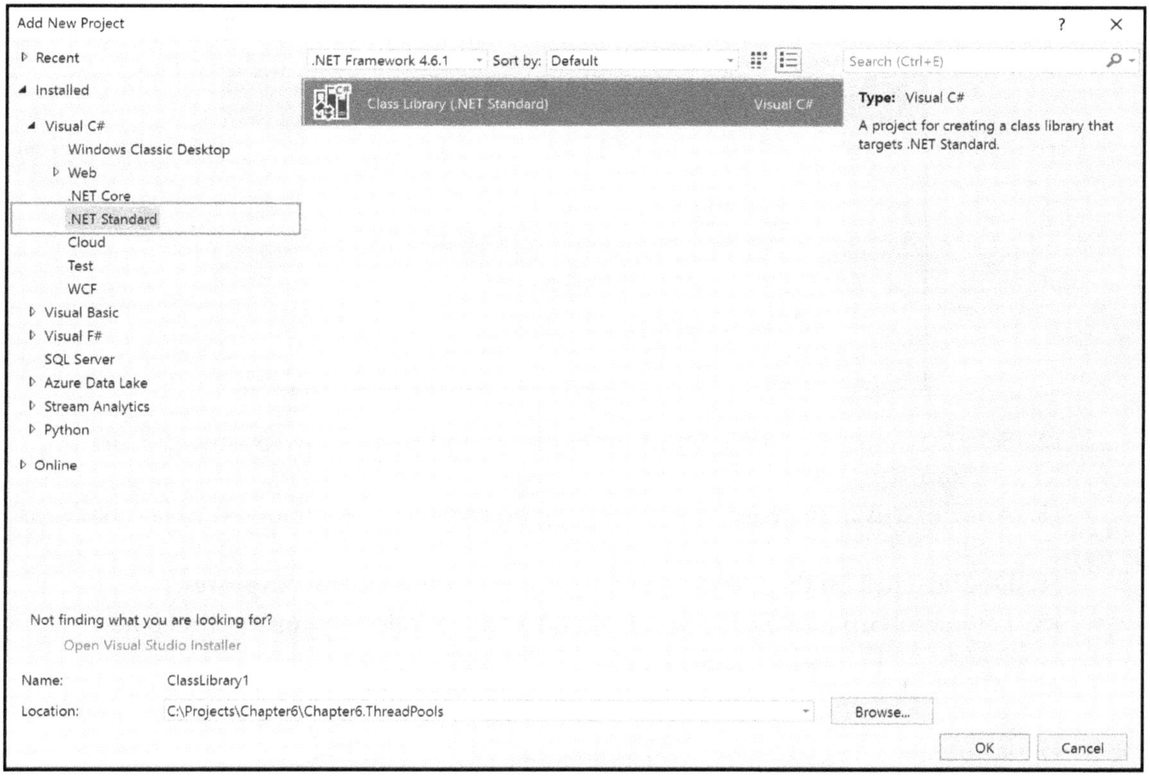

Add New Project

▷ Recent
◢ Installed
◢ Visual C#
Windows Classic Desktop
▷ Web
.NET Core
.NET Standard
Cloud
Test
WCF
▷ Visual Basic
▷ Visual F#
SQL Server
▷ Azure Data Lake
▷ Stream Analytics
▷ Python
▷ Online

.NET Framework 4.6.1 Sort by: Default

Search (Ctrl+E)

Class Library (.NET Standard) Visual C#

Type: Visual C#

A project for creating a class library that targets .NET Standard.

Not finding what you are looking for?
Open Visual Studio Installer

Name: ClassLibrary1
Location: C:\Projects\Chapter6\Chapter6.ThreadPools
Browse...
OK Cancel

10. In the **Name:** textbox, type `Chapter6.ThreadPools.PoolLib`. Leave the other defaults as they are and click **OK**:

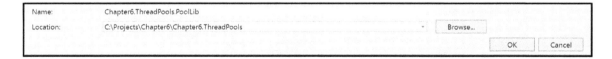

11. Now, the **Solution Explorer** (*Ctrl* + *Alt* + *L*) should look like this:

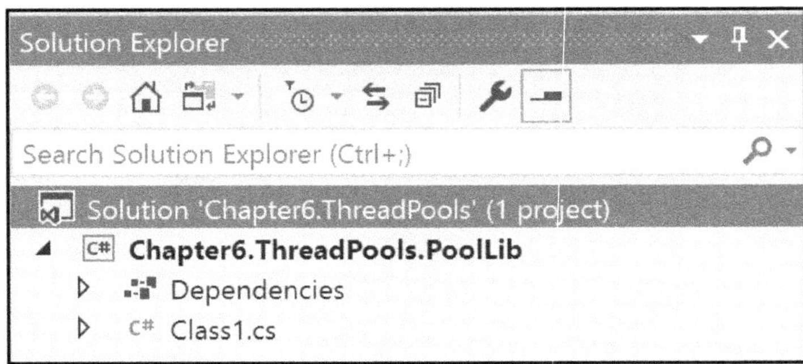

12. Select `Class1.cs` in the **Solution Explorer** and press *F2* to rename the file `ThreadList.cs`.
13. Answer **Yes** in the confirmation dialog box that asks to rename the class name as well.
14. Double-click on the `ThreadList.cs` label in the **Solution Explorer**.
15. Let's scroll up in the code window and add the following using directive:

```
using System.Text;
using System.Threading;
```

16. Let's add a class-level variable that holds a `StringBuilder`:

```
StringBuilder messages = new StringBuilder();
```

17. Add a main `ProcessPool()` method to the class:

```
public StringBuilder ProcessPool()
{
    for (int i=0; i<5; i++)
    {
        ThreadPool.QueueUserWorkItem(new WaitCallback(Process));
    }

    for (int k=0; k<10; k++)
    {
        messages.AppendLine($"Main Thread - {k + 1}");
    }

    return messages;
}
```

18. Finally, let's add the helper method to process the thread:

```
private void Process(object callback)
{
    for (int j=0; j<10; j++)
    {
        messages.AppendLine($"Thread - {j + 1}");
    }
}
```

19. Let's perform a quick build by pressing *Ctrl* + *Shift* + *B*.

How it works...

In steps 1 to 10, we created a blank solution and added a .NET Standard 2.0 library to the project. In between, we assigned meaningful names to the project and to the solution. In step 12, we renamed the default class created by Visual Studio. In step 15, we added the namespaces required to build the library.

In step 16, we created a variable to hold the messages using the `StringBuilder` class. This is a class-level variable that is shared across methods inside the class. In step 17, we created a method that creates a thread pool using a helper method in step 18. Inside that method, we use the `messages` variable to store the messages during the process.

Finally, in step 19, we performed a quick build to check for the correct syntax.

Creating a .NET console application to use the library

In this recipe, we will be looking at a .NET console-based application to use the library. This console app will reference the library created in the previous recipe and use it.

Getting ready

Make sure you have completed the previous recipe. If you have completed it, open it using Visual Studio 2017 and perform a quick build to check that everything is fine.

How to do it...

1. Open Visual Studio 2017.
2. Now, open the solution from the previous recipe. Click **File** | **Open** | **Open Project/Solution**, or press *Ctrl* + *Shift* + *O*, and select the `Chapter6.ThreadPools` solution.
3. Press *Ctrl* + *Shift* + *B* for a quick build to check that everything is fine.
4. Click on the `Chapter6.ThreadPools` solution label. Click **File** | **Add** | **New Project**.
5. In the **Add New Project** template dialog box, expand the **Visual C#** node in the left-hand pane.
6. Select **Windows Classic Desktop** and select **Console App (.NET Framework)** in the right-hand pane:

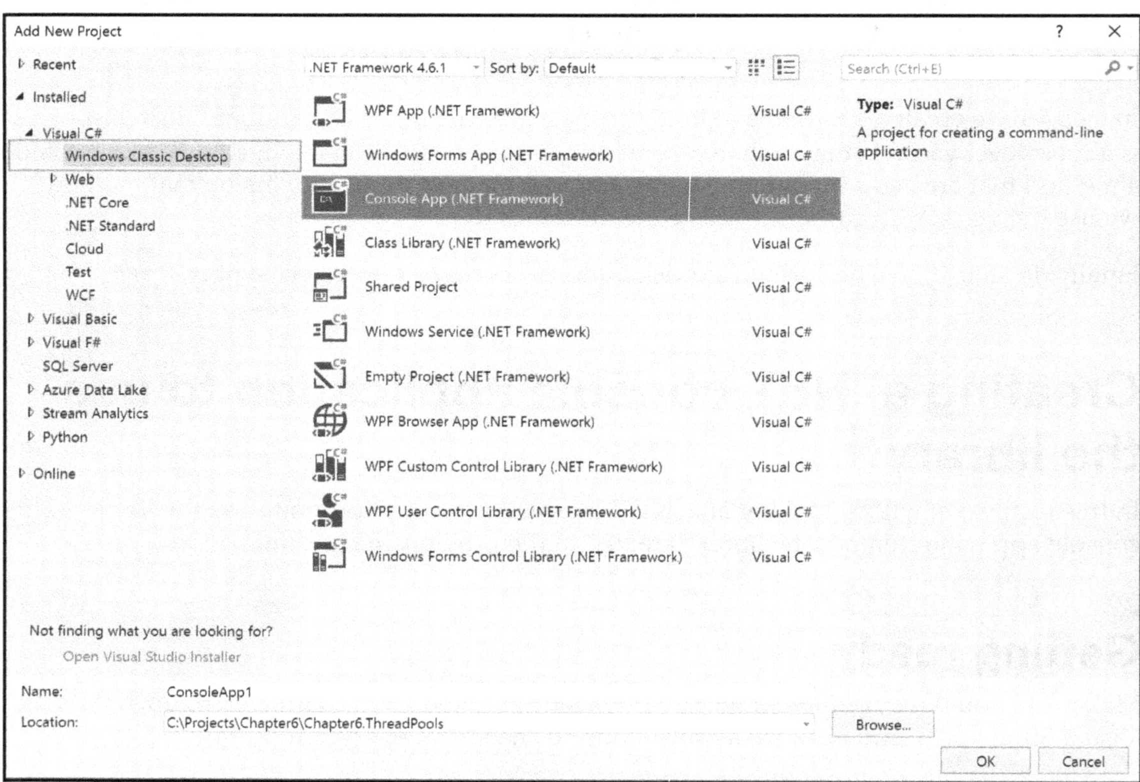

7. In the **Name:** textbox, type `Chapter6.ThreadPools.PoolConsole` as the name of the project. The rest of the fields can be left as they are:

8. Click **OK**.
9. Now, the **Solution Explorer** (press *Ctrl* + *Alt* + *L*) should look like this:

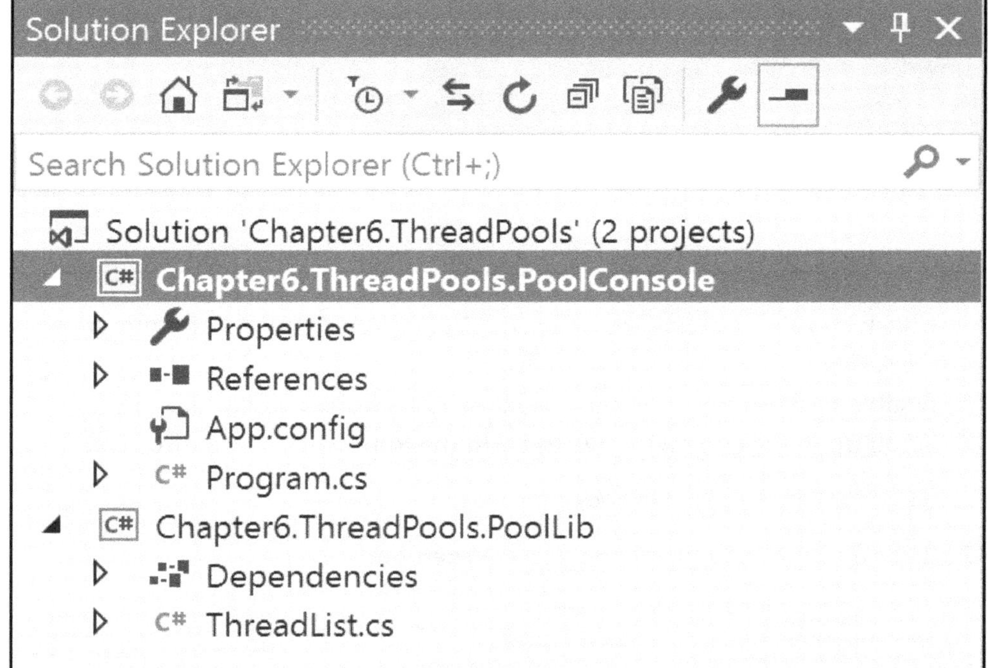

10. Right-click on the **References** label in the `Chapter6.ThreadPools.PoolConsole`.
11. Select **Add Reference**.

12. In the **Reference Manager**, click on the **Projects** label in the right-hand pane:

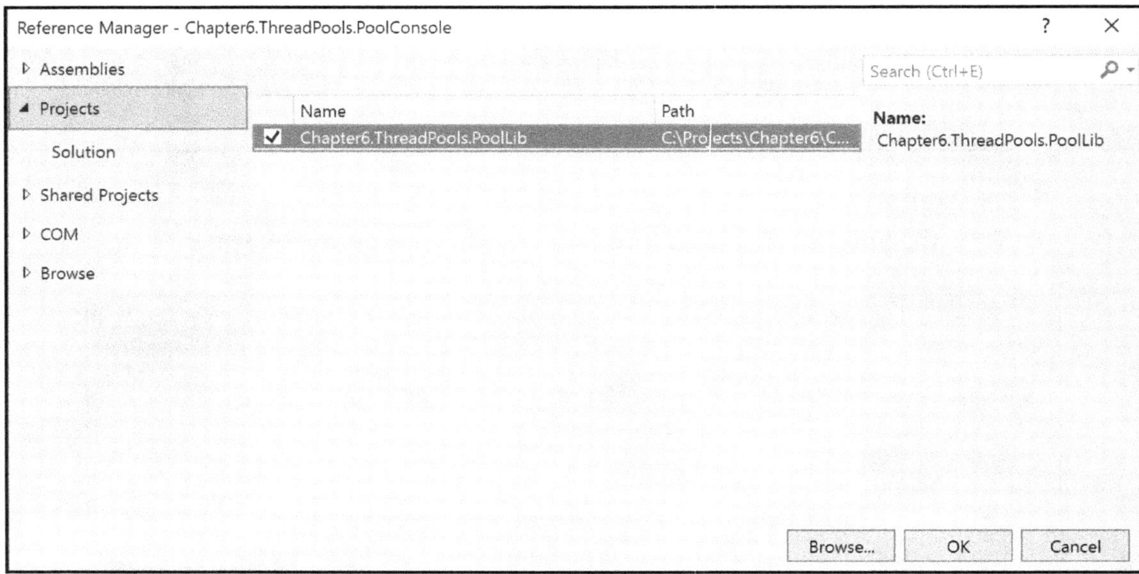

13. Check `Chapter6.ThreadPools.PoolLib` project in the left-hand pane.
14. Click **OK**.
15. Double-click on the `Program.cs` label in the **Solution Explorer**.
16. Scroll up in the code window and add the following `using` directive:

```
using Chapter6.ThreadPools.PoolLib;
```

17. Let's add the code inside the `Main()` method:

```
var pool = new ThreadList();
var output = pool.ProcessPool();

Console.WriteLine(output);

Console.ReadLine();
```

18. Now, press *F5* to test our application:

19. Press *Enter* to exit the application.

How it works...

In steps 1 to 9, we opened the solution created in the previous recipe. Then, we added a .NET console application to the project. In steps 10 to 14, we added a reference to the library we created in the previous recipe. In step 16, we created the reference in the code for the library. In step 17, we added code to create an instance of the `ThreadList` class. We called the `ProcessPool()` and stored the return value in a variable.

Finally, we displayed the output in the console window and, in steps 18 and 19, we tested the application.

7
Networking

In this chapter, we will be looking at these recipes:

- A library that displays an IP address and the name using sockets
- Creating a classic Windows application to use the library
- Creating a library that sends mail
- Creating a WPF application to use the library
- Creating a library to call a REST API
- Creating an ASP.NET MVC application to use the library

Technical requirements

Readers should have a basic knowledge of C#. They should also have a basic knowledge of using Visual Studio, installing packages using NuGet, and referencing libraries within projects from other projects.

The code files for this chapter can be found on GitHub:
`https://github.com/PacktPublishing/DotNET-Standard-2-Cookbook/tree/master/Chapter07`

Check out the following video to see the code in action:
`https://goo.gl/Wj2VD9`

Introduction

Microsoft .NET Framework provides you with a set of class libraries that make it easy to work with internet services. These libraries allow you to easily integrate services with your applications. In this chapter, we will be using a few of these classes within the System.Net namespace. We will be looking at how to get these into a .NET Standard 2.0 library, and use it across different flavors of .NET applications.

A library that displays an IP address and the name using sockets

In this recipe, we will be building a .NET Standard 2.0 class library that displays the IP address of the current machine you are on. Then, we will be creating an application that uses the library.

Getting ready

Make sure you have the latest Visual Studio 2017 installed and configured for creating a .NET Standard 2.0 library before you start building the library.

How to do it...

1. Open Visual Studio 2017.
2. Click **File** | Project to create a project.
3. In the **New Project** dialog box, expand the **Other Project Types** node in the left pane and select **Visual Studio Solutions**. In the right pane, select **Blank Solution**.

4. In the **Name:** textbox, type `Chapter7.Networking` and in the **Location:** textbox select a path from the drop-down box or click on the **Browse...** button to locate a path:

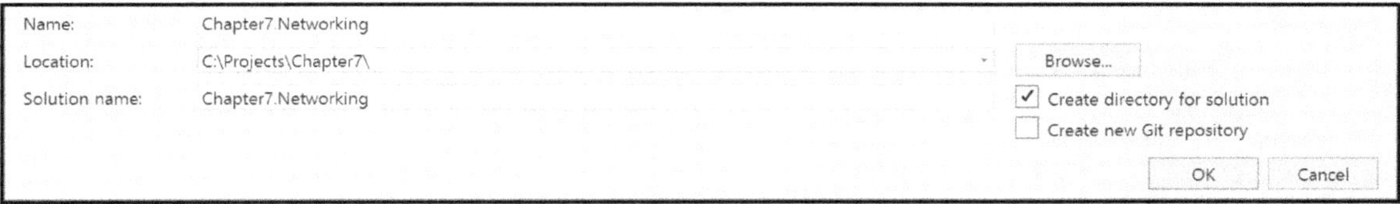

5. Click **OK**.
6. Now your **Solution Explorer** (*Ctrl* + *Alt* + *L*) should look like this:

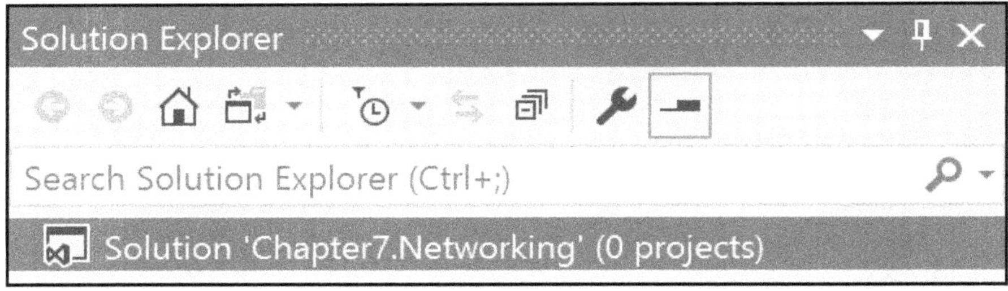

7. Now, click the right mouse button on the `Chapter7.Networking` label in the **Solution Explorer** and select **Add** | **New Project**.
8. In the **New Project** dialog box, expand the **Visual C#** node.

9. Select **.NET Standard** in the left pane and **Class Library (.NET Standard)** in the right pane:

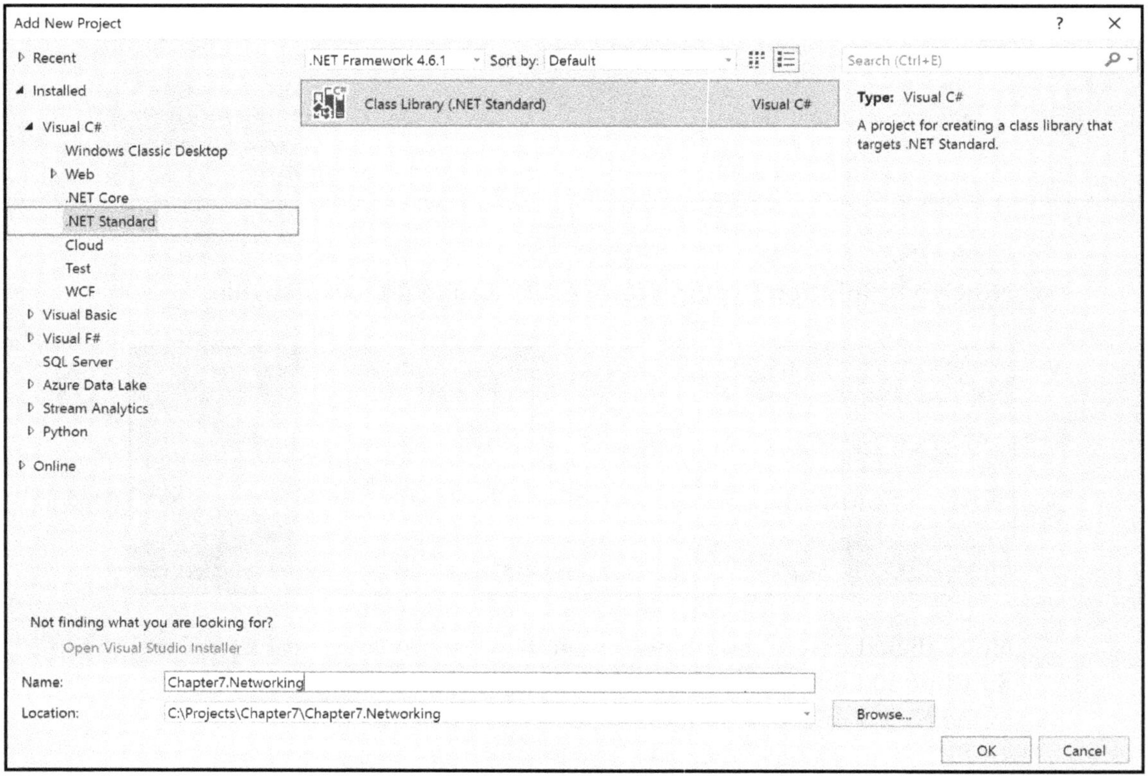

Add New Project ? ×

▷ Recent
◢ Installed
◢ Visual C#
Windows Classic Desktop
▷ Web
.NET Core
.NET Standard
Cloud
Test
WCF
▷ Visual Basic
▷ Visual F#
SQL Server
▷ Azure Data Lake
▷ Stream Analytics
▷ Python
▷ Online

.NET Framework 4.6.1 Sort by: Default
Search (Ctrl+E)
Class Library (.NET Standard) Visual C#
Type: Visual C#
A project for creating a class library that targets .NET Standard.

Not finding what you are looking for?
Open Visual Studio Installer
Name: Chapter7.Networking
Location: C:\Projects\Chapter7\Chapter7.Networking
Browse...
OK Cancel

10. In the **Name:** textbox, type `Chapter7.Networking.ReadIPLib`, leave the other defaults as is, and click **OK**:

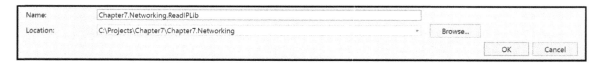

11. Now the **Solution Explorer** (*Ctrl* + *Alt* + *L*) should look like this:

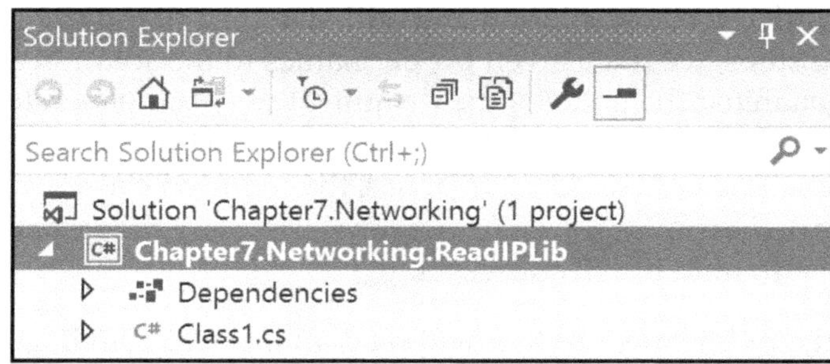

12. Now, select `Class1.cs` in the **Solution Explorer** and press *F2* to rename the file to `IPReader.cs`.
13. Answer **Yes** to the confirmation dialog box that asks to rename the class name as well.
14. Double-click on the `IPReader.cs` label in the **Solution Explorer**.
15. Let's scroll up in the code window and add the following `using` directive:

```
using System.Net;
using System.Net.Sockets;
using System.Collections.Generic;
```

16. Now, let's create this `public` method inside the `IPReader` class:

```
public List<string> GetMyIPAddress()
{
    var hostName = Dns.GetHostName();
    var hostAddress = Dns.GetHostAddresses(hostName);

    var ipList = new List<string>();

    foreach (var ipaddres in hostAddress)
    {
        if (ipaddres.AddressFamily == AddressFamily.InterNetwork)
        {
            ipList.Add(ipaddres.ToString());
        }
    }

    return ipList;
}
```

17. Press *Ctrl* + *Shift* + *B* for a quick build to check the syntax.

How it works...

In steps 1 to 11, we added a blank solution and added a .NET Standard 2.0 class library to the solution. In these steps, we have given proper names to the solution and the project. Then, in step 12 we changed the name of the default `Class1.cs` generated from Visual Studio. In step 15, we added the required `using` directive to the code. We have mainly used `System.Net` and `System.Net.Sockets` to access the required classes and read the IP address, and then added the `System.Collecitons.Generic` namespace to create a generic `string List` to hold the IP addresses.

In step 16, we added a public method that will read all the available IP addresses of the local machine you are on. In the first line, we stored the host name of the system in a variable and in the second line we used it to get the host addresses. Then, we created an empty list to store the IP addresses.

After that, we used a `foreach` loop to go through all the IP addresses we found and store them in the list after checking whether it was an IP address on the internal network. Finally, we returned the list of IP addresses we stored.

In step 17, we did a quick build to check syntax.

Creating a classic Windows application to use the library

In this recipe, we will be creating a classic Windows application to use the library. We will be creating a UI using the Visual Studio designer, adding code to use the library, and displaying the list of IP addresses picked from the library itself.

Getting ready

Make sure you have the latest version of Visual Studio 2017 and have completed the previous recipe. We will be using the solution we built in the previous recipe.

How to do it...

1. Open Visual Studio 2017.
2. Now open the solution from the previous recipe. Click **File** | **Open** | **Open Project/Solution** or press *Ctrl* + *Shift* + *O* and select the `Chapter7.Networkings` solution.
3. Press *Ctrl* + *Shift* + *B* for a quick build to check everything is fine.
4. Now, click on the `Chapter7.Networking` solution label. Click **File** | **Add** | **New Project**.
5. In the **Add New Project** template dialog box, expand the **Visual C#** node in the left pane.
6. Select **Windows Classic Desktop** and select **Windows Forms App (.NET Framework)** in the right pane:

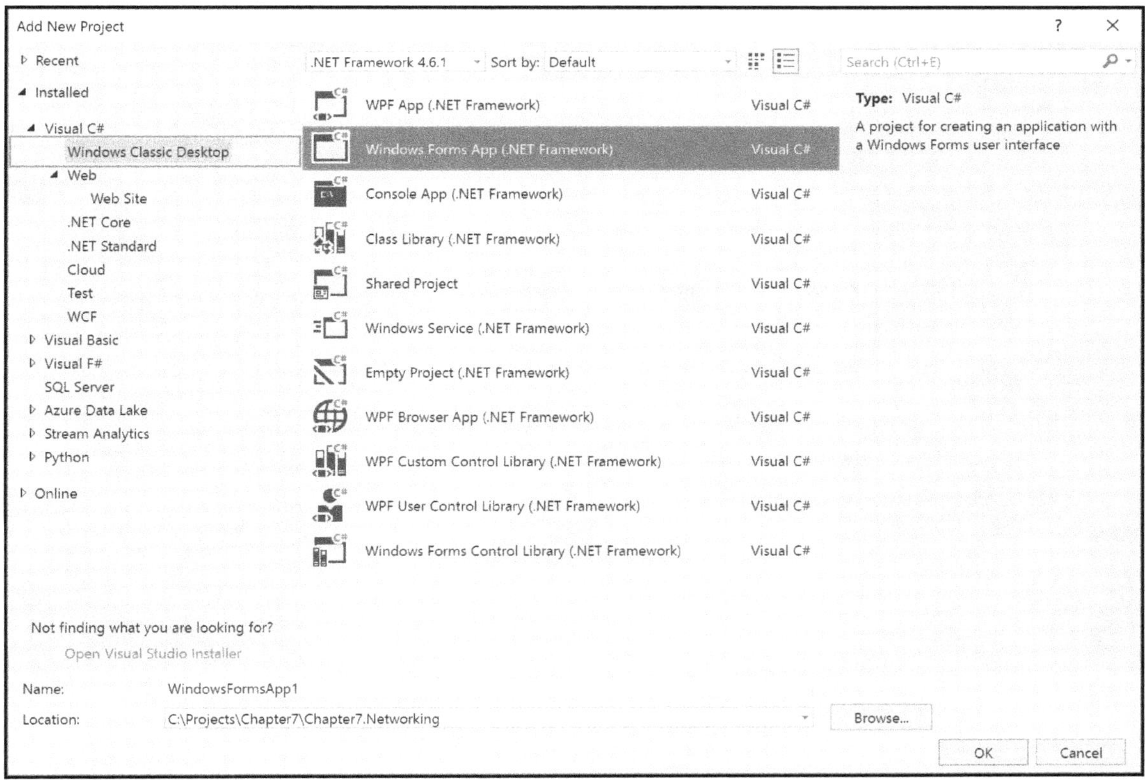

7. In the **Name:** textbox, type `Chapter7.Networking.IPListWindows` as the name of the project. The rest of the fields can be left at the defaults:

8. Click **OK**.
9. Now the **Solution Explorer** (press *Ctrl* + *Alt* + *L*) should look like this:

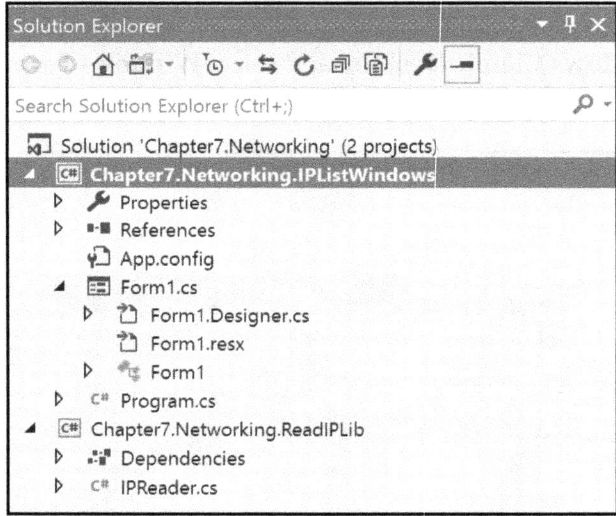

10. Click the right mouse button on the **References** label in `Chapter7.Networking.IPListWindows`.
11. Select **Add Reference**.

12. In the **Reference Manager**, click on the **Projects** label in the right pane:

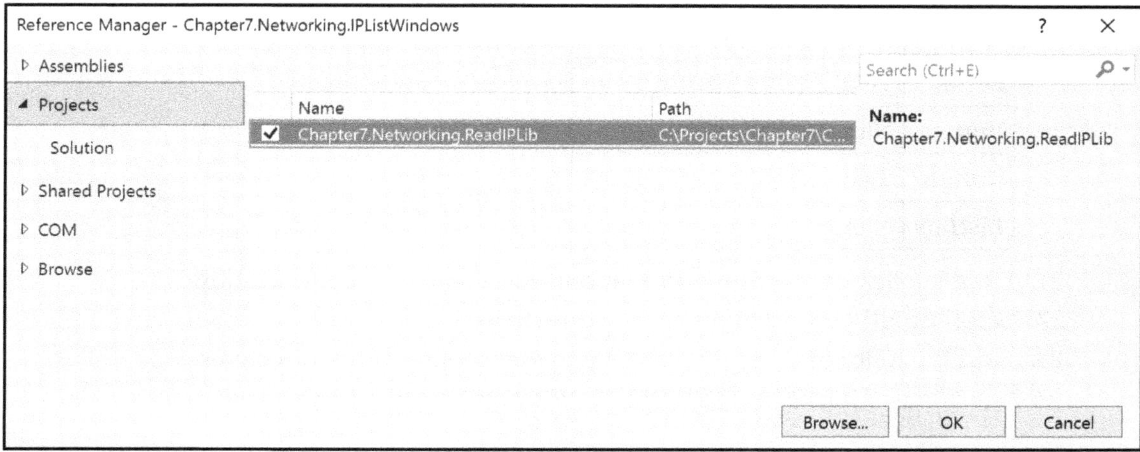

13. Check the `Chapter7.Networking.ReadIPLib` project in the left pane.
14. Click **OK**.
15. Now click on the `Form1.cs` from the project list and rename it to `MainForm.cs`.
16. Answer **Yes** to the confirmation dialog box.
17. Now click on the **MainForm.cs[Design]** tab.
18. From the toolbox, add a **Button** control and a **ListBox** control to the **MainWindow** form:

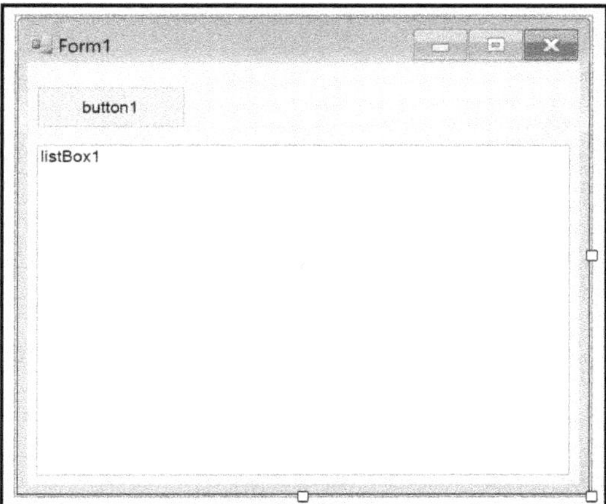

19. Select the button and press *F4* to load the **Properties** window.
20. Now change the following properties:

Control	Property	Value
Form	Text	IP List
Button	Name	ShowButton
Button	Text	Show IP List
ListBox	Name	IPListBox

21. Double-click on the **Show IP List** button to reach the code window.
22. Scroll up till you reach the `using` directives.
23. Add the following `using` directive to the last line of the directives:

```
using Chapter7.Networking.ReadIPLib;
```

24. Now, again scroll down till you reach the `ShowButton_Click()` method.
25. Type the following code inside the method:

```
var ipLib = new IPReader();
IPListBox.Items.AddRange(ipLib.GetMyIPAddress().ToArray());
```

26. Now press *F5* to debug the code.
27. Click on the **Show IP List** button.
28. You should see output like this:

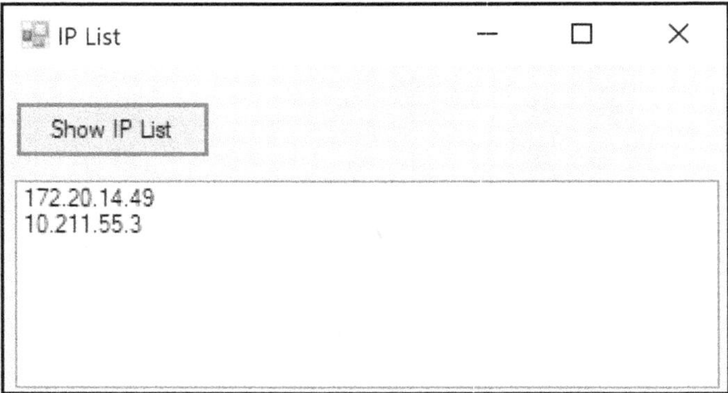

29. Close the window.

How it works...

In steps 1 to 10, we opened the previously built solution and did a quick build to check everything was intact. Then, we added a Classic Windows Forms application to the solution. In steps 11 to 14, we added the reference to the .NET Standard 2.0 class library that we built in the previous recipe. In steps 15 to 20, we renamed the main window and then we added the UI. Finally, we changed the properties of the controls in a meaningful way.

In step 23, we referenced the class library in the code. In step 25, we created an instance of the `IPReader` class and then used the `GetMyIPAddress()` method. In the same line, we output the return `List<string>` as an array and used the `ListBox`, `AddRange` method to populate the list box.

In steps 26 to 29, we executed the code and tested the results.

Creating a library that sends mail

In this recipe, we will be looking at another area of the `System.Net` namespace. We will be using it to create and send an email. Mainly, we will be looking at the `SmptClient` class to do the hard work for us.

Getting ready

Make sure you have the latest version of Visual Studio 2017 and all the updates installed. We will be building a .NET Standard 2.0 library to send an email.

How to do it...

1. Open Visual Studio 2017.
2. Click **File** | **New** | **Project** to create a project.
3. In the **New Project** dialog box, expand the **Other Project Types** node in the left pane and select **Visual Studio Solutions**. In the right pane, select **Blank Solution**.

4. In the **Name:** textbox, type `Chapter7.MailBox` and in the **Location:** textbox select a path from the drop-down box or click on the **Browse...** button to locate a path:

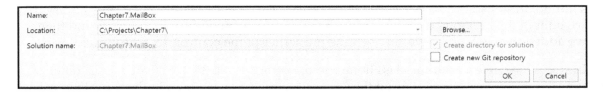

5. Click **OK**.
6. Now your **Solution Explorer** (*Ctrl* + *Alt* + *L*) should look like this:

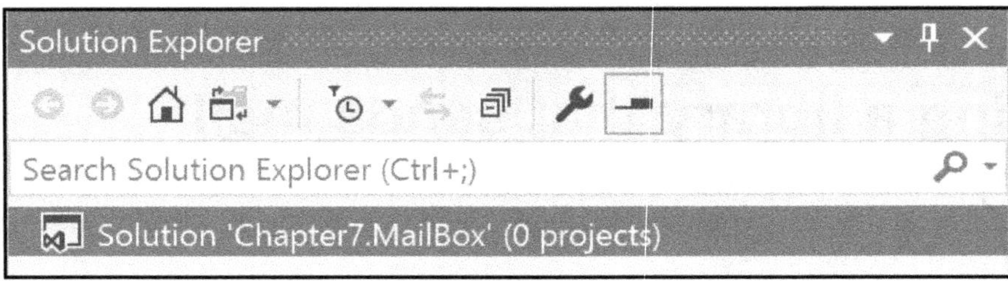

7. Now, click the right mouse button on the `Chapter7.MailBox` label in the **Solution Explorer** and select **Add** | **New Project**.
8. In the **New Project** dialog box, expand the **Visual C#** node.
9. Select **.NET Standard** in the left pane and **Class Library (.NET Standard)** in the right pane:

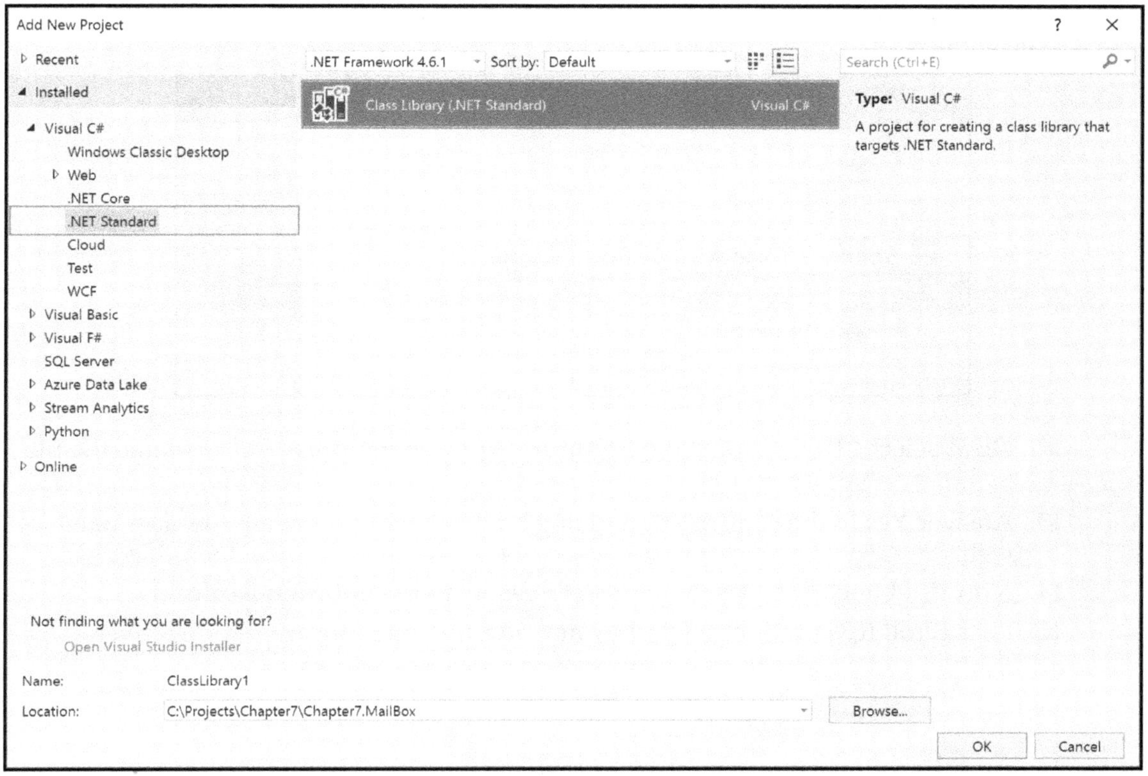

Add New Project
Recent
Installed
Visual C#
Windows Classic Desktop
Web
.NET Core
.NET Standard
Cloud
Test
WCF
Visual Basic
Visual F#
SQL Server
Azure Data Lake
Stream Analytics
Python
Online
.NET Framework 4.6.1
Sort by: Default
Class Library (.NET Standard)
Visual C#
Search (Ctrl+E)
Type: Visual C#
A project for creating a class library that targets .NET Standard.
Not finding what you are looking for?
Open Visual Studio Installer
Name: ClassLibrary1
Location: C:\Projects\Chapter7\Chapter7.MailBox
Browse...
OK
Cancel

10. In the **Name:** textbox, type `Chapter7.MailBox.MailerLib`, leave the other defaults as is, and click **OK**:

Name: Chapter7.MailBox.MailerLib
Location: C:\Projects\Chapter7\Chapter7.MailBox
Browse...
OK
Cancel

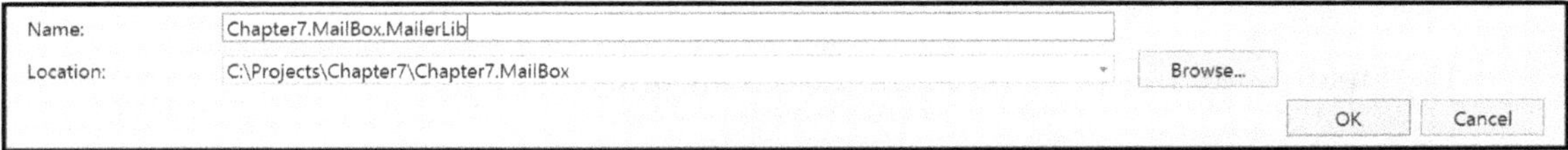

11. Now the **Solution Explorer** (*Ctrl* + *Alt* + *L*) should look like this:

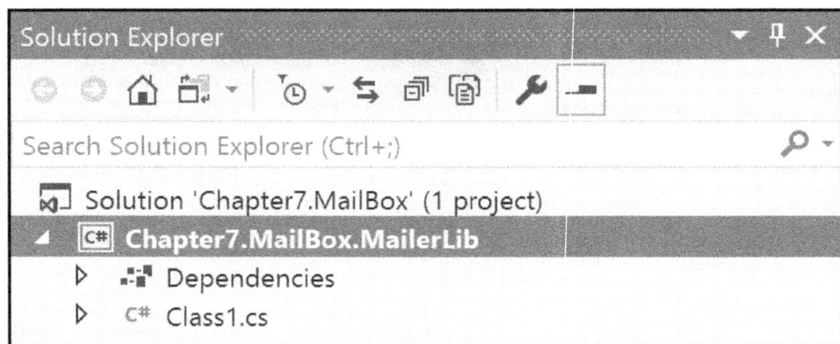

12. Now, select `Class1.cs` in the **Solution Explorer** and press *F2* to rename the file to `SendMail.cs`.
13. Answer **Yes** to the confirmation dialog box that asks to rename the class name as well.
14. Now double-click on the `SendMail.cs` label in the **Solution Explorer**.
15. Let's scroll up in the code window and add the following `using` directive:

```
using System.Net;
using System.Net.Mail;
```

16. Add the following four properties to the `SendMail` class:

```
public string From { get; set; }
public string To { get; set; }
public string Subject { get; set; }
public string Body { get; set; }
```

17. Finally, add this `public` method to create and send mail:

```
public void Send()
{
    var toAddress = new MailAddress(To);
    var fromAddress = new MailAddress(From);
    var message = new MailMessage(fromAddress, toAddress);
    message.Subject = Subject;
    message.Body = Body;

    var credentials = new NetworkCredential("<your_smtp_username>",
"<your_smtp_password>");
    var smtp = new SmtpClient();
    smtp.Host = "<smtp_host>";
```

```
        smtp.Port = <port>;
        smtp.EnableSsl = true;
        smtp.Credentials = credentials;
        smtp.DeliveryMethod = SmtpDeliveryMethod.Network;

        smtp.Send(message);
    }
```

18. Let's press *Ctrl* + *Shift* + *B* for a quick build.

How it works...

In steps 1 to 11, we created a blank solution and added a .NET Standard 2.0 class library project to it. Then, we properly named the solution and its project. In steps 12 to 14, we renamed the default class generated from Visual Studio. In step 15, we added the necessary namespaces to send a mail in the `using` directive section. In step 16, we added four properties to the main class. These properties will store the mail addresses, subject, and the body of the mail.

In step 17, we wrote the actual code to prepare and send the mail. In the first two lines, we used the from and to addresses and converted them to `MailAddress` type. Then, we created a `MailMessage` and attached the body and the subject, along with the addresses. Then, we created the network credentials required to access the given SMTP server.

Then, we created an `SmtpClient` object, attached the credentials, and sent the mail. Finally, we did a quick build to check the syntax.

Creating a WPF application to use the library

In this recipe, we will be creating a Windows Presentation Foundation application to use the library we have created. We will be creating a UI to send an email using the library.

Getting ready

Make sure you have completed the previous recipe for sending an email. If you have completed it, open it up and do a quick build to check everything works fine.

How to do it...

1. Open Visual Studio 2017.
2. Now open the solution from the previous recipe. Click **File** | **Open** | **Open Project/Solution** or press *Ctrl* + *Shift* + *O* and select the `Chapter7.MailBox` solution.
3. Press *Ctrl* + *Shift* + *B* for a quick build to check everything is fine.
4. Click on the `Chapter7.MailBox` solution label. Click **File** | **Add** | **New Project**.
5. In the **Add New Project** template dialog box, expand the **Visual C#** node in the left pane.
6. Select **Windows Classic Desktop** and select **WPF App (.NET Framework)** in the right pane:

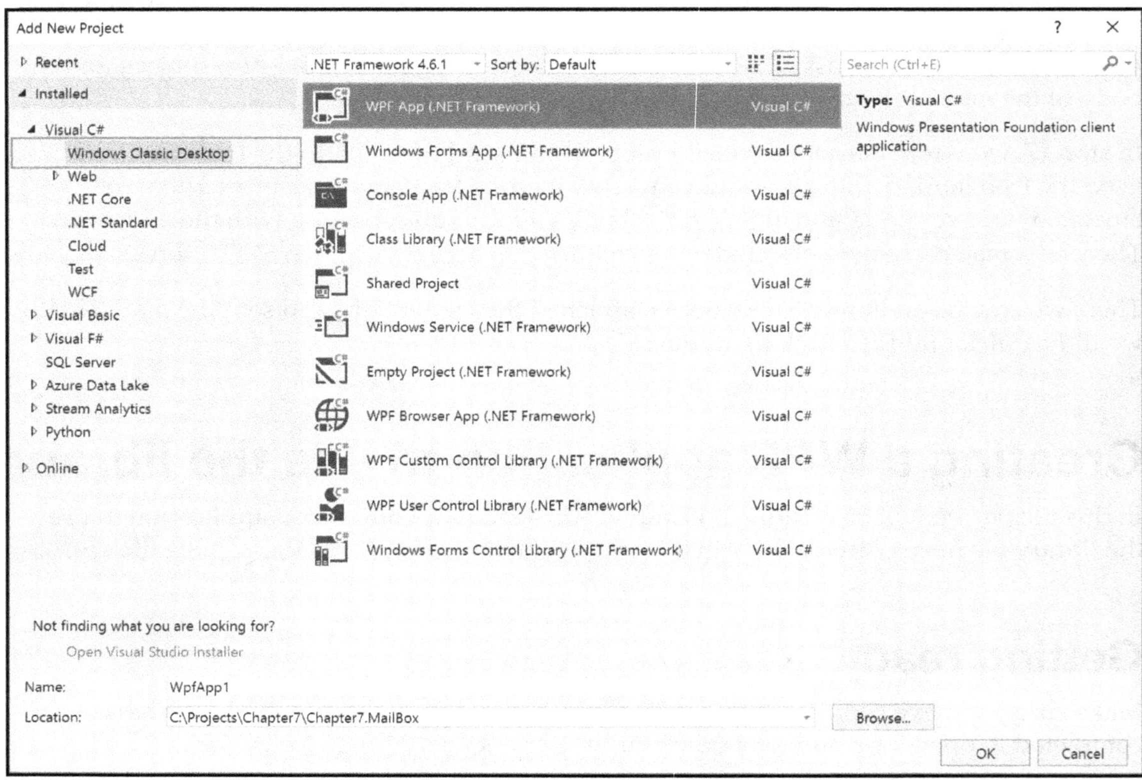

7. Now, in the **Name:** textbox type `Chapter7.MailBox.WPFMail` as the name of the project. The rest of the fields can be left at the defaults:

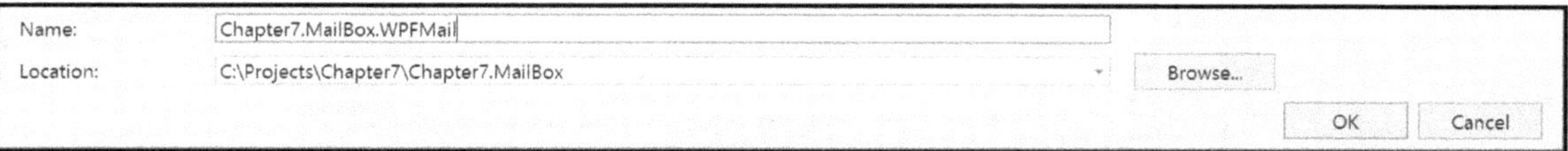

8. Click **OK**.
9. Now the **Solution Explorer** (press *Ctrl* + *Alt* + *L*) should look like this:

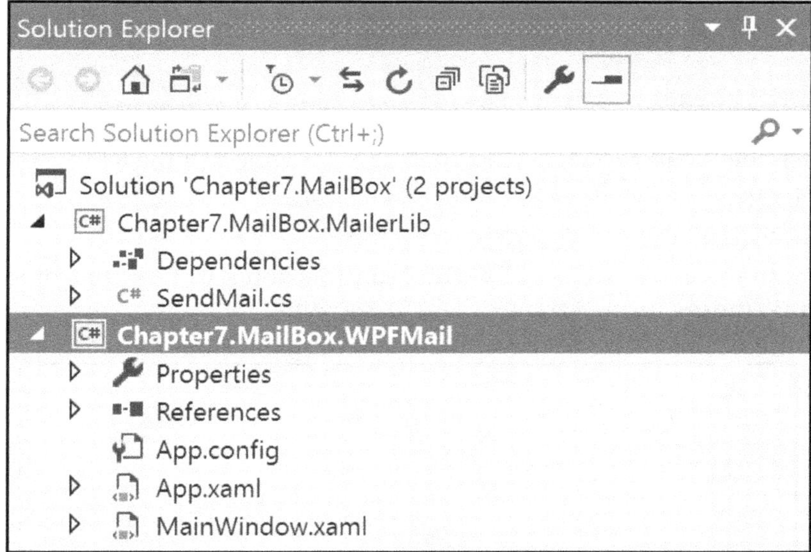

10. Click the right mouse button on the **References** label in `Chapter7.MailBox.WPFMail`.
11. Select **Add Reference**.

12. In the **Reference Manager**, click on the **Projects** label in the right pane:

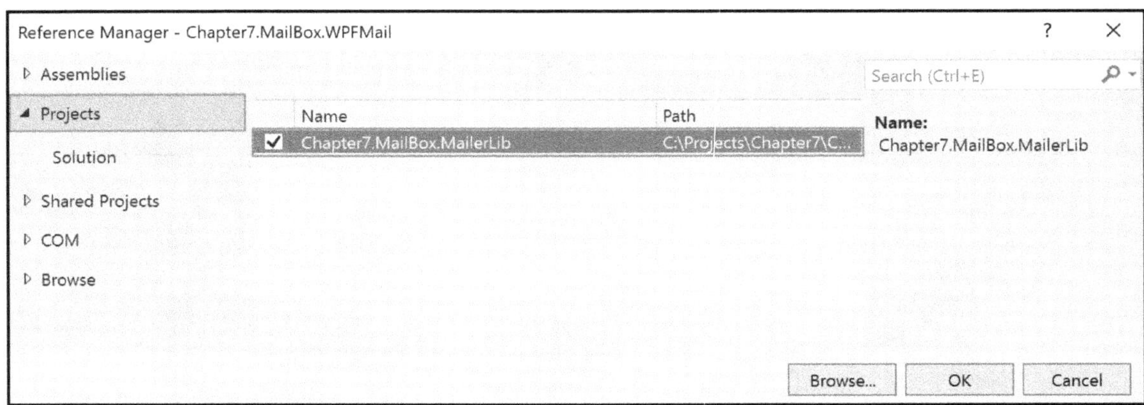

13. Check the `Chapter7.MailBox.MailerLib` project in the left pane.
14. Click **OK**.
15. Now click on the `MainWindow.xaml` tab.
16. From the toolbox, add four **TextBox** controls and a **Button** control to the **MainWindow** form. Arrange them as shown:

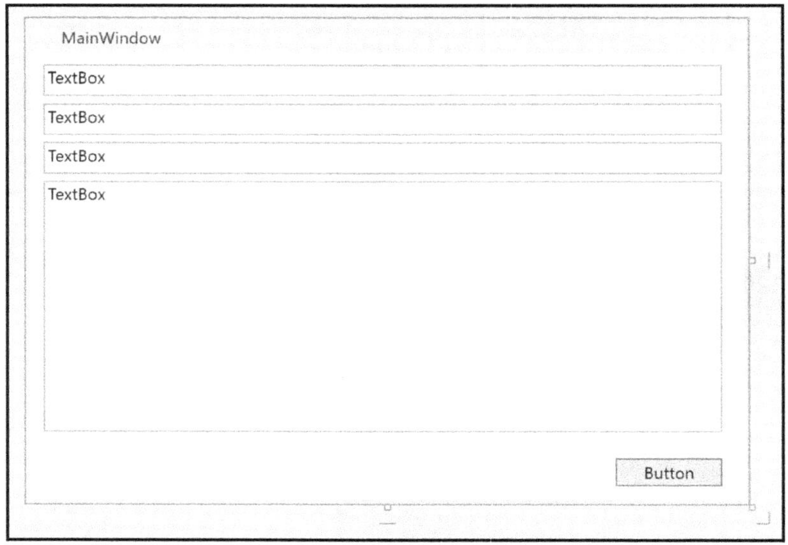

17. Select the **TextBox** and press *F4* to load the **Properties** window.

18. Now change the following properties (from the top as per the previous UI):

Control	Property	Value
TextBox	**Name**	`FromTextBox`
TextBox	**Text**	`From Address`
TextBox	**Name**	`ToTextBox`
TextBox	**Text**	`To Address`
TextBox	**Name**	`SubjectTextBox`
TextBox	**Text**	`Subject`
TextBox	**Name**	`BodyTextBox`
TextBox	**Text**	`Body`
TextBox	**AcceptReturn** (*turning on this property will make the text box multi-line*)	**True**
Button	**Name**	`SendButton`
Button	**Text**	`Send`

19. Now your UI should look like this:

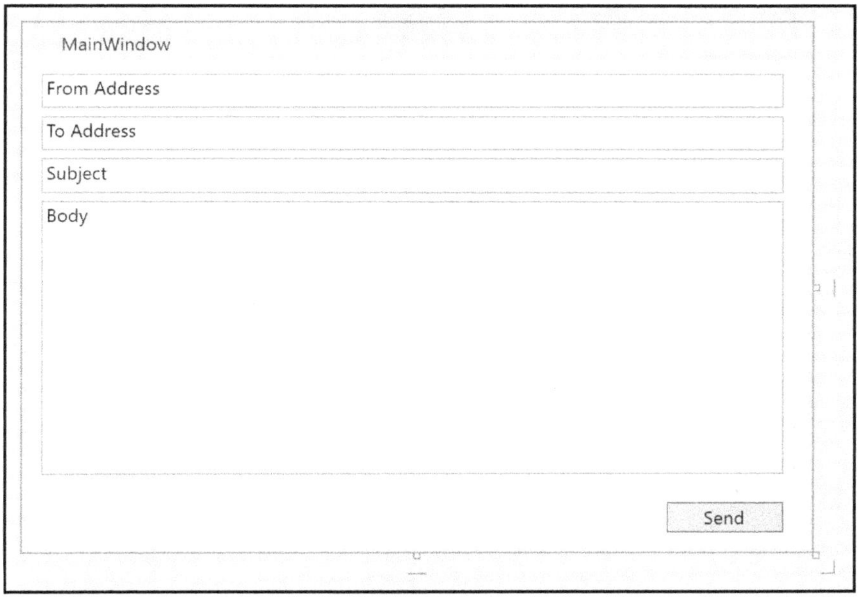

20. Double-click on the **Send** button to open up the code window.
21. Scroll up till you reach the `using` directives.
22. Add the following `using` directive to the last line of the directives:

```
using Chapter7.MailBox.MailerLib;
```

23. Scroll down until you reach the `SendButton_Click()` method and add the following code:

```
var mailer = new SendMail();

mailer.From = FromTextBox.Text;
mailer.To = ToTextBox.Text;
mailer.Subject = SubjectTextBox.Text;
mailer.Body = BodyTextBox.Text;

mailer.Send();

MessageBox.Show("Your mail has been sent");
```

24. Make sure you have changed the required credentials in the library for your SMTP server.
25. Let's test our application by pressing *F5*:

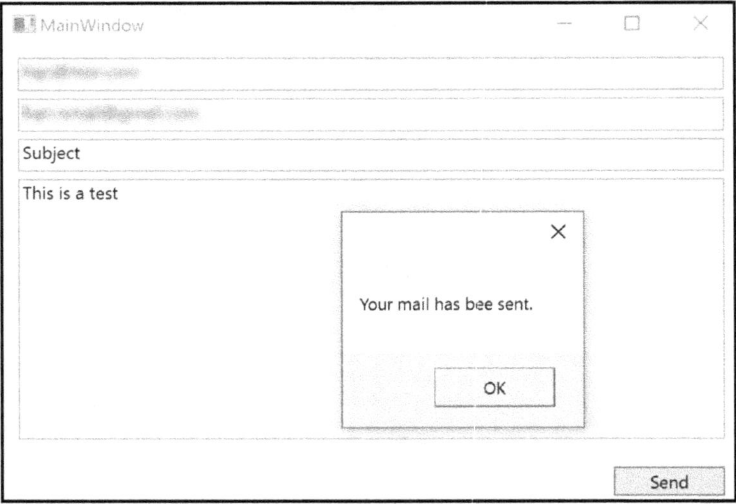

26. Click **OK** and close the window.

How it works...

In steps 1 to 14, we opened the solution with the library. Then, we added a WPF application project to the solution. Later, we added the reference to the class library. In steps 16 to 20, we built the UI and changed a few properties. In step 22, we created the reference to the library at the code level.

Finally, we added the code for a button click, which is straightforward, created an instance of the `SendMail` class, and then populated the properties from the UI itself. Finally, in steps 24 and 25 we tested the output.

Creating a library to call a REST API

In this recipe, we will be looking at a .NET Standard 2.0 library that calls a REST API. RESTful APIs are services that allow you to access its functionality through HTTP. We will be using the `System.Net.Http` namespace inside the library to send a message to an API and get back the results.

Getting ready

Make sure you have the latest version of Visual Studio 2017. Also make sure you have a basic understanding of accessing a web service, what a `GET` method is, what a `POST` method is, and so on. We will be using a test API service provided by `JSONPlaceHolder`. It's a simple REST API test bed for developers.

How to do it...

1. Open Visual Studio 2017.
2. Click **File** | **New** | **Project** to create a project.
3. In the **New Project** dialog box, expand the **Other Project Types** node in the left pane and select **Visual Studio Solutions**. In the right pane, select **Blank Solution**.

4. In the **Name:** textbox, type `Chapter7.RestAPI` and in the **Location:** textbox select a path from the drop-down box or click on the **Browse...** button to locate a path:

5. Click **OK**.
6. Now your **Solution Explorer** (*Ctrl* + *Alt* + *L*) should look like this:

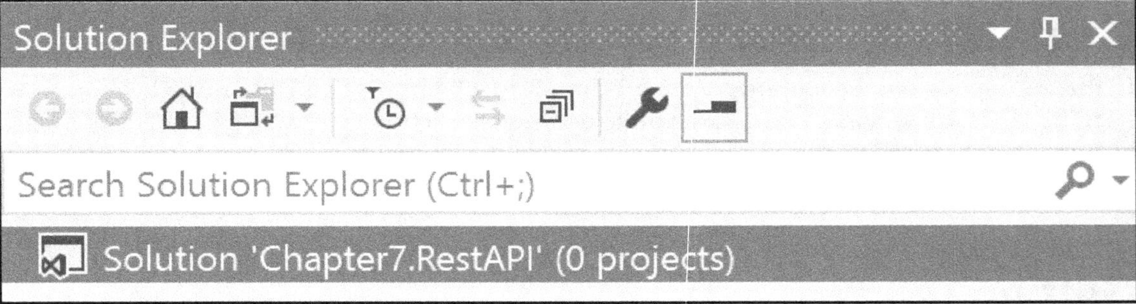

7. Now, click the right mouse button on the `Chapter7.RestAPI` label in the **Solution Explorer** and select **Add** | **New Project**.
8. In the **New Project** dialog box, expand the **Visual C#** node.

9. Select **.NET Standard** in the left pane and **Class Library (.NET Standard)** in the right pane:

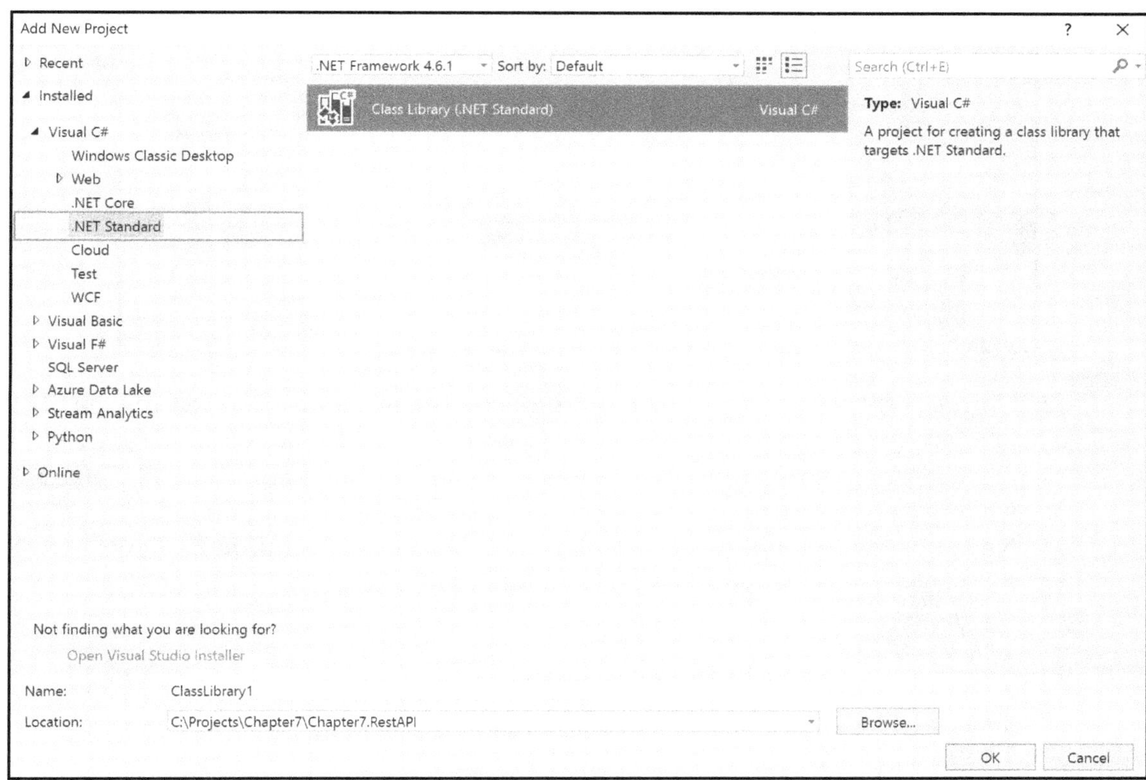

10. Now, in the **Name:** textbox type `Chapter7.RestAPI.RestLib`, leave the other defaults as they are, and click **OK**:

11. Now the **Solution Explorer** (*Ctrl* + *Alt* + *L*) should look like this:

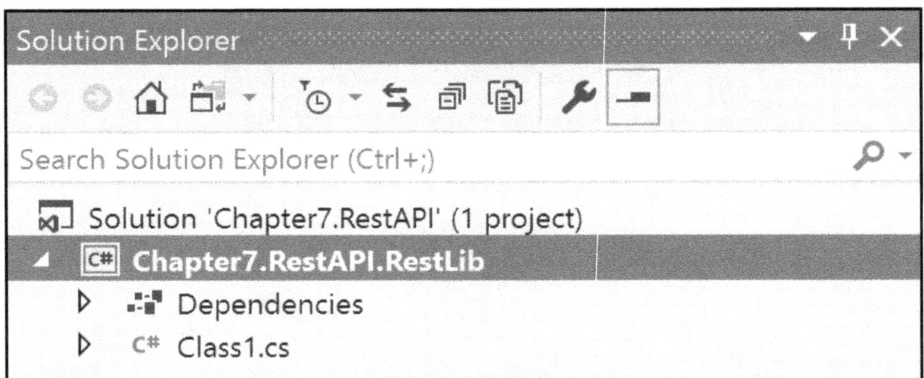

12. Now, select `Class1.cs` in the **Solution Explorer** and press *F2* to rename the file to `PostsReader.cs`.
13. Answer **Yes** to the confirmation dialog box that asks to rename the class name as well.
14. Now, double-click on the `PostsReader.cs` label in the **Solution Explorer**.
15. Let's scroll up in the code window and add the following `using` directive:

```
using System.Net.Http;
using System.Threading.Tasks;
```

16. Now, create this class-wide `private` variable to hold the URL:

```
private string _serviceURL;
```

17. Let's create the default constructor to update the previous variable:

```
public PostsReader(string serviceURL)
{
    _serviceURL = serviceURL;
}
```

18. Finally, let's add the method to read from the REST service:

```
public async Task<string> GetPostById(int id)
{
    string output;

    using (var httpClient = new HttpClient())
    {
```

```
            Uri uri = new Uri($"{_serviceURL}/posts/{id}");
            using (HttpResponseMessage response =
                await httpClient.GetAsync(uri))
            {
                output = await response.Content.ReadAsStringAsync();
            }
        }
        return output;
    }
```

19. Press *Ctrl* + *Shift* + *B* for a quick build to check the syntax.

How it works...

In steps 1 to 11, we created an empty solution. Then we added a .NET Standard 2.0 library to that solution. Again, as a good practice we properly named the solution and the class library project. In steps 12 and 13, we changed the name of the default `Class1.cs` created by Visual Studio. In step 15, we added `using` directives required for our task. In step 16, we created a class-wide private variable to hold the service URL. Then, in step 16 we created the default constructor with a `string` parameter that updates the private variable in step 15.

In step 18, we created the `public` method that did the actual work of reading the RESTful API. In the first line of code, we created a `string` variable that held the output from the service. Then, we created an instance of the `HttpClient` class inside a `using` statement. This is a good practice that will make sure the class is destroyed after we exit the `using` statement.

Then we populated the **Universal Resource Indicator** (**URI**) to the service. After that, we did the actual call to the service and stored it inside a `HttpResponseMessage` variable. Finally, we got the output from the response and returned the output.

Creating an ASP.NET MVC application to use the library

In this recipe, we will be creating an ASP.NET MVC application to use the library we have created.

Getting ready

Make sure you have completed the previous recipe. If not, you need to complete it before going through this one. If you have already done it, open it and do a quick build before we start.

How to do it..

1. Open Visual Studio 2017.
2. Now open the solution from the previous recipe. Click **File** | **Open** | **Open Project/Solution** or press *Ctrl* + *Shift* + *O* and select the `Chapter7.RestAPI` solution.
3. Press *Ctrl* + *Shift* + *B* for a quick build to check everything is fine.
4. Now click on the `Chapter7.RestAPI` solution label. Click **File** | **Add** | **New Project**.
5. In the **Add New Project** template dialog box, expand the **Visual C#** node in the left pane.
6. Select **Web** and select **ASP.NET Web Application (.NET Framework)** in the right pane:

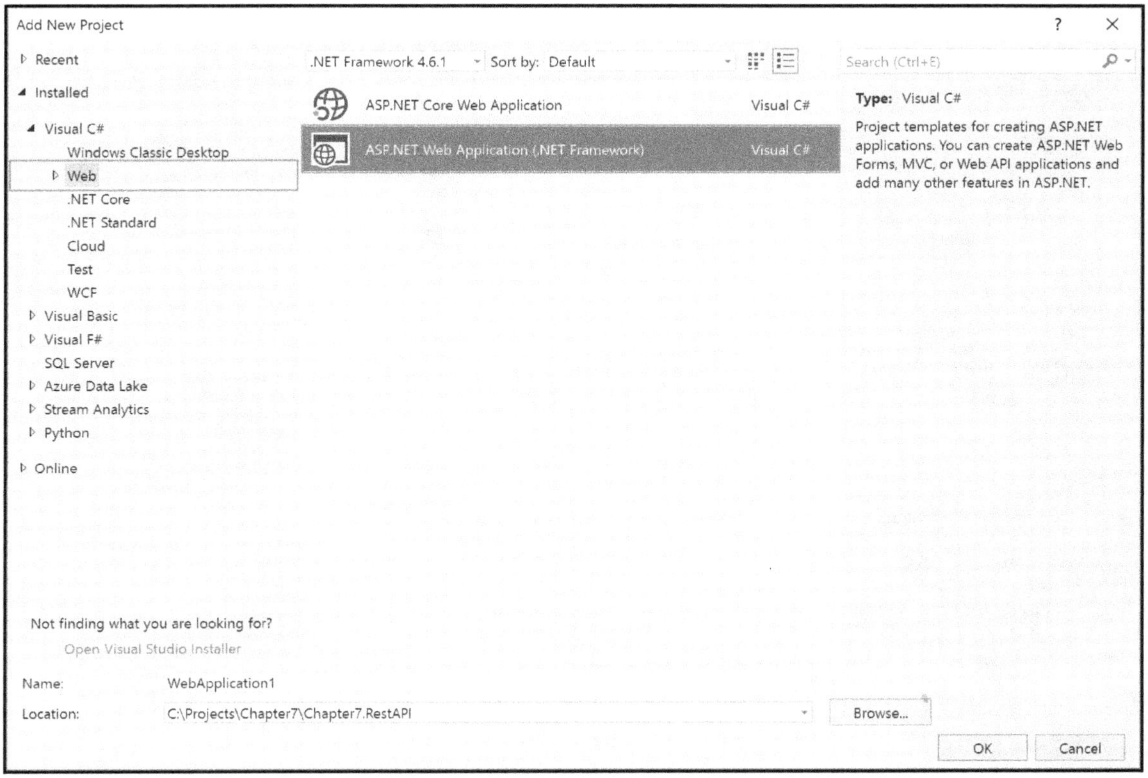

Add New Project

▷ Recent
◢ Installed
◢ Visual C#
Windows Classic Desktop
▷ Web
.NET Core
.NET Standard
Cloud
Test
WCF
▷ Visual Basic
▷ Visual F#
SQL Server
▷ Azure Data Lake
▷ Stream Analytics
▷ Python
▷ Online

.NET Framework 4.6.1 Sort by: Default

ASP.NET Core Web Application Visual C#
ASP.NET Web Application (.NET Framework) Visual C#

Search (Ctrl+E)

Type: Visual C#

Project templates for creating ASP.NET applications. You can create ASP.NET Web Forms, MVC, or Web API applications and add many other features in ASP.NET.

Not finding what you are looking for?
Open Visual Studio Installer

Name: WebApplication1
Location: C:\Projects\Chapter7\Chapter7.RestAPI
Browse...
OK Cancel

7. Now, in the **Name:** textbox type `Chapter7.RestAPI.RestMVC` as the name and leave the **Location:** textbox at its default value:

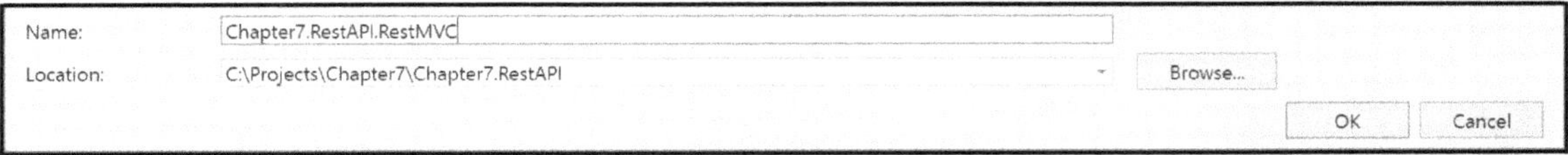

8. In the **New ASP.NET Web Application** dialog box, select **Empty** from the template list.

9. Select **MVC** for the **Add folders and core references for:** option:

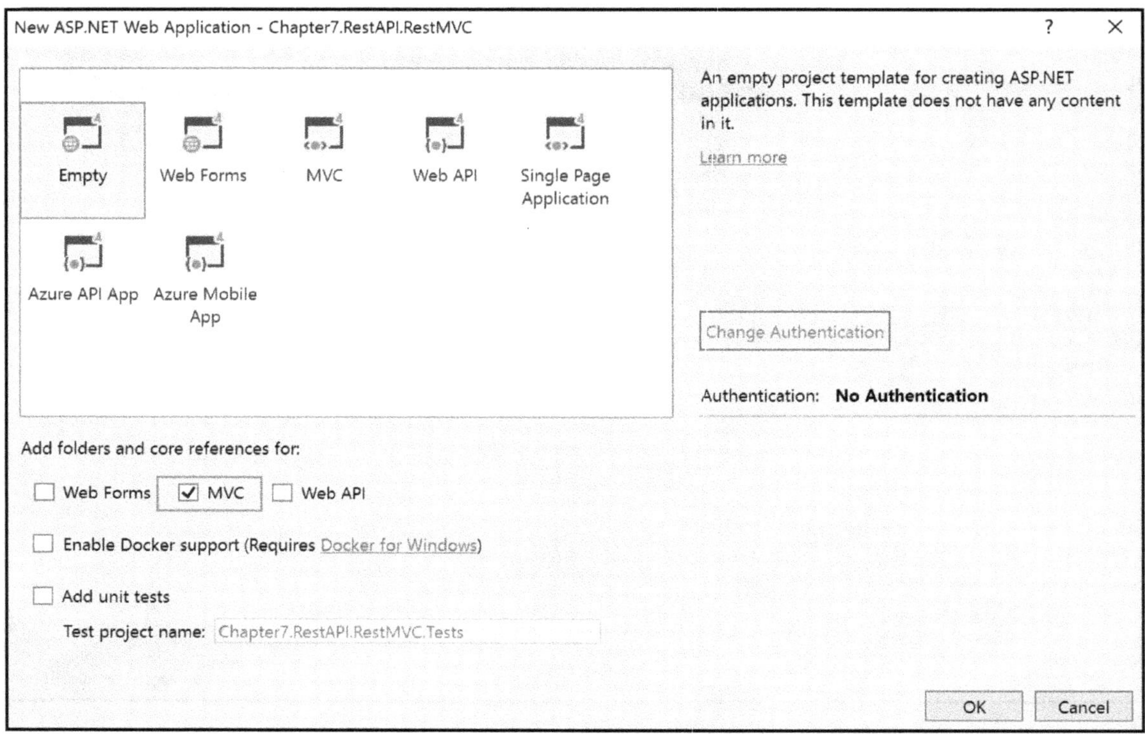

10. Leave the rest as is and click **OK** to create the default **ASP.NET MVC Web** application template.

11. Now **Solution Explorer** should look like this:

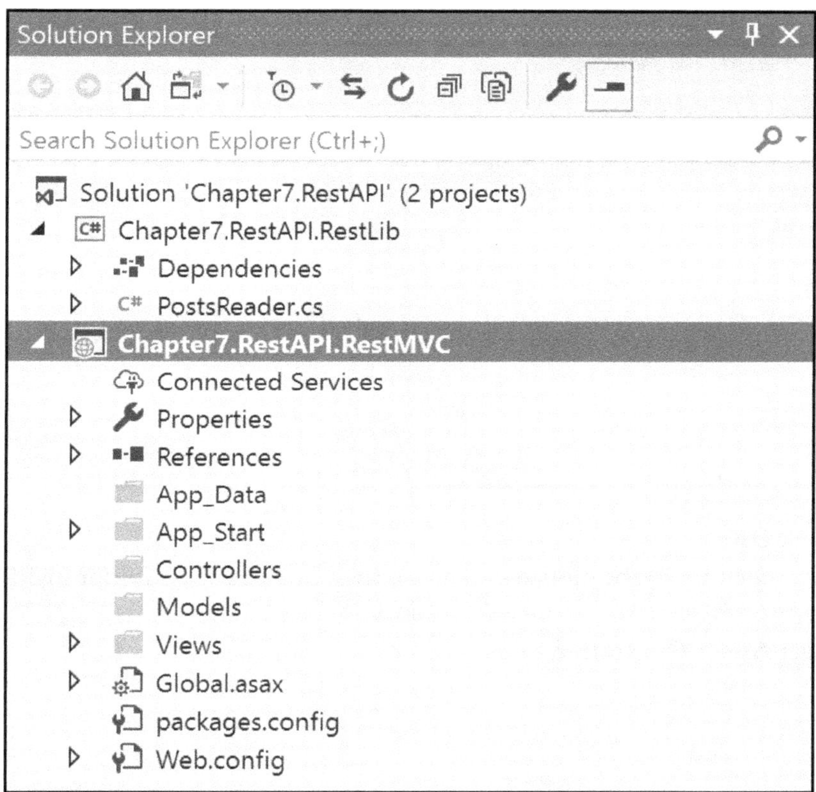

12. Now, click the right mouse button on the **References** label under the `Chapter7.RestAPI.RestMVC` project and select **Add Reference**.

13. In the **Reference Manager** dialog box, select **Projects** in the left pane and select `Chapter7.RestAPI.RestLib` in the right pane:

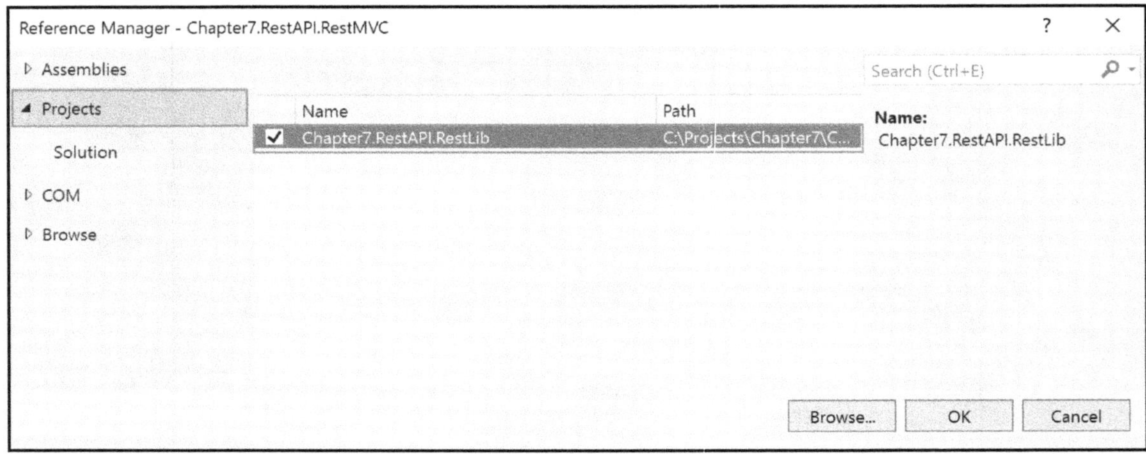

14. Click **OK**.
15. Now, click the right mouse button on the `Controllers` folder inside the `Chapter7.RestAPI.RestMVC` project.
16. Select **Add** | **Controller**.

17. In the **Add Scaffold** dialog box, select **MVC 5 Controller - Empty** from the template list and click **Add**:

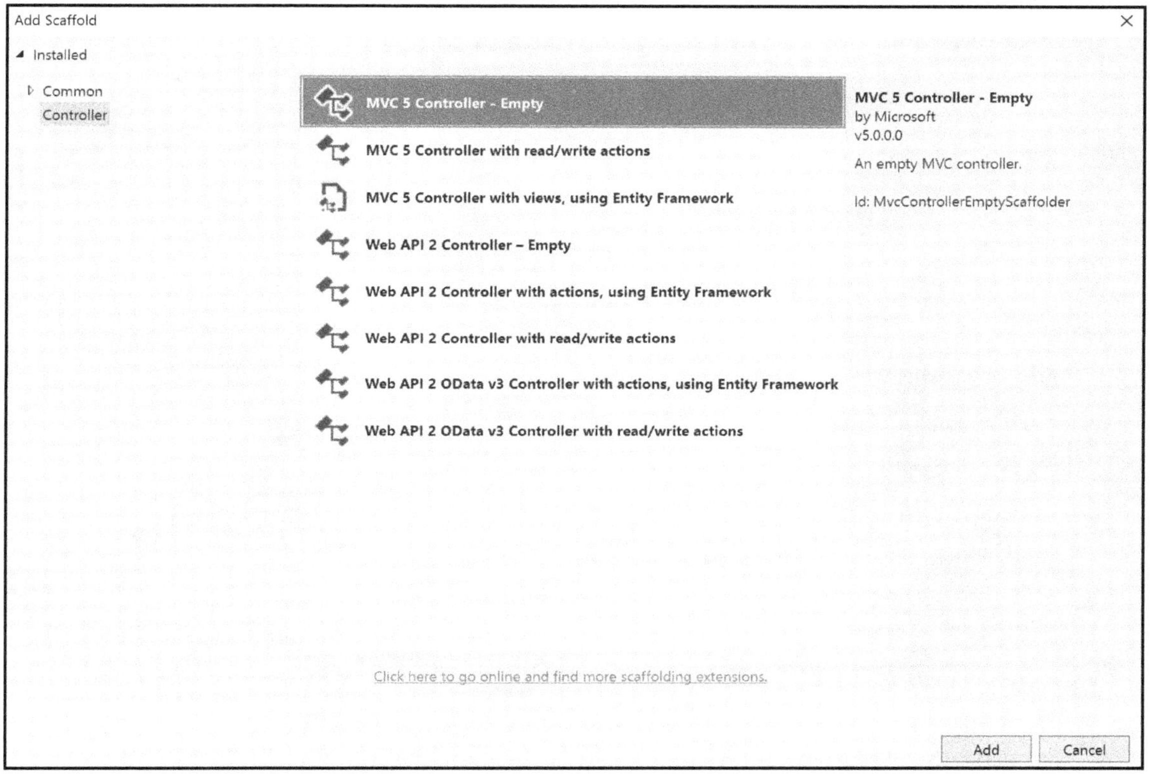

Add Scaffold
Installed
Common
Controller
MVC 5 Controller - Empty
MVC 5 Controller with read/write actions
MVC 5 Controller with views, using Entity Framework
Web API 2 Controller – Empty
Web API 2 Controller with actions, using Entity Framework
Web API 2 Controller with read/write actions
Web API 2 OData v3 Controller with actions, using Entity Framework
Web API 2 OData v3 Controller with read/write actions
MVC 5 Controller - Empty
by Microsoft
v5.0.0.0
An empty MVC controller.
Id: MvcControllerEmptyScaffolder
Click here to go online and find more scaffolding extensions.
Add
Cancel

18. Now, in the **Add Controller** dialog box type `HomeController` in the **Controller name:** textbox:

Add Controller
Controller name:
HomeController
Add
Cancel

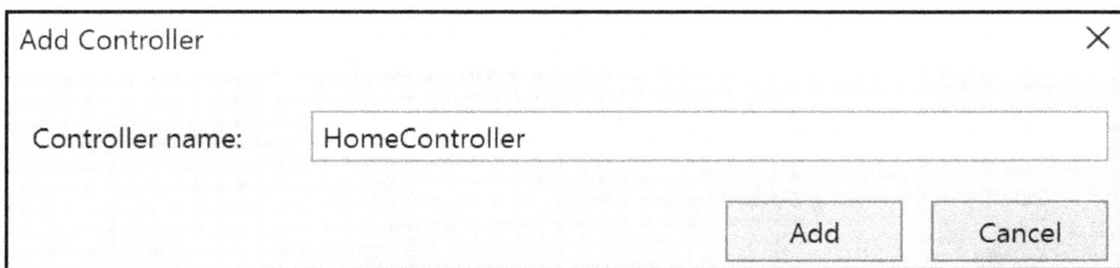

19. Click **Add**.
20. Double-click on the `HomeController.cs` label under the `Controllers` folder.

21. In the code window, click the right mouse button on the `Index()` method name and select **Add View**.
22. Leave the defaults in the **Add View** dialog box and click **Add**:

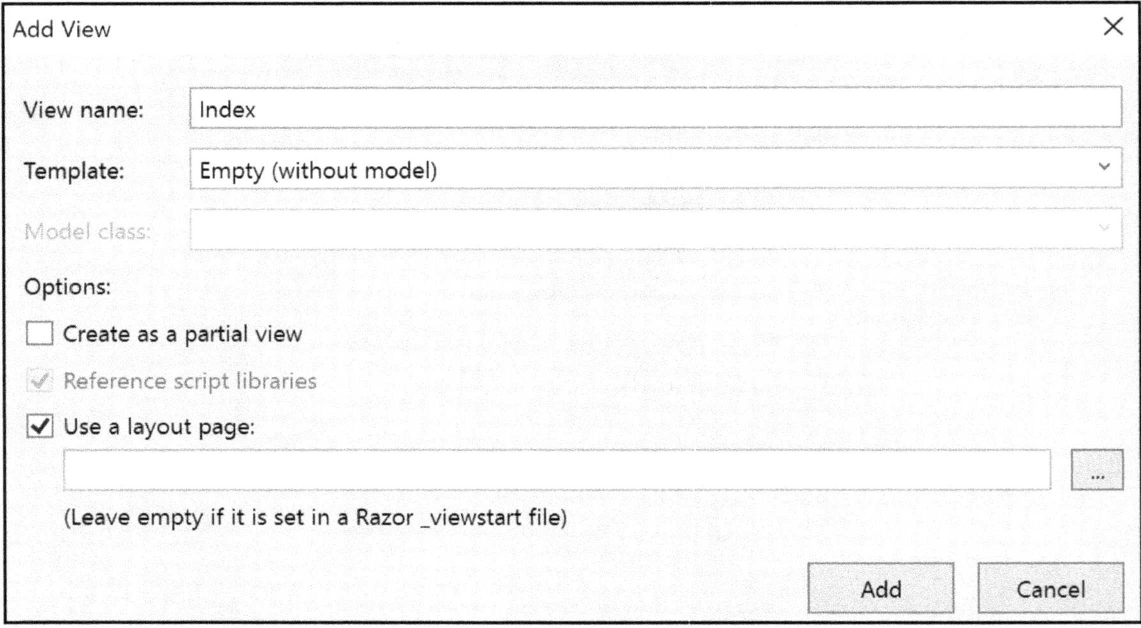

23. Click on the `HomeController.cs` tab in the code window.
24. Add this `using` directive at the top of the code, next to the last line of all the directives:

```
using System.Threading.Tasks;
using System.Web.Script.Serialization;
using Chapter7.RestAPI.RestLib;
```

25. Now change the `default Index()` action to the following:

```
public async Task<ActionResult> Index()
```

26. Add the following code inside the `Index()` method:

```
var service = "https://jsonplaceholder.typicode.com";
var restClient = new PostsReader(service);

var result = await restClient.GetPostById(1);
```

```
ViewBag.Post = new JavaScriptSerializer().Deserialize<Dictionary
    <string, string>>(result);

return View();
```

27. Now, let's open up the `Index.cshtml` file and add the following code beneath the `<h2>Index</h2>` tag:

```
@{
    var post = (Dictionary<string, string>)ViewBag.Post;
}

@foreach (var item in post)
{
    <p>
        <strong>@item.Key</strong> : @item.Value
    </p>
}
```

28. Now, make sure you have set your **MVC project** as the default project.
29. Press *F5* and you should see an output like this:

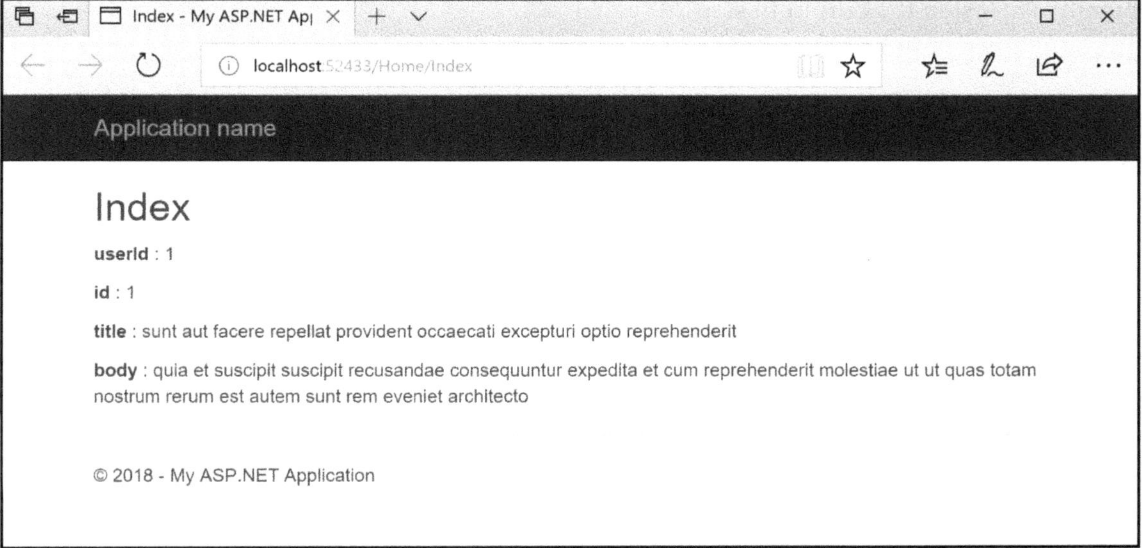

How it works...

In steps 1 to 11, we opened the solution and added an ASP.NET MVC project. Then, we gave a proper name to the project. In steps 12 and 13, we added the reference to the library we built in the previous recipe. In steps 16 to 18, we added an empty controller to the project. Then, in steps 21 and 22 we added a view to the `Index()` action in the `HomeController`.

In step 23, we added the code-level reference to the library itself and added two more namespaces required for our task. In step 24, we changed the `Index()` action to an `async` method. This is required since we will be using an `async` method from the library itself. In step 26, we created the service URL for our test bed. Then, we created an instance of the `PostsReader` class. In the third line, we used the `GetPostById()` method to get the result from the service. Again, in the fourth line of code, we used a method from the `JavaScriptSerializer` class to deserialize the output that came from the service to a Dictionary.

Finally, we stored the result in a `ViewBag` and passed it to the `Index` view. In step 27, we got the Dictionary out of the `ViewBag` and displayed the content using `Razor` syntax.

Finally, we tested the output in step 29.

8
To iOS with Xamarin

In this chapter, we will be looking at these recipes:

- Installing Visual Studio for Mac
- Hello iOS – creating a Xamarin iOS app
- Creating the .NET Standard 2.0 library
- Putting things together and testing the application

Technical requirements

Readers should have a basic knowledge of C#. They should also have a basic knowledge of using Visual Studio, installing packages using NuGet, and referencing libraries within projects from other projects.

The code files for this chapter can be found on GitHub:
`https://github.com/PacktPublishing/DotNET-Standard-2-Cookbook/tree/master/Chapter08`

Check out the following video to see the code in action:
`https://goo.gl/fG1ErJ`

Introduction

Xamarin is a development platform that allows you to build native applications for iOS, Android, and Windows. The most amazing thing about Xamarin is that you can use your existing C# skills to develop these applications. At the beginning, Xamarin was called Xamarin Studio and was used for building applications in both macOS and Windows. Windows users had the extra privilege of using Visual Studio. After its acquisition by Microsoft, Xamarin Studio became Visual Studio for Mac. In this chapter, we will be using Visual Studio for Mac to build our applications, throughout the recipes.

Installing Visual Studio for Mac

In this recipe, we will be looking at how to get Visual Studio for Mac and install it. We will also be looking at setting up a few other things.

Getting ready

Make sure you have a Mac to complete this recipe. Currently, I am using macOS High Sierra version 10.13.3. Also make sure you have already installed the latest version of XCode. XCode is required, alongside Visual Studio, for Mac to build iOS applications.

How to do it...

1. Let's open up your favorite browser.
2. Type `https://www.xamarin.com/download` in the address bar and press *Enter*.
3. You should see a screen similar to this:

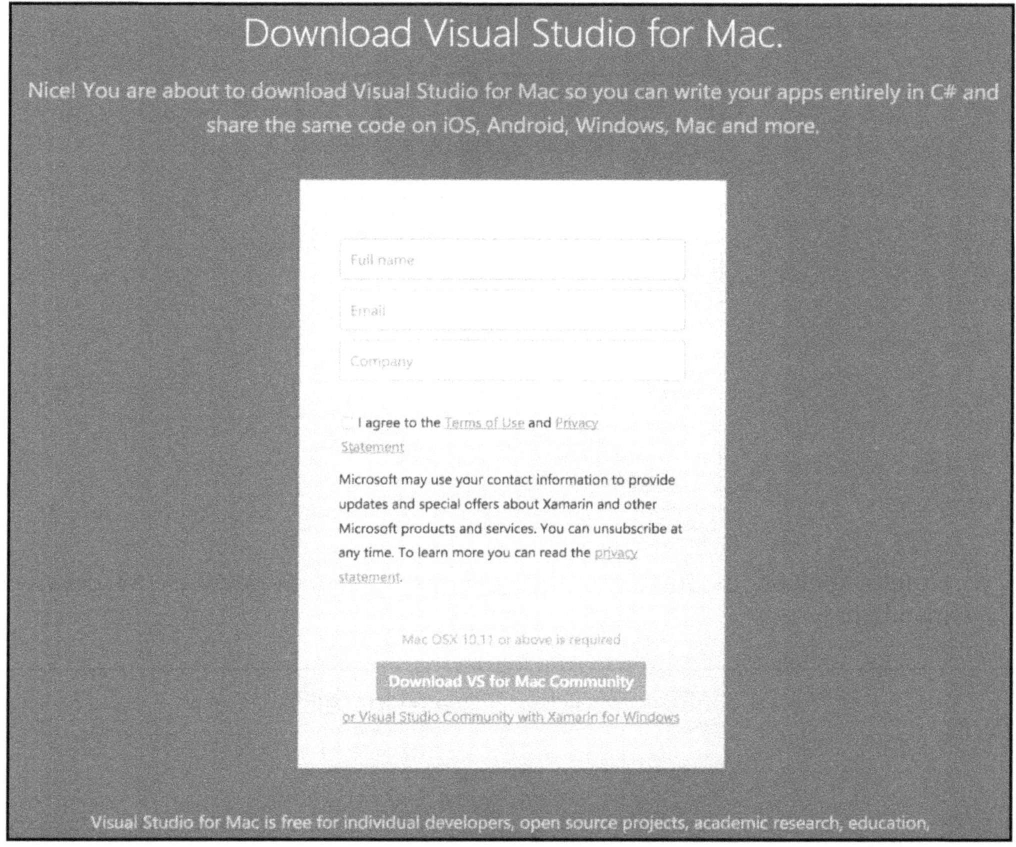

4. Now, fill in your details and press the **Download VS for Mac Community** button.
5. This will download a file to the `Downloads` directory by default, named `VisualStudioForMacInstaller__215259590.1517557727.dmg` or something similar (the end numbers might change when you download it.)
6. Double-click on that file.

7. You should see a window similar to this:

8. Double-click on the down arrow. In the next screen, choose the components to be installed:

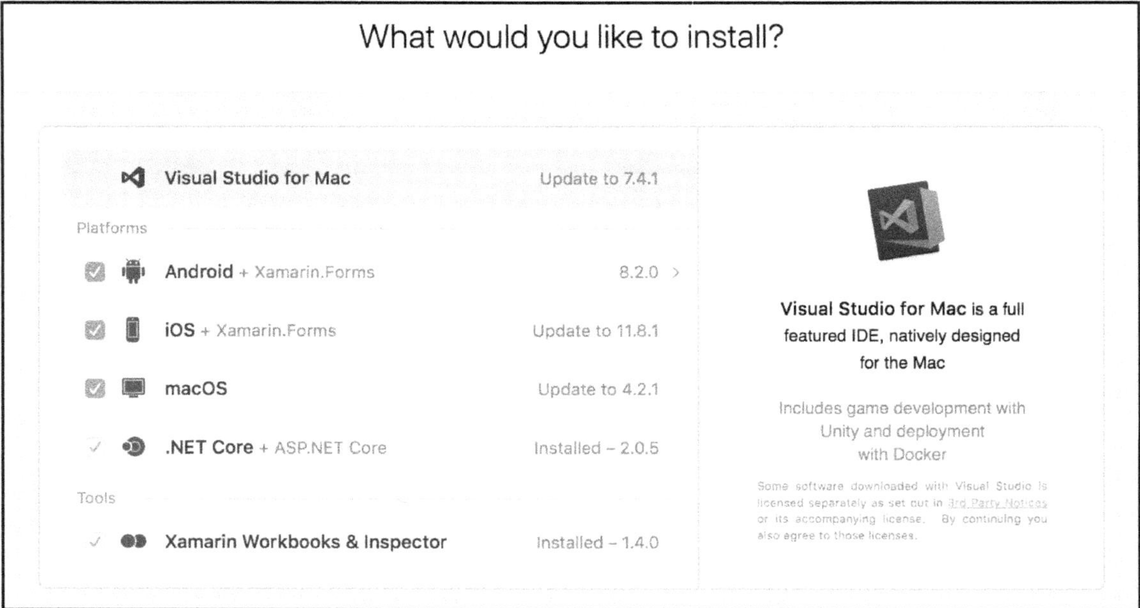

9. Click the **Install** button to install all the components. Make sure you have selected **Android** and **iOS**.
10. After a successful installation, you should see this:

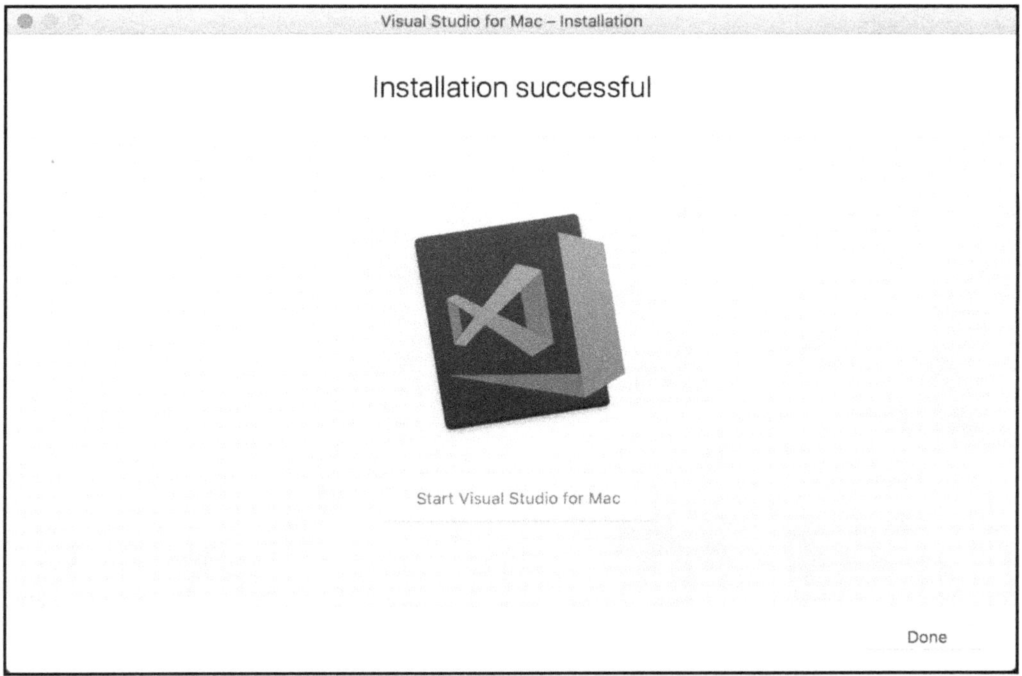

11. Now, you can click **Done** to exit and start **Visual Studio for Mac** to launch the IDE:

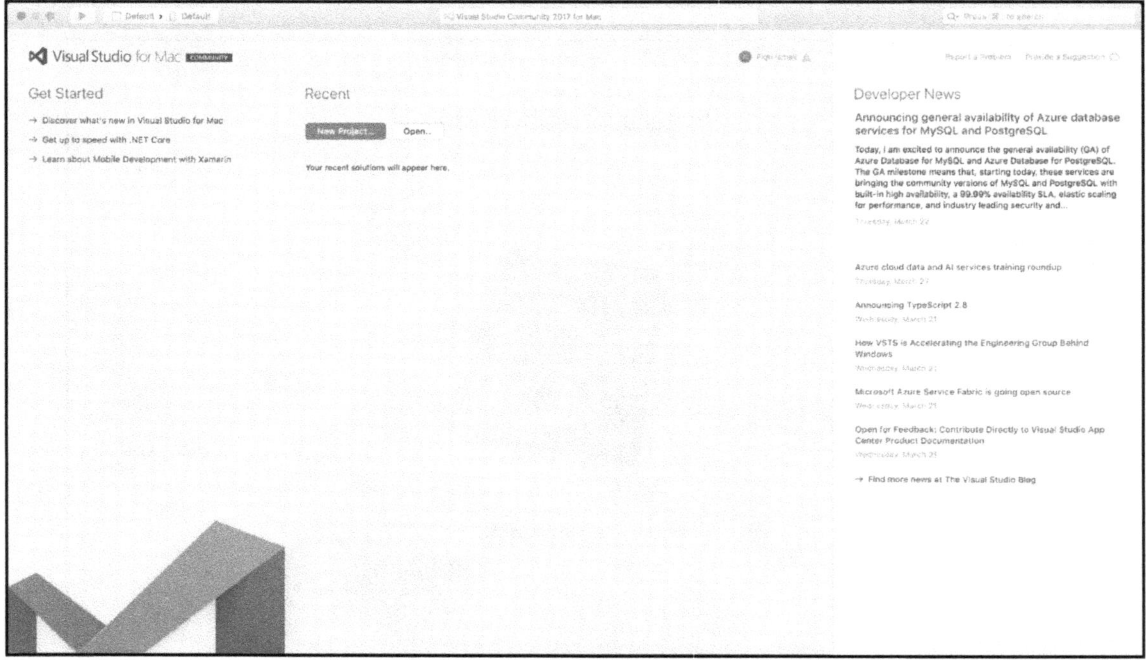

Visual Studio for Mac

How it works...

These are simple steps for installing Visual Studio for Mac. In step 8, you should see **Install** instead of **Update**. This screen appeared because I already have a version of Visual Studio for Mac installed.

Hello iOS – Creating a Xamarin iOS app

In this recipe, we will be creating our first iOS application. This will be a `Hello World` type of application. Later on, we will change this application to use a .NET Standard 2.0 library.

Getting ready

Make sure you have completed the previous recipe and installed Visual Studio for Mac. Also, make sure you have XCode installed alongside Visual Studio for Mac.

How to do it...

1. Open **Finder**.
2. Click **Applications** in the left-hand pane.
3. Now, double-click on the Visual Studio icon.
4. Now, click on the **New Project** button.
5. In the **Choose a template for your project** dialog box, scroll down till you reach the **other** section.
6. Select **Miscellaneous** and, under **Generic**, select **Blank Solution**:

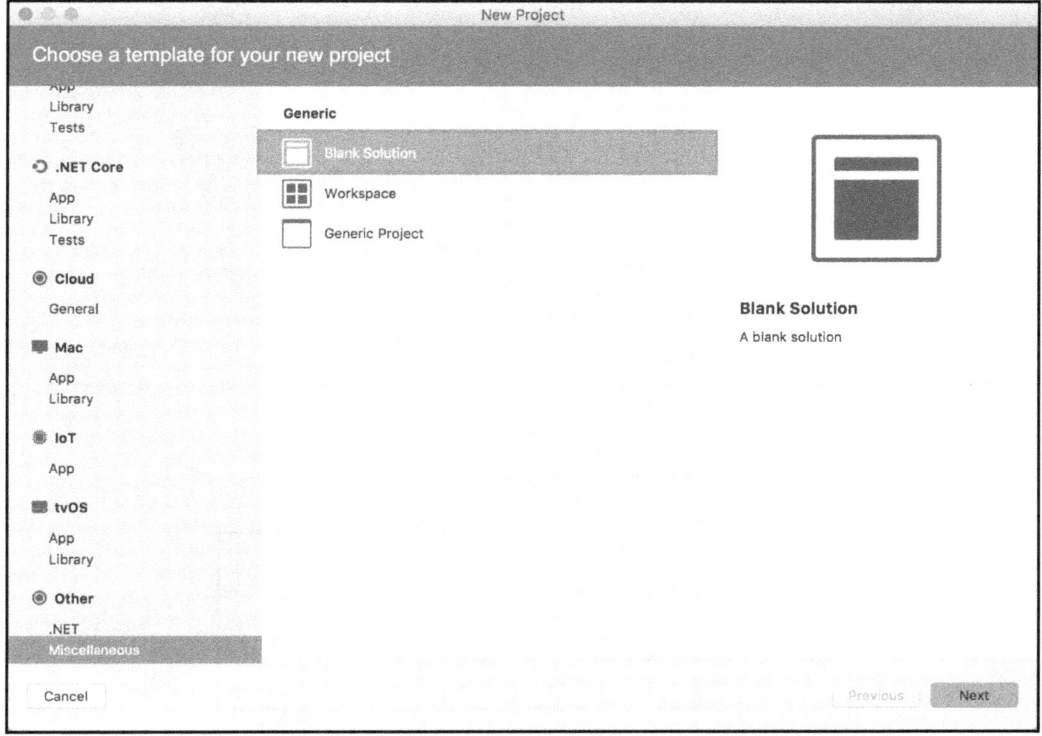

7. Now, click the **Next** button.
8. In the **Solution Name:** textbox, type `Chapter8.Xamarin`. Also make sure you have selected a proper location:

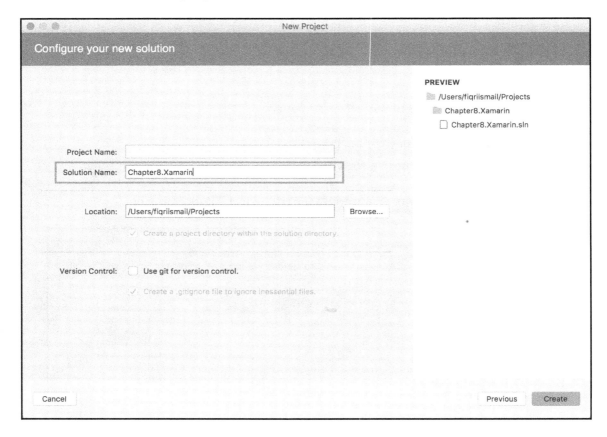

9. Now, click **Create**.
10. Now, the **Solution Explorer** should look like this:

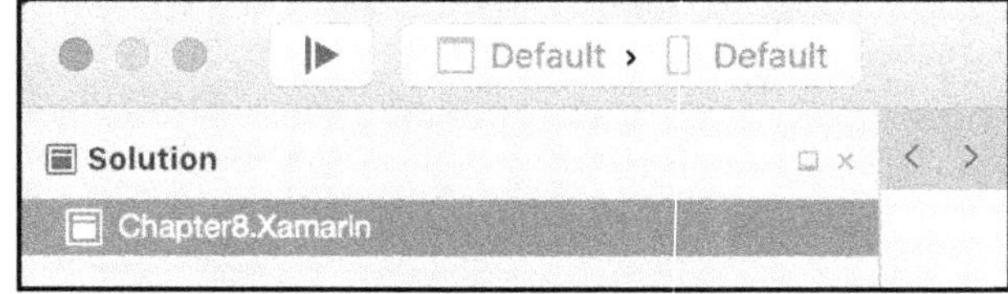

11. Now, *Ctrl* + click on the **Chapter8.Xamarin** label and select **Add** | **New Project**.
12. Select **App** under the iOS section in the left-hand pane and select **Single View App** in the right-hand pane.
13. Make sure **C#** is selected as the programming language:

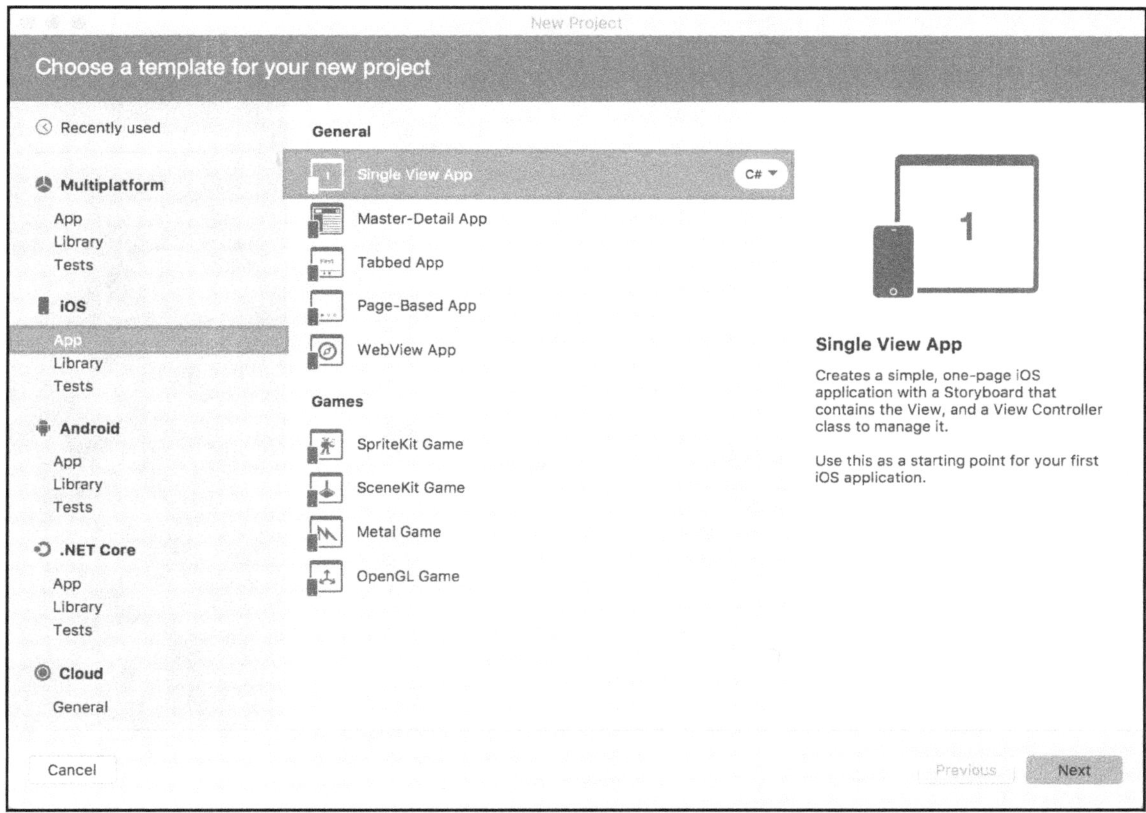

14. Click the **Next** button.
15. The **New Project** dialog box will be displayed.
16. Type `Chapter8.Xamarin.iOSApp` in the **App Name:** textbox, `com.chapter8` in the **Organization Identifier:** textbox, and uncheck **iPad** from the devices. Leave the **Target:** OS as it is:

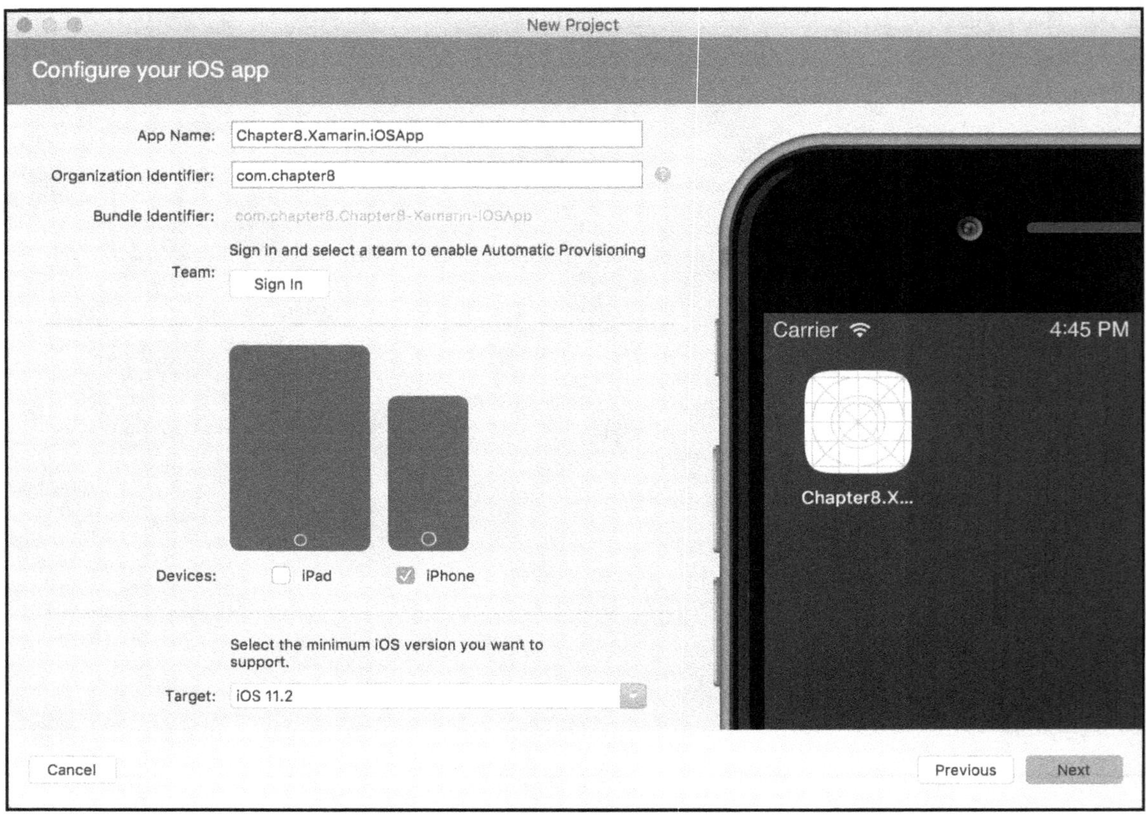

17. Click **Next**.
18. Leave everything as it is and click **Create**:

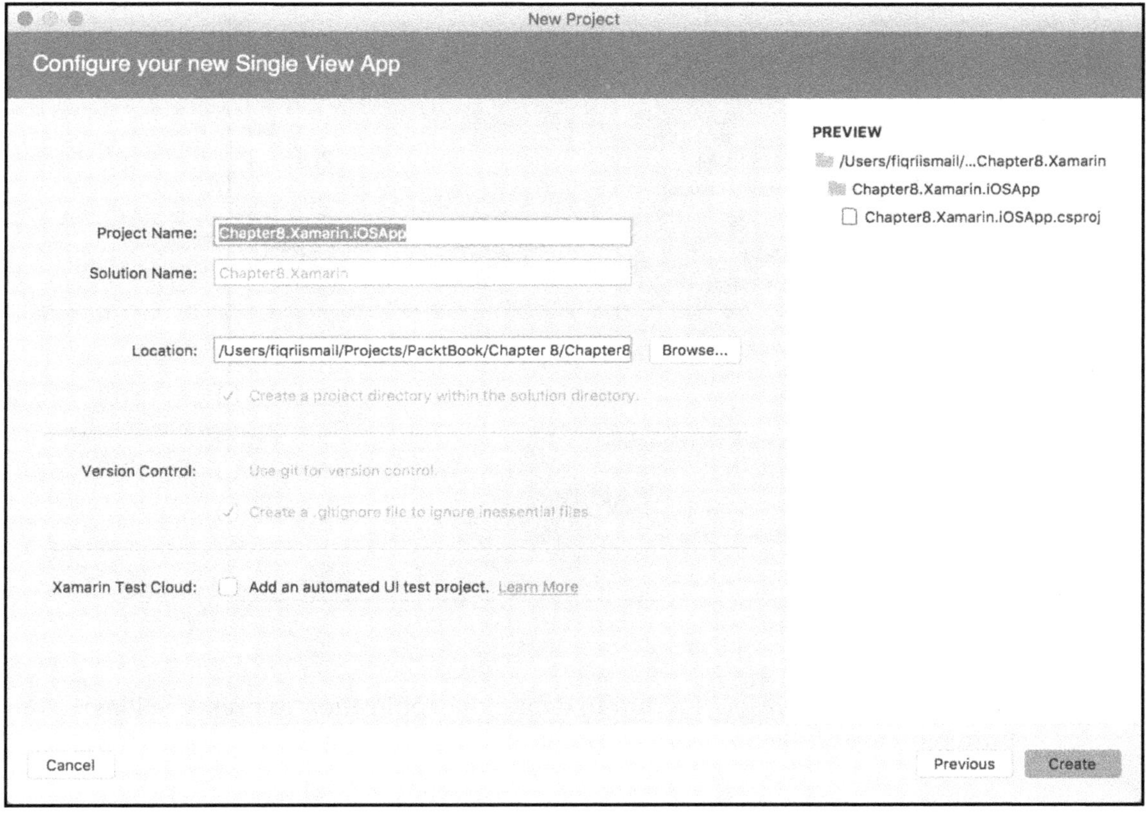

19. Now, the **Solution Explorer** should look like this:

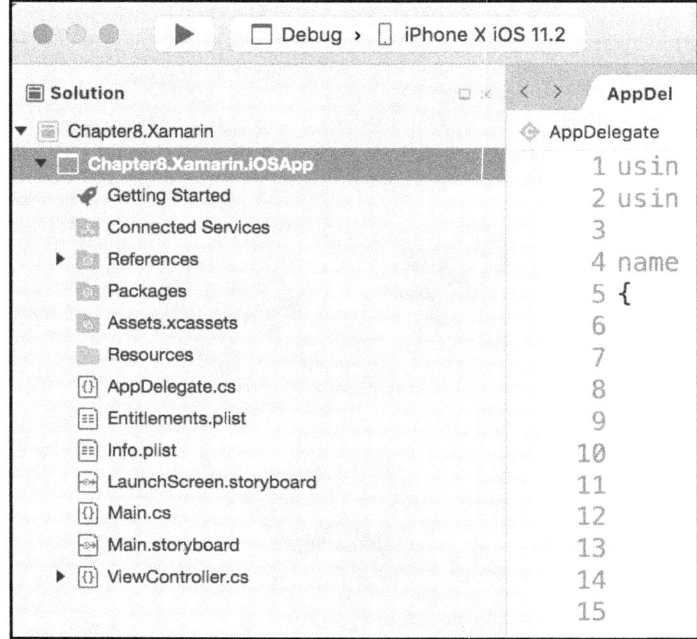

Solution Explorer

20. Now, press the *command* + *return* to debug the application or press the Play button on top of the **Solution Explorer**.

21. Now, you should see the iOS emulator kicking in, which displays the first screen of the app:

22. Congratulations! You have tested your first iOS application.
23. Now, stop the debugger by pressing *shift* + *command* + *return*.

How it works...

In steps 1 to 3, we opened Visual Studio for Mac and, in steps 6 to 9, we created a blank solution. We assigned a proper name to the solution as well. This blank solution will act as the base throughout this chapter. In steps 11 to 18, we added an iOS Single View app to the solution. In step 16, we added an **Organization Identifier**, which is a unique identifier for recognizing your app when you deploy to the app store. A single view app is a starter template to help developers build for iOS and has one custom `ViewController` to start with. We gave it a proper name too. At the end, in steps 20 to 23, we tested the default template generated by Visual Studio for Mac.

We will come back to this application in a later recipe and add a few controls and some code.

Creating the .NET Standard 2.0 library

In this recipe, we will be building a .NET Standard 2.0 library using Visual Studio for Mac. We will be using the same solution from the previous recipe.

Getting ready

Make sure you have completed the previous recipe that added an iOS project. If so, let's get started with adding the library and writing some code.

How to do it...

1. Open Finder.
2. Click **Applications** in the left-hand pane.
3. Now, double-click on the Visual Studio icon.

4. Now, click on **Open**, locate the `Chapter8.Xamarin` solution, and open it.
5. The **Solution Explorer** should look like this:

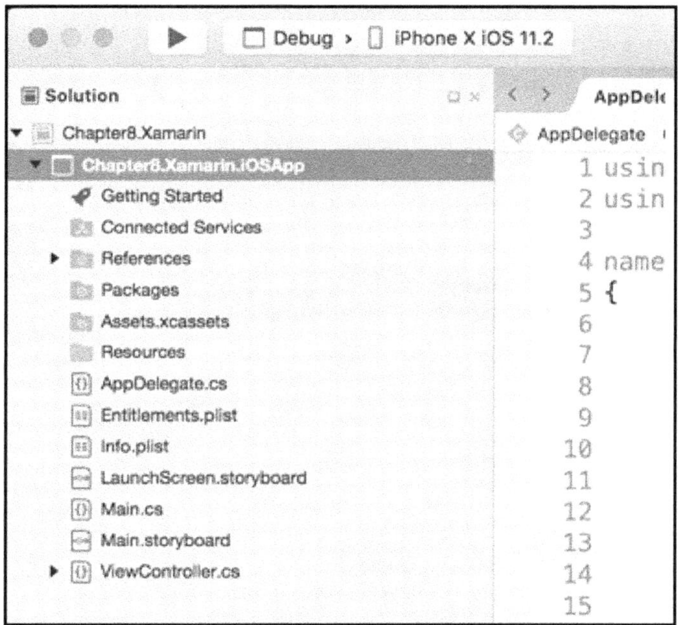

6. Now, *control (^)* + click on the `Chapter8.Xamarin` label and select **Add** | **New Project**.
7. In the **New Project** dialog box, scroll down the left-hand pane till you see the **Multi Platform** section.

8. Click on **Library** and select **.NET Standard Library** under **General** in the right-hand pane. Also make sure **C#** is selected:

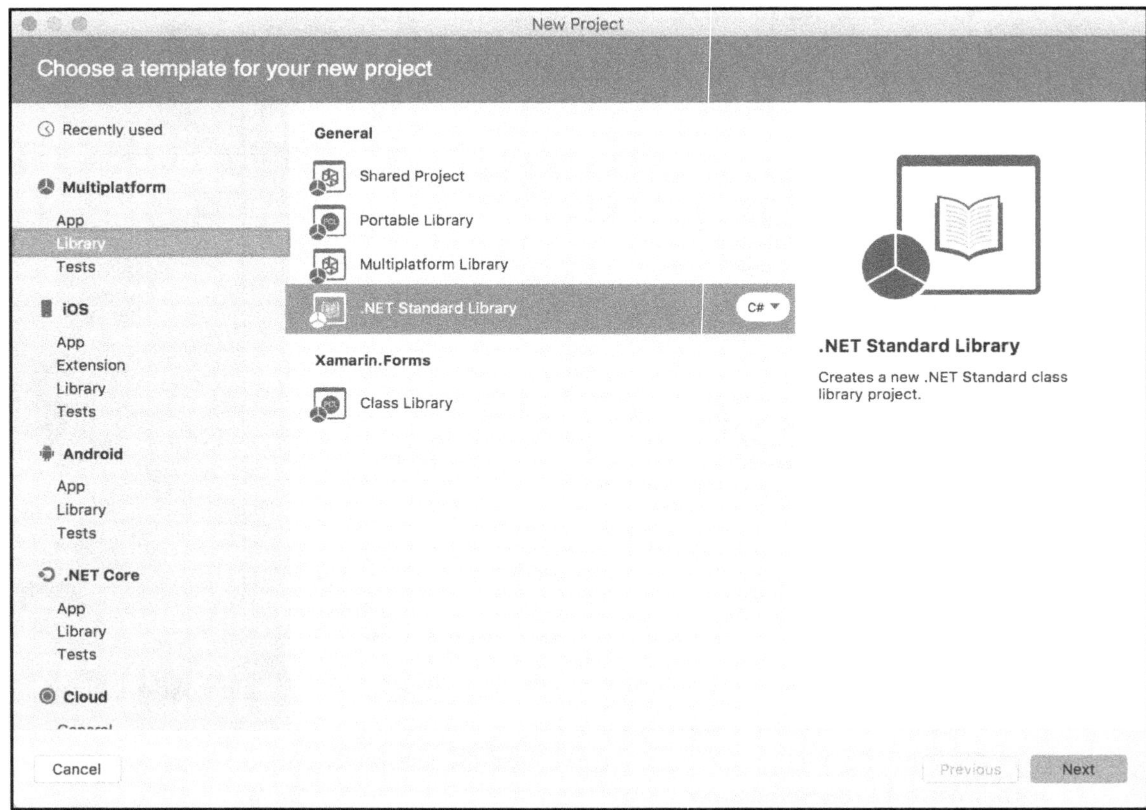

9. Click **Next**.
10. Select **Target Framework:** as **.NET Standard 2.0** and click **Next**:

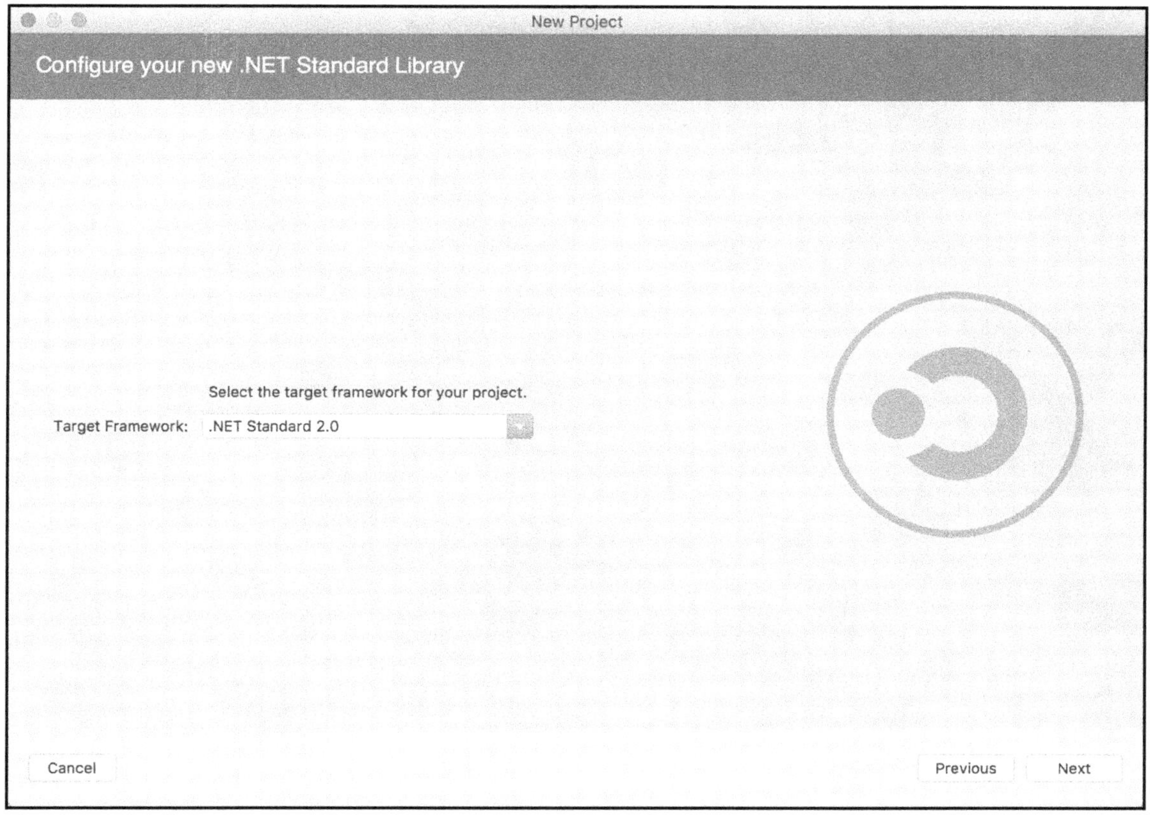

11. In the **Project Name:** textbox, type `Chapter8.Xamarin.iOSLib` as the name and leave the rest:

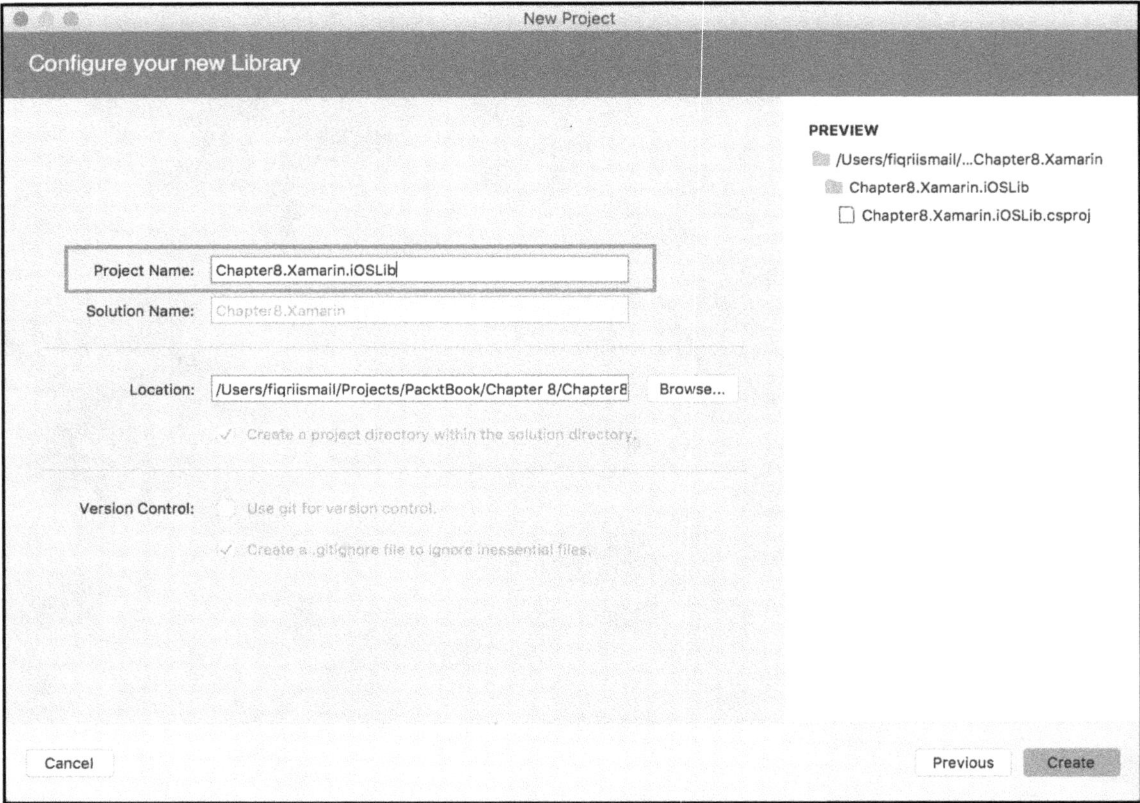

12. Click **Create**.

13. Now, the **Solution Explorer** should look like this:

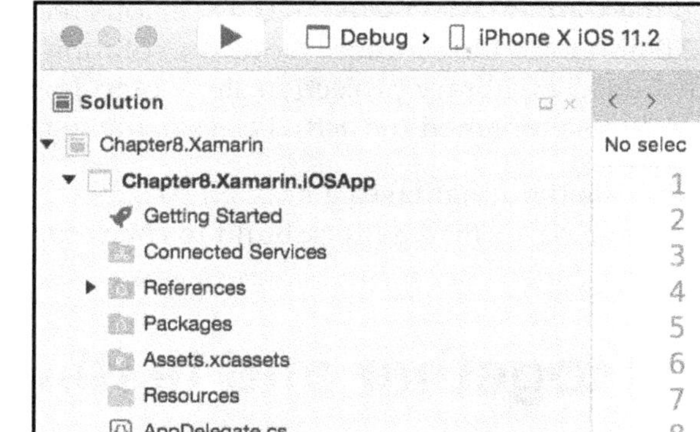

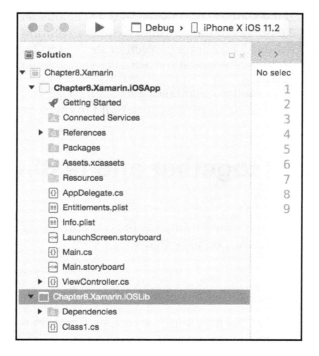

14. Select the `Class1.cs` label and press *command* + *R* to rename.
15. Rename it `HelloLib.cs`.
16. Make sure you change the class name as well from `Class1` to `HelloLib`.
17. Now, inside the `HelloLib` class, add the following code:

```
public string SayHello(string yourName)
{
    return $"Hello {yourName}, Greetings from iOS";
}
```

18. Click **Build** | **Build All** to check that all syntax is correct.

How it works...

In steps 1 to 4, we opened the solution we created in the previous recipe. In steps 6 to 12, we added a .NET Standard 2.0 library to the solution. Now, the solution has two projects, an iOS project and a .NET Standard 2.0 library project. In steps 14 to 16, we renamed the class created by Visual Studio. We also renamed the actual class name to match the file name.

In step 17, we added a public method that takes a `string` parameter and returns a string as a welcome message. Finally, we performed a quick build to check for the correct syntax.

Putting things together and testing the application

In this recipe, we will be adding some controls to the iOS application and using the .NET Standard 2.0 library created in the previous recipe.

Getting ready

Make sure you have completed the previous two recipes. They are required in order to continue. If you have already completed them, let's perform a quick build and start.

How to do it...

1. Open Finder.
2. Click **Applications** in the left-hand pane.
3. Double-click on the Visual Studio icon.
4. Click on **Open**, locate the `Chapter8.Xamarin` solution, and open it.

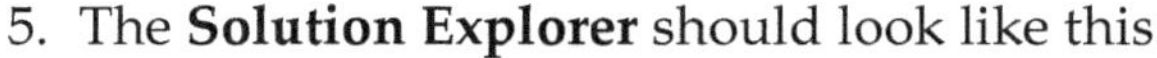

5. The **Solution Explorer** should look like this:

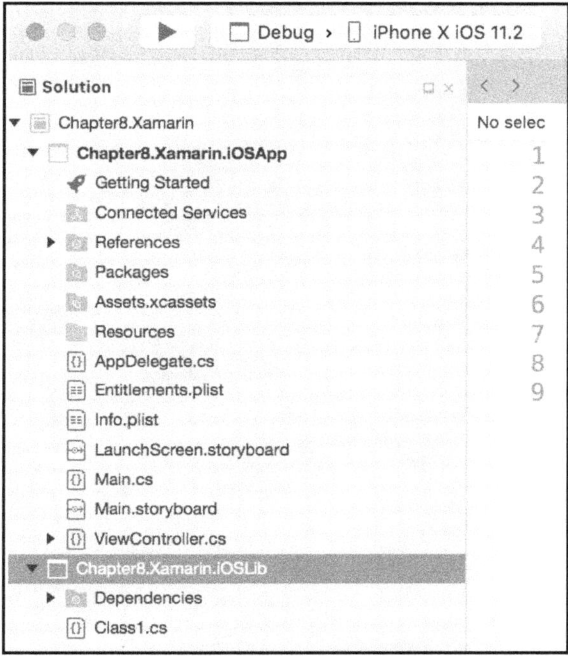

6. Now, expand the `Chapter8.Xamarin.iOSApp` project node.
7. Double-click on the `Main.storyboard` file.
8. This will open the storyboard tab for your application.

9. You should see the default layout of the iOS application as follows:

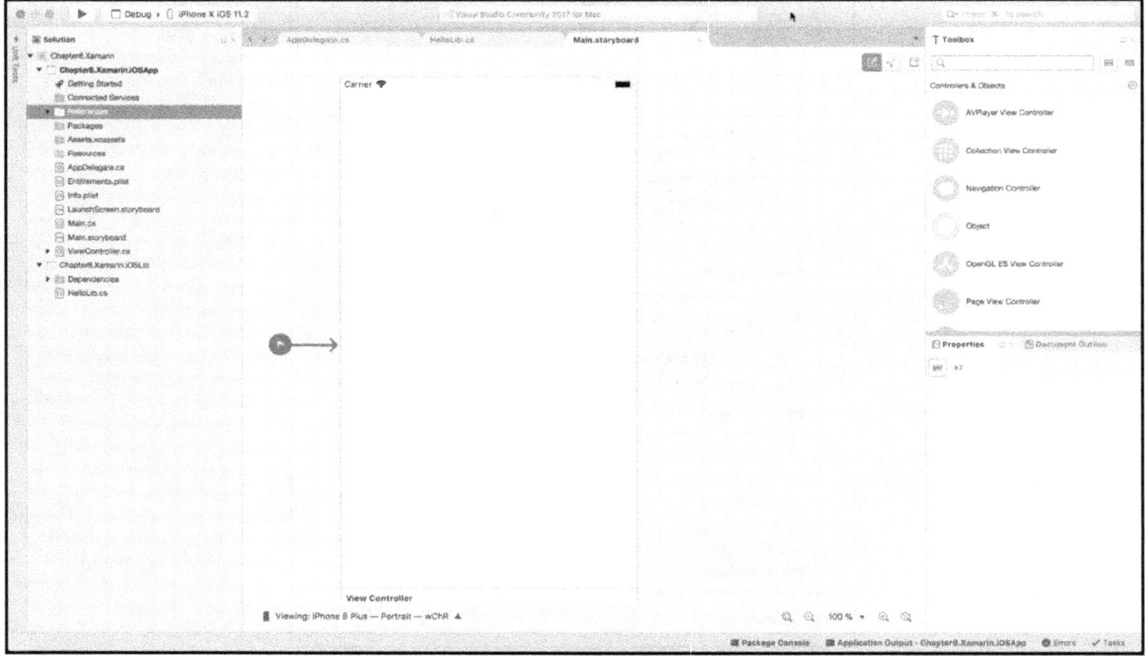

Default layout of the iOS application

10. Now, select the **Toolbox** window.
11. Click inside the `search` textbox and type `Button`.
12. Now, drag a **Button** control to the main white area of the canvas, in the middle.
13. Select the button. In the **Properties** window, type `Say Hello` under the **Title** label and type `HelloButton` in the **Name** property.

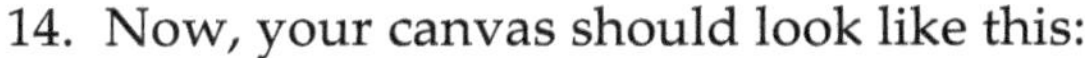

14. Now, your canvas should look like this:

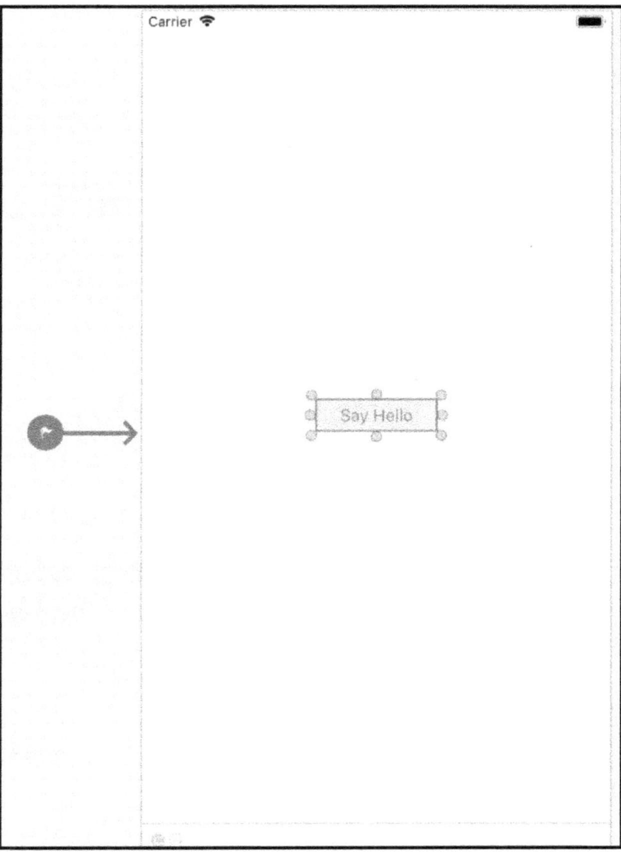

15. Now, in the **Solution Explorer**, *control (^)* + click on the **References** label and select **Edit References**.
16. In the **Edit References** dialog box, click on the **Projects** tab.

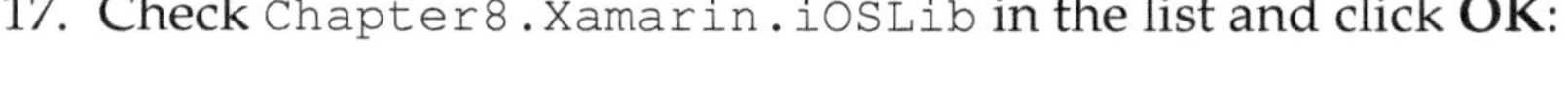

17. Check `Chapter8.Xamarin.iOSLib` in the list and click **OK**:

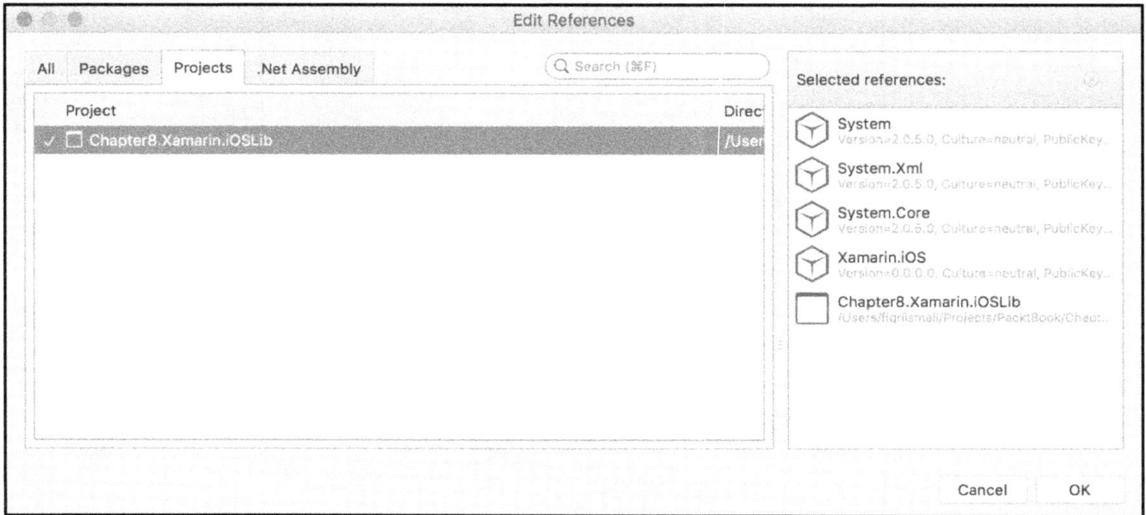

18. Now, double-click on the `VeiwController.cs` file to open its code.
19. Scroll up till you reach the `using` directives and add the following `using` directive to access the library:

```
using Chapter8.Xamarin.iOSLib;
```

20. Now, scroll down till you reach the `ViewDidLoad()` method.
21. Add the following code next to the `base.ViewDidLoad()` line:

```
HelloButton.TouchUpInside += (object sender, EventArgs e) =>
{
    var greetings = new HelloLib();
    var message = greetings.SayHello("Fiqri Ismail");

    //Create an alert box
    var greetingsAlert = UIAlertController.Create("Hello",
        message, UIAlertControllerStyle.Alert);
    greetingsAlert.AddAction(UIAlertAction.Create("OK",
        UIAlertActionStyle.Default, null));

    PresentViewController(greetingsAlert, true, null);
 };
```

22. Now, let's press *command* + *return* to debug the application.
23. You should see the following output:

24. Now click on the **Say Hello** button:

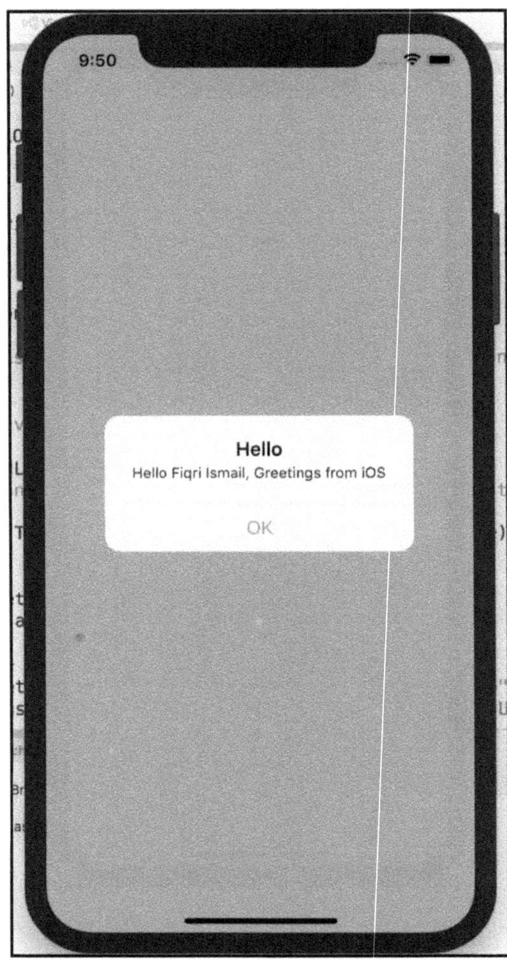

25. Now, click **OK** and stop debugging.

How it works...

In steps 1 to 6, we opened an existing project solution. In steps 10 to 13, we added a simple button control to the canvas. After that, we changed the **Title** and **Name** properties of the button. In step 17, we added the reference to the library from the iOS project. Again, in step 19, we added a reference to the .NET Standard library from the code level.

In step 21, we added code to trigger the button touch up event. This event triggers when you touch and move up your finger on an actual device, but in the emulator it triggers when you click the button. We added the code inside the `ViewDidLoad()` method. This method triggers after the View is loaded. In the first two lines of the code, we created an instance of the `HelloLib` class from the library. Then, we executed the `SayHello` method and saved the return value in a variable.

Then, we created an alert box to display the **Calcutta** message with an **OK** button. Finally, in steps 23 and 24, we tested the iOS application we had just built.

9
To Android with Xamarin

In this chapter, we will be looking at these recipes:

- Hello Android – creating a Xamarin Android app
- Adding a .NET Standard 2.0 library to the Xamarin project
- Putting things together and testing the application

Technical requirements

Readers should have a basic knowledge of C#. They should also have a basic knowledge of using Visual Studio, installing packages using NuGet, and referencing libraries within projects from other projects.

The code files for this chapter can be found on GitHub:
`https://github.com/PacktPublishing/DotNET-Standard-2-Cookbook/tree/master/Chapter09/Chapter9.Xamarin`

Check out the following video to see the code in action:
`https://goo.gl/dMi9PZ`

Introduction

In this chapter, we will be looking at building an Android application using Visual Studio for Mac. We will also be building a .NET Standard 2.0 class library that the Android application will use. Visual Studio for Mac allows you to build Xamarin-based applications for iOS, Android, and Windows using your favorite C# programming language. It also has F# support by default. In the previous chapter, `Chapter 8`, *To iOS with Xamarin*, we talked about how to install Visual Studio for Mac.

Hello Android – Creating a Xamarin Android app

In this recipe, we will be looking at support for Android-based applications in Visual Studio for Mac. We will be looking at an Android project, setting up a solution for it, and checking for all the bits and pieces required.

Getting ready

Make sure you have installed Visual Studio for Mac for your macOS system. If not, follow the *Installing Visual Studio for Mac and preparation* recipe, which shows you how to install it.

How to do it...

1. Open **Finder**.
2. Click **Applications** in the left-hand pane.

3. Now, double-click on the Visual Studio icon:

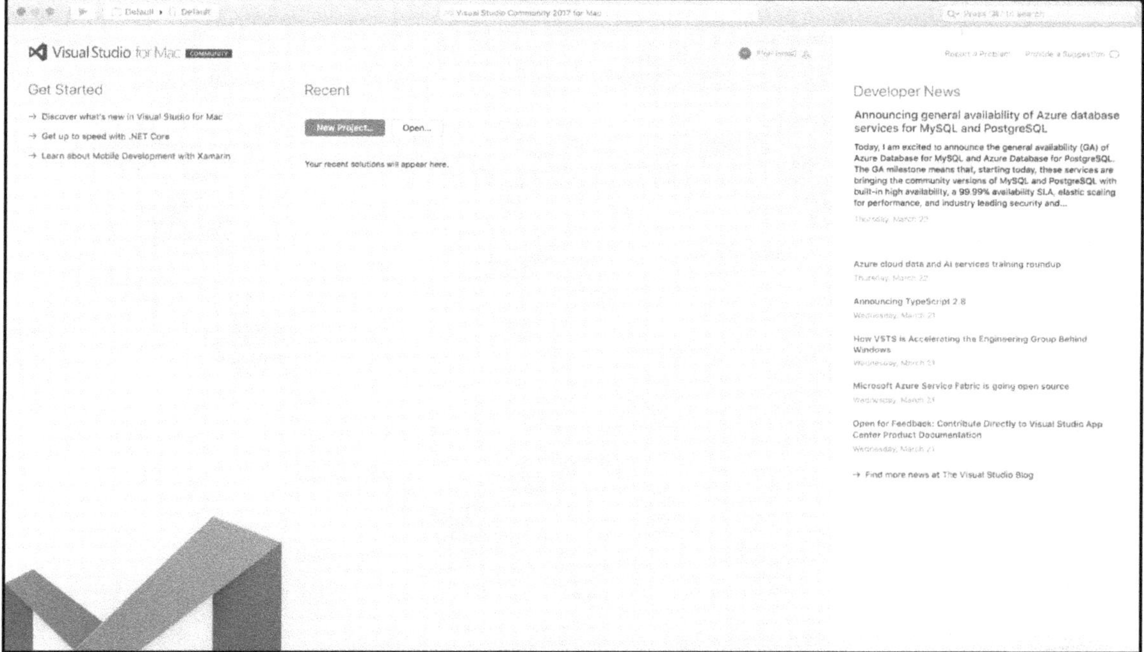

Visual Studio

4. Click on the **New Project** button.
5. In the **Choose a template for your project** dialog box, scroll down till you reach the **other** section.

6. Select **Miscellaneous** and, under **Generic**, select **Blank Solution**:

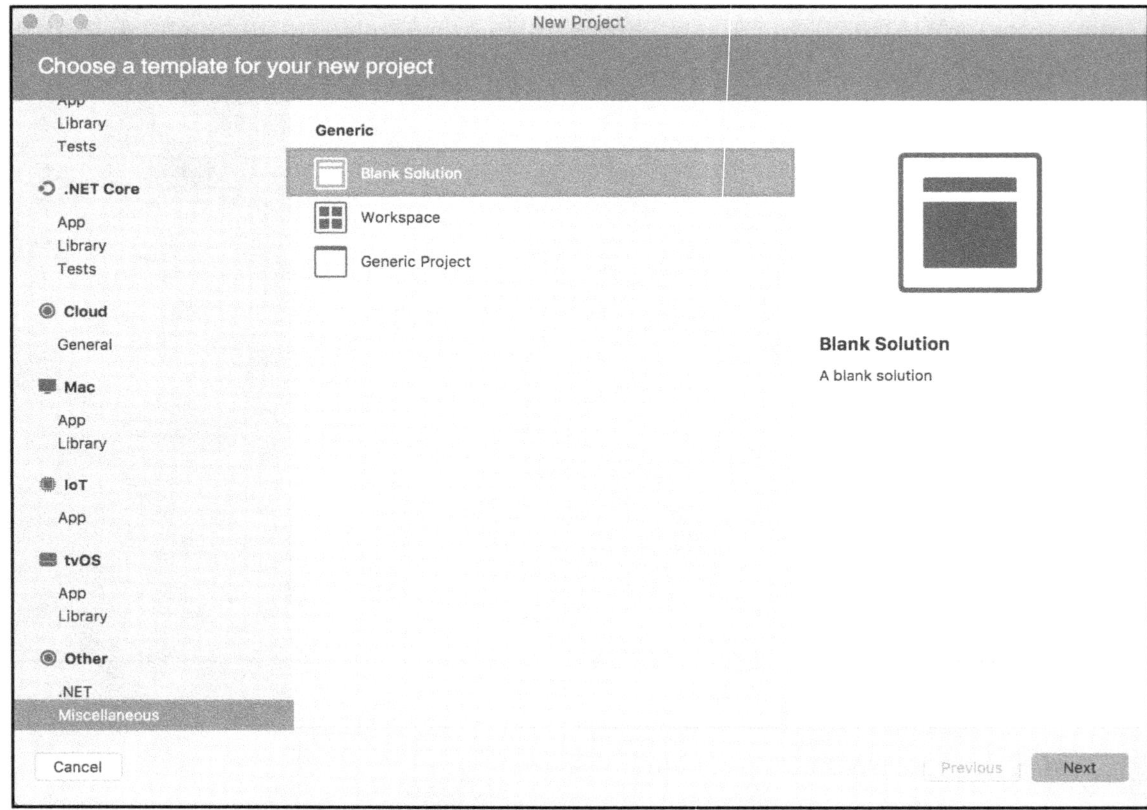

7. Now, click the **Next** button.

8. In the **Solution Name:** textbox, type `Chapter9.Xamarin`. Also make sure you have selected a proper location:

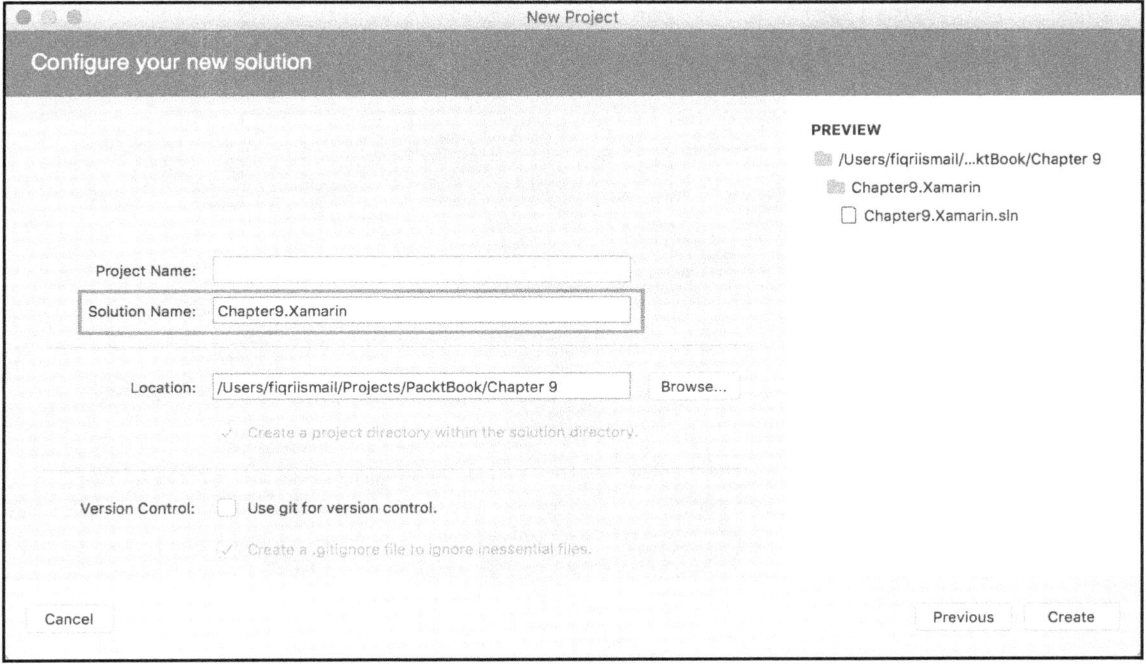

9. Now, click **Create**.
10. Now, the **Solution Explorer** should look like this:

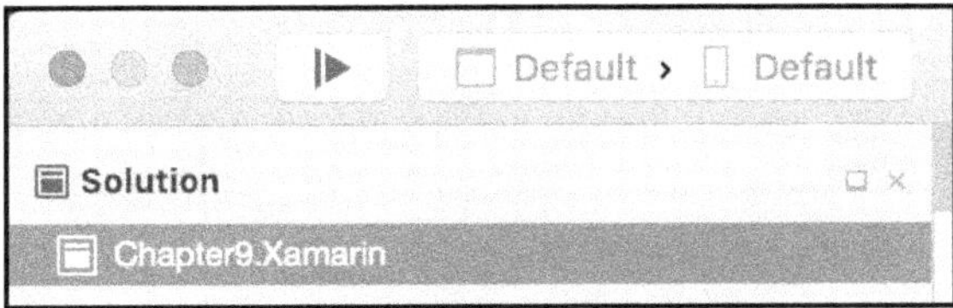

11. Now, *control (^)* + click on the `Chapter9.Xamarin` label and select **Add** | **New Project**.
12. Select **App** under the **Android** section in the left-hand pane. Select **Android App** in the right-hand pane.
13. Make sure **C#** is selected as the programming language:

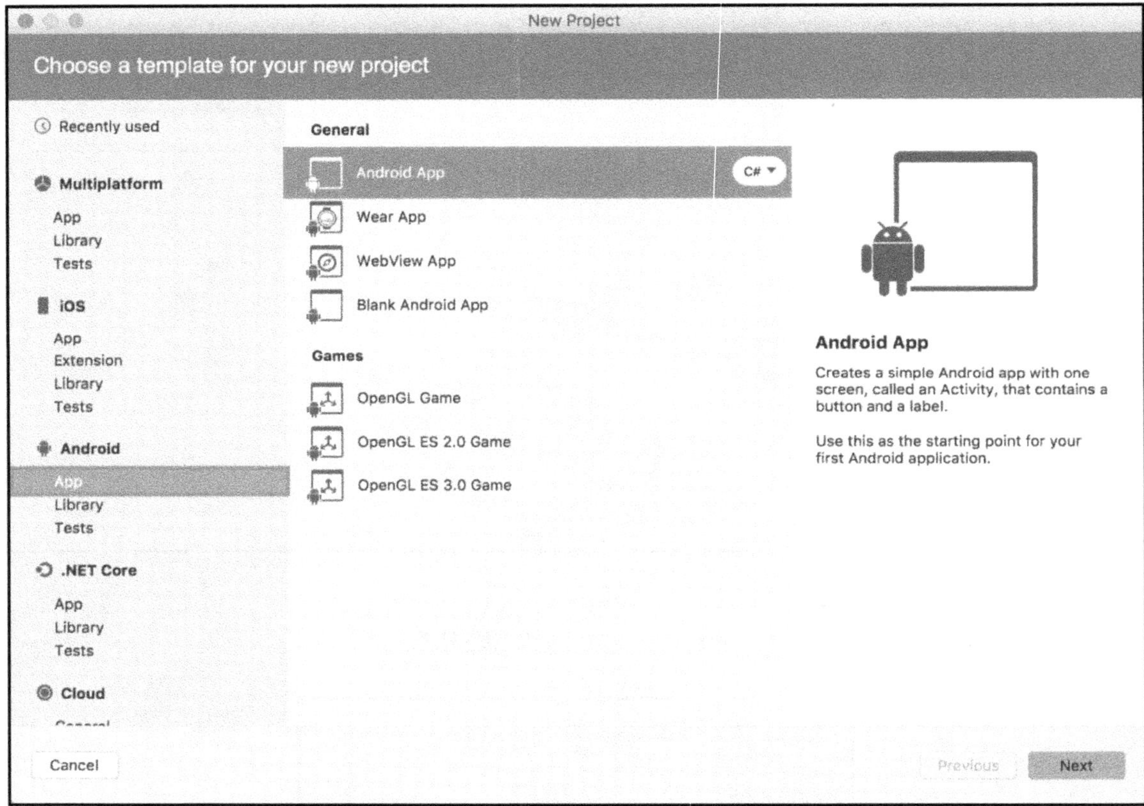

14. Click **Next**.
15. Now, in the **App Name:** textbox, type `Chapter9.Xamarin.AndroidApp` and, in the **Organization Identifier:** textbox, type `com.chapter9`. Leave the rest as it is:

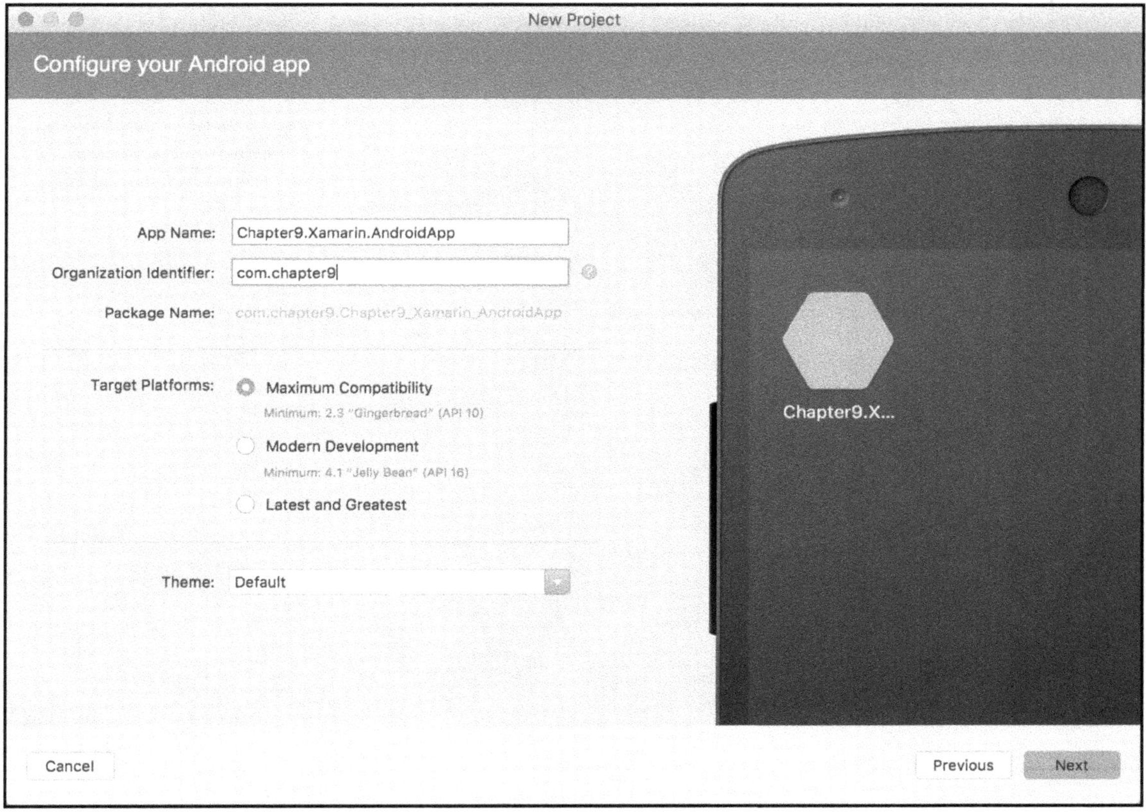

16. Click **Next**.
17. Leave everything as it is and click **Create**:

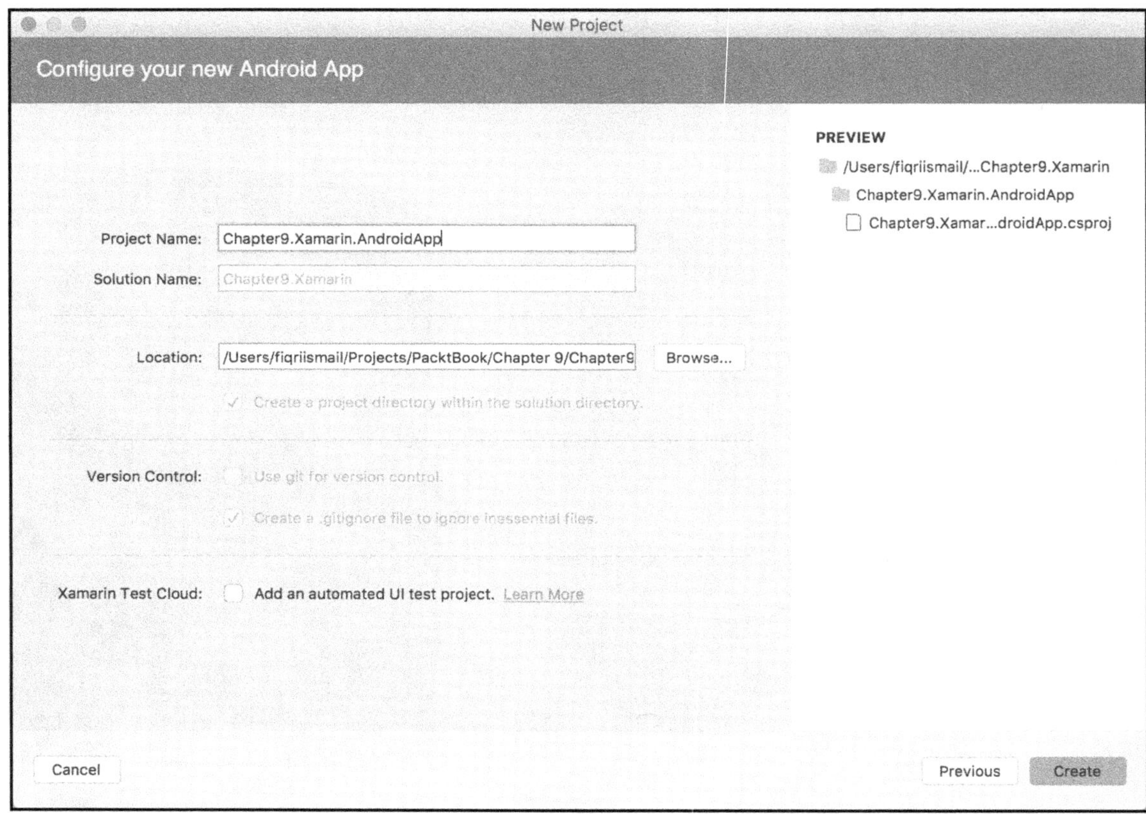

18. Now, the **Solution Explorer** should look like this:

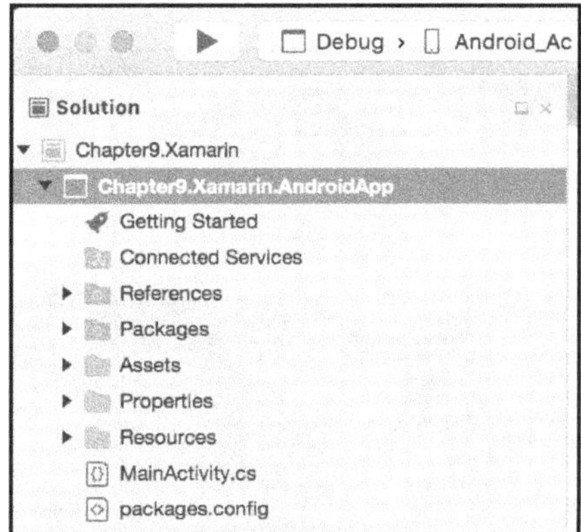

19. Now, you should see that the default template already has a working application.
20. Press the *command* + *return* keys to debug the application.
21. Now, you should see the default `HelloWorld` application running in the emulator:

22. Click on the button to see it in action. Press *shift* + *command* + *return* to stop debugging.

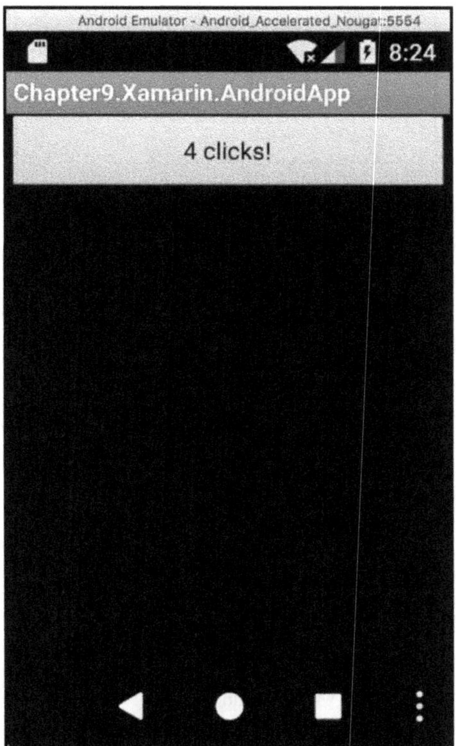

How it works...

In steps 1 to 10, we created a blank solution and gave it a proper name. In step 10, we added an **Android App** project to that solution. The **Android App** project is a default template created by Visual Studio for Mac. It's a working prototype application for testing that everything is intact.

If you look at the **Solution Explorer** and click on the `MainActivity.cs` file, you will see all the action. Inside the `OnCreate()` method, the code looks like this:

```
base.OnCreate(savedInstanceState);

// Set our view from the "main" layout resource
SetContentView(Resource.Layout.Main);

// Get our button from the layout resource,
// and attach an event to it
Button button = FindViewById<Button>(Resource.Id.myButton);

button.Click += delegate { button.Text = $"{count++} clicks!"; };
```

You can see a simple button. When you click on the button, its increments are counted and it updates the button label. `FindViewById` will locate the button and create a `Button` class. Finally, the `button.Click` event triggers the process of counting and storing it in the button caption.

Adding a .NET Standard 2.0 library to the Xamarin project

In this recipe, we will be looking at creating a .NET Standard 2.0 library and moving the default count code into the library. The counting code was created by Visual Studio for Mac as a default template for the Android app.

Getting ready

Make sure you have completed the previous recipe that creates a default Android Application. If you have already completed it, let's open up that solution and get started.

How to do it...

1. Open **Finder**.
2. Click **Applications** in the left-hand pane.
3. Now, double-click on the Visual Studio icon.
4. Click on **Open**, locate the `Chapter9.Xamarin` solution, and open it.
5. The **Solution Explorer** should look like this:

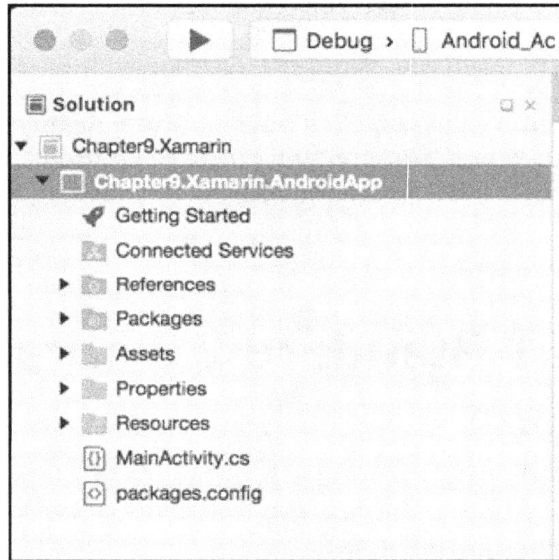

6. Now, *control (^)* + click on the `Chapter9.Xamarin` label and select **Add** | **New Project**.
7. In the **New Project** dialog box, scroll down the left-hand pane until you see the **Multi Platform** section.

8. Click on **Library** and select **.NET Standard Library** under **General** in the right-hand pane. Also make sure **C#** is selected:

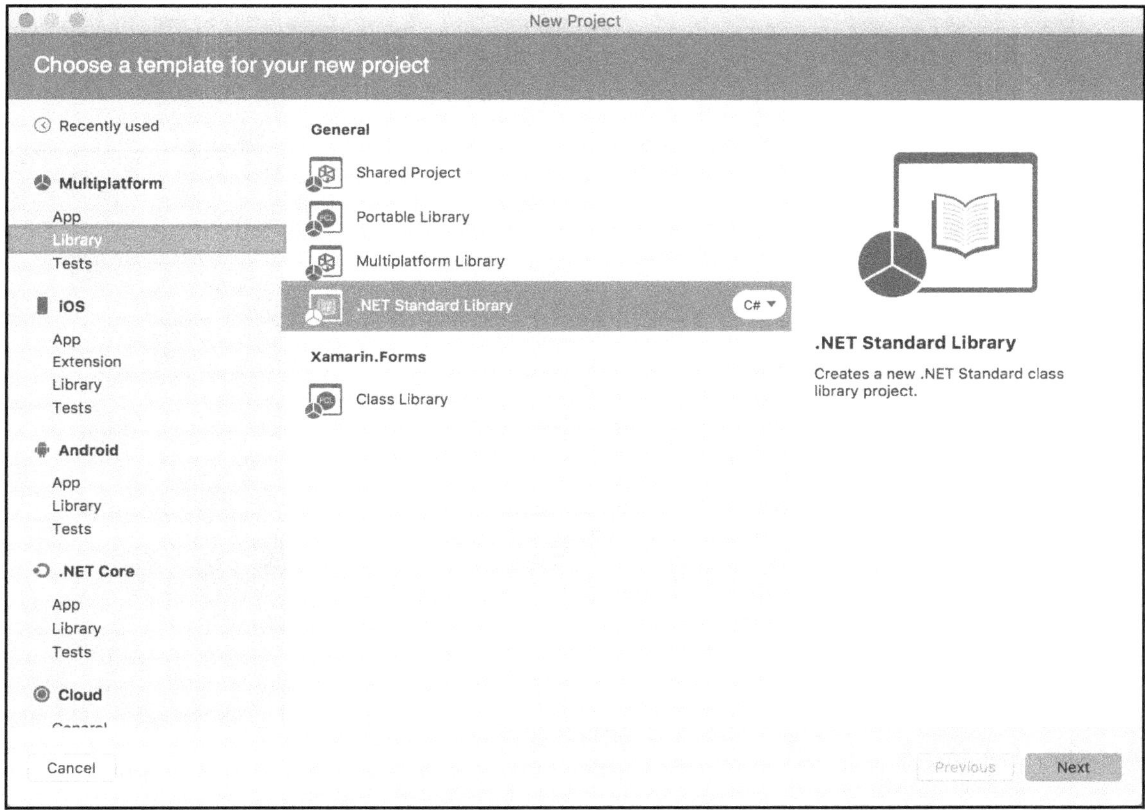

9. Click **Next**.

10. Select **Target Framework:** as **.NET Standard 2.0** and click **Next**:

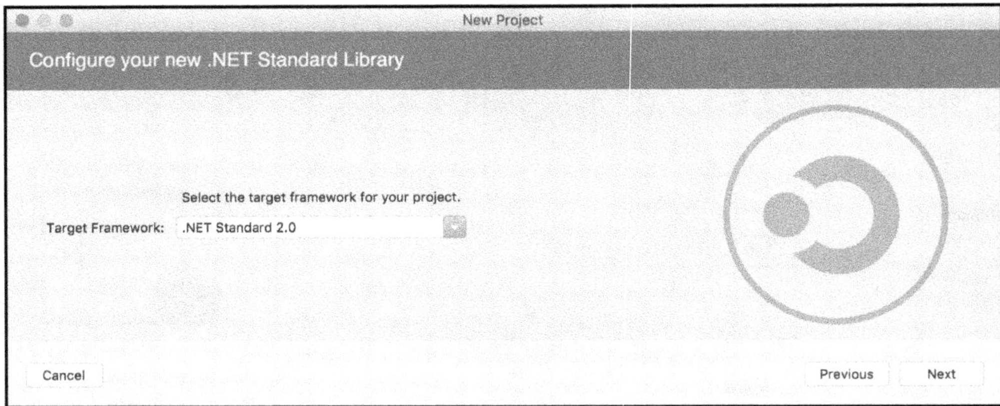

11. In the **Project Name:** textbox, type `Chapter9.Xamarin.AndroidLib` as the name and leave the rest:

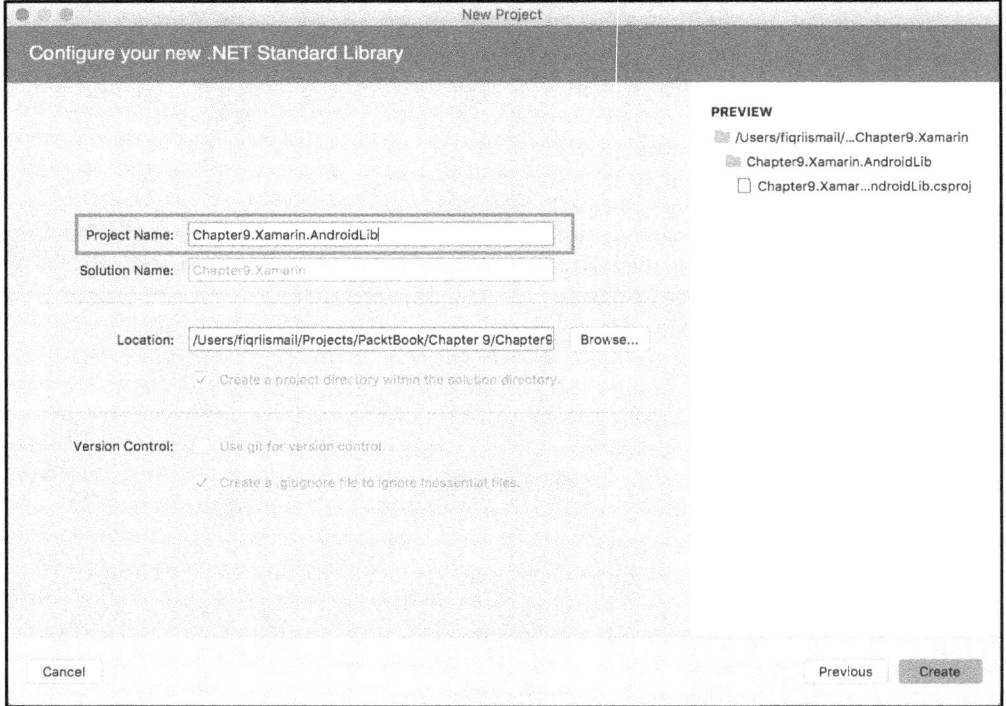

12. Click **Create**.
13. Now, the **Solution Explorer** should look like this:

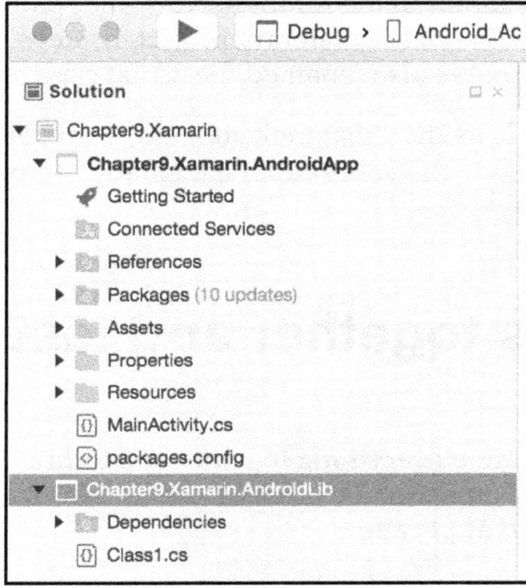

14. Now, select the `Class1.cs` label and press *command* + *R* to rename.
15. Rename it `CounterLib.cs`.
16. Make sure you change the class name as well from `Class1` to `CounterLib`.
17. Now, inside the `CounterLib` class, add the following code:

```
public int IncrementByOne(int value)
{
    return value++;
}
```

18. Click **Build** | **Build All** to check that all syntax is correct.

How it works...

In steps 1 to 4, we opened the solution created in the previous recipe. In steps 6 to 12, we added a .NET Standard 2.0 library to the solution. Now, the solution has two projects: an Android project and a .NET Standard 2.0 library project. In steps 14 to 16, we renamed the class created in Visual Studio. We also renamed the actual class name to match the filename.

In step 17, we added a public method that took an `integer` parameter and returned an integer value with one added to the value supplied. Finally, we performed a quick build to check for the correct syntax.

Putting things together and testing the application

In this recipe, we will be putting everything together and testing the final application. We will be referencing the .NET Standard 2.0 library from the Android application and using the library from the Android application.

Getting ready

Make sure you have completed the previous recipe that builds the .NET Standard 2.0 library. If you have, open up the solution and get started on this application.

How to do it...

1. Open **Finder**.
2. Click **Applications** in the left-hand pane.
3. Now, double-click on the Visual Studio icon.

4. Click on **Open**, locate the `Chapter9.Xamarin` solution, and open it.
5. The **Solution Explorer** should look like this:

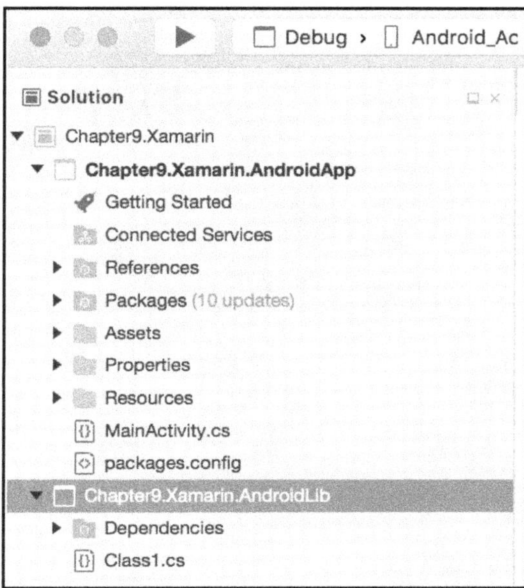

6. Now, expand the `Chapter9.Xamarin.AndroidApp` project node.
7. In the **Solution Explorer**, *control (^)* + click on the **References** label and select **Edit References**.
8. In the **Edit References** dialog box, click on the **Projects** tab.

9. Check `Chapter9.Xamarin.AndroidLib` in the list and click **OK**:

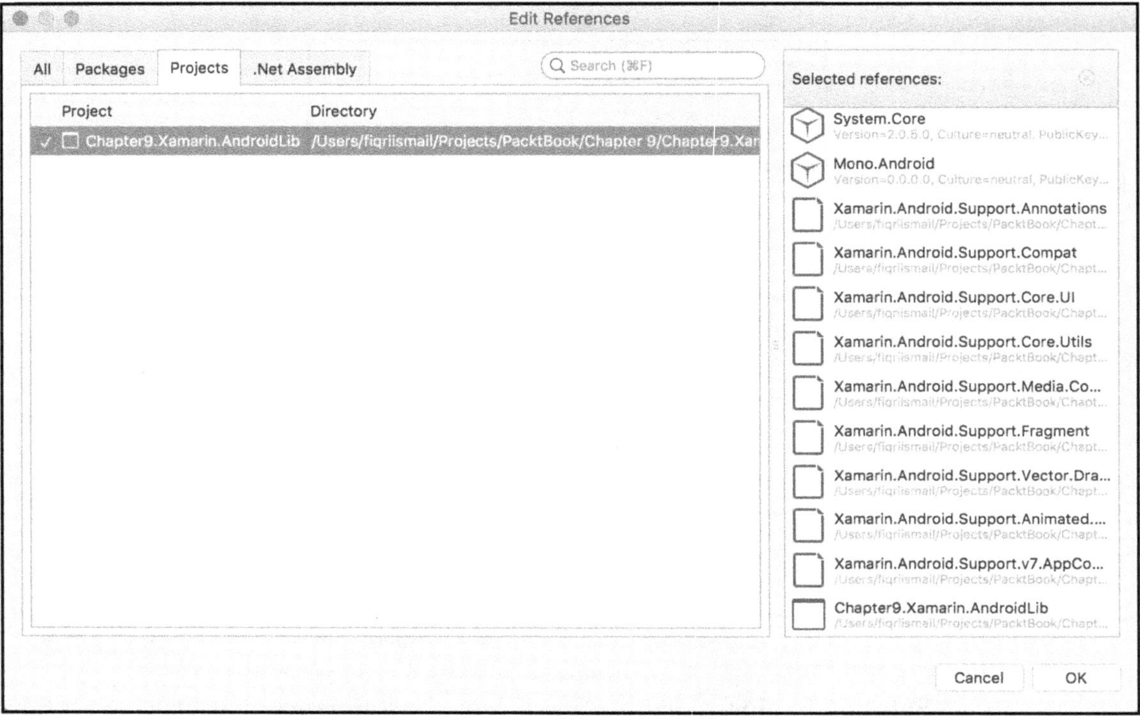

10. Scroll up until you reach the `using` directives and add the following `using` directive to access the library:

```
using Chapter9.Xamarin.AndroidLib;
```

11. Now, double-click on the **MainActivity.cs** file to open its code.
12. Under the `MainActivity` class, find this code:

```
int count = 1;
```

Replace the previous code with the following:

```
int count = 0;
```

13. Now, scroll down until you reach the `OnCreate()` method.
14. Add the following code next to the `base.OnCreate()` line:

```
CounterLib counter = new CounterLib();
```

15. Now, replace the default button click code with the following:

```
button.Click += delegate {
    count = counter.IncrementByOne(count);
    button.Text = $"{count} clicks!";
};
```

16. Press *command* + *return* to debug the application.
17. Click the button a few times and you should see the following output:

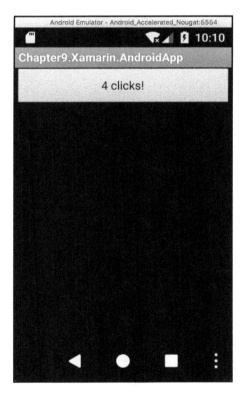

18. Press *shift* + *command* + *return* to stop debugging.

How it works...

In steps 1 to 6, we opened the existing solution we created in previous recipes. In step 9, we added a reference to the library from the Android application. In step 10, we added the code-level reference to the library. This will allow us to grab all the available methods from the library. In step 12, we changed the existing code. In step 14, we created an instance of `CounterLib()` and stored it in a variable.

In step 15, again, we made a small change to the button's existing click code to use the `IncrementByOne()` method from the class library. Finally, in steps 16, 17, and 18, we tested our new code.

10
Let's Fine-Tune Our Library

In this chapter, we will be looking at these recipes:

- Logging the library
- Creating a .NET Core console application to use the library
- Informing the end user – exception handling and error messages
- Using Visual Studio 2017 diagnostics and debugging tools

Technical requirements

Readers should have a basic knowledge of C#. They should also have a basic knowledge of using Visual Studio, installing packages using NuGet, and referencing libraries within projects from other projects.

The code files for this chapter can be found on GitHub:
`https://github.com/PacktPublishing/DotNET-Standard-2-Cookbook/tree/master/Chapter10/Chapter10.Logging`

Check out the following video to see the code in action:
`https://goo.gl/HNVQMh`

Introduction

In this chapter, we will be looking at how to fine-tune our .NET Standard 2.0 library, how to create a log, and how to use the debugging tools available in Visual Studio 2017. We will also look at exception handling. Throughout previous chapters, we have been looking at how to build a library and its utilization. In this chapter, we are going to make that library good and solid.

A library logs things itself

In this recipe, we will be using a text log file to store details about how the library interacts with other programs. This is a good practice; to log things as you go. Then, you will be able to pinpoint errors and other important things, such as usage of the library.

Getting ready

Make sure you have the latest version of Visual Studio 2017 installed on your system. Let's get started on our recipe.

How to do it...

1. Open Visual Studio 2017.
2. Click **File** | **New** | **Project** to create a project.
3. In the **New Project** dialog box, expand the **Other Project Types** node in the left-hand pane and select **Visual Studio Solutions**. In the right-hand pane, select **Blank Solution.**
4. In the **Name:** textbox, type `Chapter10.Logging`, and, in the **Location:** textbox, select a path from the drop-down box or click on the **Browse...** button to locate a path:

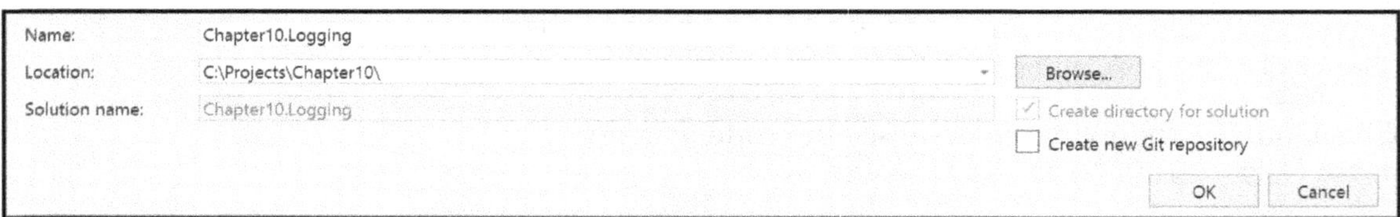

5. Click **OK**.
6. Now, the **Solution Explorer** (*Ctrl* + *Alt* + *L*) should look like this:

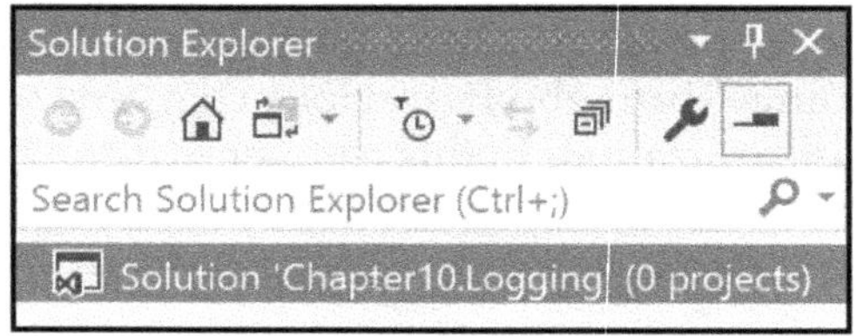

7. Now, right-click on the `Chapter10.Logging` label in the **Solution Explorer** and select **Add** | **New Project**.
8. In the **New Project** dialog box, expand the **Visual C#** node.
9. Select **.NET Standard** in the left-hand pane and **Class Library (.NET Standard)** in the right-hand pane:

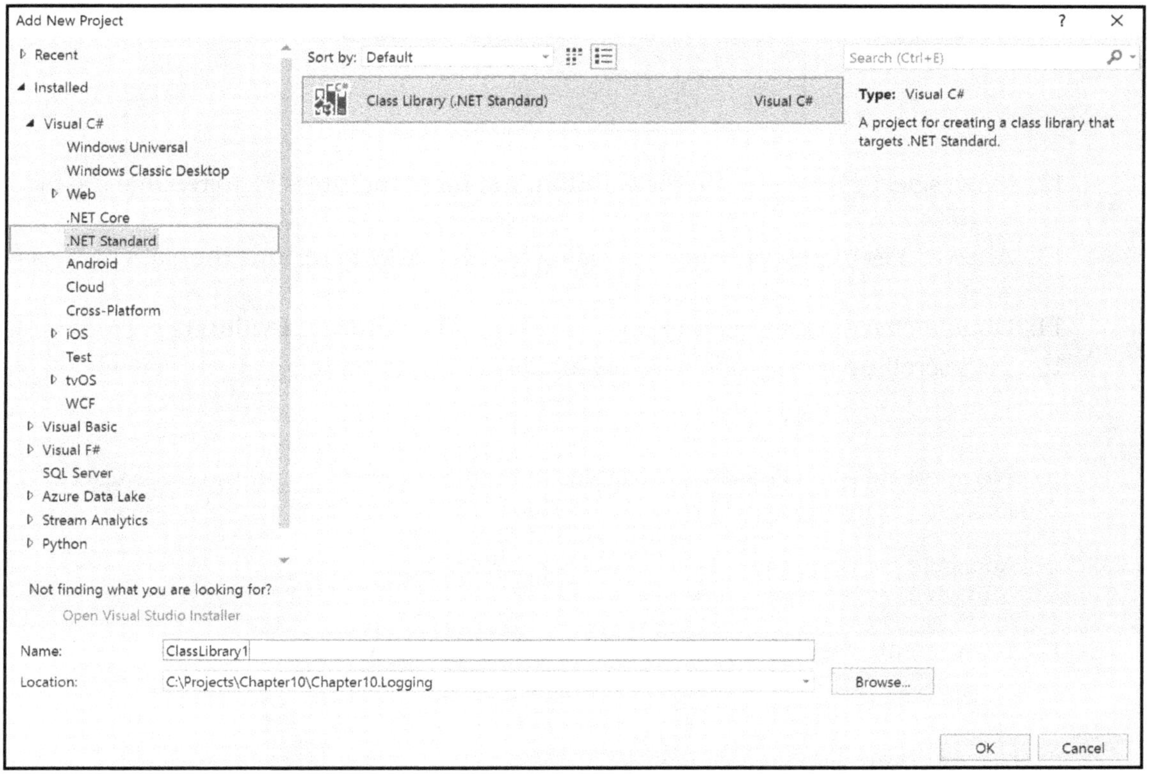

10. In the **Name:** textbox, type `Chapter10.Logging.LogLib`, leave the other defaults as they are, and click **OK**:

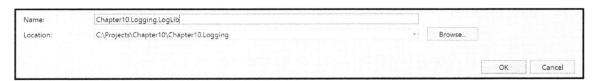

11. Now, the **Solution Explorer** (*Ctrl* + *Alt* + *L*) should look like this:

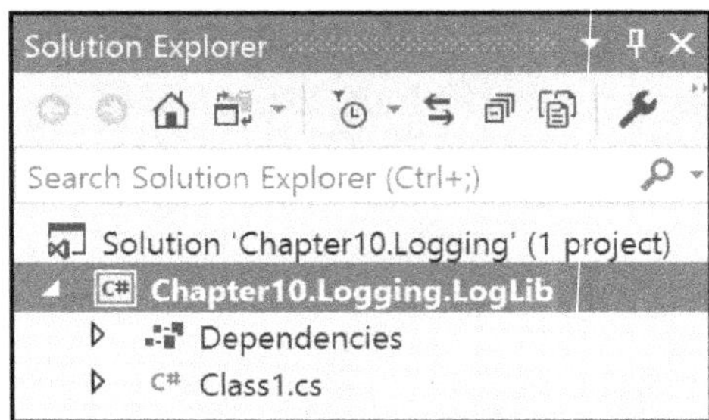

12. Now, select `Class1.cs` in the **Solution Explorer** and press *F2* to rename the file `LoggerDemo.cs`.
13. Answer **Yes** in the confirmation dialog box that asks to rename the class name as well.
14. Double-click on the `LoggerDemo.cs` label in the **Solution Explorer**.
15. Let's scroll up in the code window and add the following `using` directive:

```
using System.IO;
```

16. Now, create two class-level variables to hold the filename and the `StreamWriter` class:

```
private string logFileName = "lib_log.txt";
private StreamWriter logFile;
```

17. Now, create the default constructor method as follows:

```
public LoggerDemo()
{
    WriteLog("Constructor Called.");
}
```

18. Again, create this `private` method to write log details to the file:

```
private void WriteLog(string message)
{
    if (!File.Exists(logFileName))
    {
        logFile = File.CreateText(logFileName);
    }
    else
    {
```

```
            logFile = File.AppendText(logFileName);
        }

        logFile.WriteLine($"{DateTime.Now} Log Message: {message} ");
        logFile.Close();
    }
```

19. Create these three `public` methods:

```
public void CallMethod1()
{
    WriteLog("Method 1 Called");
}

public void CallMethod2()
{
    WriteLog("Method 2 Called");
}

public void CallMethod3()
{
    WriteLog("Method 3 Called");
}
```

20. Press *Ctrl* + *Shift* + *B* to build the solution.

How it works...

In steps 1 to 11, we created a blank solution and added a .NET Standard 2.0 library to the solution. In these steps, we assigned proper names to the solution and to the library. In steps 12 and 13, we renamed the existing `Class1.cs` created by Visual Studio. In step 15, we created a `using` directive to access the file operations.

In step 16, we created two `private` variables to hold the filename and the `StreamWriter` class. In step 17, we created the default constructor and we are calling the `WriteLog()` method we created in step 18. In step 19, we created three test methods to demonstrate logging. Finally, in step 20, we performed a quick build to check for syntax.

Creating a .NET Core console application to use the library

In this recipe, we will be creating a .NET Core console application to use the library from the previous recipe. You can also try this recipe in macOS or Linux, since .NET Core is cross-platform.

Getting ready

Make sure you have completed the previous recipe and that it builds successfully. Let's open the solution and get ready.

How to do it...

1. Open Visual Studio 2017.
2. Now, open the solution from the previous recipe. Click **File** | **Open** | **Open Project/Solution**, or press *Ctrl* + *Shift* + *O*, and select the `Chapter10.Logging` solution.
3. Press *Ctrl* + *Shift* + *B* for a quick build to check that everything is fine.
4. Click on the `Chapter10.Logging` solution label. Click **File** | **Add** | **New Project**.
5. In the **Add New Project** template dialog box, expand the **Visual C#** node in the left-hand pane.
6. Select **.NET Core** and select **Console App (.NET Core)** in the right-hand pane:

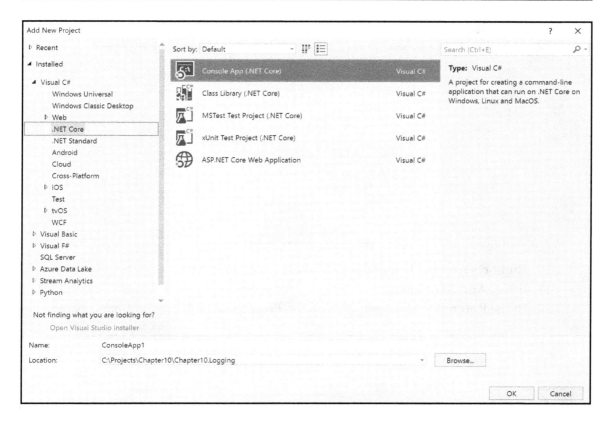

7. In the **Name:** textbox, type `Chapter10.Logging.LogCore` as the name of the project. The rest of the fields can be left as they are:

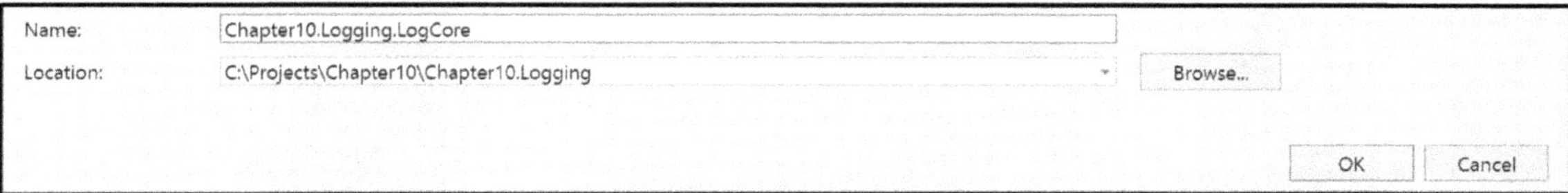

8. Click **OK**.
9. Now, the **Solution Explorer** (press *Ctrl* + *Alt* + *L*) should look like this:

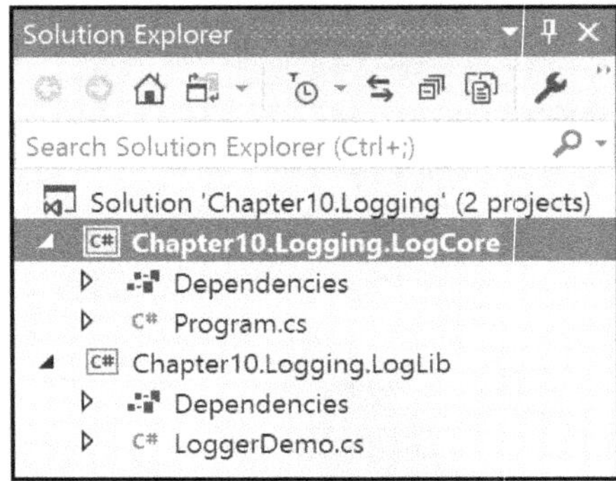

10. Right-click on the **Dependencies** label under `Chapter10.Logging.LogCore`.
11. Select **Add Reference**.
12. In the **Reference Manager**, click on the **Projects** label in the right-hand pane:

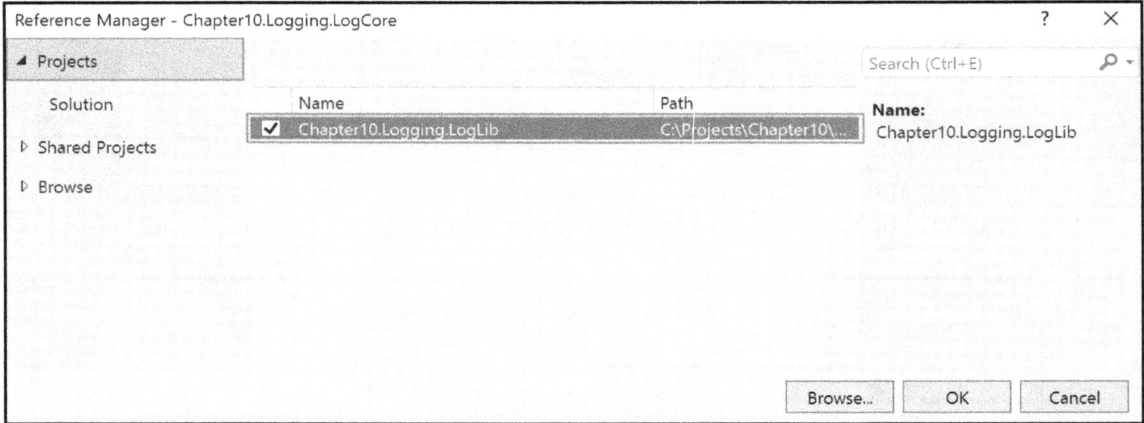

13. Check the `Chapter10.Logging.LogLib` project in the left-hand pane.
14. Click **OK**.
15. Now, double-click on the `Program.cs` label in the **Solution Explorer**.
16. Scroll up until you see the `using` directives.
17. Add the following reference next to the last line of `using` directives:

```
using Chapter10.Logging.LogLib;
```

18. Now, replace the existing code in the `Main()` method with this code:

```
var logDemo = new LoggerDemo();

Console.WriteLine("Executing method 1");
logDemo.CallMethod1();

Console.WriteLine("Executing method 2");
logDemo.CallMethod2();

Console.WriteLine("Executing method 3");
logDemo.CallMethod3();

Console.WriteLine("Press ENTER to exit.");
Console.ReadLine();
```

19. Press *F5* to debug the code.
20. You should see the following output:

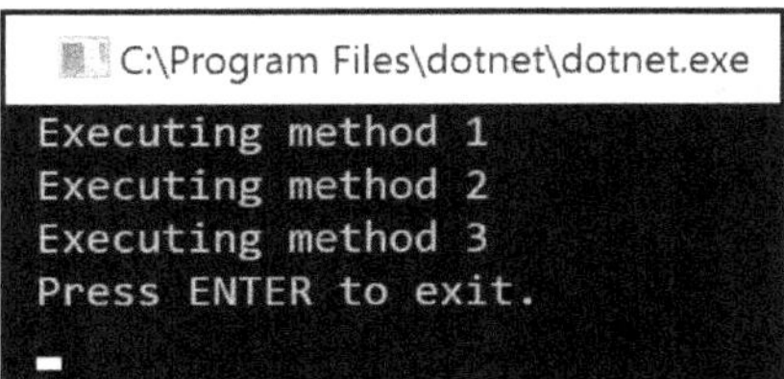

21. Press *Enter* to exit.
22. You will also see a `lib_log.txt` file created inside the `bin/Debug` folder (make sure you have clicked Show All Files):

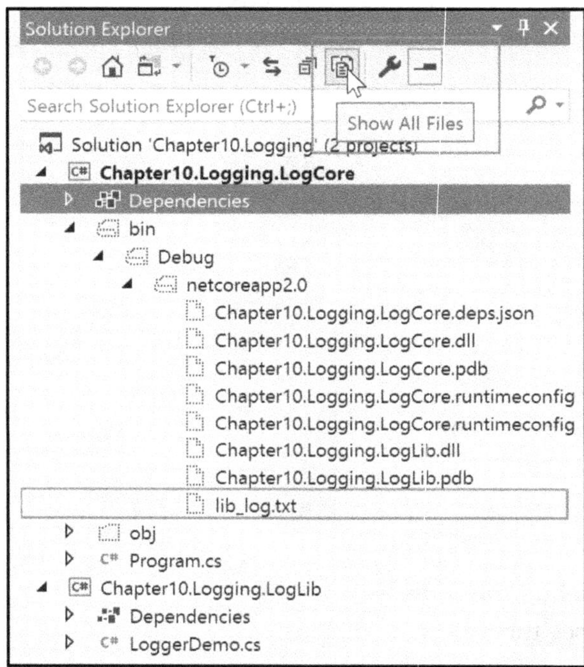

23. The `lib_log.txt` file should have the following output:

```
lib_log.txt    Program.cs    LoggerDemo.cs
4/3/2018 8:19:09 PM Log Message: Constructor Called
4/3/2018 8:19:09 PM Log Message: Method 1 Called
4/3/2018 8:19:09 PM Log Message: Method 2 Called
4/3/2018 8:19:09 PM Log Message: Method 3 Called
```

How it works...

In steps 1 to 10, we opened the solution from the previous recipe and added a .NET Core console application. In these steps, we gave it a proper name. In step 17, we added the code-level reference to the library. In step 18, we created the code inside the `Main` method. In the first line, we created an instance of the `LoggerDemo` class and stored it in a variable. In the next few lines, we executed the `public` methods of `CallMethod1()`, `CallMethod2()`, and `CallMethod3()`.

Finally, in steps 19 and 20, we executed the code and tested it. In steps 21 and 22, we investigated the text file created from the library.

Informing the end user – Exception handling and error messages

In this recipe, we will be looking at exception handling inside a .NET class library. We will be reusing the same library created in the first recipe of this chapter.

Getting ready

Make sure you have completed the two recipes from this chapter. Open the solution and perform a quick build to check that everything is fine and compiles well.

How to do it...

1. Open Visual Studio 2017.
2. Now, open the solution from the previous recipe. Click **File** | **Open** | **Open Project/Solution**, or press *Ctrl* + *Shift* + *O*, and select the `Chapter10.Logging` solution.
3. Press *Ctrl* + *Shift* + *B* for a quick build to check that everything is fine.

4. The **Solution Explorer** should look like this:

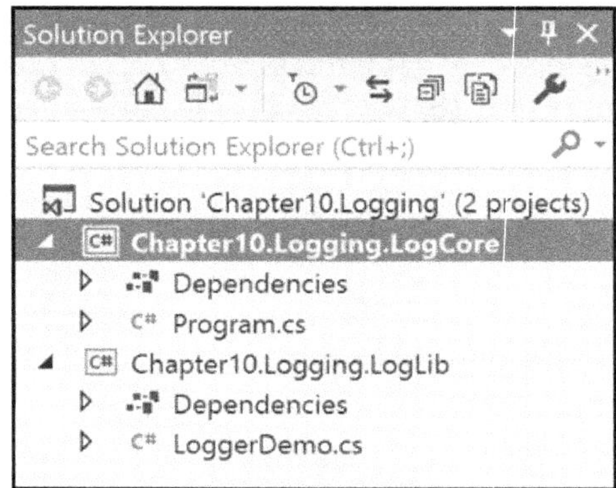

5. Now, double-click on the `LoggerDemo.cs` label to open the code window.
6. Scroll down until you reach the `WriteLog()` method.
7. Replace the current code with the following:

```
try
{
    if (!File.Exists(logFileName))
    {
        logFile = File.CreateText(logFileName);
    }
    else
    {
        logFile = File.AppendText(logFileName);
    }

    logFile.WriteLine($"{DateTime.Now} Log Message: {message} ");
}
catch (FileNotFoundException)
{
    //Cannot find the file you are looking for
}
catch (Exception ex)
{
    //Catch any exception
}
finally
{
    logFile.Close();
}
```

8. Now, click on the .NET Core console application project and press *F5* to test.

How it works...

In steps 1 to 5, we opened the existing solution. In step 7, we added exception handling to the `WriteLog()` method in the library. In the first line of code, we added the keyword `try`. Inside it, we created the code that creates the text file. Then, we caught a `FileNotFoundException` in the first `catch` clause. This is a good practice; to catch the exact exception. If you have caught all exceptions, then you can catch the default `exception`.

Finally, we have used a `finally` clause to close the file stream. The `finally` clause will always execute inside a `try...catch` block. It's a good practice to include the code for a cleanup inside a `finally` clause.

Using Visual Studio 2017 diagnostics and debugging tools

In this recipe, we will be looking at how to debug a .NET Standard 2.0 library using Visual Studio 2017 and its debugging tools. We will be using the same solution we created in the previous recipes.

Getting ready

Make sure you have completed the previous recipes and built them without any issues. Let's get started.

How to do it...

1. Open Visual Studio 2017.
2. Now, open the solution from the previous recipe. Click **File** | **Open** | **Open Project/Solution**, or press *Ctrl* + *Shift* + *O*, and select the `Chapter10.Logging` solution.

3. Press *Ctrl* + *Shift* + *B* for a quick build to check that everything is fine.
4. The **Solution Explorer** should look like this:

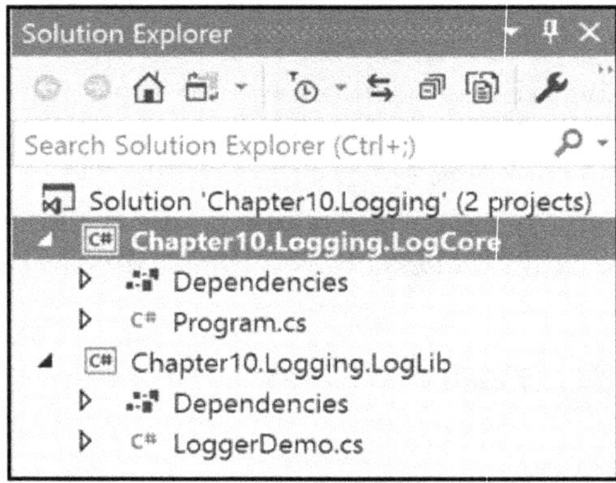

5. Now, double-click on the `LoggerDemo.cs` label to open the code window.
6. Scroll down until you reach the `WriteLog()` method.
7. Now, as shown in the following, click on the gray bar on the left side of the code window to add a debug point:

lib_log.txt Program.cs LoggerDemo.cs

Chapter10.Logging.LogLib Chapter10.Logging.LogLib.LoggerDemo

```
4 references
private void WriteLog(string message)
{
    try
    {
        if (!File.Exists(logFileName))
        {
            logFile = File.CreateText(logFileName);
        }
        else
        {
            logFile = File.AppendText(logFileName);
        }
        logFile.WriteLine($"{DateTime.Now} Log Message: {message} ");

    }
```

8. Again, click on the `Program.cs` tab.
9. Press *F5* to debug the code.
10. As you can see, the cursor will stop at the debugging point:

```
lib_log.txt    Program.cs    LoggerDemo.cs
Chapter10.Logging.LogLib    Chapter10.Logging.LogLib.LoggerDemo    WriteLog(string message)
        4 references
        private void WriteLog(string message)
        {
            try
            {
                if (!File.Exists(logFileName))
                {
                    logFile = File.CreateText(logFileName);
                }
                else
                {
                    logFile = File.AppendText(logFileName);
                }
                logFile.WriteLine($"{DateTime.Now} Log Message: {message} ");

            }
            catch (FileNotFoundException)
```

11. Now, move your mouse pointer to the `message` parameter of the `WriteLog()` method:

```
lib_log.txt    Program.cs    LoggerDemo.cs
Chapter10.Logging.LogLib    Chapter10.Logging.LogLib.LoggerDemo    WriteLog(string message)
        4 references
        private void WriteLog(string message)
        {                                   message "Constructor Called"
            try
            {
                if (!File.Exists(logFileName))
                {
                    logFile = File.CreateText(logFileName);
                }
                else
```

12. Now, you can see what is stored inside that variable.
13. Click on the small green arrow as highlighted in the following:

```
lib_log.txt    Program.cs    LoggerDemo.cs
Chapter10.Logging.LogLib    Chapter10.Logging.LogLib.LoggerDemo    WriteLog(string message)
        4 references
        private void WriteLog(string message)
        {
            try
            {
                if (!File.Exists(logFileName))
                {
                    logFile = File.CreateText(logFileName);
                }
                else
                {
                    logFile = File.AppendText(logFileName);
                }
                logFile.WriteLine($"{DateTime.Now} Log Message: {message} ");
                        logFile null

            }
            catch (FileNotFoundException)
            {
                //Cannot find the file you are looking for
            }
```

14. You should see that the debug point jumps to the `logFile.WriteLine` method.
15. On the right-hand side of the screen, you should see the **Diagnostics Tools** window:

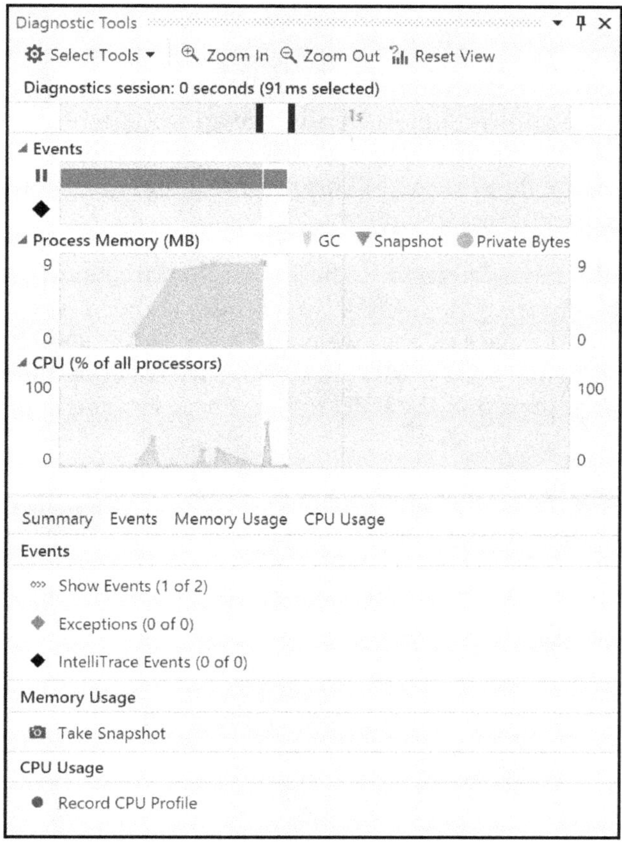

16. Also, at the bottom, you should see the **Watch** windows and the **Call Stack** window:

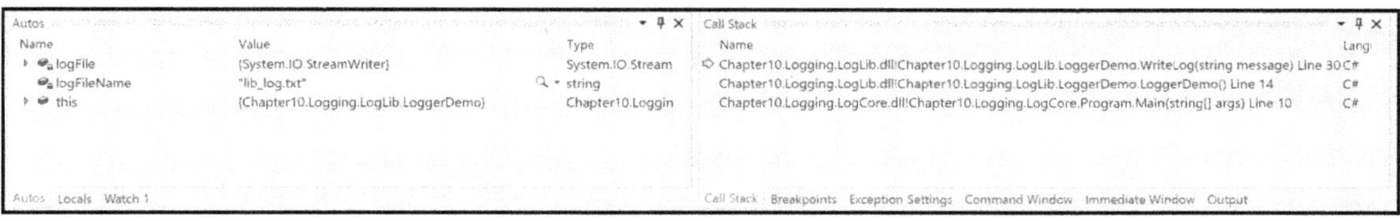

17. Now, stop debugging by pressing *Shift* + *F5*.

How it works...

In steps 1 to 5, we opened the existing solution with the .NET Standard library and its accompanying .NET Core application. In step 10, we added a debugging point to the code. In step 11, we could see that it had stopped at the debugging point, at the .NET Standard 2.0 library itself. From then on, it performed like a normal debugging application. Visual Studio knew we were looking for code in the library.

In step 13, we moved the mouse pointer to the `string` parameter of the `WriteLog()` method, which is in the library code itself. Visual Studio showed us the value inside that parameter. Again, in step 13, we saw that we could jump to any area in the code we desired. This is a new feature in Visual Studio 2017. In step 15, we saw the diagnostic tools available, including the Events, Memory, and the CPU usage. These tools help us to fine-tune our library as normal C# code.

Finally, we looked at the **Watch** and **Call Stack** windows, which are self-explanatory.

11 Packaging and Delivery

In this chapter, we will look at the following recipes:

- Creating a .NET Standard 2.0 library
- Creating a NuGet package of your library
- Submitting the package to NuGet package manager
- Creating a classic Windows application and testing the NuGet package

Technical requirements

Readers should have a basic knowledge of C#. They should also have a basic knowledge of using Visual Studio, installing packages using NuGet, and referencing libraries within projects from other projects.

The code files for this chapter can be found on GitHub:
`https://github.com/PacktPublishing/DotNET-Standard-2-Cookbook/tree/master/Chapter11`

Check out the following video to see the code in action:
`https://goo.gl/XuznM7`

Introduction

In this chapter, we will look at how to create a NuGet package of your library. We will create a basic library, and after that, we will create a NuGet package and submit it. Finally, we will use that package in two different applications.

NuGet is a package delivery tool for your .NET-based applications. It avoids the hassle of finding all the dependencies required for a package or library. For example, if you are looking for Library A, and it requires a few other libraries such as Library B and Library C, you just need to get Library A. NuGet will save you the time of searching for Libraries B and C, as well as installing and configuring them for you.

Creating a .NET Standard 2.0 library

In this recipe, we will create a basic .NET Standard 2.0 library for packaging; for demonstration purposes, we will create a small calculator library.

Getting ready

Make sure you have the latest version of Visual Studio 2017 installed and updated on your system. This recipe assumes you have a fair amount of knowledge of creating a .NET Standard 2.0 library.

How to do it...

1. Open Visual Studio 2017.
2. Click **File** | **New** | **Project** and, in the **New Project template** dialog box, select **Visual Studio Solutions** under **Other Project Types** in the left-hand pane and select **Blank Solution** in the right-hand pane.
3. In the **Name:** textbox, type `Chapter11.Packaging` as the name of the solution, as shown in the screenshot. Select a preferred location under the **Location:** drop-down list, or click the **Browse...** button and select a location. Leave the defaults as they are:

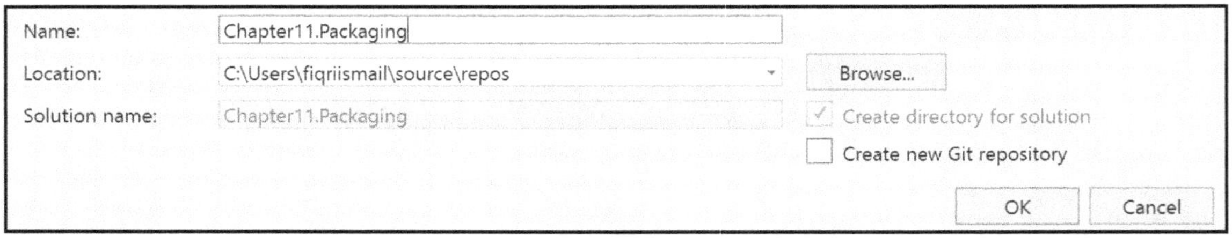

Name: Chapter11.Packaging
Location: C:\Users\fiqriismail\source\repos
Browse...
Solution name: Chapter11.Packaging
Create directory for solution
Create new Git repository
OK
Cancel

4. Click **OK**.

5. Now, in the **Solution Explorer** (or press *Ctrl* + *Alt* + *L*), select `Chapter11.Packaging`. Right-click and select **Add** | **New Project.**
6. In the **Add New Project** dialog box, expand the **Visual C#** node and select **.NET Standard** in the left-hand pane.
7. In the right-hand pane, select **Class Library (.NET Standard),** as shown here:

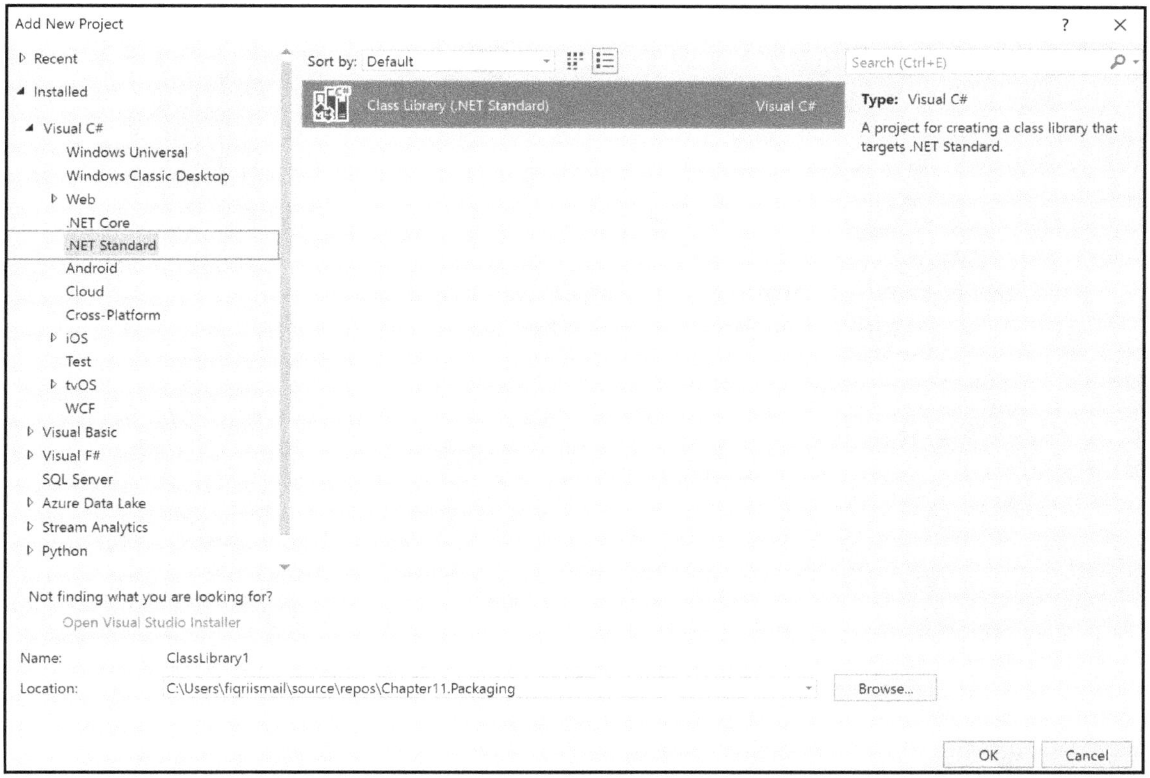

8. Now, in the **Name:** textbox, type `Chapter11.Packaging.CalcLib` and leave the **Location:** textbox as it is:

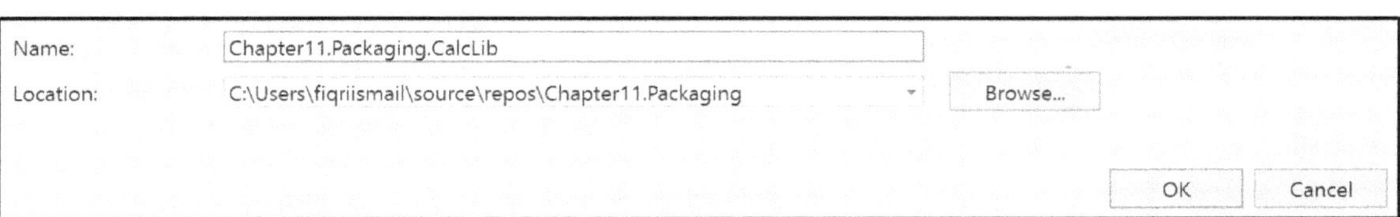

9. Click **OK**.
10. Now, the **Solution Explorer** should look like this:

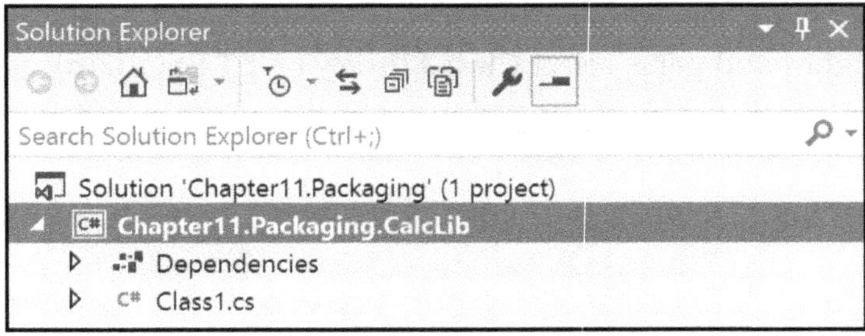

11. Click on `Class1.cs` and press *F2* to rename it. Type `Calculator.cs` as the new name.
12. Select **Yes** to confirm the renaming of the class name, too.
13. Now, add these two public methods to the class body:

```
public int Add(int num1, int num2)
{
    return num1 + num2;
}

public int Subtract(int num1, int num2)
{
    return num1 - num2;
}
```

14. Press *Ctrl* + *Shift* + *B* for a quick build.

How it works...

In steps 1 to 10, we created a blank solution and gave it a proper name. And then we added a .NET Standard 2.0 class library to the solution. In steps 11 and 12, we renamed the default `Class1.cs` to something more meaningful. Yes, you can always delete this class and create a new one. And, in step 13, we created two simple methods for the addition and subtraction of two integers.

Finally, we performed a quick build in step 14 for syntax checking.

Creating a NuGet package of your library

In this recipe, we will look at how to create a NuGet package out of the library you have just built in the previous recipe.

Getting ready

Make sure you have completed the previous recipe or that you have a .NET Standard library already with you. Let's get started.

How to do it...

1. Open Visual Studio 2017.
2. Now, open the solution from the previous recipe. Click **File** | **Open** | **Open Project/Solution**, or press *Ctrl* + *Shift* + *O*, and select the `Chapter11.Packaging` solution.
3. Now, the **Solution Explorer** should look like this:

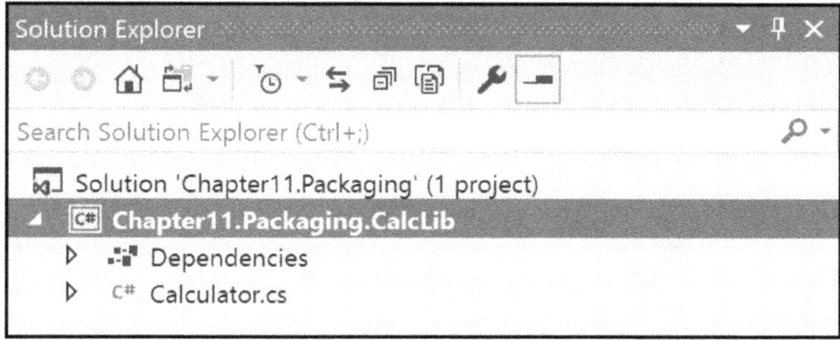

4. Now, click on the `Chapter11.Packaging.CalcLib` project label to select it.
5. Right-click and select **Properties**.
6. In the **Properties** tab, click on the **Packages** label:

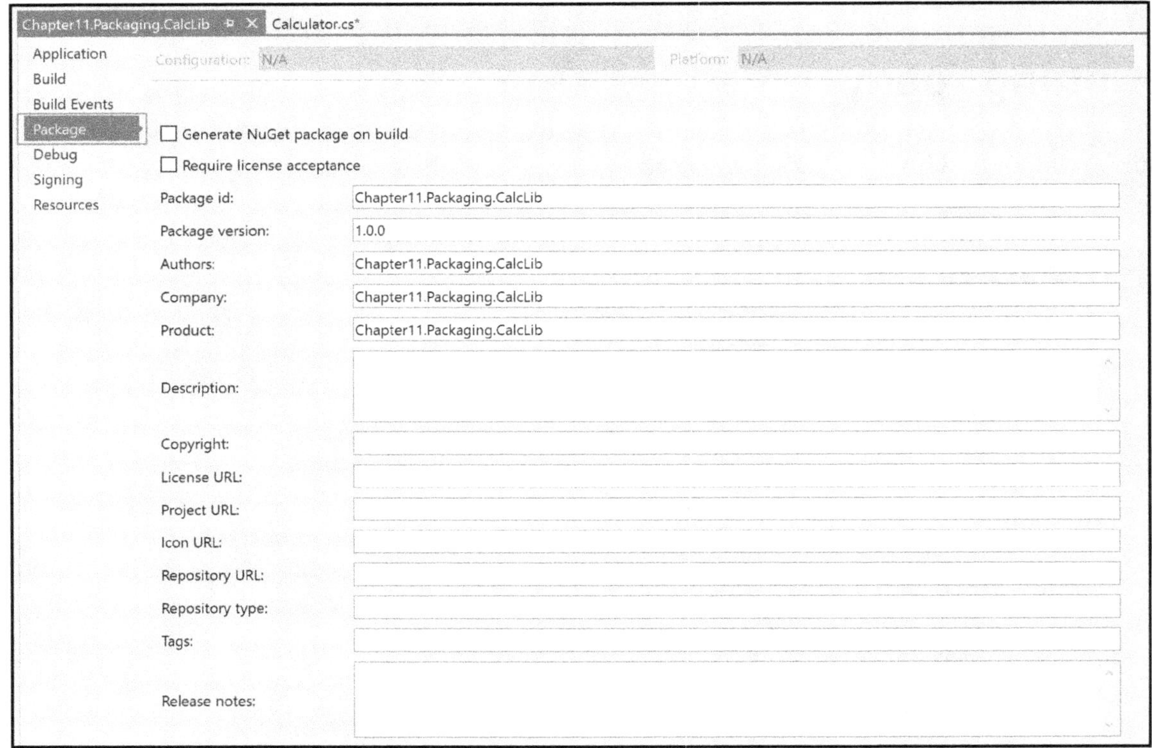

7. Now, fill in the information and it should look like this:

Chapter11.Packaging.CalcLib | Calculator.cs

Application
Build
Build Events
Package
Debug
Signing
Resources

Configuration: N/A   Platform: N/A

☐ Generate NuGet package on build

☐ Require license acceptance

Package id:	Packt_DotNetStandard_CookBook_Chap11
Package version:	1.0.0
Authors:	Fiqri Ismail
Company:	Fiqri Ismail
Product:	.NET Standard 2.0 Library Demo
Description:	This is a sample library created to demonstrate NuGet Packaging
Copyright:	
License URL:	
Project URL:	
Icon URL:	
Repository URL:	
Repository type:	
Tags:	
Release notes:	

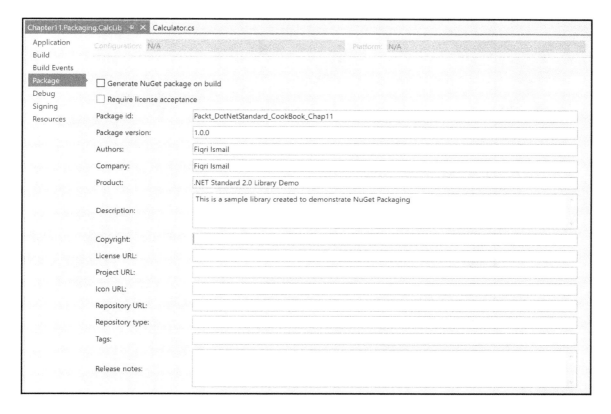

8. Now, **Save** and close.
9. Again, in the toolbar, select **Release** from the debugging area:

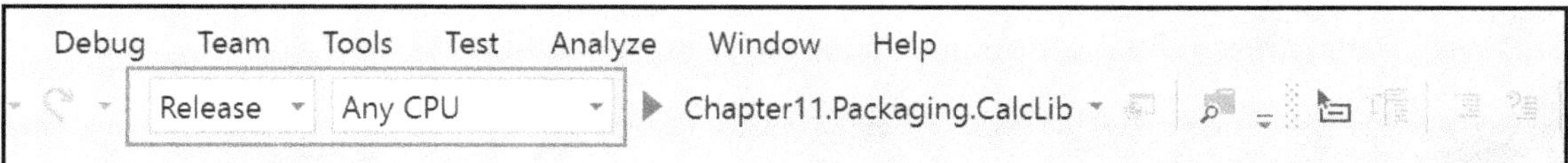

10. Now, again in the **Solution Explorer**, right-click on the `Chapter11.Packaging.CalcLib` label.

11. Select **Pack**:

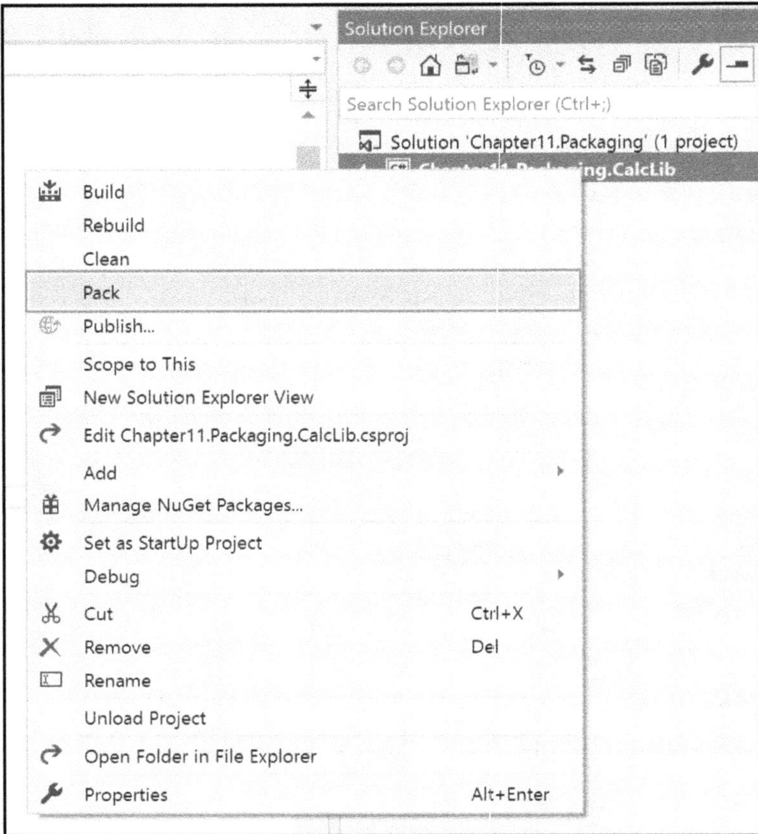

12. This should build and create a NuGet package in your location.
13. You can see the location in the output window, as shown:

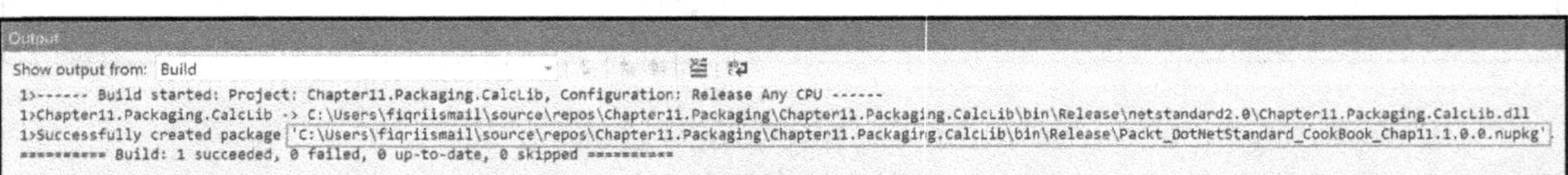

How it works...

The steps are self explanatory. As you follow these steps, you will be able to see the NuGet package is selected. In step 7, you can check **Require License Acceptance** to true, if you really want your customers to accept the license terms explicitly to your module. The most important step is step 9, in which you set the build option to **Release**. Make sure you have done this when you get your library up there—not the debug version, always the release version.

Submitting the package to NuGet package manager

In this recipe, we will look at how to submit our NuGet package created in the previous recipe. To submit a package to NuGet, you will be required to sign in. It's easy if you have a Microsoft Live account with you, otherwise you can always create a `nuget.org` account at the NuGet site itself.

Getting ready

Make sure you have completed the previous recipe and created a NuGet package. Also, it's handy to have a Microsoft Live account to make things smoother during the login process, but yes, you can always create a NuGet account.

How to do it...

1. Open your preferred browser.
2. In the address bar, type `www.nuget.org`, and press *Enter*.

3. Now, click on the **Sign in** link in the top right-hand corner:

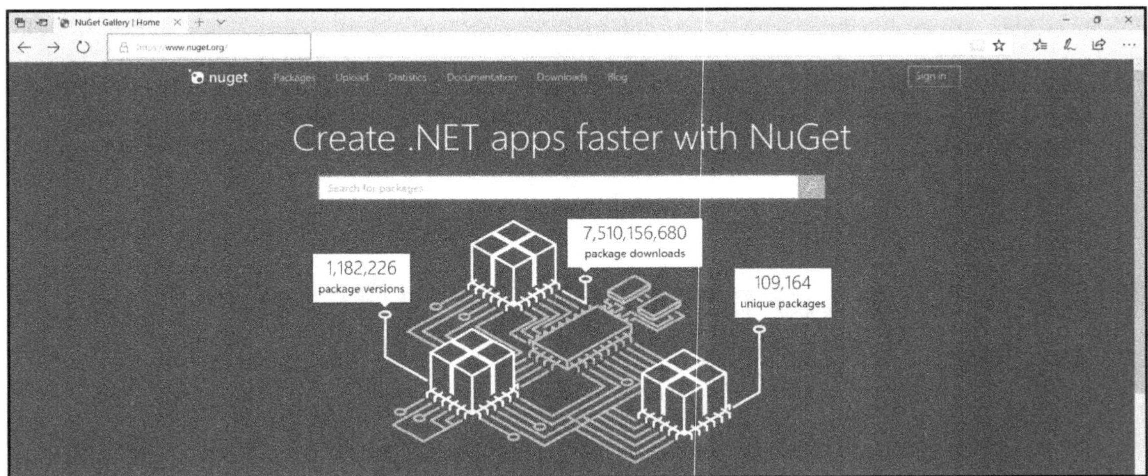

4. Use your Microsoft account or create a NuGet account and then sign in:

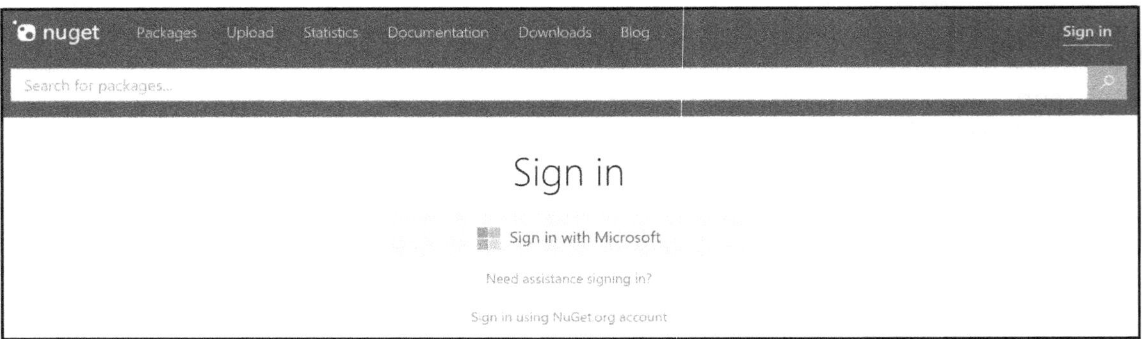

5. After a successful sign in, click the **Upload** link.

6. Now, in this screen, you can drag and drop your package or you can browse for the package:

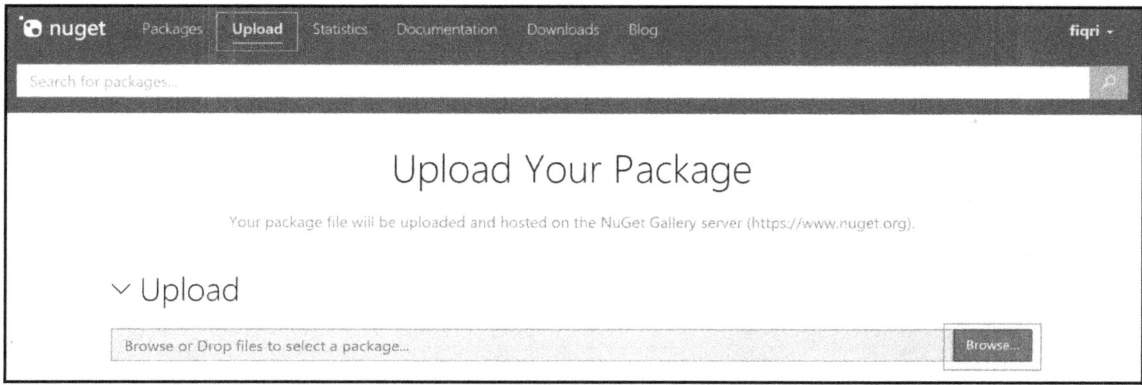

7. Now, click on the **Browse...** button and locate your package (or you can drag and drop the package here):

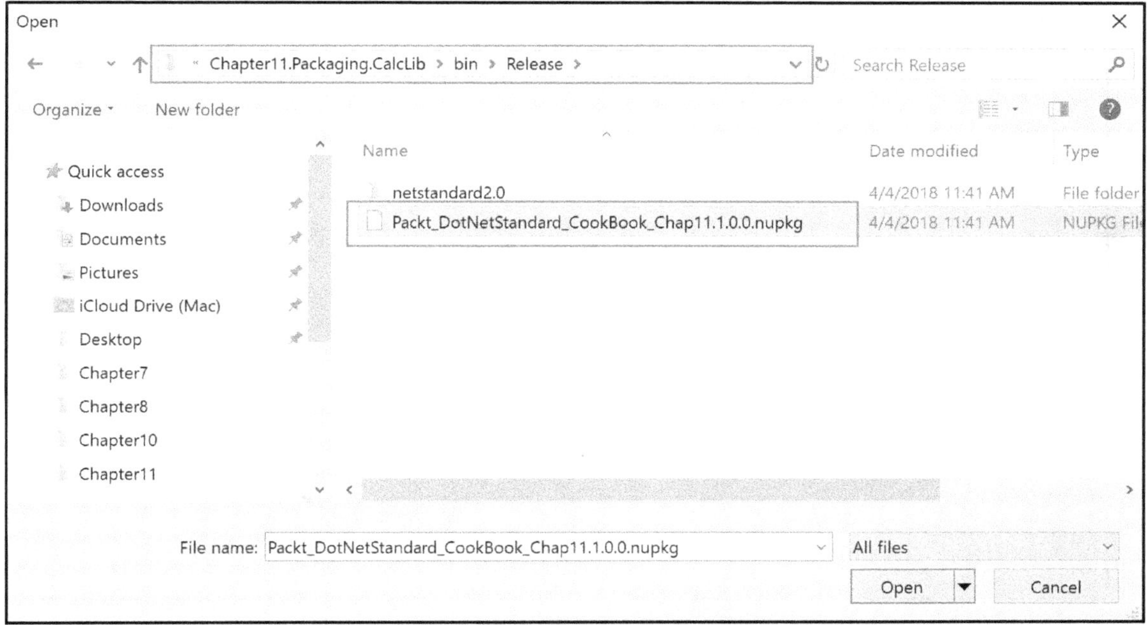

8. Click **Open.**
9. In the next screen, you will be asked to confirm the details of your package.
10. If you are happy with it, click on the **Submit** button at the bottom of the screen:

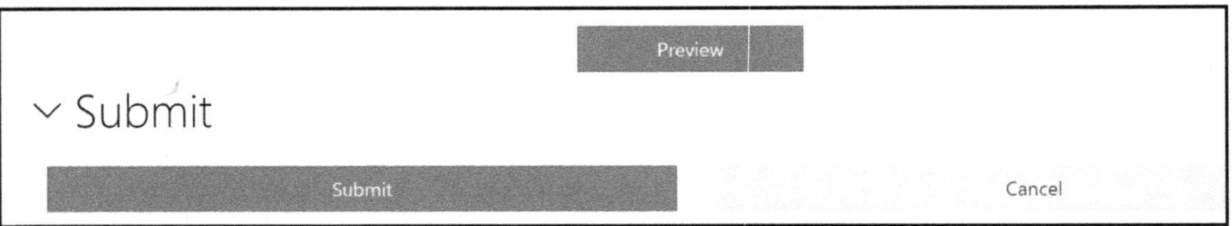

11. You should see this screen after a successful submission:

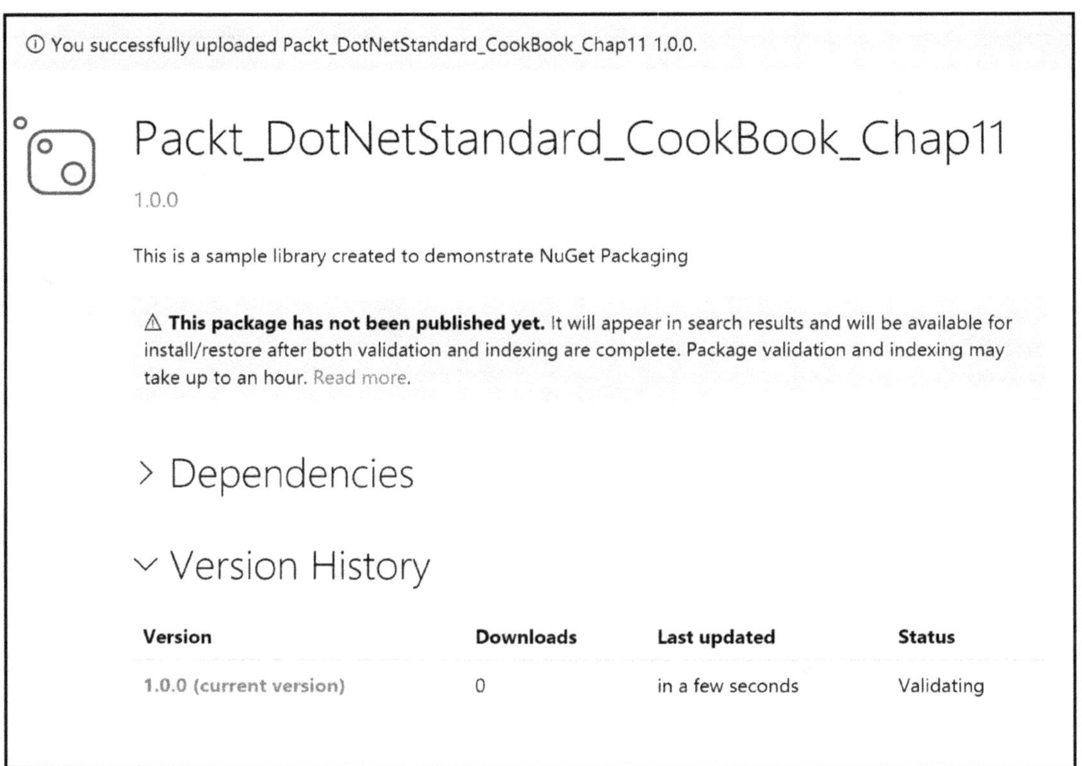

12. After a few minutes, you should see the installation instructions for your package:

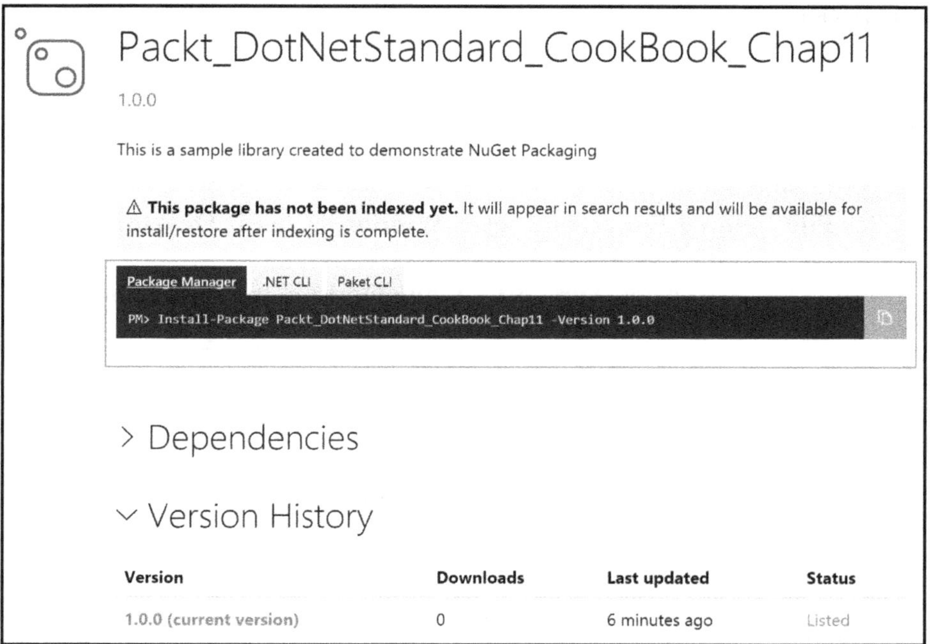

How it works...

All these steps explain how to create and submit your NuGet Package. You need to keep a few things in mind though, things such as proper naming, and testing before submitting a library. Always make sure you update the library with new versions, as they will contain bug fixes that allow you to deliver a very good product at the end of the day.

Creating a classic Windows application and testing the NuGet package

In this recipe, we will look at creating a classic Windows application and using the NuGet package submitted in the previous chapter. We will create a brand new project and use the library.

Getting ready

Make sure you have completed the previous recipe that submitted a NuGet package. Make sure that the package is ready for installation at `nuget.org`.

How to do it...

1. Open Visual Studio 2017.
2. Click **File** | **New** | **Project** and select **Windows Classic Desktop** in the right-hand pane under **Visual C#**.
3. Select **Windows Forms App (.NET Framework)** in the right-hand pane:

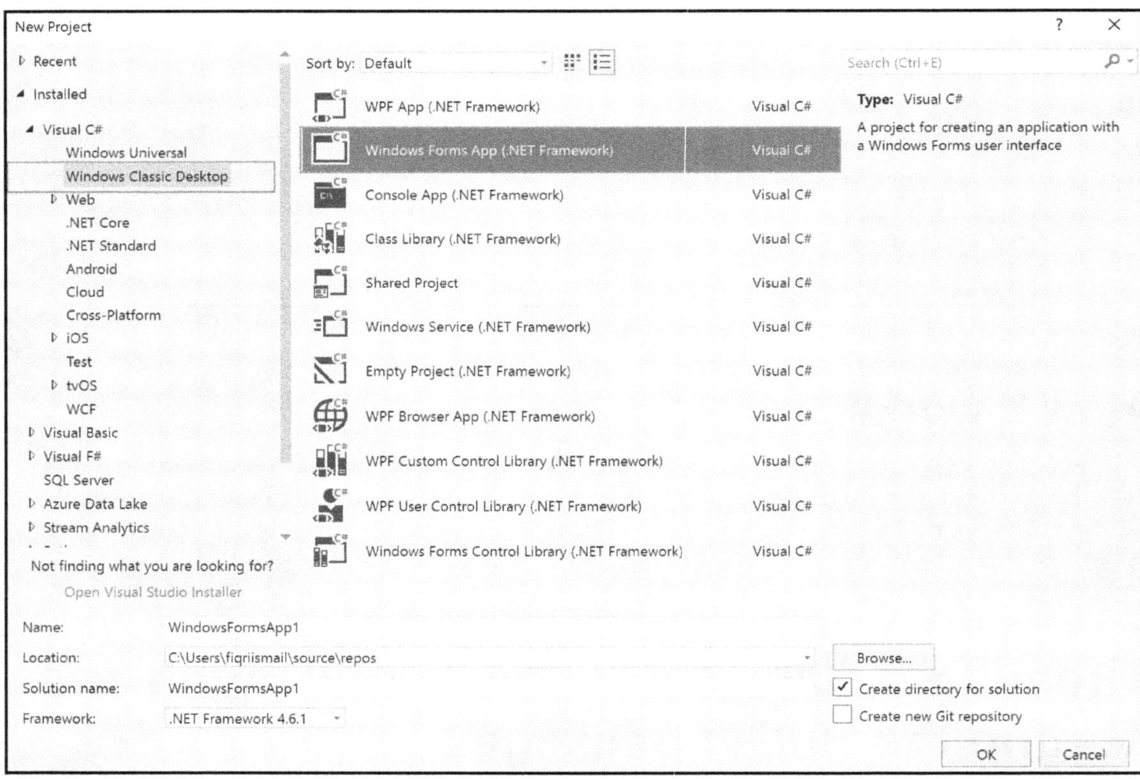

4. Now, in the **Name:** textbox, type `Chapter11.Packaging.WinAppUsage` and, under the **Location:** textbox, select a proper location and leave the other fields as they are:

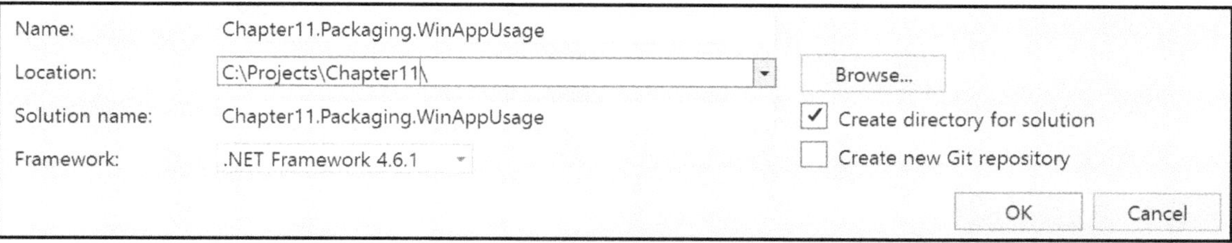

5. Click **OK**.
6. The **Solution Explorer** (*Ctrl* + *Alt* + *L*) should look like this:

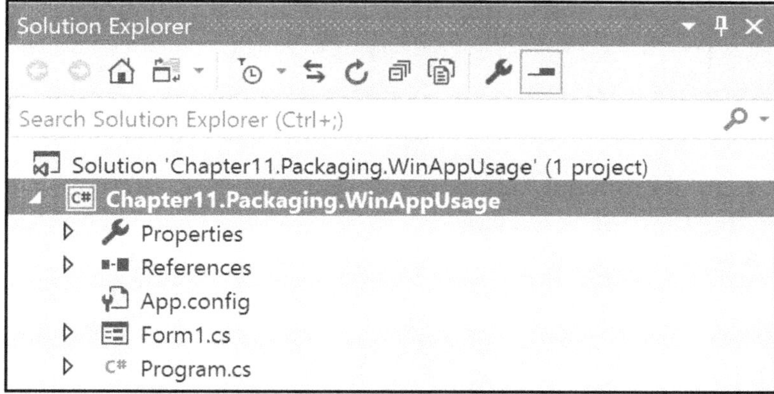

7. Now, click on `Form1.cs` and change the name to `MainForm.cs`.
8. Answer **Yes** to confirm the change to the class name as well.
9. Now, drag two buttons to the form in the designer.
10. Change the properties of the buttons as follows:

Control	Property	Value
Button	**Name**	`BtnAdd`
Button	**Text**	`Add`
Button	**Name**	`BtnSub`
Button	**Text**	`Subtract`

Form	Name	`MainForm`
Form	Text	`Simple Calculator`

11. Now, your form should look like this:

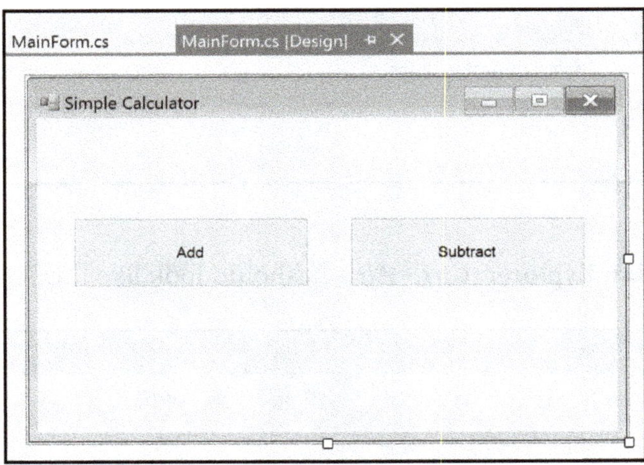

12. Now, right-click on the **References** label.
13. Select **Manage NuGet Packages.**
14. Click **Browse** and, in the search box, type the Package ID you have selected while uploading.
15. In this case, `Packt_DotNetStandard_CookBook_Chap1`, and press *Enter*:

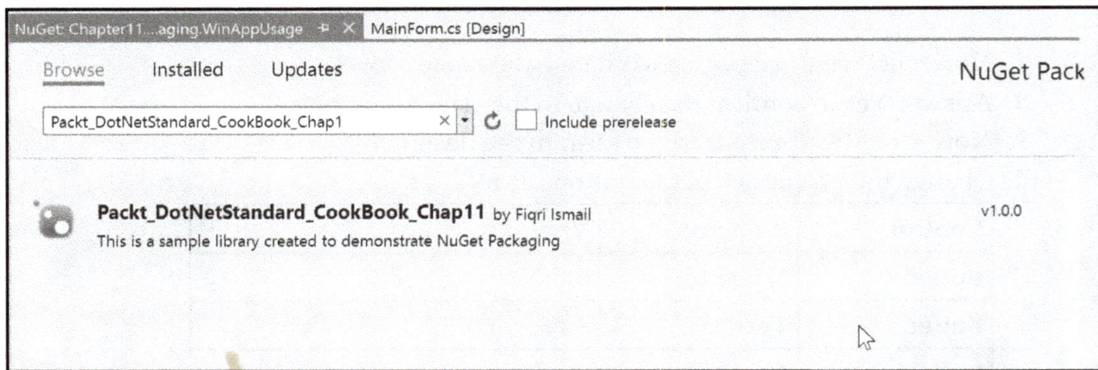

16. Now, click on the package.
17. Click the **Install** button in the right-hand pane:

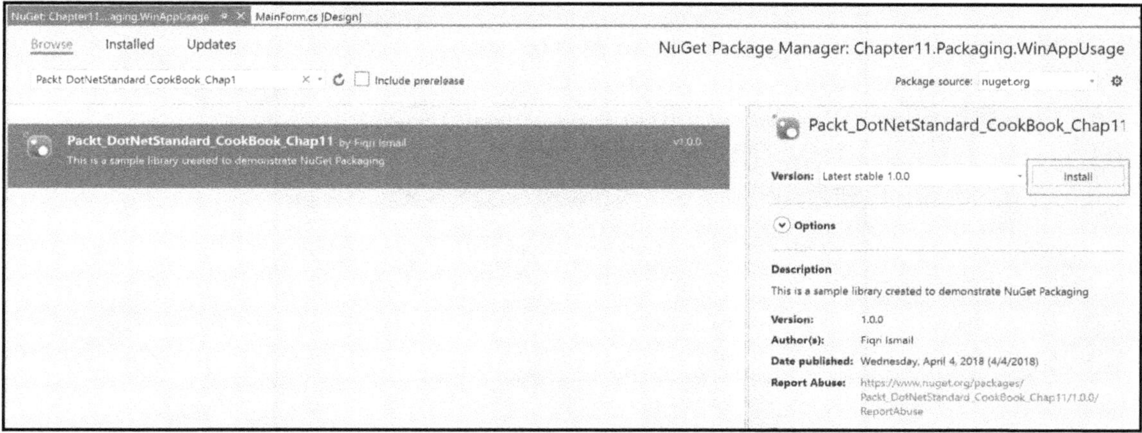

18. Click **OK** in the confirmation dialog box:

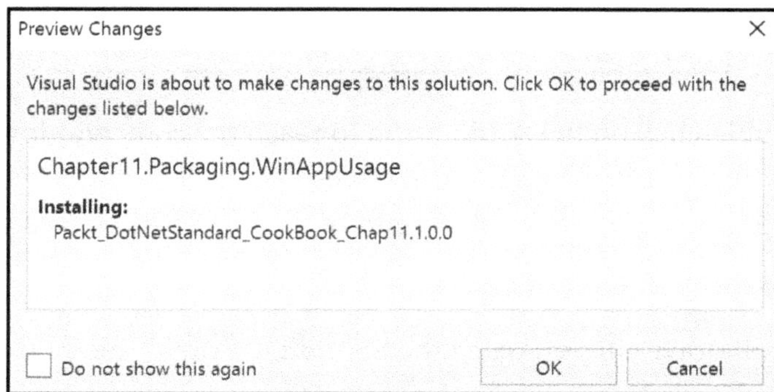

19. After a successful installation, the output window should look like this:

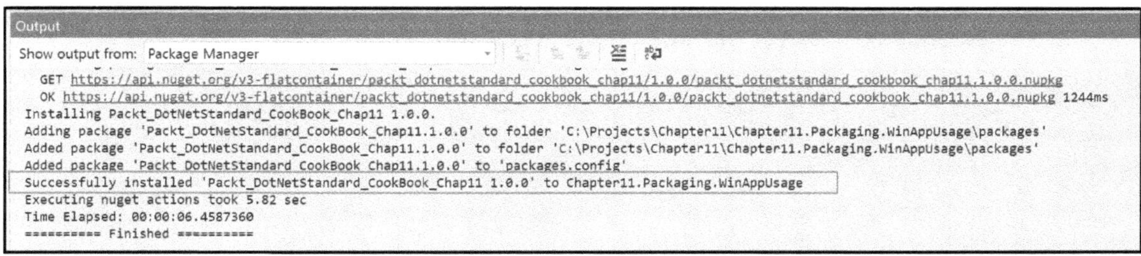

20. Now in the **Solution Explorer**, expand the **References** tab and you should see our library there:

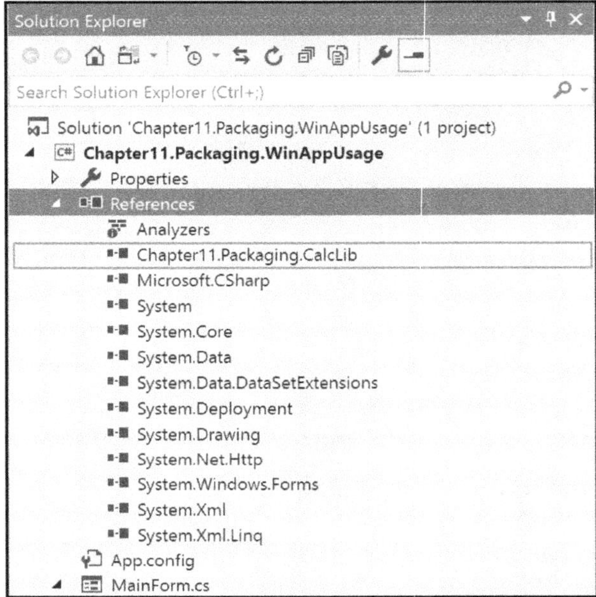

21. Now, double-click on the **Add** button to reach the code window.
22. Scroll up till you see the `using` directives.
23. Add the following directive at the end of the `using` directives.

```
using Chapter11.Packaging.CalcLib;
```

24. Now, scroll down till you reach the `BtnAdd_Click()` method.
25. Add the following code inside the method:

```
var calculator = new Calculator();
var answer = calculator.Add(10, 20);

MessageBox.Show($"The answer is {answer}");
```

26. Now, double-click on the **Subtract** button and add the following code inside the `click` method:

```
var calculator = new Calculator();
var answer = calculator.Subtract(50, 20);

MessageBox.Show($"The answer is {answer}");
```

27. Now, press *F5* to test the application.
28. Click on the **Add** button and you should see an output like this:

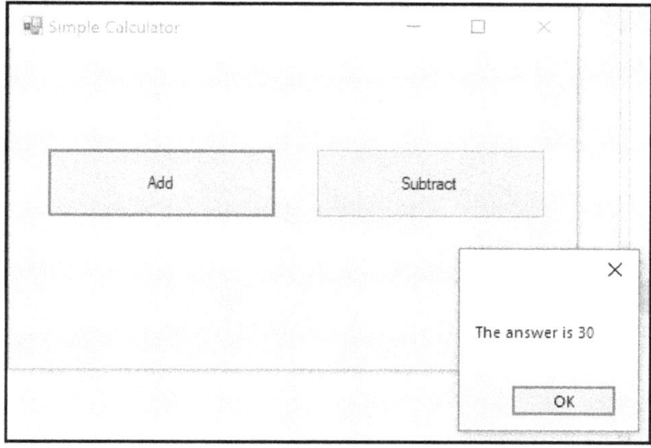

29. Do the same for the **Subtract** button.
30. Click **OK** and close the window.

How it works...

In steps 1 to 7, we created a classic Windows application project. And then, in steps 9 to 11, we created the UI for the Windows project. In steps 14 and 15, we opened NuGet Package Manager. And then we searched for our package and confirmed that it had loaded. In steps 18 to 20, we installed our package and confirmed that it had installed.

In step 24, we added the reference to our library, which is installed using NuGet Package Manager. In steps 25 and 26, we created an instance of the `Calculator` class and used its `Add()` and `Subtract()` methods. Finally, in steps 28 to 30, we tested the application.

Using the package manager is one way of installing a package from NuGet. But you can use the NuGet Package Manager Console to do the same. To access the package manager console, you can click **Tools** | **NuGet Package Manager** | **Package Manager Console:**

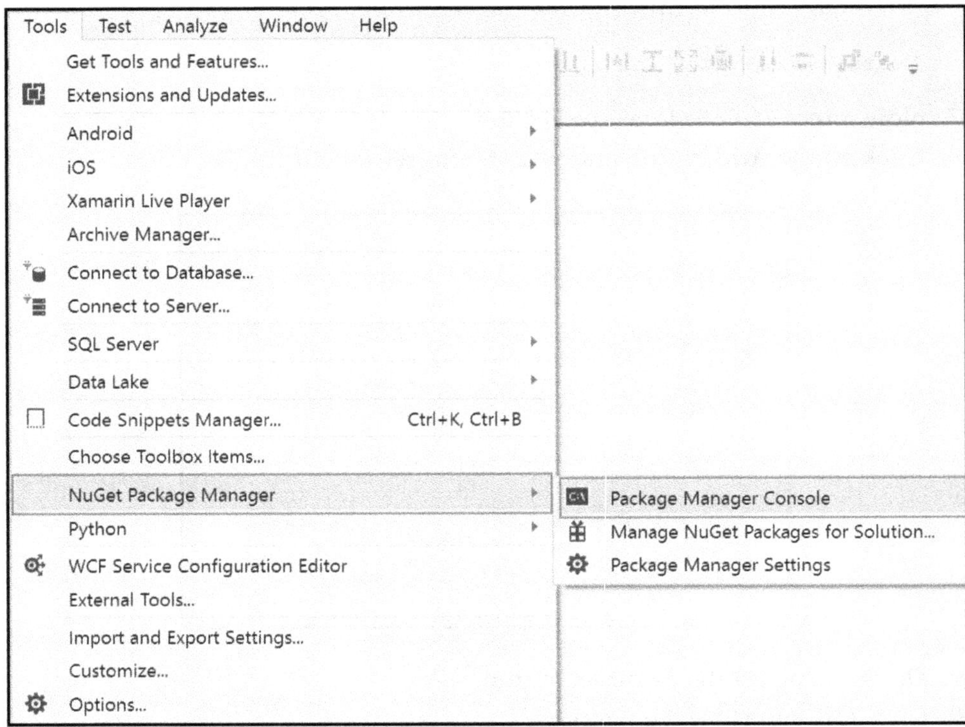

In the console, you can type:

```
Install-Package Packt_DotNetStandard_CookBook_Chap11 -Version 1.0.0
```

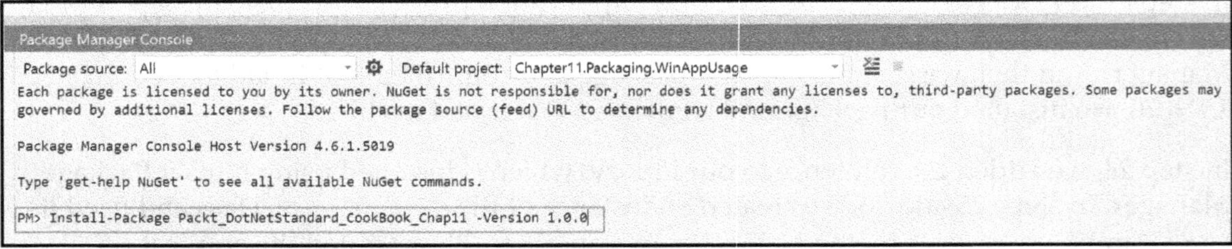

This method will do the same and install your package to the project.

12
Deploying

In this chapter, we will look at the following recipes:

- Creating a free Azure Cloud subscription
- Creating an ASP.NET Core web application to use the library from NuGet
- Deploying the application to Azure Cloud

Technical requirements

Readers should have a basic knowledge of C#. They should also have a basic knowledge of using Visual Studio, installing packages using NuGet, and referencing libraries within projects from other projects.

The code files for this chapter can be found on GitHub:
`https://github.com/PacktPublishing/DotNET-Standard-2-Cookbook/tree/master/Chapter12/Chapter12.Azure.WebAppCore`

Check out the following video to see the code in action:
`https://goo.gl/syvoGK`

Introduction

In this chapter, we will be working with a library we worked on in the previous chapter. In that chapter, we created a library and submitted it at NuGet. We will be using the same library with an ASP.NET core application and deploying it to Azure and testing it.

Creating a free Azure Cloud subscription

In this recipe, we will create an Azure free account for you. This will help you to deploy the application at Azure. We will be using Visual Studio tools for Azure to deploy our project. At the time of writing this book, Microsoft allows you to create one free account worth USD 200; it is also freely available for one year.

Getting ready

Make sure you have a valid credit card before you start this process. The credit card is only required for validation purposes.

How to do it...

1. Open your preferred browser.
2. Type `azure.microsoft.com`, and press *Enter*:

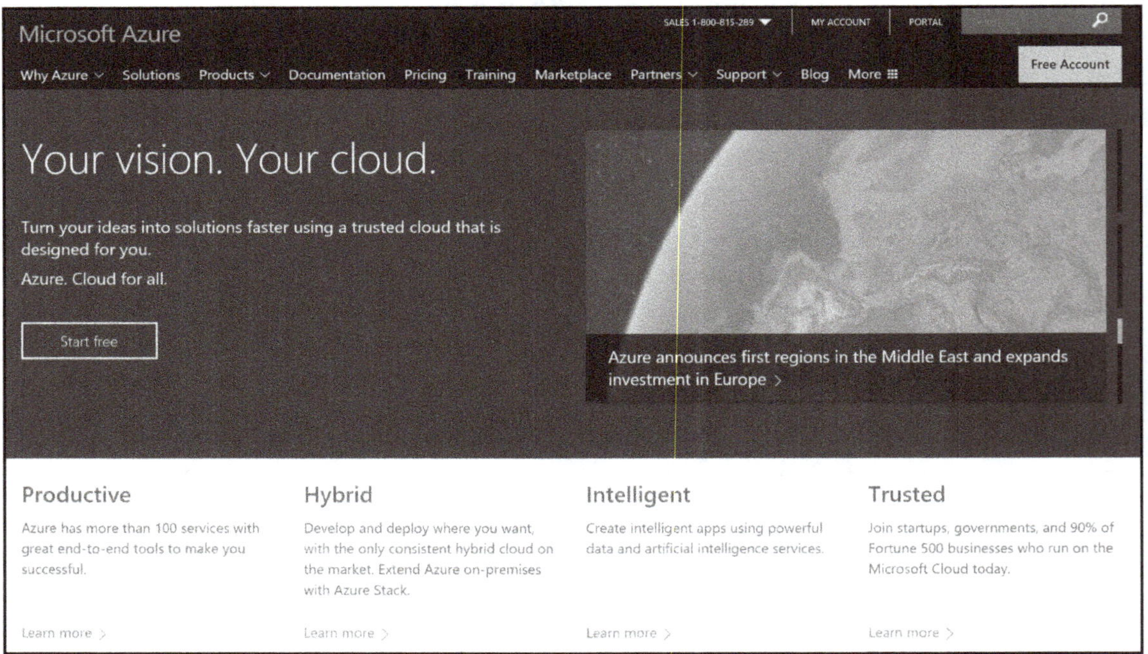

3. Now, click on the **Free Account** green button in the top right-hand corner, or click the **Start free** button at the left-hand side.
4. After that, you will get a screen of information.
5. Again, click on the **Start free** button.
6. You will then be requested to sign in using a Microsoft account or any other account.
7. After sign in, you will be asked to give payment information. Follow the instructions and you are good to go with a new Azure account.
8. After all that has been completed, you will be presented with the Azure Portal.
9. Or else, type `portal.azure.com` in the address bar, and press *Enter*.
10. You should be presented with the Azure Portal and should see a screen similar to this:

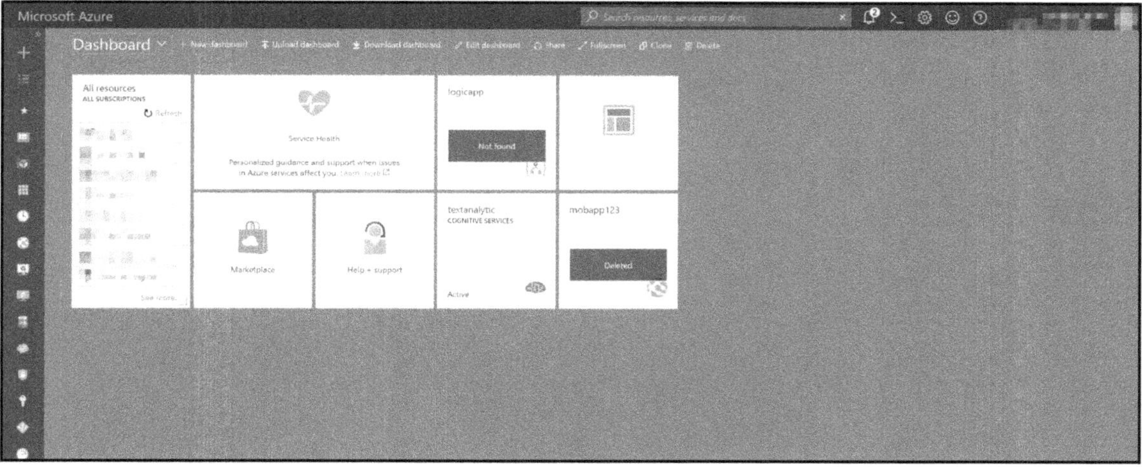

Azure Portal

How it works...

The steps are straightforward and all you need to do is follow the instructions from the Azure Portal on creating a new subscription.

Creating an ASP.NET core web application to use the library from NuGet

In this recipe, we will create an ASP.NET core web application, and then we will install the .NET Standard 2.0 library we uploaded at NuGet in the previous chapter.

Getting ready

Make sure you have the latest version of Visual Studio 2017 installed and updated, and also make sure you have completed the previous chapter.

How to do it...

1. Open Visual Studio 2017.
2. Click **File** | **New** | **Project** and select **Web** in the right-hand pane under **Visual C#**.
3. Select **ASP.NET Core Web Application** in the right-hand pane:

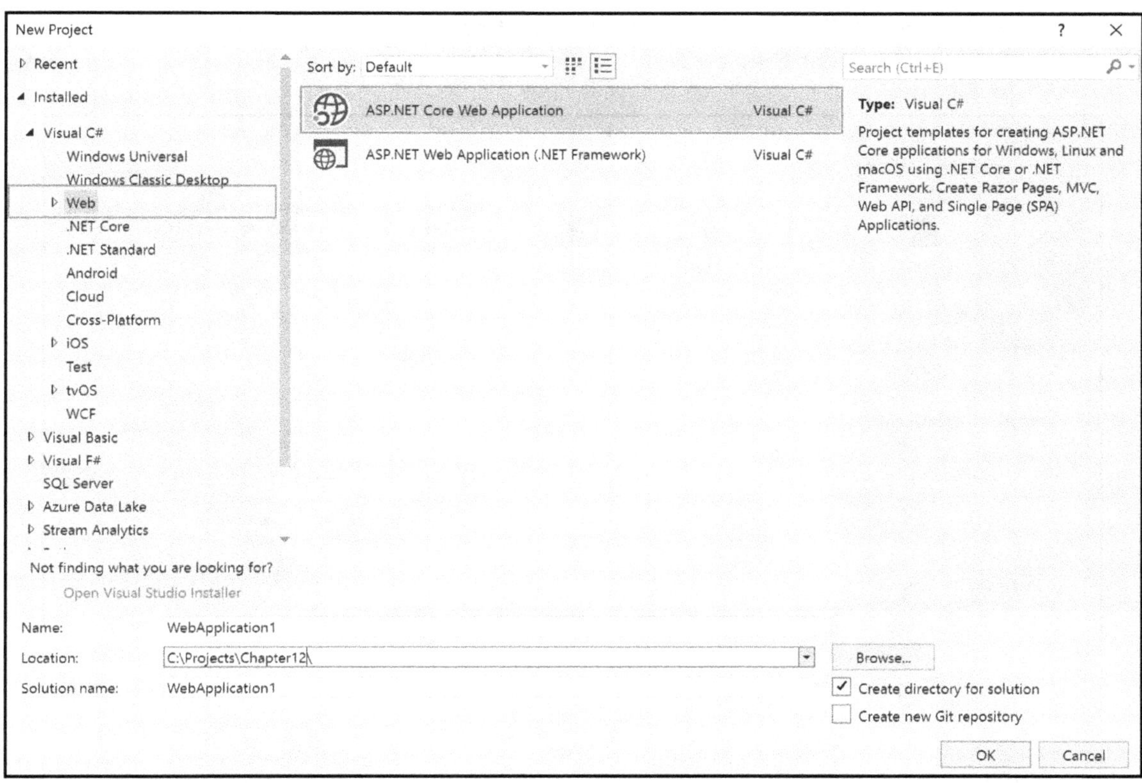

4. Now, in the **Name:** textbox, type `Chapter12.Azure.WebAppCore`, and, under the **Location:** textbox, select a proper location and leave the other fields as they are:

5. Click **OK**.

6. In the **New ASP.NET Core Web Application** dialog box, select **Empty** and leave the other fields as they are:

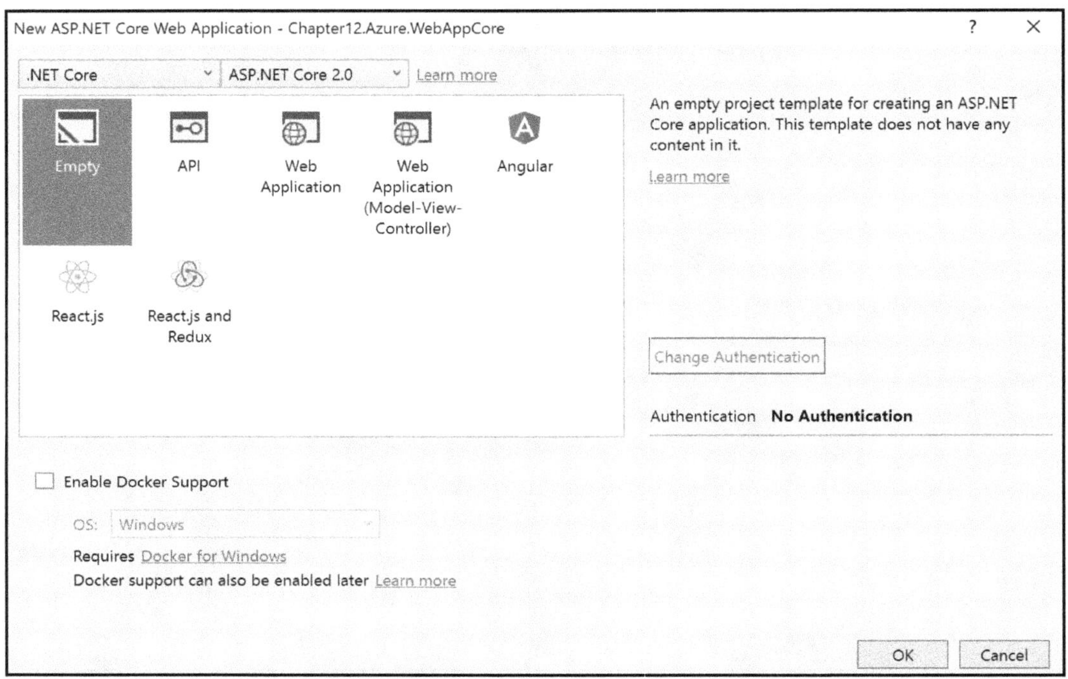

7. Click **OK.**
8. The **Solution Explorer** (*Ctrl* + *Alt* + *L*) should look like this:

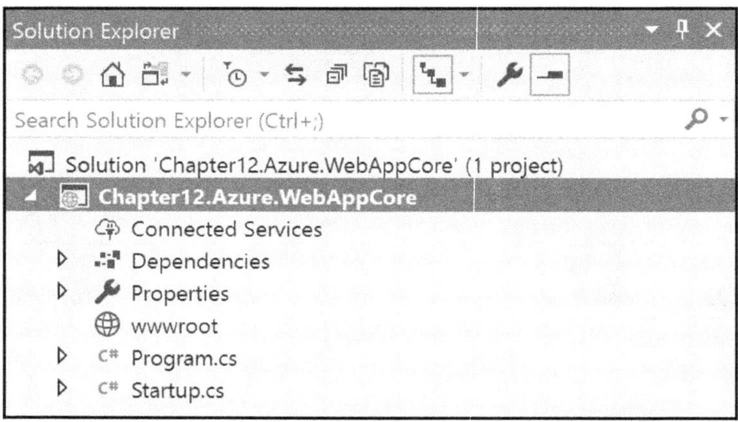

9. Now, right-click on the **Dependencies** label.
10. Select `Manage NuGet Packages`.
11. Click **Browse** and, in the search box, type the Package ID you have selected while uploading.
12. In this case, `Packt_DotNetStandard_CookBook_Chap1`, and press *Enter*:

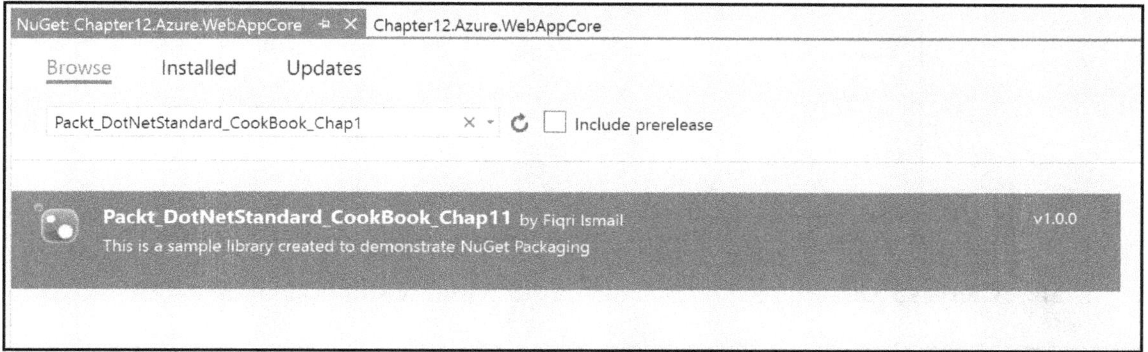

13. Now, click on the package.
14. Click the **Install** button in the right-hand pane:

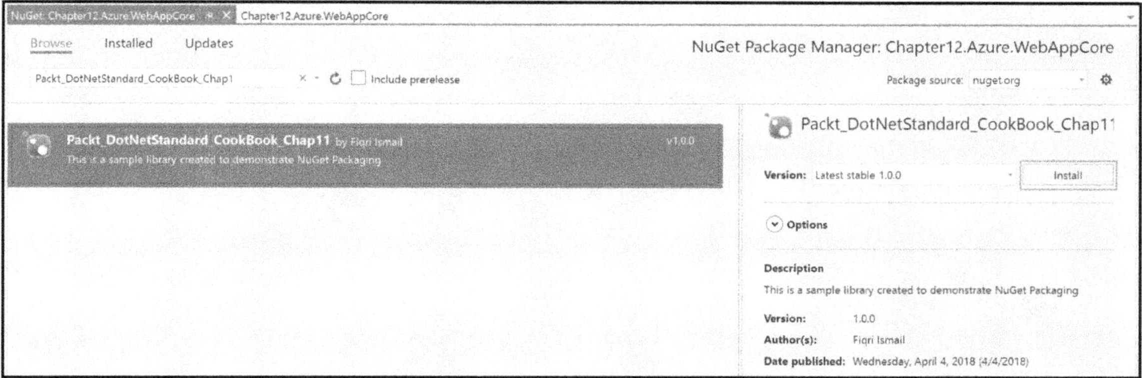

15. Click **OK** in the confirmation dialog box.

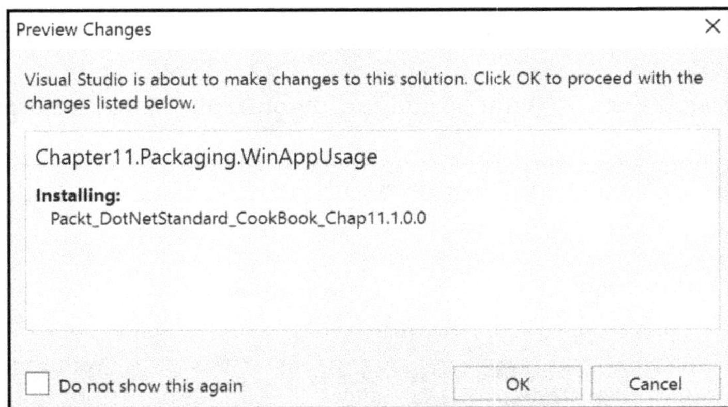

16. After a successful installation, the output window should look like this:

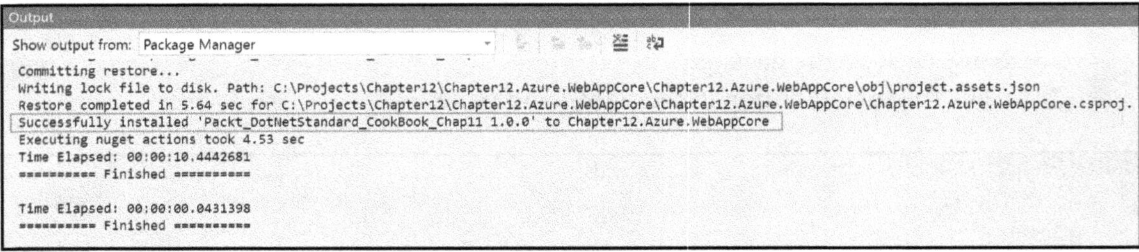

17. Now, in the **Solution Explorer**, expand the **Dependencies** | **NuGet** tab and you should see our library there:

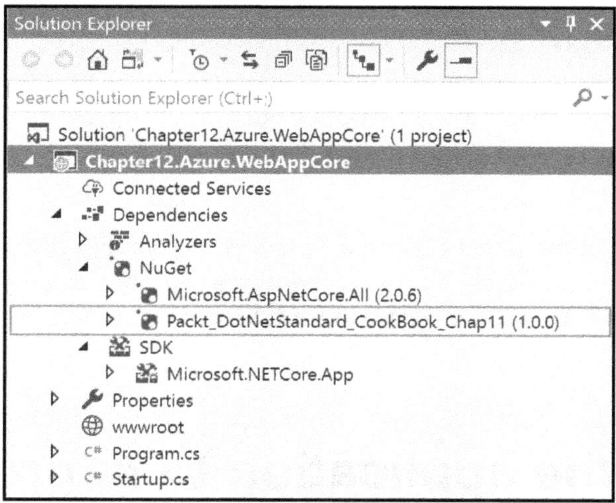

18. Now, double-click on the `Startup.cs` button to reach the code window.
19. Scroll up till you see the `using` directives.
20. Add the following directive at the end of the `using` directives:

```
using Chapter11.Packaging.CalcLib;
```

21. Now, scroll down till you reach the `app.Run()` method inside the `Configure()` method.
22. Replace the code with this:

```
var calculator = new Calculator();
var answer = calculator.Add(10, 50);

await context.Response.WriteAsync($"Answer for 10+50
    is {answer}");
```

23. Press *F5* to debug.
24. You should get an output like this:

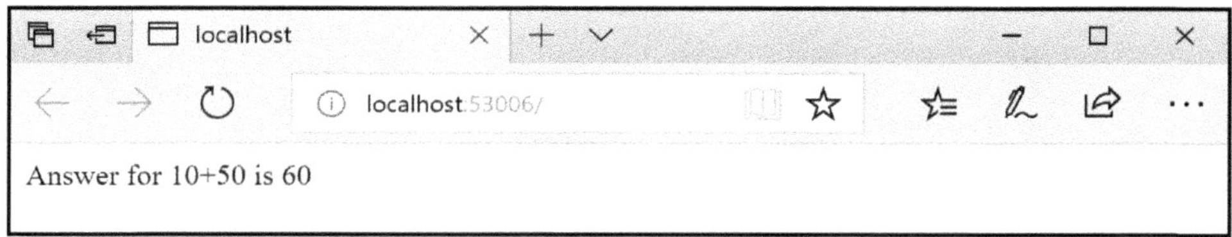

How it works...

In steps 1 to 9, we created an ASP.NET core project. We selected an empty project for this recipe. After that, in steps 10 to 17, we installed the library created in the previous chapter. We used the NuGet Package Manager to install it and we also confirmed that the library was successfully installed.

In step 20, we referenced the library using a `using` directive. Finally, in step 22, we created an instance of the `Calculator` class and stored it in a variable. Finally, we sent the output to the browser using the `WriteAsync()` method. In step 24, we tested our application in the browser.

Deploying the application to Azure Cloud

In this recipe, we will look at deploying our application to Azure. We will be using Visual Studio 2017 to deploy the application to an Azure App Service.

Getting ready

Make sure you have an Azure account. If not, you can create a free account at `azure.microsoft.com`. Also, make sure you have completed the previous recipe. We will need Visual Studio 2017, with its latest updates. Let's get going.

How to do it...

1. Open Visual Studio 2017.
2. Now, open the solution from the previous recipe. Click **File** | **Open** | **Open Project/Solution**, or press *Ctrl* + *Shift* + *O*, and select the `Chapter12.Azure.WebAppCore` solution.

3. The **Solution Explorer** (*Ctrl* + *Alt* + *L*) should look like this:

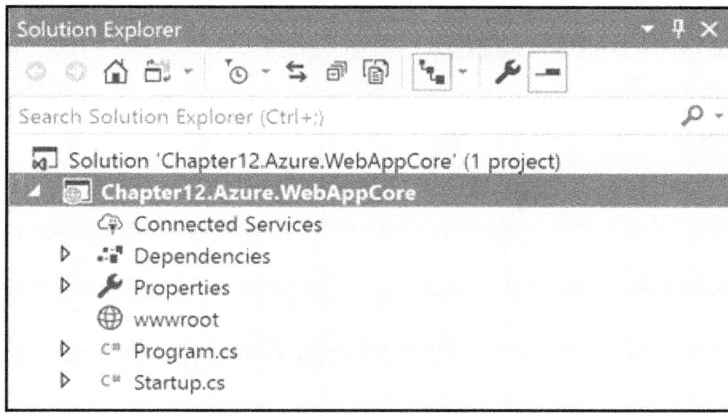

4. Now, right-click on `Chapter12.Azure.WebAppCore` and select **Publish**.
5. In the **Pick a publish target** window, select **App Service** in the left-hand pane and **Create New** in the right-hand pane:

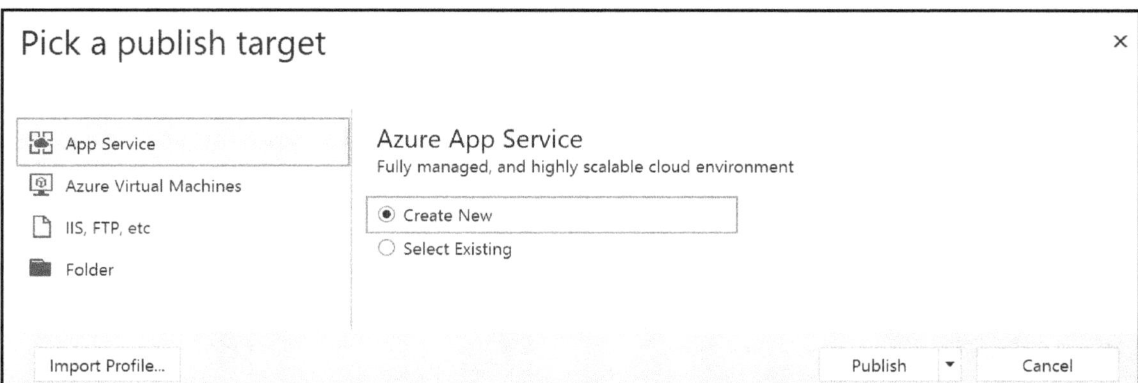

6. Click **Publish**.

7. Now, in the **Create App Service** screen, supply a proper **App Name**, and select a **Resource Group** and a **Hosting Plan**:

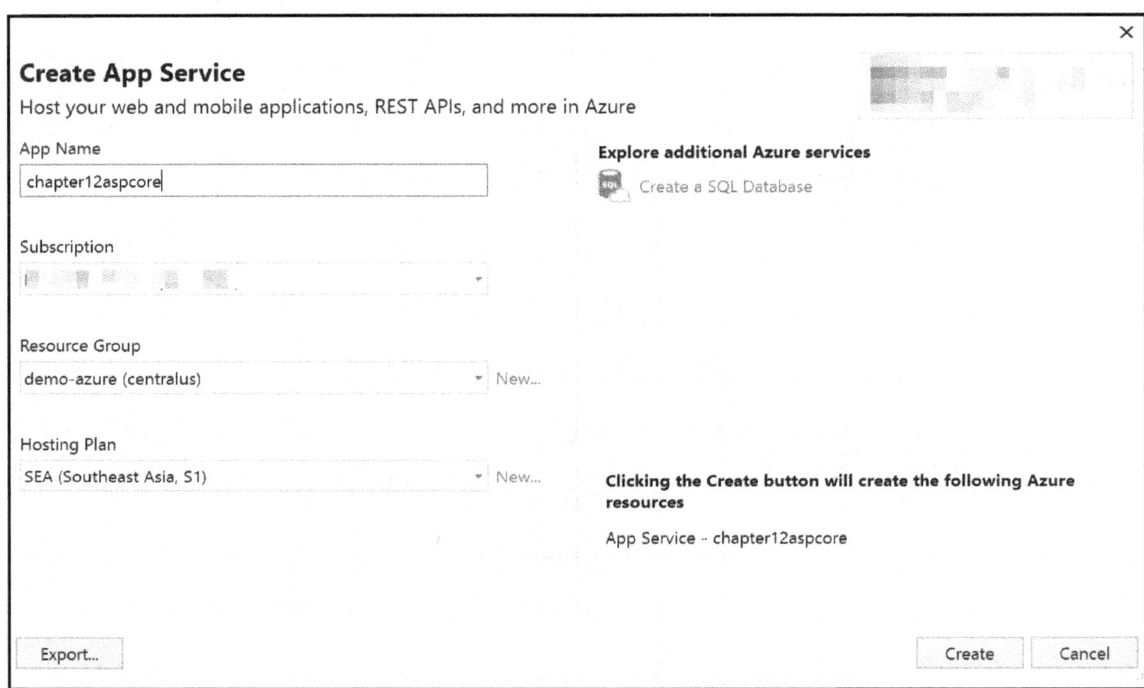

8. Click **Create**.
9. This will deploy your application to Azure.
10. If everything goes well, you should see this in the browser:

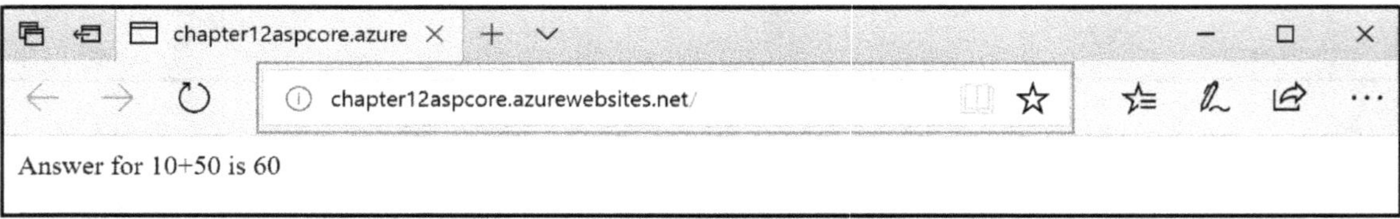

How it works...

In steps 1, 2 and 3, we opened the existing solution that we created in the previous recipe. We performed a quick build to check for any syntax errors and to confirm that everything is fine. In step 5, we used Visual Studio tools to publish the application to Azure. In this case, we selected a new App Service. In the next screen, at step 7, we had to use the Azure subscription bound with your login. This should be the account you created in the previous recipe. You can select an existing **Resource Group** here, or you can create a new one by clicking the **New** link. You will see a dialog box similar to this:

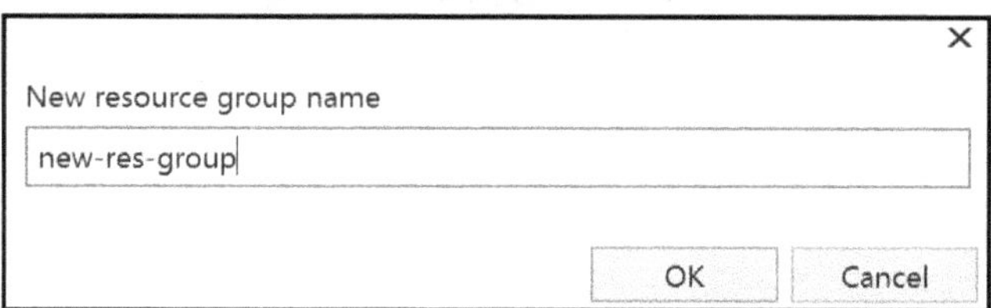

You will have to give a name for your **Resource Group** and click **OK**. A **Resource Group** is a way of categorizing your resources in Azure. And again, you can select a new **Hosting Plan** by clicking on the **New** link. Again, you should see a screen such as this to select your new plan:

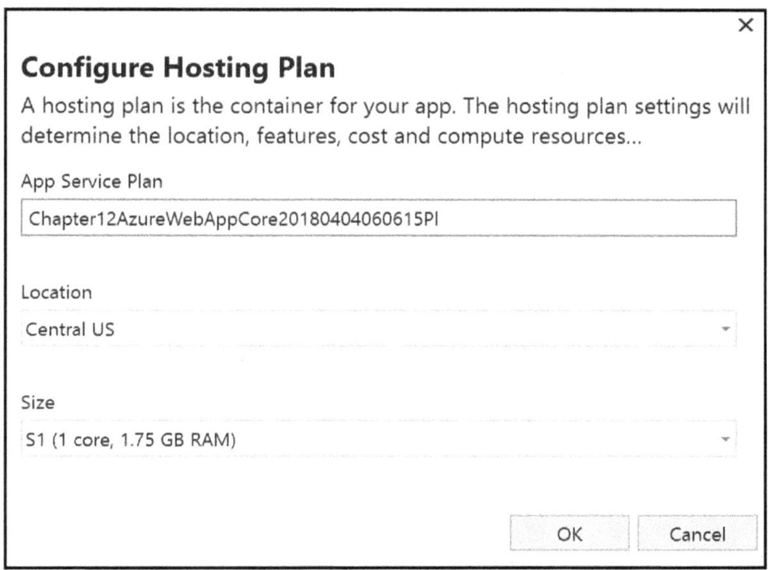

The **Location** and **Size** drop-down lists give you different options to select. **Location** will help you to select a region close to your customers. This will help you to access your website quickly. Also, **Size** will tell you the processor and RAM you are going to use for this App Service. Finally, you hit the **Create** button and Visual Studio will take care of the process. This will include uploading your files to Azure, opening the browser, and showing the final result. In the Azure Portal, your App Service should appear in the list like this:

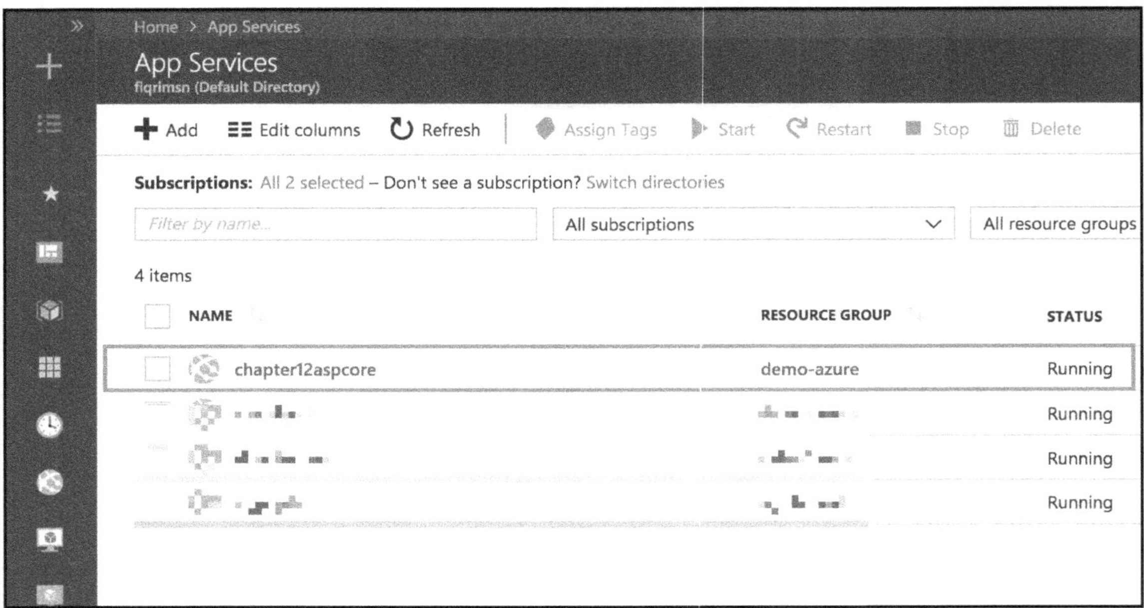

As you can see, Visual Studio has done a great job of doing all the hard work for you.

Index

www.ingramcontent.com/pod-product-compliance
Lightning Source LLC
Chambersburg PA
CBHW080609060326
40690CB00021B/4630

* 9 7 8 1 7 8 8 8 3 4 6 6 7 *